2 1765 0056 8674 9

DATE DUE

Aboriginal
and
Spanish Colonial
Trinidad

A Study in Culture Contact

Aboriginal
and
Spanish Colonial
Trinidad

A Study in Culture Contact

LINDA A. NEWSON

*Department of Geography, King's College,
University of London*

1976

ACADEMIC PRESS
London   New York   San Francisco
A Subsidiary of Harcourt Brace Jovanovich, Publishers

ACADEMIC PRESS INC. (LONDON) LTD.
24/28 Oval Road,
London NW1

United States Edition published by
ACADEMIC PRESS INC.
111 Fifth Avenue,
New York, New York 10003

972.983
NSS8a
1976

Copyright © 1976 by
ACADEMIC PRESS INC. (LONDON) LTD.

All Rights Reserved
No part of this book may be reproduced in any form by photostat, microfilm, or any other
means, without written permission from the publishers

Library of Congress Catalog Card Number: 75 46338
ISBN: 0 12 517450 0

PRINTED IN GREAT BRITAIN BY
W & J MACKAY LIMITED, CHATHAM

Preface

This book is an attempt to analyse the cultural changes that occurred in Trinidad as a result of the discovery and occupation of the island by the Spanish. The Spanish period in Trinidad has attracted little attention from historians, anthropologists and geographers and no study of the whole period has been undertaken using primary sources. Studies on the impact of Spanish colonialism in the New World have focused on the socio-economic centres of the Empire and on the nature and operation of selected institutions; few studies have looked at locationally remote areas or have compared the impact of different institutions such as the *encomienda* and the mission. It is hoped that this book will make a contribution towards an understanding of these aspects of Spanish colonialism which have been neglected so far. In addition it is hoped that, although this study is for practical reasons non-comparative, it will be able to identify cultural patterns and processes that are paralleled in other parts of the Spanish Empire and as such throw light on the culture-contact process in general.

Research in Trinidad, Venezuela and the United States was undertaken in two four-month periods in 1968 and 1970, and archival work in Spain for eight months in 1969. For financial support during the four years in which the data were collected and analysed I wish to acknowledge a three-year Parry Studentship from the Department of Education and Science and assistance from the Central Research Fund of the University of London.

I am grateful to many people in Trinidad, Venezuela, Spain and the United States who supplied me with valuable information and comment. I would like to thank Professor I. Rouse of Yale University for allowing me to use his excellent library and to examine his and John Goggin's archaeological collections from Trinidad. I am also grateful to Dr Elizabeth Wing of the University of Florida, Gainesville, for providing me with unpublished results of her investigations into aboriginal fishing in the West Indies; to Dr R. Bullen, also of the University of Florida, Gainesville, for allowing me to examine his archaeological collections from Trinidad and the Lesser Antilles; to Dr Mario Sanoja and Lic. Iraída Vargas of the Universidad Central de Venezuela, Caracas for information relating to the movement of the Neo-indians from the mainland of Venezuela to the Antilles.

I also wish to express my appreciation to Mr Enos Sewlal of the National Archives, Port of Spain and Señorita Josefina Jaimes of the Archivo General de la Nación, Caracas for the help they gave me in locating relevant documents in a variety of archives. I would also like to thank the staff of the Archivo General de Indias, Seville for their patience in helping me with the palaeography of sixteenth and seventeenth century documents.

In the preparation of the manuscript and figures I would like to thank the secretarial and cartographic staffs of King's College London and University College London.

Finally I would like to thank those without whom this study would not have been possible. Firstly, and above all, my thanks are due to Dr David Harris of University College London, who not only stimulated my interest in cultural geography but provided valuable criticism and advice both during the period of research and in the completion of the final manuscript. I would also like to thank Professors D. J. Robinson and P. Wheatley for valuable comment in the earlier phases of the research. The acknowledgements would not be complete without thanking the many friends in Trinidad, Venezuela, Spain and the United States who by their hospitality made my periods of research abroad so enjoyable, not least to Wilbert Holder, Judy Stone and Derek Walcott.

March, 1976   L.A.N.

Contents

part six
Conclusion

Appendices

part one

Introduction

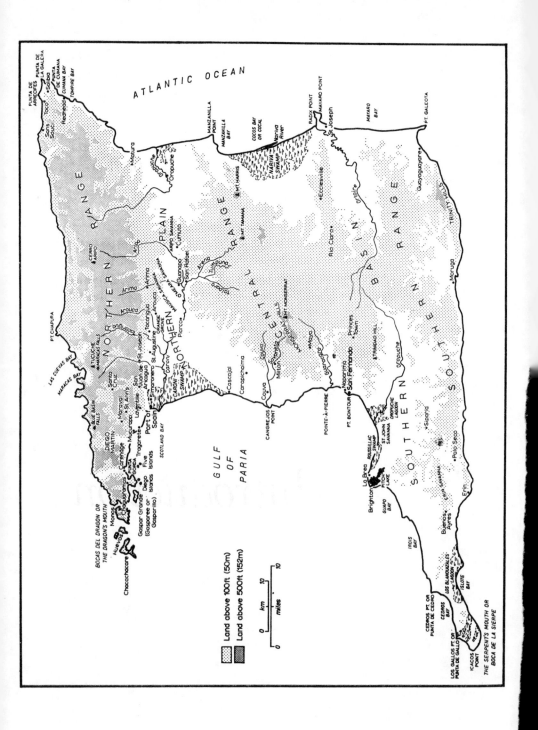

ATLANTIC OCEAN

GULF OF PARIA

Land above 100ft (50m)
Land above 500ft (152m)

km
miles

NORTHERN RANGE

CENTRAL RANGE

SOUTHERN RANGE

NARIVA BASIN

NORTHERN PLAIN

BOCAS DEL DRAGON OR THE DRAGON'S MOUTH

THE SERPENT'S MOUTH OR BOCA DE LA SIERPE

1
Methods and Sources

Trinidad's aboriginal and Spanish colonial heritage will not be apparent to the casual observer. Despite the fact that indians inhabited Trinidad for nearly 2000 years prior to the arrival of the Spanish, few, if any, descendents of the indigenous population survive in the island. All that remain are aboriginal names for prominent geographical features, such as the mountains of Aripo, Naparima, and Tamana, and the rivers of Arena, Couva, Oropuche and Caroni, and the bays of Guayaguayare and Mayaro (see Fig. 1).[1] Scarcely more evidence exists of the subsequent 300 years of Spanish rule. Fort San Andres and the ruins of Chacon's fort at Laventille survive as testimonies to the island's role as a defensive outpost of the Empire, and placenames such as San Fernando, San Juan, Diego Martin, Santa Cruz and La Brea also bear witness to the Spanish occupation of the island, but Puerto de España and San José de Oruña were anglicised long ago into Port of Spain and St. Joseph respectively. It is not surprising, therefore, that Vidya Naipaul describing Trinidad during the Second World War concluded that, "the Spanish language had died in Trinidad; there was no trace of the Spanish Empire".[2]

The lack of superficial evidence, however, belies the importance of the two cultures to the cultural history of the island; for it was on foundations laid during the aboriginal and Spanish periods that the present-day economy and society of Trinidad were built. Many present-day settlement sites and crops cultivated today had their origin in the pre-Columbian period, but the aboriginal contribution to Trinidad culture was effectively eclipsed by the subsequent 300 years of Spanish rule, when the indian population was decimated and its culture profoundly modified. By the end of the eighteenth century, the indian subsistence

---

Fig. 1 (opposite). Surface features and place names mentioned in the text.

3

economy based on the shifting cultivation of root crops, hunting and fishing, with access to resources free to all, had been replaced by the commercial production of selected domesticated plants and animals maintained on privately held land and worked by subservient members of the population; the essentially egalitarian and rural population had been incorporated into an urban and feudal society controlled by a complex secular and ecclesiastical bureaucracy; indian animism and shamanism had been replaced by monotheistic Catholicism preached by a hierarchy of priests. The basis of social and economic life in Trinidad had been laid.

The study of culture contact

The history of aboriginal and Spanish colonial Trinidad is a history of contact between two very different cultures. The Social Science Research Council Summer Seminar in 1953 was devoted to an attempt "to synthesise and codify research and theory in the field of acculturation" and for this purpose acculturation was defined succinctly but broadly as "culture change that is initiated by the conjunction of two or more cultural systems".[3] Fernando Ortiz has suggested that the term transculturation should be used in preference to acculturation to emphasise the reciprocal nature of the culture-contact process.[4] The failure of the term to be adopted may be explained perhaps by the continued emphasis of acculturation studies on the nature of the changes that have occurred in one cultural group, generally the subordinate one, with practically no discussion of the nature of the dominant culture or of cultural changes that were consequent upon contact. Foster's work on the culture of Spanish *conquistadores* and settlers is a notable exception to this rule.[5] Foster also advocates that the concept of dominance should be incorporated in any definition of culture contact, since the nature and consequences of acculturation are to a large degree dependent on the dominant role played by one of the contacting cultures.

The processual nature of culture contact was emphasised by Fortes in 1936 when he stated, "Culture contact has to be regarded not as a transference of elements from one culture to another, but as a continuous process of interaction between groups of different cultures."[6] Not all acculturation studies, however, have reflected this understanding. Earlier works such as Hunter's on the Pondo and Mair's on the Baganda were concerned with the reconstruction of tribal life prior to contact, rather than with the process of acculturation.[7] In part they reflected the current emphasis in anthropology as a whole on synchronic functionalist studies of culture in which the concept of process was relatively neglected. The latter was lamented by the Social Science Research Council Summer Seminar (1954), where it was seen as one of the major causes of the failure of empirical studies to add to the theory of culture contact.[8]

It is clear that before any analysis of cultural changes that have occurred as the result of contact may be undertaken, the nature of the cultures prior to contact needs to be determined. Since most cultures under study are already in contact at the time of investigation it is necessary to turn to historical sources to provide the required information. Some acculturation studies are prefaced with an historical introduction based on interviews and local histories but, rather than attempt to reconstruct the nature of the cultures prior to contact, they give lists of significant dates and descriptions of the cultures by contemporary observers.[9] Despite the fact that there is an abundance of documentary evidence relating to many culture-contact situations, particularly in Latin America, there has been no acculturation study so-claimed that has been based on archival material. Even the very historical studies of Albrecht, Service and Geertz have only used secondary source materials.[10] The neglect of documentary evidence may be explained in part by the anthropologists' feeling of incompetence in handling it. The challenge has not, however, been taken up by historians. Historians have been interested in culture contact from the point of view of the history of colonialism and the functioning of certain colonial institutions, but as Miranda points out, "the evolution and changes brought about in the indigenous population have held little attraction for the historian".[11] A number of acculturation studies have attempted to compensate for not using historical source materials by using comparative techniques. Eggan, for example, working in the northern Philippines examined six contemporary tribes with similar cultures located at varying distances from the coast. He assumed that distance from the coast was related to the intensity of contact, with the most intense contact occurring on the coast. From this he hoped to isolate the factors responsible for cultural changes, but he found that other factors were more important that the intensity of contact: village organisation was related more to topography and water supply, and social organisation was related more to population density and per capita wealth. He concluded, "Here is an instance where historical and comparative studies may co-operate to create a better understanding of the processes and results of culture change."[12]

By regarding culture contact as a process and taking into account the historical development of cultures, it should be possible to identify stages in the acculturation process. A number of studies have attempted to do this, notably La Farge's study of the Maya, Kubler's of the Quechua, and Services's examination of Spanish–Guaraní relations.[13] However, they form only a small proportion of acculturation studies and there have been few attempts to identify patterns and process that are duplicated in independent situations. Elkin, and Murphy and Steward have distinguished stages in the acculturation process in more general terms.[14] Elkin has identified six stages in what he calls "the process of reaction" of the aboriginal peoples of Australia to the arrival of Europeans as follows: tentative clash; clash (incipient or actual); pauperism; intelligent parasitism; intelligent appreciation; assimilation. He does not attach dates to these stages and, although he constructs his formulation on this example alone, he maintains that it has comparative potential. Murphy and Steward have undertaken a cross-cultural comparison of the effects of European culture on the Mundurucú of Brazil and the Algonkians of Canada. They distinguish four stages on the basis of changes occurring in social organisation as an index of overall cultural change as follows: pre-rubber or pre-fur (i.e. pre-contact); marginal involvement; transitional; and convergence, culmination. It would appear therefore that despite the plea at the Social Science Research Council Summer Seminar that the possibility of regularities in sequential developments over long periods should not be neglected, very little headway has been made. Service has pointed out that the colonial situation, and the establishment of the Spanish Empire in particular, offers unique advantages for the comparative study of culture contact. Colonial policies formulated in the Peninsula were to apply uniformly to all parts of the Spanish Empire. Thus, by controlling one culture any spatial or temporal variations in the nature of the culture-contact process may be regarded as the result of differences in the local cultures and environments.[15] The institutions that the Spanish introduced into Trinidad were the same as those established in other parts of the Empire but their operation and impact on the tropical rain forest peoples of the island was different from that on the indian population of the upland agricultural states of Mexico and Peru.

Numerous studies have been made by historians of the nature and impact of various institutions, such as the *encomienda* and the mission, in different parts of the Empire but several major fields of enquiry have been neglected. First, there have been few studies that have looked at overall changes in the nature of indian groups. Whilst the Social Science Research Council Summer Seminar stressed the importance of examining changes in cultures as wholes, rather than in particular aspects of culture,[16] anthropologists have been reluctant to do so, maintaining that it is methodologically impossible. The fact that the task is not easy, however, should not deter further effort directed at achieving this desirable goal. Second, there has been a lack of studies that have attempted to compare the impact of different Spanish institutions on the same culture. The opportunities for such a comparison are limited to some extent by the fact that the institutions adopted to control the indian population were largely determined by the nature of the culture; generally speaking *encomiendas* were introduced in the highland states and chiefdoms, whereas missions were established in remoter tribal areas. In Trinidad both institutions were in operation. Third, studies of indian cultural change under Spanish rule have been concerned almost exclusively with the more complex cultures of the highlands of Middle America and the Andes, with the result that the operation and impact of particular Spanish institutions have only been studied in the socio-economic centres of the Empire; more neglected and locationally remote areas have not been investigated,[17] with the notable exception of Service's study of Spanish–Guaraní relations in early colonial Paraguay.[18] It is hoped that this book, which is concerned with the differential impact of Spanish institutions on a culturally less complex indigenous group in a remote part of the Empire will also help to redress the imbalance created by former studies. It is also hoped that, although this study is for practical reasons non-comparative, it will not only reveal data formerly unknown but, through a detailed examination of the archaeological and historical data relating to contact between two cultures over a long time period, will throw light on the culture-contact process in general.

The nature of the evidence

This book is based on substantive and comparative archaeological, documentary, and ethnological evidence.

Archaeological investigations undertaken in Trinidad provide valuable evidence for the reconstruction of aboriginal culture during the pre-Columbian period when no written records were kept. The primary source of information which has attracted the attention of archaeologists is the shell midden—a mound composed mainly of shell refuse, with fragments of animal bones, implements and utensils, with occasional human remains and non-utilitarian objects. Shell middens are found throughout the island and are particularly common on the south and east coasts. From archaeological work carried out on Trinidad middens, particularly by Bullbrook, Rouse and Wing,[19] direct evidence has been obtained on the material culture of the indians and indirectly insights into non-material aspects of aboriginal culture have been gained. Finds of individual artefacts have also provided information.

Original documents are the most important source of information on the Spanish period in Trinidad, but here they have also been used together with archaeological and comparative ethnological evidence to reconstruct the economy and social organisation of the indians in the island on the eve of discovery. Certain drawbacks in the use of documentary evidence for this purpose, however, must be recognised. First, documentary evidence is only available for Trinidad from the end of the sixteenth century, by which time indian culture had already been modified by contact with the Spanish. Second, the accounts are highly subjective and were coloured by the experience of the observers in Europe. Third, many accounts were purposely biased in order to achieve an appropriate response on behalf of the Crown. The difficulty, therefore, is in judging the accuracy of accounts. This drawback applies equally to early printed chronicles based on direct observation or second-hand information, and to all periods under study, but the problem is particularly acute for the early colonial period for which few documents exist and their evaluation is made correspondingly more difficult.

Original documents found in the Archivo General de Indias in Seville form the most important source of information for the Spanish period in Trinidad. Particular use was made of both official and non-official secular and ecclesiastical documents found in the sections entitled Patronato, Audiencia de Santo Domingo, Audiencia de Caracas and Audiencia de Santa Fé. For the end of the colonial period additional information was gleaned from documents found in the Archivo General de la Nación in Caracas and the Public Record Office in London.

Extensive use was also made of contemporary accounts published during the colonial period. Of particular value were Spanish accounts which make specific reference to Trinidad, notably those of Las Casas Castellanos, Enciso, Velasco and Aguado[20] written in the sixteenth century, and of Díaz de la Calle, Simón, Espinosa, Linage, Caulín and Alcedo[21] in the later colonial period. The accounts of European voyagers, including the Englishmen Raleigh and Dudley, to Trinidad and the Caribbean,[22] that are published by the Hakluyt Society, and the accounts of the Dutchman de Laet and the French Abbé Raynal[23] also provided much valuable information.

The first books published that focused exclusively on Trinidad did not appear until the nineteenth century. The histories of Joseph and Borde, however, were based on Spanish and French documents many of which have since been destroyed; they are thus valuable sources of information particularly for the latter part of the Spanish period.[24] Fraser's book focuses mainly on the British period but contains comments on the nature and impact of French immigration at the end of the eighteenth century.[25] These three studies with that of de Verteuil have formed the source material for the well known twentieth century histories of the island.[26]

In the light of the incompleteness of the archaeological and documentary records for Trinidad, comparative evidence has been drawn on. Comparative archaeological and documentary evidence of other cultures in the Antilles and neighbouring mainland has been used, whilst comparative ethnographic evidence has been drawn from other parts of the world as well.

part two

Aboriginal Trinidad

2
The Indian Occupation of the Island

Radiocarbon evidence suggests that man was living in Venezuela by about 15 000 BC[1] having migrated through North and Central America from Asia. Fossil bones and pollen indicate that at that time the climate of Venezuela was probably cooler and wetter than at present and that the forest, though interspersed with savannas, was more widespread.[2] The livelihood of the Paleo-indians[3] was based on the hunting of large mammals such as mastodon, megatherium and glyptodon; they were neither fishers or agriculturalists. At that time Trinidad was still attached to the mainland but as yet there is no evidence of indian occupation; although the Gulf of Paria had not been formed, swampy conditions must have existed which may have precluded the passage of the Paleo-indians, who were unfamiliar with techniques of navigation, to Trinidad. If, however, as has recently been suggested, Paleo-indians did possess such techniques, then the question remains open.[4] The Paleo-indian epoch lasting from 15 000 BC to about 5000 BC was apparently characterised by a gradual increase in the warmth and dryness of climate, accompanied by a rise in sea level caused by the retreat of the Pleistocene ice sheets in the northern hemisphere. About 5000 BC the indians began to rely more on other means of subsistence, notably fishing, both riverine and marine, and collecting and thus they passed into the Meso-indian epoch.

It was the Meso-indians who were the first inhabitants of Trinidad. Having learned techniques of navigation in the rivers and coasts of eastern Venezuela they crossed to Trinidad, by then separated from the mainland, in the first millenium BC. The earliest radiocarbon date for Trinidad is for the site of Ortoire on the east coast, which has yielded a date of 810 $\pm$ 130 BC.[5] So far ten Meso-indian sites have been identified in Trinidad of which six are non-ceramic shell middens and the other four non-ceramic flint deposits, the presence and use of which has not been accounted for. Little evidence is available for the non-ceramic sites of Tortuga and San Juan but the other four sites—Cocal, Ortoire, St. John and Banwari Trace—are all situated in or near swampy terrain and consist of relatively thick middens, which with the presence of ash, charcoal and animal remains suggests that they were permanent habitation sites.[6]

The beginning of cultivation in Trinidad was not spontaneous: agricultural techniques were introduced to the island from Venezuela by the Neo-indians about 300 BC.[7] The Neo-indians, or more specifically

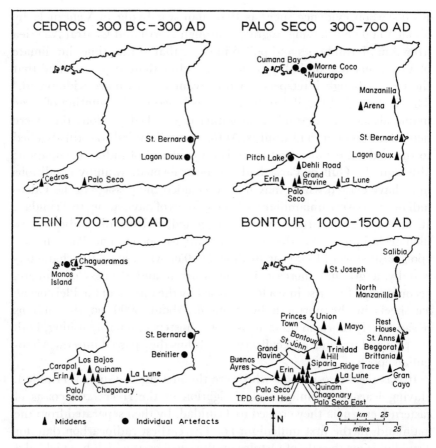

FIG. 2. Archaeological sites dating from the Neo-indian epoch.

Saladoid people, probably originally inhabited the flood plain of the Central Amazon[8] from whence they migrated to Venezuela. It has been postulated that the movement of Saladoid people from Venezuela to Trinidad was brought about by the encroachment of Barrancoid people, also agriculturalists, into the lower Orinoco, where the former are thought to have lived. Recent work in Venezuela has suggested, however, that Saladoid people may have lived further north, possibly in the Paria Peninsula.[9] From about 300 BC until the discovery of the island by Columbus in 1498, Trinidad was continuously inhabited by Neo-indians (see Fig. 2 for distribution of Neo-indian sites). This epoch in Trinidad has been divided into four periods on the basis of variations in ceramic styles, which represent minor changes in Neo-indian culture. The four successive periods have been called Cedros, Palo Seco, Erin and Bontour after their type sites.

The first agricultural inhabitants of Trinidad made pottery in the Cedros style.[10] This later developed into the more elaborate but less sinuous Palo Seco style. The change to Erin-style pottery was abrupt and it is postulated that it developed from Los Barrancos style introduced to Trinidad by Barrancoid people who migrated to the island from the lower Orinoco (see Fig. 3). From Trinidad certain Barrancoid traits spread to the Greater Antilles, where they contributed to the development of a new series.[11] Erin-style pottery is characteristically a thicker and heavier, yet refined ware with complicated incised and incised-modelled designs. During the predominance of the Erin-style, Palo Seco-style pottery persisted as a minority ware, which may have developed into the later Bontour style.[12] The Bontour style does, however, show resemblances to the Guayabita style developed in the Paria Peninsula and may have been introduced from there. The lack of a transitional style between the Palo Seco and Bontour styles suggests that the latter proposition is the most likely.[13] Bontour-style pottery is characteristically a thin soft ware with ornament limited to crude appliqué work, incision and punctuation. It lacks the slip and glaze characteristic of earlier periods.[14] It may thus be regarded as a simplification and degeneration of an earlier Saladoid style, either Irapa or Palo Seco. The reason for the disappearance of the Erin style and the appearance of a degenerative pottery style is unknown. It has been suggested that migrations from the mainland to the Antilles about AD 1000 effectively isolated Trinidad from the higher cultural developments occurring in central Venezuela and the Greater Antilles. Since

Trinidad is the most southerly island in the West Indian chain it is difficult to explain why it should have been avoided in favour of the more northerly Lesser Antilles. It has been suggested that at the time migrations were occurring, Trinidad was highly populated and as such was bypassed on the way to uninhabited or more thinly populated islands.[15]

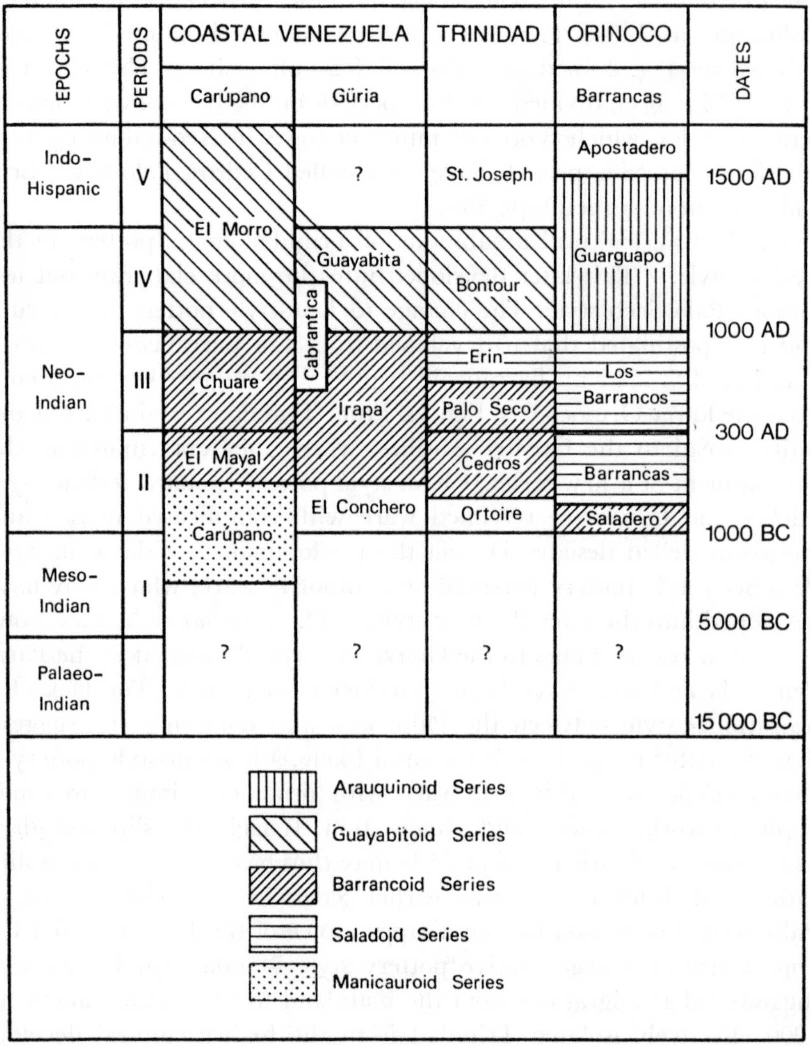

EPOCHS	PERIODS	COASTAL VENEZUELA		TRINIDAD	ORINOCO	DATES
		Carúpano	Güria		Barrancas	
Indo-Hispanic	V	El Morro	?	St. Joseph	Apostadero	1500 AD
Neo-Indian	IV		Guayabita	Bontour	Guarguapo	
		Cabrantica				1000 AD
	III	Chuare	Irapa	Erin	Los Barrancos	
				Palo Seco		300 AD
	II	El Mayal		Cedros	Barrancas	
		Carúpano	El Conchero	Ortoire	Saladero	1000 BC
Meso-Indian	I					5000 BC
Palaeo-Indian		?	?	?	?	15 000 BC

Legend:

- Arauquinoid Series
- Guayabitoid Series
- Barrancoid Series
- Saladoid Series
- Manicauroid Series

Fig. 3. Relative chronology of the coasts of eastern Venezuela and Trinidad.

Arawaks or Caribs?

The terms Arawak and Carib have been most commonly used to describe two linguistic-cultural groups that inhabited the Antilles, including Trinidad at the time of discovery. The difficulties of correlating groups of indians with pottery series have been described by Rouse and Cruxent.[16] Nevertheless, such correlations may provide valuable supporting evidence when considered with documentary, linguistic and cultural data.

The Neo-indians who migrated to the Antilles about 300 BC were probably Arwak-speaking, whereas Carib-speaking indians are thought to have arrived about AD 1000.[17] At the time of conquest, the latter were expanding into territories formerly occupied by the Arawaks and they may have secured a foothold in Trinidad. The migration of Arawak-speaking indians from the mainland to the Antilles had been correlated with the spread of Saladoid pottery[18] but the migration of Carib-speaking indians is less easily determined by a distinctive pottery style since Carib men often took captive Arawak women for wives, who made pottery according to their own traditions.[19] Nevertheless, a distinctive type of pottery has been found in great quantities in certain of the islands of the Lesser Antilles, which Caribs are known to have inhabited.[20] Insufficient work has been done on this pottery to determine its origin or distribution, though Rouse and Cruxent have reluctantly correlated the Dabajuroid pottery series in western Venezuela and its offshore islands with Carib-speaking indians,[21] whilst Lathrap has correlated the expansion of Caribs at the expense of their Arawak neighbours with the distribution of three pottery styles—Guarguapo, Late Marumba and Apostadero.[22]

Pottery remains from Trinidad middens are exclusively Arawak[23] and distinctive Carib pottery found in the Lesser Antilles is conspicuously absent.[24] Certain Carib stone implements have been found in the north-western peninsula and in the south-west of the island[25] but they may have been trade items. Further archaeological investigations in the island would help to clarify the picture.

Documentary evidence conflicts as to whether the aboriginal inhabitants of Trinidad were Arawak or Carib, apart from two accounts which indicate that the island was occupied by both groups.[26] Caribs were identified by the Spanish by their warlike nature and cannibalism[27] but since many of the indian groups were provoked into attack by bad treatment at the hands of the Spanish, and since indians designated as Carib or "cannibal" could be enslaved whereas Arawaks could not, the extent of Carib settlement is likely to have been exaggerated. Other indian groups appear to have been distinguished by their leaders and by their affinities with similar groups on the mainland. Accounts of "Aruacas" or "Araucas" are common in sixteenth-century documents[28] but several suggest that they shared the island with another group, the "Nepuyos"[29] and there is a reference to three *encomiendas* of "indians of the nations araucas and nipuyos in the island of Trinidad".[30] Walter Raleigh visiting the island in 1595 said that "Arawacas" were to be found in the south-east around Point Galeota and between there and Curiapan (Los Gallos Point) they were called "Saluaios". The "Nepoios" occupied the east coast whilst on the west, probably near San Fernando, were the "Iaos"[31] who according to Borde had links with the Nepuyos on the mainland.[32] "Carinepagotos" around "the Spanish citie" were possibly Caribs[33] brought from the mainland as slaves by the Spanish. The presence of the two groups, "Aruacas" and "Nipuyos", was also noted by Juan Troche Ponce de León in 1573[34] but Espinosa said that the island was divided between Nepuyos and Guayanes.[35] Castellanos noted the presence of two rival groups of indians, Camucuraos and Chacomares, between whom the island was divided;[36] a division that Antonio Sedeño considered a complicating factor in the conquest of Trinidad. The fact that the two groups fought together against the Caribs suggests that they were both Arawak and that they were the same groups as those variously called Aruacas, Nepuyos and Guayanes, which Lovén considers were all Arawak.[37]

Whether Carib indians were present in Trinidad at the time of discovery is more difficult to ascertain. As indicated earlier, the Spanish were anxious to designate areas as Carib since they were then permitted to enslave the indians. In 1510 it was said that there were no peaceful indians along the whole coast of the Tierra Firme, except in Trinidad, but in 1511 the island was declared Carib.[38] Vociferous complaints were made by Las Casas that Trinidad had been wrongly designated as Carib[39] and in 1518 the Crown appointed Rodrigo de Figueroa to determine which islands and parts of the mainland were in fact inhabited by Caribs. After considerable investigation he reported in 1520 that all the islands were occupied by Caribs except Trinidad, the Lucayas, Barbados, Gigantes and Margarita.[40] Nevertheless, in 1532

Sedeño petitioned the Crown for permission to enslave the indians of Trinidad on the grounds that they were "caribs and people who eat human flesh and have other rites and evil customs and are very war-like".[41] A number of accounts mention the presence of Caribs in Trinidad[42] but most evidence points to the indians being friendly rather than hostile,[43] although they are now considered to have been a more warlike branch of the Arawak stock.[44] Evidence against the presence of Carib settlements in Trinidad is seen in reports of attacks on the indians of the island by Caribs from "las islas de barlovento, dominica, matalino [Martinique], sancta lucia y la granada".[45] The *Escribano* of Margarita in 1554 related how "The said indians of the island [Trinidad] are guaiquiris and not caribs, on the contrary they are subject to great injury from the caribs".[46] Sedeño, however, met some Caribs in the Orinoco who said they lived in Trinidad[47] and Scott noted the presence of Caribs in the northern part of the island in 1645.[48] The late date of the latter observation would have allowed for the migration of Caribs to Trinidad in the sixteenth or early seventeenth century. If there were Carib settlements in Trinidad at the time of discovery, they were probably temporary and did not account for a large proportion of the indian population. Linguistic evidence from early documents does, however, suggest that both Arawaks and Caribs were present in the island in the sixteenth century. Word lists given by de Laet, Dudley and Wyatt are Arawak, whilst that of Espinosa is Carib.[49]

Cultural evidence is also inconclusive. Certain Carib techniques such as the use of poisoned arrows[50] were present in the island in the sixteenth century but the ease of inter-island communication would have made some cultural interchange inevitable.[51] The importance of cultivation in the economy of the indians of Trinidad and the siting of villages away from the immediate vicinity of the seashore would seem to indicate the presence of Arawak agriculturalists rather than of Carib fishers.

Altogether the evidence suggests that Trinidad on the eve of being discovered by Columbus was predominantly Arawak. The evidence is, however, inconclusive and the presence of some Carib settlements remains a possibility.

3
Trinidad on the Eve of Discovery

The ecology of the island

Vivid descriptions of the Trinidad landscape were sent back to Europe by early visitors to the island. Columbus was impressed by the verdancy of the forests, which he described as, "superior to the gardens of Valencia in May",[1] whilst de Vera reported that, "there is in this island the greatest quantity of cedars I have ever seen in my life".[2] Such accounts, however, only give a generalised picture of the landscape, which, if the intimate relationship of indian groups to their natural environment is to be understood, needs elaboration. The lack of documentary detail has not been compensated for by scientific inquiries into the island's ecological history; the following reconstruction of the natural environment at the time of discovery therefore relies on inference from the nature and distribution of present-day ecosystems, and from the results of zooarchaeological investigations.[3]

The tropical seasonal climate of Trinidad today probably differs insignificantly from that of pre-Columbian times.[4] The "dry" season normally lasts from January to April, and the "wet" season, during which 75% of the annual rainfall occurs, is from June to December, with May as a transitional month. The mean annual rainfall varies from under 50 in. (1259 mm) on the west coast to over 80 in. (2032 mm) in the Northern and Central Ranges, with a maximum of over 120 in. (3048 mm) occurring in the north-eastern part of the Northern Range. Unlike the rainfall, temperatures in Trinidad show little seasonal or spatial variation: the mean monthly maximum is about 86°F (22·2°C) and the mean monthly minimum seldom falls below 70°F (21·1°C).

Similarly, the physiography of the island has changed little since the time of discovery; only minor differences exist as the result of land clearance and drainage. The vegetation, soils and animal life, however, have been altered considerably. In the post-conquest years the distribution, structure, and composition of various vegetation types was modified by land clearance, the selective felling of trees for timber, and the introduction of alien plants and animals, both domesticated and wild. These activities had profound effects on the structure and composition of soils and the size and distribution of animal populations.

Trinidad consists of three ranges of mountains and hills separated by two plains, which together form the five major physiographic regions of the island (Fig. 4).[5] The Southern Range was the first part of Trinidad to be sighted by Europeans. Columbus, on his third voyage to the New World in 1498, had previously determined that the first land he should discover would be named after the Trinity; he thus regarded it as a miracle, when he sighted the three hills of the Southern Range, now known as the Trinity Hills. These sandstone hills, which rise to about 1000 ft (305 m), form the highest land in the Southern Range. The relief may be accounted for by an anticlinal structure, which east of Erin strikes towards the sea, where there is a corresponding decrease in relief. The anticlinal structure is complicated by subsidiary folding and faulting, evidenced by steeply dipping beds, that often form vertical cliffs, where erosion has removed the less resistant interbedded shales. The land is thus very dissected and there are locally precipitous slopes. Most of the drainage is to the south coast, but rivers are short and active marine erosion prevents the accumulation of alluvial deposits. In some places, notably at Guayaguayare, marine erosion amounts to 10 ft (3 m) a year, in which case the position of the coastline in pre-Columbian times must have been further south than at present.

The lack of sheltered bays or inlets, except at Moruga and near Erin, together with the highly forested nature of the coast combined to make it inhospitable to early explorers.[6] These southern slopes of the Southern Range were probably covered by semi-evergreen forest,[7] characterised either by purpleheart (*Peltogyne porphyrocardia*) or acurel (*Trichilia smithii*) and moussara (*Brosimum alicastrum*). The lower rainfall and more freely draining sandy soils in this part of the island may explain the more deciduous nature and lower height of the canopy layer of the forest— rising to about 20–40 ft (6–12 m), with emergent trees at 60–80 ft (18–24 m). However, in some areas of acurel–moussara forest, the dry

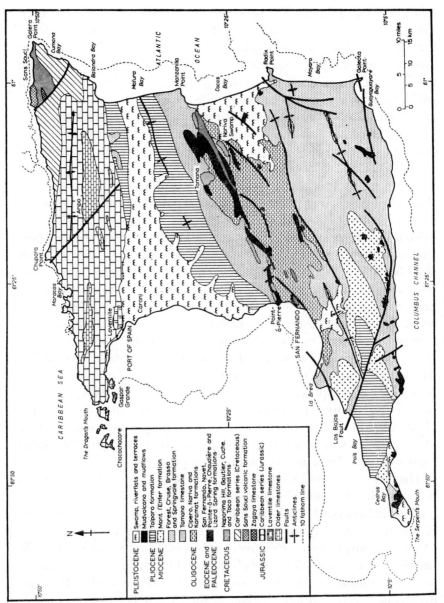

FIG. 4. Geology.

conditions were probably related to forest clearance associated with shifting cultivation in pre-Columbian times. The presence of aboriginal middens in these areas and of cedar trees, which are indicative of firing, and were noted by sixteenth-century observers, supports this view.[8] This area of open semi-evergreen forest formed one of the most important hunting grounds of pre-Columbian man in Trinidad. Zooarchaeological investigations in this area indicate that the most important species hunted there were the small brocket deer (*Mazama americana*), agouti (*Dasyprocta aguti*) and the collared peccary (*Tayassu pecari*). The presence of these species, which are inhabitants of open-forest environments, provides additional evidence that the forest cover in this area was more open than the evergreen forest found throughout the greater part of the island. Today agoutis and peccaries, which were formerly more widespread, occur most commonly in the Southern Range.[9] The higher and more inaccessible parts of the Southern Range were probably covered by evergreen forest dominated by the bois-mulatre (*Pentaclethra macroloba*) –carat (*Sabal* sp.) floristic association, giving way to mora forest dominated by *Mora excelsa* in the vicinity of Mayaro and Guayaguayare. The presence of the mora forest has been the subject of considerable discussion, since the distribution of the forest does not appear to coincide with any obvious physical or cultural feature.[10] As Fig. 5 shows, on the eve of discovery it probably accounted for about 10% of the evergreen forest in the island; it has since been heavily exploited for timber and thereby reduced in extent.[11]

A structural syncline forms the Southern Basin, which separates the Southern and Central Ranges. Over the greater part of the Basin greenish-grey Cretaceous clays outcrop and during the rainy season landslides are prevalent. In the west San Fernando hill, formed of argiline, a siliceous fissile shale, and bounded on three sides by faults, is a prominent landscape feature. Further south the Cedros peninsula is composed of Quaternary deposits, which form gently undulating land about 75 ft (23 m) above sea level. Soil variations within the Southern Basin are considerable within a short distance; they vary between clay, silt and sand, the latter being the most infertile. The greater part of the Southern Basin was probably covered by evergreen forest; this is suggested by the predominance of bones of closed-forest mammalian species, notably the red howler monkey (*Alouatta seniculus*), lape (*Agouti paca*) and nine-banded armadillo (*Dasypus novemcinctus*), found at the aboriginal middle site of St. John.

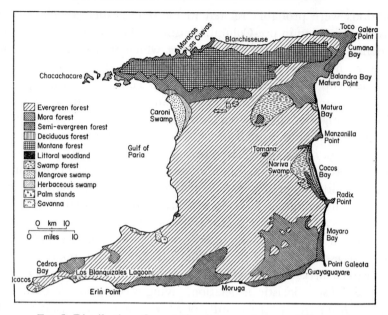

FIG. 5. Distribution of vegetation types on the eve of discovery.

Dominant features of the landscape of the Southern Basin at the time of discovery were swamps which had been formed during the Pleistocene and are still present today. Although the east coast is undergoing active marine erosion, two extensive swamps are present at the mouths of the Nariva and Ortoire rivers, where sand bars break the force of the surf. The west coast, conversely, is experiencing deposition by rivers entering the Gulf both from Trinidad itself and by waters coming from the Orinoco and entering the Gulf through the Serpent's Mouth, and here there are extensive swamps. On the west coast, five miles south of San Fernando, is the Oropuche Lagoon. This tidal swamp is covered with mangrove trees near the coast but further inland the level surface is broken up by occasional hills. Further south near Icacos and on the south coast near Islote Bay there are other less extensive swamps below the general level of 50 ft (15 m). It was at Icacos that Columbus noted oysters (*Ostrea* sp.) growing on the roots of mangrove trees.[12] Inland from the mangrove swamps herbaceous swamp characterised by mota grass (*Cyperus giganteus*), white roseau (*Gynerium sagittatum*) and elephant's ear (*Montrichardia arborescens*) is found. Within the herbaceous swamp palm stands, particularly of palmiste (*Roystonea oleracea*) or moriche (*Mauritia setigera*), sometimes develop, but, although individual trees reach a height of 80 ft (24 m) they do not form a continuous canopy layer. During the sixteenth century herbaceous swamp was probably more limited in its distribution, having since spread at the expense of the swamp forest as a result of burning during the dry season. The swamp forest found in the Nariva swamp is dominated by crappo (*Carapa guianensis*), roseau (*Bactris major*), palmiste, cocochat (*Hirtella racemosa*) and bloodwood (*Pterocarpus rohrii*). At the time of discovery this forest probably also characterised part of the Caroni swamp, which has since been drained.

A variety of animals is found in the swamps of the Southern Basin but most of them are not edible. The most important mammalian species, that was hunted during pre-Columbian times, was the crab-eating racoon (*Procyon cancrivorous*), which is found mainly in mangrove swamps, particularly the Oropuche Lagoon. Several animals found in rivers and open stretches of water, were more common throughout the island in the sixteenth century. The freshwater otter (*Lutra* sp.) is now rare in Trinidad, whilst the manatee (*Trichechus manatus*), once very common in the island's rivers, and hunted during the pre-Columbian period, had become a rarity in the larger rivers of the east and south coasts by the middle of the nineteenth century due to over-exploitation.[13]

The east coast of Trinidad had a very different appearance in the sixteenth century than it has today. The coconut palm (*Cocos nucifera*) which fringes the beaches was not introduced into Trinidad until the early seventeenth century. Turtles, particularly green turtles (*Chelonia mydas*), however, were probably more common at the time of discovery than at present. The over-exploitation of nesting females and marine erosion, which has exposed the roots of littoral trees and created a less favourable environment for females to make their nests, has resulted in a considerable decline in their numbers.[14]

The Central Range, stretching south-west–north-east across the island from Pointe-à-Pierre to Manzanilla Point, is composed of low hills with an average height of between 200 and 500 ft (61–152 m) but rising in the east where the peaks of Montserrat, Tamana and Mt. Harris reach 918 ft (280 m), 1009 ft (308 m) and 884 ft (269 m) respectively. The northern part of the Range is composed of moderately soft, massive, arenaceous limestone Miocene in age, which forms some of the most fertile soil in the island: the southern part of the Range is composed of poorly drained Oligocene clays. At both ends of the Range are rugged sandstone hills, and at the north-eastern end Upper Cretaceous shales also outcrop; they all form poor sandy soils. The mean annual rainfall in the Central Range is heavy—over 80 in. (2032 mm)—and the soils are poorly drained.

The Central Range remained remote during the pre-Columbian period; economic activity was concentrated in the coastal areas and only occasional hunting expeditions ventured into the more elevated and densely forested parts of the Range. During the eighteenth and nineteenth centuries sugar-cane lands were carved out of the forest leaving only small remnants of the "monstrous thicke wood" which Dudley noted covered most of the island in the sixteenth century.[15] The present-day composition of the forest remnants suggests that the Central Range was covered by evergreen forest with a canopy layer at 40–90 ft (13–27 m) dominated by bois mulatre, a lower layer at 10–20 ft (3–6 m) characterised by carat palm or cocorite (*Maximiliana elegans*), and emergent crappo and guatecare (*Eschweilera subglandulosa*) trees rising to over 100 ft (30 m). At the time of discovery the forest would have been inhabited by closed-forest species such as the lape, nine-banded armadillo, the red howler monkey (*Alouatta seniculus*) and the capuchin monkey (*Cebus* sp.); these species, as attested by bones found at Mayo, were all hunted during the pre-Columbian period. They have since declined drastically in numbers, owing to over-exploitation, land clearance and changes in the forest environment; so much so that the lape is now protected by hunting laws.

The Central Range is separated from the Northern Range by an almost featureless plain composed of old alluvial terraces, probably Pleistocene in age. The plain is deeply dissected by river channels, whose rivers flow both east and west from the centre of the basin near Cumuto. The Caroni river is the main drainage feature of the Northern Plain. It is fed by tributaries flowing from the Northern Range and meanders across the plain to the Caroni swamp, where it breaks up into many distributaries before entering the Gulf of Paria. The Caroni swamp, like most other swamps in Trinidad, represents the last stage of land formation, Pleistocene in age.[16] Along the coast where deposition is occurring and tidal mud flats are building up, mangrove forest is well developed but inland it gives way to herbaceous swamp and swamp forest. Jaques Ousiel reporting to the Dutch West India Company in 1637 described the land around the Caroni river as "entirely open and produces nothing but rushes".[17] At the time of discovery the Caroni swamp was more extensive than at present, having been partially drained in the last 200 years. As such, it is likely that swamp animals and particularly water birds, which were intensively exploited in the nineteenth century, were more common than today. Along the banks of the rivers alluvial deposits form very fertile soils, but for the most part the Plain is composed of sandy or clayey soils of indifferent fertility; at the eastern end of the Plain, where sandstone outcrops, the land has been noted as being "the worst land in the colony".[18] The savannas of the Northern Plain were conspicuous landscape features in the sixteenth century. Velasco noted that "the land is good and fertile and there are many savannas and rivers"[19] and another sixteenth century observer commented on their suitability for cattle breeding.[20] Beard maintains that the savannas of the Northern Plain are remnants of a formerly more widespread vegetation cover that developed during the Pleistocene but is being destroyed by a more recent cycle of erosion, which rejuvenates the soil and allows the invasion of woody species.[21] It seems more likely, however, that the increased number of fires associated with shifting cultivation in recent times has encouraged the spread of herbaceous species thereby extending the area of savanna.[22] The main grass species that compose the savannas are *Leptocoryphium lanatum* and *Paspalum pulchellum*, and the dominant tree species are *Byrsonima crassifolia* and *Curatella americana*, which grow to about 10 ft (3 m). The importance of fire in the savanna environment is indicated by the fire-resistant nature of the bark of the latter two species. The mammalian fauna of the savannas is limited— the small brocket deer being the most common species found there; the avifauna is more varied with falcons, hawks, and buzzards amongst its inhabitants.

The southern flank of the Northern Range rises sharply from the Northern Plain. It is dissected by V-shaped valleys containing perennial streams, which feed the Caroni after having flowed over numerous waterfalls—the highest being Maracas falls and Blue Basin falls. On the upper slopes of the mountain range the soil is thin and in places absent due to the stripping action of the heavy rainfall and runoff on the steep slopes, but the valleys are filled with rich loamy deposits washed down from the surrounding hills, which form well drained and rich agricultural soils.

The suitability of the soils of the foothills of the Northern Range for cultivation had been recognised prior to the arrival of Europeans, who also made this area their centre of agricultural activity. The colonisation of the foothills during the pre-Columbian period is attested by the presence of shell middens and finds of individual artefacts, as well as by the fact that savannas existed in the sixteenth century; the savannas are considered to have resulted from continued land clearance and burning at an earlier period.[23]

The mountains of the Northern Range compose the highest land in Trinidad rising to an average height of 1500–2000 ft (457–762 m); the peaks of Tucuche and Cerro Aripo rise to 3075 ft (935 m) and 3085 ft (940 m) respectively. Geologically it is composed almost exclusively of indurated Jurassic and Cretaceous metamorphic rocks, mainly schists, which have a complex history of faulting and folding.[24] To a height of between 700 and 800 ft (213–244 m), the Range is clothed with ever-green forest similar to that found in the Central Range but with wild debasse (*Licania biglandulosa*) replacing carat and cocorite as the characteristic constituent of the lower layer. In these more inaccessible parts of the island the larger mammalian species may be found in small numbers: the tiger cat or ocelot (*Felis pardalis*) and two anteaters, the tamandua (*Tamandua longicaudata*) and the silky anteater (*Cyclopes didactylus*). At heights of over 800 ft (244 m) the canopy layer of the forest lowers to 70–100 ft (21–30 m) and becomes more closed and the lower layer correspondingly more open. Many of the species found in the evergreen forest are represented in the montane forest but the dominants are different. They include serrette (*Byrsonima coriacea* var. *spicata*), wild debasse (*Licania biglandulosa*), bois gris (*Licania ternatensis*) and mahoe (*Sterculia caribaea*). As the altitude increases the number of tree species decreases and the lower layer becomes dominated by palms and large tree ferns, which at altitudes of over 2800 ft (853 m) form a canopy at 20–25 ft (6–8 m). At this height the main species is *Clusia intertexta*.

The mountains of the Northern Range rise steeply from the coast making access from the sea virtually impossible, except at the small bays of Maracas and Las Cuevas. Towards the east the mountains are lower and descend more gently to the coast, where anticlinal and synclinal valleys form open bays separated by rugged headlands. Littoral wood-land forms a narrow band along the sandy beaches and cliffs of the northern and eastern coasts. Here the prevailing winds are quite strong and trees on the exposed headlands show evidence of wind trimming and are xerophytic, with cutinised leaves that are tolerant of sea blast and salty conditions. The most important species is the sea grape (*Coccoloba uvifera*), which grows inland from the high water mark. It is usually found in association with seaside mahoe (*Thespesia populnea*) and manchineel (*Hippomane mancinella*); palmiste (*Roystonea oleracea*) and balata (*Manilkara bidentata*) take over where conditions are less severe. The most common animal that is hunted in this environment at the time of discovery, would have been the iguana (*Iguana iguana*).

In contrast to north and east coasts, which have experienced uplift in recent times, the western extremity and southern coast of the Northern Range, have been submerged creating the islands of the Bocas and the deep bays at Chaguaramas and Carenage. In the western part of the Range exposures of limestone may be seen at Laventille, Diego Martin and the islands of Gaspar Grande, Gasparillo, Diego islands and the Five islands. Not only are the underlying rocks more permeable in this part of the Range, but the rainfall only averages 50–70 in. (1259–1802 mm) a year compared with over 110 in. (2794 mm) in the more elevated parts. Although drier conditions do prevail in the west it is unlikely that natural conditions alone can account for the presence of deciduous forest dominated by saltfishwood (*Machaerium robinifolium*). It would appear that it was degraded from evergreen forest characterised by naked indian (*Bursera simaruba*) and yellow savonette (*Lonchocarpus latifolius*), which still occurs today in Tobago, the Lesser Antilles and Venezuela.[25] Human interference is indicated by the presence of bread and cheese (*Pithecollobium unguis-cati*), and cactaceous species, notably *Cephalocereus smithians* and *Acanthocereus pentagonus*. To what extent the deciduous forest existed at the time of discovery is difficult to ascertain in the absence of both documentary and archaeological evidence.

The aboriginal population

Estimates of the aboriginal population of South America on the eve of discovery have been the subject of considerable discussion centred on the reliability and interpretation of documentary evidence.[26] It is generally considered that population figures given by early chroniclers were exaggerated to magnify their achievements or to spur the Spanish authorities into some required action. Sauer, however, maintains that "there was neither reason of vanity or of practical ends to inflate the native numbers".[27] It would appear that neither case was consistently true, for South America as a whole or even for the same area at the same

TABLE 1

Population estimates for Trinidad on the eve of discovery

DOCUMENTARY EVIDENCE

Population	Date	Source
200 000	1534	Estimate of Antonio Sedeño. ANHC *11–31* no. 15 15.9.1534
100 000	1570	Estimate of Miguel Diosdado. AGI SD *71–1–526* 15.1.1570
50 000	1589	Estimate of Pedro de Angulo. BM ADD *36,315* ff. 122–5 24.11.1589
35 000	1593	Estimate of Antonio de Berrío AGI EC *1011A* 1.1.1593
40 000	1595	Estimate of Domingo de Ibargoyen y Vera, camp-master to Antonio de Berrío. AGI EC *1011A* September 1595
40 000	*c.* 1612	ANHC *11–32* no. 7 f. 60 In a testimony on the Caribs it was stated that of the 40 000 indians that there were in Trinidad and the neighbouring mainland only 4000 remained

COMPARATIVE DOCUMENTARY EVIDENCE

Population estimate	Density per 100 km²	Source
c. 25 000	555	Population density for the Greater Antilles calculated by Steward from figures estimated by Rosenblat.[a]
c. 22 500	500	Population density for the Lesser Antilles calculated by Steward from figures estimated by Rosenblat.[a]
c. 66 500	1470	Calculated from the figure of 1 130 000, which is accepted by Sauer for Hispaniola.[b]

COMPARATIVE CULTURAL EVIDENCE

Population estimate	Density per 100 km².	Source
c. 2000	45	Population density given by Steward for tropical forest indians amongst whom he includes the indians of Trinidad.[c]
c. 11 500	250	Population density given by Rouse for tropical forest indians.[d]

COMPARATIVE CULTURAL EVIDENCE—*continued*

Population estimate	Density per 100 km²	Source
c. 45 000	1000	Population density given by Clarke and Haswell for groups supported by simple agriculture.[e]
c. 90 000	2000	Population density given by Clarke and Haswell for groups supported by shifting cultivation.[e]

[a] Steward, "South American Cultures", map on p. 659, 661, and 664
[b] Sauer, "The Early Spanish Main", p. 65
[c] Steward, "South American Cultures", map on p. 676
[d] Rouse, "Settlement Patterns", p. 169
[e] Clarke and Haswell, "The Economics of Subsistence Agriculture", p. 111

time. Each estimate would have been subjective and dependent on the availability of information and the purposes for which it was recorded. It is not surprising therefore that figures for the same time and place often do not agree. In these circumstances, archaeological and ecological evidence may be valuable in assessing the reliability of estimates.

There is no doubt that, relative to the other West Indian islands, Trinidad was densely populated at the time of discovery (Table I). Many early reports, whilst not giving numerical estimates of the aboriginal population, mentioned the great number of indians there were in the island.[28] The numerical estimates given by sixteenth century observers show a consistent decline in the aboriginal population throughout the century. The earliest estimate was given by Antonio Sedeño in 1534 who said that 20 Spaniards defended the fort they had built in Trinidad from 200 000 indians.[29] The 200 000 indians may possibly have been inhabitants not of Trinidad alone, but also of Guyana,[30] and the figure may have been exaggerated in an effort to obtain reinforcements from Spain or other parts of the Indies. In 1570 a Spanish priest, Miguel Diosdado, who accompanied Juan Troche Ponce de León in his attempted settlement of the island, estimated that there were more than 100 000 indian inhabitants[31] but in 1589 Pedro de Angulo reported that there were only 50 000 indians in Trinidad.[32] The first count of indians was undertaken by Antonio de Berrío who established a settlement on the island in 1592. In 1593 he reported "the whole island has been explored and an inventory of the natives compiled, of whom about 7000 have been found and as many married indians, so there are probably more than 35 000 inhabitants".[33] This figure was increased by his camp master Domingo de Ibargoyen y Vera to 40 000, presumably to magnify the achievements of his governor.

In the Greater Antilles there are historical reports of villages with populations of up to 5000[34] but it is unlikely that villages in Trinidad were so large. Steward has suggested that villages located on the coast or river banks and supported largely by fishing could contain populations of up to 1000.[35] Carneiro, however, using the example of the Kuikuru, whose economy is based primarily on the shifting cultivation of bitter manioc, proposed that the maximum village size was 500–600.[36] The greater availability of animal protein in Trinidad would probably have permitted higher concentrations of population, of which there is some documentary evidence. Juan Bono in 1516 built a house in Trinidad in which he intended to capture the indians of a village and then transport them to Puerto Rico. The plan succeeded in part, for 180–200 indians were taken, but in the process 100–200 were killed and many escaped.[37] This would suggest that the village exceeded 500 in population. It is reasonable, therefore, to assume an average of about 400–500 people per village. Archaeological investigations have revealed the presence of 24 permanently occupied settlement sites in the period prior to the conquest, which would place the aboriginal population at about 12 000. Since it is likely that as many midden sites have been destroyed or not been discovered this figure could be doubled to give a population of 24 000.

Population density estimates for other areas at the time of conquest and for groups with a similar culture may throw light on the aboriginal population of Trinidad. Steward assigns Trinidad a population density of 45 per 100 km^2, equating it with northern Venezuela. Whilst this figure may well apply to northern Venezuela where the savanna areas would have been sparsely populated, it is absurd for Trinidad whose population works out at barely 2000; even more so since Steward himself notes the presence of villages of up to 1000 people.[38] Rouse similarly assigns Trinidad a low population density of 250 per 100 km^2, classifying the indians of Trinidad as Tropical Forest Indians.[39] This density estimate would give Trinidad a population of just over 11 000, an estimate which seems low when the large population losses due to enslaving, Carib raids, diseases and disruption of the aboriginal economy in the sixteenth century are taken into account. The population density figures for the Lesser Antilles and Hispaniola given by Rosenblat and accepted by Steward and based on historical sources are 500 and 555 per 100 km^2, respectively. These density figures would seem to be equally applicable to Trinidad, where sources of food were as varied and reliable as those of Hispaniola and where the indians were more sedentary than in the Lesser Antilles. Assuming an overall density of 500 per 100 km² Trinidad's population works out at nearly 23 000.

In the light of the foregoing discussion, the earliest population estimate of 200 000 by Antonio Sedeño in 1534 would appear to be exaggerated, for it even exceeds the high population density accepted by Sauer for Hispaniola which worked out for Trinidad would be 66 500.[40] The high estimates of the early observers were probably influenced by the difficulty the Spanish had in conquering the island and by the great number of indians from the Tierra Firme and of Caribs from the Lesser Antilles, who were to be found in Trinidad waters. Archaeological and comparative evidence would seem to suggest that on the eve of discovery the population of Trinidad was between 20 000 and 30 000.

The aboriginal population was distributed in villages identified by the presence of middens; the variation in the depth and extent of the deposit indicating the temporary or permanent nature of the settlement. Permanent settlement sites are present through all archaeological periods of the Neo-indian epoch. It is sometimes assumed that shifting cultivation necessarily involves the shifting of settlement sites at periodic intervals, but archaeological evidence seems to suggest that sites in Trinidad were occupied continuously for long periods, although the sites of individual houses within the settlement may have been moved. The large size of the middens indicates that the settlement pattern was nucleated, though there may have been a few isolated huts in the hills that were used as bases for hunting. The nucleated nature of the settlements would have enabled co-operation that was occasionally required in warfare and in cultivation, particularly in the clearance of primary forest. Temporary or bivouac sites occupied during hunting and trading expeditions and characteristically located along watershed trails only made their appearance at the end of the Neo-indian epoch, in the Bontour period.

As shown in Fig. 6, settlement sites throughout the Neo-indian epoch show a concentration in the southern part of the island, forming two main clusters: at Mayaro Bay and on the south coast near Palo Seco. Another cluster may be identified in the hills in the vicinity of San Fernando in the Bontour period.[41] These concentrations were noted by early visitors to the island.[42] In 1532, however, Sedeño reported that he had pacified the "province of camucurabo and chacomari [in the

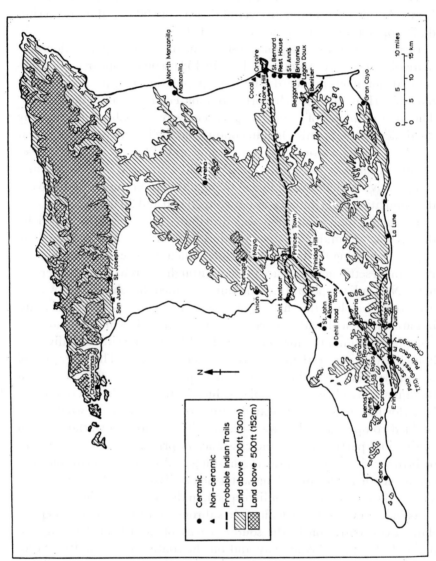

Fig. 6. Aboriginal midden sites.

foothills of the Northern Range] where many *caciques* have their seats and lands".[43] It would appear therefore that the northern part of the island was also inhabited and that the relative absence of midden sites reflects the lack of archaeological investigations and the intensive cultivation of the area.

All known midden sites in Trinidad are below 250 ft (76 m) but often on small hills and terraces. Such locations would have been drier than the surrounding land and free from mosquitos if they were present at that time. It is possible that malaria was only introduced into Trinidad in relatively recent times.[44] Land over 500 ft (152 m) would have been unsuitable for cultivation, as would the swamps and savanna lands. Most of the settlements were located on the banks of rivers or within half a mile of freshwater resources. The two exceptions were the settlements at Point Bontour and Erin, whose freshwater supplies were over a mile away at the Cipero and Galap rivers respectively. Given the availability of fresh water, access to food resources probably played an important role in determining the actual location of settlement sites. During the Neo-indian epoch in Puerto Rico the location of settlement sites gradually changed. Originally located on the coast, the population moved inland along the major rivers so that on the eve of conquest it was well established several miles inland.[45] This change in the location of settlement sites has been regarded as an expression of changes in the indian economy, involving an increase in the role played by cultivation and a decrease in that part played by hunting, fishing and collecting, and superimposed on that the effect of Carib raids. As yet there is insufficient evidence to indicate that a similar change in the location of settlements occurred in Trinidad, where the situation is complicated by the changing position of the coastline during the Neo-indian epoch. Many of the middens on the east coast appear originally to have been located on the coast but recent deposition has resulted in their present location about 800 ft (243 m) inland.[46] Conversely, parts of the southern coast have undergone active marine erosion and it seems likely that sites at present located on the coast were originally sited 2–3 miles inland, whilst others may have been eroded away completely.[47] As yet too few ceramic middens characterised by Cedros, Palo Seco and Erin pottery have been found in Trinidad for valid generalisations about their locations to be made. Suffice to say that, with the exception of Arena and Los Bajos located 15 miles and 3½ miles inland respectively, all middens dating from these periods are found within 2 miles of the coast.

More evidence is available on middens dating from the Bontour period. Of the 24 sites identified, 20 are located within 3 miles of the coast, but four—St. Joseph, Mayo, Siparia and Princes Town—are located over 5 miles from the coast. The latter four sites may be regarded as the most recent of the aboriginal middens found in Trinidad since none of them shows evidence of indian occupation prior to AD 1000 whereas one third of the other 20 sites were formerly occupied and three of them were continuously occupied from about AD 300. Also, three of the four sites have yielded ceramic evidence of Spanish occupation— indeed, St. Joseph was the Spanish capital and the other three were missions. Of the other 20 sites, however, only one—Buenos Ayres—has yielded any Spanish pottery. If the four midden sites described are regarded as the most recent of the aboriginal middens then there is some evidence to suggest that the location of settlement sites did change during the Neo-indian epoch from the coast to inland. Additional evidence for the movement of the population inland at the end of the epoch may be seen in the presence of bivouac sites located on inland watersheds. Unfortunately, there is little evidence available to suggest that this change accompanied changes in the economy. What is known is that prior to the arrival of the Neo-indians in Trinidad cultivation was unknown in the island, but that by the end of the Neo-indian epoch it had become well established,[48] whilst midden evidence suggests that hunting declined relative to fishing.[49] On the eve of discovery the indian economy was based on cultivation supplemented by fishing, hunting and collecting, so that settlement sites on the banks of rivers several miles inland would have been well located to minimise the labour in- volved in assembling necessary food items. Here alluvial soils would have been good for the cultivation of manioc and other crops, whilst the diverse flora and fauna found in the vicinity of river banks would have favoured collecting and hunting. Freshwater fishing would have been possible and easy access to the sea would have rendered marine resources exploitable.

How far defence was an important consideration in the choice of settlement sites at that time is not known. Carib-speaking indians had migrated to the Lesser Antilles about AD 1000 and during the fifteenth and sixteenth centuries they carried out frequent raids on other Antillean islands and on the mainland. If raiding occurred at an earlier period then the defence may have been a consideration, though the location of settlement sites would seem to suggest otherwise.[50]

The form of aboriginal settlements is unknown but comparative and documentary evidence suggests that each village contained a large rectangular house (such as that built by Juan Bono[51]) which was used for village meetings and ceremonies. Around it would have been circular huts housing a group of related families.[52] All houses were probably built of wooden poles covered with palm or grass leaves.

The aboriginal economy

The livelihood of the Meso-indians, who were the first inhabitants of Trinidad, was based on hunting, fishing and collecting; techniques of cultivation were unknown to them. An investigation of the non-ceramic site of St. John suggests that the most important animals hunted were the collared peccary (*Tayassu tajacu*), the nine-branded armadillo (*Dasypus novemcinctus*) and the lape (*Agouti paca*), all forest-loving species, whilst most of the fishing was carried out in estuaries and along the shore, where shellfish were also collected. Unfortunately the shellfish remains have not been examined, but their presence in large quantities suggests that their importance in the indian diet should not be underestimated.

Cultivation began in Trinidad about 300 BC when agricultural techniques were introduced to the island from the mainland by the Neo-indians. During the early part of the Neo-indian epoch the economy was probably still relatively dependent on hunting, fishing, and collecting but by the end of the epoch cultivation had become a well established economic activity. Indirect archaeological evidence for cultivation exists in the form of sherds of griddles used for the baking of cassava, which is made from bitter manioc (*Manihot esculenta*),[53] and in the form of chips of stone, similar to those found on manioc graters from Guiana and Cuba, which have been found in several middens dating from the Palo Seco period.[54] There is, however, insufficient evidence to substantiate changes in the structure of the indian economy during the Neo-indian epoch and in particular the increasing importance of the role played by cultivation. Faunal remains found in middens representative of successive periods in the Neo-indian epoch suggest, however, that hunting declined relative to fishing, which extended to the offshore environment. The relative importance of collecting at the beginning and the end of the Neo-indian epoch is not known.

The lack of archaeological evidence for the nature of the aboriginal

economy is in part compensated for by documentary evidence available
for Trinidad and other parts of the Caribbean for the sixteenth century
and by comparative ethnographic evidence mainly from the New World
but also from the Old. Whilst it would be extremely difficult, if not
impossible, to ascertain the changing nature of the economy throughout
the Neo-indian epoch, such a task may be undertaken with varying
degrees of success for different aspects of the economy at the end of the
epoch.

The diversity of resources exploited by the indians of Trinidad was
noted by Martín López, who in 1550 wrote, "they live by sowing and
harvesting their crops of maize and cassava, and other fruits of the land;
and from fishing and the hunting of deer and wild hogs [peccaries]".[55]
The relative importance of each of these activities is difficult to ascertain.
Carneiro describing the manioc-based economy of the Kuikuru of
Amazonia estimated that manioc in the form of cassava comprised about
80–85% of the indian diet, while other cultivated plants accounted for
only 5% or less; 10–15% came from fishing, while hunting was of almost
no importance providing less than 1% of the food supply.[56] In Trinidad,
while manioc was clearly established as the dominant crop, it seems
likely that with the abundance of wild faunal resources, particularly
fish and shellfish, it accounted for a less significant percentage of the
indian diet than that estimated for the Kuikuru by Carneiro—probably
between 60% and 70%. Other crops, including maize and beans,
probably provided less than 5% of the diet. In Trinidad the protein
deficiency of the crops cultivated was compensated for by the availability of animal protein. The abundant remains of fish and shellfish
found in Trinidad middens[57] suggests that in comparison with the
Kuikuru, fishing, including the collection of shellfish, accounted for a
higher percentage of the indian diet—probably about 20%. An investigation of the faunal remains found at the immediate pre-conquest site
of St. John has shown that under 25% of the individuals were terrestrial.[58] Taking into account the relative size of animals and fish, it is
estimated that hunting provided about 4–5% of all food products. In
Trinidad the contribution of collecting and trading to food production
would have been small, but collecting would have made available
raw materials for the manufacture of implements, utensils, canoes,
and houses, while trade would have been an important source of
already worked goods, particularly those of ornamental or ceremonial
value.

Cultivation and crops

In Trinidad in pre-Columbian times crops were evidently grown under a system of shifting cultivation. There is no direct archaeological or documentary evidence for the abandonment of plots after several years of cultivation, but the fact that the term *conuco*, which is used by shifting cultivators in northern South America to denote a plot of land in active cultivation was also used in the early Spanish period to describe culti-vated lands in Trinidad,[59] suggests that shifting cultivation was practised in the island.

Conklin, describing the shifting cultivation system of the Hanunóo in the Philippines, has distinguished five phases in the shifting cultivation cycle: site selection, cutting, burning, cropping and fallowing. These phases may be applied to the aboriginal system of shifting cultivation in Trinidad.[60]

The selection of plots of land or *conucos* for cultivation was probably dependent on both physical and cultural factors. Despite generally favourable climatic conditions, the physiography of the island would have militated against certain areas being cultivated. The upper slopes of the Northern Range would probably have been considered too steep, whilst lowland swamp areas would have been unsuitable for burning— an integral part of the shifting cultivation cycle. Apart from these areas, most of the island would probably have been considered cultivable. The foothills of the Northern Range were described as "densely popu-lated with cultivators"[61] and Columbus noted fields in the Southern Range.[62] For the reasons of accessibility fields were probably located near the permanent village sites. Sauer considers that for regular pro-visioning fields need to be sited not more than 10 miles from the village,[63] and in practice they are located much nearer. The Kuikuru grow most of their crops within 3–4 miles of the village[64] and Conklin found that the Hanunóo rarely located a field more than 1 km from the village and that 80% of the fields were less than 500 m away.[65] Given that the fields were sited near the village, their actual location would have been dependent on local physical conditions. The use of certain slopes, particularly east-facing slopes, may have been limited by exposure to both wind and sun, although manioc can be grown in quite open areas that would be too dry for most crops.[66] It seems likely that the most favoured areas for cultivation would have been undulating foothills and valley slopes, where soils would have been well drained. Although manioc can grow and produce on any but the poorest soils as long as they are loose and not waterlogged,[67] light soils would have been preferred since planting and harvesting would have been easier. It is difficult to assess how far the indians were able to appreciate soil differences, but comparative evidence suggests that they would probably have been aware of variations in soil moisture.[68]

Once the sites of the *conucos* had been selected, the land would probably have been cleared by ring barking, cutting and firing. Larger trees were probably felled by ring barking and repeated burning,[69] since stone axes available to the indians were probably not effective enough;[70] smaller trees and shrubs were cut, piled and burned when dry, whilst the very largest trees would have been left standing.

The ease of clearance would have depended on whether the vegetation cover was grassland, primary, or secondary forest. Grasslands would have been the most difficult to clear due to the sod-forming nature of the roots[71] and as such would probably have been avoided in favour of primary and secondary forest. Although data from the Philippines suggest that secondary-forest clearance only takes two-thirds of the time required to clear primary forest,[72] the soils underlying the latter are generally more fertile and subject to less rapid weed invasion.[73] However, due to the easy access of secondary-forest areas, generally located near settlements, and the lower labour inputs required in their clearance, such areas would have been favoured for cultivation. The actual amount of land cleared at any one time would have varied with local physical and cultural conditions. Carneiro, in his discussion on settlement patterns associated with shifting cultivation, assumes that one acre per person per year is needed where the land is planted with manioc for $2\frac{1}{2}$ years and is left to rest for 30 years.[74] Leeds considers this figure too high for an economy substantially dependent on wild food resources and favours an estimate of $\frac{1}{2}$ acre per person per year.[75] Unfortunately no evidence exists for the size of plots cleared in pre-Columbian Trinidad.

To take advantage of the dry conditions and the oncoming rains, firing would probably have occurred at the end of the "dry" season. As well as clearing much of the vegetation debris, firing would have made the soil more friable for planting. Comparative evidence from Africa, Ceylon and Venezuela suggests that burning would also have led to an increase in available phosphorus and exchangeable calcium and magnesium, thereby reducing the acidity of the soil.[76] The avowed simultaneous destruction of the humus has not been proved,[77] indeed recent data from Venezuela suggests that whilst organic carbon decreases with burning, the incompleteness of clearing and burning associated with manioc *conucos* indirectly lends to an increase in organic carbon, since a considerable amount of vegetation debris remains on the surface, and is incorporated into the soil during cultivation.[78] Continued clearance and burning in pre-Columbian times would have inhibited the growth of hardwood species and favoured that of herbaceous species, but how far burning was responsible for the creation of the savannas in Trinidad is difficult to ascertain. Savannas in the foothills of the Northern Range were probably created by burning in the pre-Columbian period, whereas the lowland savannas probably had an edaphic origin and were only maintained by firing.[79] Even if firing did not ultimately lead to the establishment of a grass cover, it must have altered the structure and composition of many Trinidad forests.

Cropping would have included three activities: planting, weeding and harvesting. After the land had been cleared, the soil would probably have been heaped into mounds, called *montones* by the Spanish, using digging sticks.[80] In the Greater Antilles the *montones* were generally 1–2 ft high and several feet wide; they were probably constructed to loosen the soil for the planting of tubers, to improve soil drainage, and in areas of thin soil, to provide sufficient humus. In areas where the soil was naturally light and well drained *montones* may not have been constructed.[81] In the areas cleared a varied assemblage of crops would have been planted. In Trinidad planting probably occurred throughout the year but was at a maximum in April and October, taking advantage of the forthcoming rains in May and November. The root crops manioc (*Manihot esculenta*), sweet potato (*Ipomoea batatas*), tania (*Xanthosoma* spp.), arrowroot (*Maranta arundinacea*), llerén (*Calathea alluia*), yams (*Dioscorea* spp.) and *Canna* spp. would have been grown in the *conucos* with maize (*Zea mays*), beans (*Phaseolus* spp.) and squashes (*Cucurbita* spp.) probably finding subordinate places. Comparative evidence suggests that root crops would have been grown in the central areas, with beans and gourds at the margins.[82] Annual pepper (*Capsicum annuum*), pineapple (*Ananas comosus*), peanut (*Arachis hypogaea*) and cotton (*Gossypium* spp.) may have been included in the *conucos* also, although Sauer thinks that cotton was grown in separate clearings in the Antilles as was tobacco in Trinidad.[83] The fruit trees and squashes, accompanied by dye-producing plants, were probably grown in small gardens near the villages.[84]

Weeds would have grown very quickly and the difficulty of weeding during the growing season may have been a limiting factor in the amount of land cultivated.[85] Conklin, in discussing the number of man hours needed per hectare in various activities in the shifting cultivation cycle, found that weeding in a former secondary-forest area took twice as long as in an area of former primary forest and in fact accounted for one-fifth of the man hours spent in the complete cultivation cycle.[86] Investigations of present-day shifting cultivation systems in South America have also indicated that excessive weeding may be an important factor in the abandonment of *conucos*.[87]

Most of the root crops would have been harvestable throughout the year,[88] since rhizomes, roots and tubers could be left in the soil until required. The process of harvesting root crops may also have had the beneficial effect of incorporating organic matter left on the surface after partial clearance and burning, thereby improving the physical condition of the soil. This has been demonstrated for root-crop shifting cultivation systems in Venezuela.[89] The seasonal variation in climate would have permitted two crops of maize a year—in December and April—the former being by far the larger. Although maize produces seasonally, once cropped it can be stored for long periods. Altogether, it is unlikely that there were any periods during the year when no crops could be harvested from the *conucos*. Tobacco was harvested in November and December.[90]

An essential feature of the shifting cultivation cycle is the abandonment of plots to fallow after they have been cultivated for a number of years.[91] How quickly this occurs after the commencement of cultivation depends on the soil fertility, the crops grown and the amount of land available to the shifting cultivator. In areas of fertile soil crops were probably grown continuously for up to 15–20 years but in areas of poor soil plots would have been abandoned sooner. The fact that manioc was the staple crop meant that soil fertility would have declined more slowly than if seed crops, which are more demanding of soil nutrients, had been the most important crops grown.[92] Where there was plenty of land available to the cultivator, the plots were probably abandoned to fallow after only short periods of cultivation: in areas of easy access and land pressure they were probably cultivated for longer periods.[93] Comparative evidence suggests that even in areas of fertile soil continuous cultivation would have led to a depletion in soil nutrients though not as rapidly as formerly envisaged.[94] As indicated weed encroachment was probably a decisive factor in the abandonment of *conucos*; the time-consuming nature of weeding would probably have made weed encroachment more apparently oppressive to the indians than soil depletion. Where land was available this may have encouraged the abandonment of plots despite the relative fertility of the soil.

Carneiro, in calculating the size of settlements associated with shifting cultivation based on manioc, assumes that the land is left to fallow for 30 years.[95] This figure would have varied, however, with local physical and cultural conditions. The actual length of the fallow period would have depended on the rate of regeneration of the forest cover and of the recovery of soil fertility, as well as on land pressure. Where there was plenty of land available for cultivation, the fallow period was probably long, allowing re-establishment of the forest to almost climax status; where there was land pressure the vegetation was probably only allowed to regenerate to the stage where, when burned, it could produce a good supply of ash for the re-cultivation of the soil. This would have occurred near villages, encouraged by easy access.

Most tasks in the shifting cultivation cycle were probably undertaken on an extended family basis with men responsible for the more arduous task of land clearance and women for the planting, weeding and harvesting of crops. Although shifting cultivation is a labour-intensive system it is unlikely that it demanded joint action involving the continuous co-operation of more than one family. An exception may have been when new *conucos* were cleared.[96]

The indians who migrated to Trinidad in 300 BC took with them an assemblage of crop plants that had been domesticated on the South American mainland; others were subsequently introduced in the pre-Columbian period. At the time of discovery a great variety of crops were grown for food, dye, spices, fruits, drugs, fibres and for use as utensils.

The most important crop grown in the *conucos* was manioc. All varieties of manioc (*Manihot esculenta*) are now considered to belong to one species, the toxicity of the variety varying with climatic and edaphic conditions.[97] The most important variety grown in Trinidad was bitter manioc: sweet manioc was not common. Archaeological evidence for the cultivation of bitter manioc exists in the form of manioc graters and cassava griddles,[98] and sixteenth-century accounts note its cultivation.[99] Manioc has the advantage that it can be grown on a great variety of soils provided they are well drained; it can also be harvested throughout the year. Stem cuttings planted in the *conucos* would have provided tubers within a year but they could have been left to grow for two or more years to allow repeated harvestings.[100] Once harvested, the poisonous roots of the bitter variety would have been grated and the gratings squeezed to remove the poisonous juice and baked into unleavened bread called cassava. In this form manioc could be stored for long periods.

Second in importance to manioc was probably sweet potato (*Ipomoea batatas*). It had the advantage of being able to produce a crop in 4 months[101] but it could only be grown in lowland areas where moister conditions prevailed. Its yield and storage capacity were also lower than manioc. "Potatoes of all kinds" were growing in Trinidad in 1570.[102]

Other important root crops grown in the *conucos* probably included arrowroot (*Maranta arundinacea*), llerén or alluia (*Calathea alluia*), yautia, ocumo or tania (*Xanthosoma* sp.), yam (*Dioscorea* sp.) and *Canna* sp. The cultivation of arrowroot in the Antilles in pre-Columbian times has not been fully investigated. It was only introduced to the Greater Antilles in the seventeenth century, when it was taken there by Europeans from the Lesser Antilles.[103] If it was present in the more southerly West Indian islands at an earlier date, it was probably more important as an antidote for poisons than a source of food, due to the low-yielding nature of the rhizome. Tania, on the other hand was high-yielding and, like manioc, could be grown at any time of the year and stored. It was present in the Greater Antilles at the time of discovery[104] and it is possible that a very nutritious root called guapo grown in Trinidad in the early seventeenth century was in fact tania.[105] It is also possible that the New World domesticated yam (*Dioscorea trifida*) was grown in pre-Columbian times.[106]

Other crops grown in the *conucos* would have included the peanut,[107] annual pepper[108] and the calabash gourd (*Crescentia cujete*). Rouse notes the use of the fruits of the latter to catch birds in the Greater Antilles[109] whilst Columbus on his third voyage was offered "calabashes of chicha" by the indians of the coast of Paria.[110] The "calabashes" probably came from the calabash gourd though they may have come from the bottle gourd (*Lagenaria siceraria*).

The cultivation of maize, beans and squashes in Trinidad in pre-

Columbian times has not been proved. Grindstones, *metates* and *manos*, indicative of maize cultivation have not been found in Trinidad for any period. Since maize is known to have been cultivated during the Spanish period, it has been suggested that it was a soft variety that did not need grinding.[111] Documentary evidence indicates that maize was grown in Trinidad in the sixteenth century and that a number of varieties were known.[112] Also, chicha and macato, fermented drinks, probably made from maize, were drunk by the indians on the eve of a battle against the Spanish in 1533.[113] Seed-crop cultivation, however, as a dominant system of agriculture, failed to spread further east than western Venezuela, where it was established about 1000 BC.[114] Its failure to spread further east has been seen as a reflection of the limited agricultural potential of those areas,[115] but the presence of maize as a minor crop indicates that ecological conditions did not preclude its cultivation.[116] Harris has recently suggested that a system of shifting cultivation based on manioc cultivation is inherently better adapted to tropical rain-forest conditions than one based on maize and other seed crops, and that this may account for the failure of the latter to diffuse far into the tropical forests of lowland South America.[117]

It seems likely that if maize was cultivated in Trinidad in pre-Columbian times, beans and squashes would have been also, since the three are often found in close association. Columbus noted beans growing in Cuba and they were probably present in the more southerly West Indian islands, having been introduced to Cuba from Central America via the South American mainland and the Lesser Antilles.[118] The common bean (*Phaseolus vulgaris*) was probably cultivated and possibly the lima bean also (*Phaseolus lunatus*).[119] The cultivation of squashes and the bottle gourd in pre-Columbian times is undetermined.[120] If squashes were present then it was probably the species *Cucurbita moschata*.[121]

A great variety of other crops were grown for food and dyes. Cultivated fruits probably included pineapple, sweetsop (*Annona squamosa*), soursop (*Annona muricata*), guava (*Psidium guajava*), hog plum (*Spondias mombin*), mamey (*Mammea americana*) and possibly the pawpaw (*Carica papaya*) and cashew (*Anacardium occidentale*).[122] Pineapples were almost certainly cultivated in pre-Columbian times and were present in Trinidad at the end of the sixteenth century.[123] They were probably introduced into the West Indies with soursop, sweetsop, guava, hog plum and mamey at an early date having been domesticated on the mainland.[124] Pawpaw may have been cultivated in Trinidad in pre-Columbian times, though it was not introduced to the Lesser Antilles until the seventeenth century.[125] Espinosa noted it growing in Trinidad in the early seventeenth century[126] so, if it was not a pre-Columbian introduction, it must have arrived in the early post-conquest period. The cashew has a similar history. It was probably introduced to the Leeward Islands by Europeans in the seventeenth century but it may have been taken there by Caribs in pre-Columbian times.[127] Since Trinidad was not permanently occupied by Caribs it may not have been introduced till the post-conquest period. The sapodilla (*Achras zapota*) was probably grown in the Antilles prior to discovery. Oviedo noted it growing there in the early sixteenth century.[128]

Bixa orellana, Genipa americana and *Indigofera suffructicosa*, which produced red, black and blue dyes respectively, were also cultivated. The dyes were used in the Antilles as body paint and for dyeing cloth.[129] Castellanos noted that the indians in Trinidad painted themselves with "bija" before going to battle.[130] These dye plants may have been grown in small gardens near the houses rather than in the *conucos*. Tobacco (*Nicotiana tabacum*) was also grown in exclusive patches.[131] It had probably been introduced to Trinidad from the mainland with manioc, with which it is commonly associated.[132] It was taken in the form of a paste which was licked and as snuff breathed through the nostrils, but it is unlikely that it was smoked.[133]

Other crops which may have been present include the perennial shrub cotton (probably varieties of both *Gossypium barbadense* and *G. hirsutum*),[134] the plantain (*Musa paradisiaca*), coconut (*Cocos nucifera*), sugar cane (*Saccharum officinarum*) and cacao (*Theobroma cacao*). Cotton was almost certainly a pre-Columbian introduction. Columbus noted that the indians of Trinidad wore clothes made of cotton and in 1532 Sedeño was given permission to trade with the indians for cotton.[135] The introduction of the south-east Asian plantain to the West Indies is generally ascribed to the Spanish, but it is possible that it reached the American mainland via a Pacific route in pre-Columbian times.[136] The great number of varieties present on the mainland would seem to suggest its early arrival in that area,[137] in which case it may have arrived in Trinidad before Columbus. Coconuts were grown on the Pacific coast of America in pre-Columbian times[138] but their presence on the Atlantic coast is uncertain. Oviedo does not mention coconut growing in the West Indies and, since it is a conspicuous tree, it was probably not present.[139] It was found in Barbados in 1650 and since the coconut is a rapid coloniser in coastal areas, its introduction probably did not long precede this date, taking place possibly in the 1640s.[140] An early seventeenth-century introduction by the Spanish would seem likely for Trinidad, as for other West Indian islands.[141] Sugar cane was taken to the New World by Columbus on his second voyage in 1493, but it did not prosper. It was reintroduced to Hispaniola in the early sixteenth century from where it was taken to other islands and to the mainland.[142] There is a possibility, however, that sugar cane reached America via a Pacific route prior to Columbus.[143] It was certainly cultivated in Trinidad in 1570 and was noted to be abundant in 1593.[144] Cacao was found growing wild in Trinidad in 1617 but it is not known whether the trees were wild or cultivated forms.[145]

Fishing

Although the combined contribution of fishing and hunting to food production decreased during the Neo-indian epoch, the contribution made by fishing increased relative to hunting. At the end of the Neo-indian epoch fish, shellfish and other aquatic animals probably accounted for about 20% of the indian diet. At that time archaeological evidence suggests that inshore waters and estuaries were the preferred environments for fishing though the indians did venture offshore. Shellfish, crabs and turtles were collected from the shore but freshwater fish did not make a large contribution to food production (Tables II, III).

An investigation of faunal remains at the immediate pre-conquest site of St. John has revealed that 65% of all faunal remains came from inshore and estuarine environments. In these environments demersal fish were the most important fish caught. Sea catfishes (Ariidae) accounted for over 90% of the individuals found at St. John. The most important ariid caught was probably the bagre (*Bagre* sp.) found particularly on the north and east coasts.[146] Demersal weakfish, croakers and corvinas (Sciaenidae) were also well represented at St. John, being common on the estuaries of the west coast.[147] Toadfish or crapauds were probably caught at low tide in estuaries and on mudflats, where they would have been left embedded in the mud or under stones.[148] Inshore pelagic fish were probably also relished, particularly mullet (*Mugil curema*), querinam (*M. liza*) and two species of herring (*Harengula*

TABLE II

Habitats of animal species found in certain aboriginal middens, Trinidad

Site	Land		Fresh-water		Beach		Estu-arine Inshore		Banks Reefs		Off-shore Pelagic		TOTAL
	M	%	M	%	M	%	M	%	M	%	M	%	
St. John 1	97	58	–	–	–	–	59	36	10	6	–	–	166
Cedros	88	75	1	1	5	4	23	20	–	–	–	–	117
Palo Seco	243	61	2	1	28	7	124	31	3	1	–	–	400
Quinam	172	69	–	–	40	10	38	15	–	–	–	–	250
Erin	91	46	–	–	20	10	84	43	1	1	–	–	196
St. John 2	55	21	9	3	–	–	174	65	29	11	1	–	268

TABLE III

Remains of aquatic animals found in certain aboriginal middens, Trinidad

Site	Chelomidae		Ariidae		Caranx		Sciaenidae		TOTAL
	M	%	M	%	M	%	M	%	
St. John 1	–	–	17	71	4	17	3	13	24
Cedros	5	24	11	52	5	24	–	–	21
Palo Seco	28	24	81	69	9	8	–	–	118
Quinam	40	61	23	35	3	5	–	–	66
Erin	20	29	37	54	12	17	–	–	69
St. John 2	–	–	98	91	3	3	7	6	108

Source: Elizabeth Wing, Personal communication 1970
Chelomidae=sea turtles
Ariidae=sea catfishes
Sciaenidae=croakers and weakfishes

M=Minimum number of individuals
%=Percentage of all individuals
St. John 1 is pre-ceramic and St. John 2 is proto-historic

pensacolae and *Opisthonema oglinum*). Rayfish, both sting rays (Dasyatidae) and eagle rays (Mylobatidae) were caught and their bones used by the indians as arrow heads.[149]

A small number of fish were caught on inshore banks and on the continental shelf. The most important two species caught were probably couvalli (*Caranx hippos*) and carite or Spanish mackerel (*Scomberomerus maculatus*). A number of sharks (Squaliformes) were caught in the offshore environment and archaeological and documentary evidence indicates that their teeth and vertebrae were used as arrow heads and for ornamental purposes.[150] Other species caught offshore probably included most of those caught at present.[151]

Marine mollusca were a vital source of food to the indians. The importance of shellfish in the economy is indicated by the thousands of shells which compose the middens. The most important constituent was chip-chip (*Donax* sp.), which accounts for over 50% of the shells found in middens on the south and east coasts. Other shellfish collected included *Cyrena carolinensis*, conches (*Strombus gigas*) and the gastropods *Melongena melongena* and *Neritina* sp.[152] These mollusca would have been found in the surf zone a few inches beneath the surface of the sand, from which they could be collected by hand. Oysters (*Ostrea* sp.) were collected from the roots of mangrove trees to which they were attached. The relative absence of chip-chip shells at St. Joseph and the importance of conches and oysters may be related to its inland location.[153]

In addition to shellfish, turtles and crabs would have been caught on the beach. Turtle bones and shell account for over 20% of all aquatic faunal remains found in four of the five middens examined in Trinidad, and crabs also figure significantly.[154] Turtles would have been used as a source of food in the form of meat and eggs, and the shell for practical and ornamental purposes. The turtle may also have played a part in aboriginal ceremonies: two turtle effigy vases have been found in Trinidad.[155] Turtles probably visited Trinidad in July and August laying their eggs on the beaches of the north and east coasts.[156] Huevos island at the north-west tip of Trinidad is said to have been so named because of the abundance of turtle eggs found there.[157] In addition occasional whales and sharks may have been washed up onto the beach.

Marine resources were so rich, that even with fairly simple techniques annual and seasonal yields would have been high; freshwater resources, however, were poor, due to the muddy nature of Trinidad rivers and the small size of the species living in them. Bones of freshwater fish accounted for a maximum of only 3% of all faunal remains recorded at the site of St. John, where ecological conditions would have favoured the exploitation of freshwater resources. The total number of species found at the five sites examined was also very small. The most important freshwater species caught were probably river pike (*Gerres* sp.), anne marie (*Hypotomus* sp.), cutlass fish (*Trichiurus* sp.), guabine and yarrao (*Erythrinus* sp.), cascadura (*Callicthys* sp.). Freshwater sardines were probably too small to warrant fishing.[158]

Large fish and aquatic animals would have been caught with bows and arrows, and nets; the harpoon was probably a colonial introduction.[159] Suckerfish, probably *Echeneis naucrates*, which attach themselves to large fish, turtles and manatees, may also have been used in aboriginal times together with fish stupefacients such as *Lonchocarpus latifolius*. The latter technique may have been a Carib introduction.[160] Lines and hooks were also used to catch fish; the hooks being made of bone and shell. Nets were used both inshore and offshore and were equipped with floats and sinkers. Aboriginal net sinkers have been found at Ortoire and St. John.[161] Offshore fishing would have been carried out from canoes, which had been hewn out of single tree trunks and could carry 25–50 people.[162] They were propelled by paddles; the sail was unknown.[163]

Hunting

The contribution of hunting to food production declined during the Neo-indian epoch; the indians by then had learnt fishing techniques and preferred to exploit aquatic resources which were more reliable. Nevertheless, animal bones from aboriginal middens in Trinidad suggest that at all periods the indians were skilled and regular, rather than sporadic, hunters.[164]

Mammal bones are most common in middens of all periods followed by bones of turtles and tortoises; bones of birds and reptiles are scarce. Changes in the kind of species hunted and the number of individuals of each species caught during the Neo-indian epoch are difficult to ascertain and appear to be more related to the ecological conditions at the sites investigated than to the period at which the hunting occurred.[165] Archaeological evidence exists, however, of two species which are not found in the present-day fauna of Trinidad. Bones of a deer, *Odocoileus gymnotis*, have been found at St. Bernard.[166] A relic of the Pleistocene savanna fauna, it is common in the llanos of Venezuela and is hunted by the Warrau in the delta of the Orinoco.[167] Since only one specimen of *Odocoileus gymnotis* has been found of nearly 300 individuals examined from Trinidad, it seems likely that it was acquired during a hunting trip to the mainland,[168] or by trade, rather than being an indicator of faunal extinction. Bones of a tapir (*Tapirus* sp.) have been found at Palo Seco[169] and its single occurrence would seem to suggest a similar origin to *Odocoileus gymnotis*. A sixteenth-century account, however, specifically mentions the hunting of tapirs in Trinidad "and the meat which they eat is from the hunting of deer, pigs [peccaries], tapirs and other sorts of animals which there are in the island".[170] The question of faunal extinction therefore remains open.

Comparative evidence suggests that most hunting probably occurred within a 10 mile radius of the settlements, though small hunting parties may have ventured up to 20 or 30 miles and even to the mainland, erecting temporary camps as they went.[171] Castellanos noted that one of the *caciques* of Trinidad wore some "tiger's claws" which he had obtained during a hunting trip to the mainland.[172] Such expeditions would explain the occurrence of bones of animal, not known in Trinidad, in some of the island's middens. Hunting was probably carried out by individuals as well as in groups. The Warrau, living in the Orinoco delta, hunt alone during the day but form small groups for hunting at night.[173] In Trinidad deer, anteater and opossums would have been better hunted at night.[174]

The mammalian species most commonly represented in Trinidad middens (Tables IV, V) would have been hunted in the open forest, particularly along streams and around *conucos*, where they came to drink and forage. The most important species hunted were the small brocket deer, the agouti and the collared peccary, which (as shown in Table V) together account for over 30% of mammalian individuals found in immediate pre-conquest middens. The higher percentages recorded for these species at Erin, Palo Seco and Quinam at earlier periods may be related to the ecological conditions at those sites. Deer prefer more open forest than peccaries, which live in closed-forest areas but venture into open-forest areas in search of food and water. Of the two species of peccary known to the indians the collared peccary was by far the more important species hunted, accounting for about 25% of the mammal bones found in immediate pre-conquest middens. The absence of

TABLE IV

Faunal remains from certain archaeological sites, Trinidad

Species	St. John 1	Cedros	Palo Seco	Erin	Quinam	Chagonary	Mayaro	St. John 2	Mayo	St. Joseph	Total number of individuals
Primates											
Red howler monkey	5	1	2	3	2			2	6		21
Carnivores											
Ocelot	1		1	2	2						6
Trinidad otter				1	1						2
Crab-eating racoon	1	2		1				2			6
Rodents											
Bank rat				1							1
Aboreal rat	1										1
Bristle rat	9	1	2	2		1	1	1			17
Spiny rat	2			2				1			5
Prehensile porcupine	1		6	4				1	2	1	15
Agouti	4	14	47	59	26	1	1	6	5	3	166
Lape	11	16	41	14	16	1	1	8	12	1	121
Squirrel				1							1
Ungulates											
Small brocket deer	10	23	76	61	77	2	2	7	8	2	268
Collared peccary	27	14	26	11	23	3	3	12	17		136
White-lipped peccary					5						5
Tapir			1								1
Edentates											
9-banded armadillo	15	15	18	10	10	1	2	6	14		91
Tamandua				2	2				3		7
Marsupials											
Large opossum	3	5	14	18	4			4			48
Woolly opossum				2							2

TABLE IV—*contd.*

Species	St. John 1	Cedros	Palo Seco	Erin	Quinam	Chagonary	Mayaro	St. John 2	Mayo	St. Joseph	Total number of individuals
Whales			1						1		2
Sirenians											
Manatee		2	1	1							4
TOTAL	90	93	236	195	168	9	10	50	67	8	

Numbers refer to the minimum number of individuals found at each site.
From: Elizabeth S. Wing, "Succession of Mammalian Faunas on Trinidad, West Indies", Ph.D. dissertation, University of Florida 1962.

TABLE V

Five mammalian species as a percentage of the total number of individuals found in certain archaeological sites, Trinidad

Species	St. John 1	Cedros	Palo Seco	Erin	Quinam	Chagonary	Mayaro	St. John 2	Mayo	St. Joseph
Agouti	4·4	15·0	19·9	30·2	15·4	11·1	10·0	12·0	7·4	37·5
Lape	12·2	17·2	17·3	7·1	9·5	11·1	10·0	16·0	17·9	12·5
Small brocket deer	11·1	24·7	32·2	31·1	45·8	22·2	20·0	14·0	25·0	
Collared peccary	30·0	15·0	11·0	5·6	13·6	33·3	30·0	24·0	25·7	–
9-banded armadillo	16·6	16·1	7·6	5·1	5·9	11·1	20·0	12·0	20·8	–
Total percentage	74·3	88·0	88·0	79·2	90·2	88·8	90·0	78·0	82·2	75·0

peccary bones in the St. Joseph midden may be a reflection of the smaller number of individuals collected there and their relative scarcity in that part of the island.[175] The white-lipped peccary, however, is far-ranging and would not have been a dependable source of food;[176] the only evidence of its being hunted is from Quinam. The importance of both deer and peccaries is shown by modelled figurine handles of the two animals on bowls found at midden sites.[177] The agouti, also an open-forest species, was commonly hunted in the aboriginal period. It may be native to the island or it may have been introduced by the Neo-indians from the mainland at an early date.[178] Other mammalian species hunted in small numbers in the open-forest environment included the large opossum, the prehensile porcupine, the large bank rat and the bristle rat. They would probably all have been hunted for their meat, but in addition porcupine quills would probably have been used for ornament.[179] Two other species, a tree-living squirrel and a tree-living rat, would have been common in the vicinity of *conucos* but their arboreal habit would have made them difficult to catch; they are not abundant in the middens. A squirrel-shaped whistle has been found at Erin.[180]

Several species were hunted in closed-forest areas but apart from the lape and the nine-banded armadillo they are not common in Trinidad middens. The preference of the lape and armadillo for denser forest areas would explain their relative importance at St. John and Mayo. Both species were prized for their meat, but in addition the carapaces of armadillo may have been used as containers.[181] Several large mammalian inhabitants of the closed forest which were hunted occasionally included the red howler monkey, the ocelot or tiger cat and the taman-dua. A necklace made from part of a monkey's skull has been found at Palo Seco,[182] and this find suggests that monkey bones may have had some mystical significance. The ocelot was probably hunted for its meat though it may have been kept as a pet since it is tameable when young.[183] Today it is mainly found in the Northern Range,[184] but midden evidence suggests that in aboriginal times it was distributed throughout the island. Tortoises, similarly, would have been common throughout the deeper forest areas and midden evidence suggests that they were not an un-common constituent of the indian diet.[185] The noted presence of "a great store of tortyses" in "sandie banks" probably refers to turtles, but "morrocoys" were specifically mentioned as being given to the Spanish by indians in 1595.[186]

Birds would have been generally available in the forest but midden evidence suggests that they did not form a vital part of the indian diet. They were probably hunted as much for their feathers and for keeping as pets, as for food. Castellanos noted that the indians wore feather headresses when going into battle.[187] For such purposes, parrots, particularly the Amazon parrot (*Amazona amazonica*), parakeets, macaws, and toucans would have been important. Two species of pigeon, *Columba speciosa* and *C. cayennensis*, and three species of ground dove, *Columbigallina passerina*, *C. minuta*, and *C. talpacoti*, were probably the most important avifaunal sources of food. Others probably included paui or white-headed guan (*Pipile pipile*), hunted today in the Northern and Southern Ranges,[188] and the oil bird (*Steatornis caripensis*), which would also have been used as a source of oil.

Despite their presence in forest areas certain mammalian species, including bats, and amphibia do not seem to have been hunted. Most of the mammalian species not hunted, notably the capuchin monkey, the mouse opossum, Carr's mouse opossum and rice rats, were probably too small to warrant hunting, whilst the silky anteater was probably avoided because of the mournful wail emitted by the animal.[189] There is no evidence that toads or frogs were eaten but they may have had some mystical significance. Some tribes living in the Orinoco basin believe that the croaking of the tree frog (*Hyla venulosa*) indicates forthcoming rain,[190] whilst Arawak indians of Guiana use frog spawn and parts of the frog's body as a hunting charm, rubbing it into their sense organs and scarified skin.[191]

Few animals were hunted in the swamps. The only mammal hunted in that environment was the mangrove dog or crab-eating racoon. Snakes and the caiman were not hunted, though pot handles in the form of the latter indicate an awareness of its existence.[192] Various ducks, teals, herons and the pelican (*Pelicanus occidentalis*) may have been hunted in the swamps and other water surfaces and it is possible that hunting during the aboriginal period contributed to the extermination of Audubon's shearwater (*Puffinus iherinieri*), the horned screamer (*Anhima cornuta*)[193] and possibly the roseate flamingo (*Phoenocopterus ruber*), which was formerly widespread in the Caribbean.[194] The scarlet ibis (*Eudocimus ruber*) was probably also reduced in numbers, being a source of attractive feathers.

The riverine environment was similarly not a very favourable environment for hunting. Only two mammalian species from that environment are represented in Trinidad middens—the Trinidad otter and the manatee. The latter species was probably most abundant on the south and east coasts,[195] where it would have been hunted from canoes using nets and suckerfish.[196] The beach environment in addition to being a source of shellfish, crustaceans and turtles was also the nesting place of the iguana. It was prized for its meat, and its eggs may also have been eaten.[197]

Many techniques of varying complexity were employed in hunting. Most of the larger animals would have been chased into traps from which they would have been taken by bow and arrow.[198] Although stone arrow heads are noticeably absent from the middens, the indians of Trinidad did use the bow and arrow; instead of metal arrow heads they used fish bones and teeth.[199] Worked bone projectiles have also been found in many Trinidad middens.[200] There is some doubt as to whether the indians used poisoned arrows;[201] poison would have been available from vegetable sources and it appears to have been used against the Spanish in 1533.[202] The blow-gun, however, was not known.[203] Nets were probably also used to capture animals once they had been cornered. Peccaries, agoutis and lapes could be driven into hollows at the bases of trees or logs from which they could be taken by hand or smoked out. How far fires were used as a hunting device is not known. Quick-moving animals, such as the iguana, squirrel and monkey, would have been difficult to catch, whilst those less fleet of foot, including the armadillo, opossum and turtle would have been relatively easily taken by hand.[204] Birds for food were probably hunted with the bow and arrow, whilst those desired as pets would have been captured as fledglings or lured into the open using decoying noises.[205] Eggs may also have been collected and hatched under adult birds kept in the villages.

So far no archaeological evidence has been found of domesticated animals in Trinidad in pre-Columbian times. If they were present they would have been of minor significance. The Muscovy duck (*Cairina moschata*) was kept by the Caribs in the Lesser Antilles,[206] where it was noted by Columbus.[207] Guinea pigs (*Cavia porcellus*) have also been found in middens in both the Greater and Lesser Antilles,[208] where they were used primarily for meat but may also have had some ritual significance. There is no evidence of either species being kept in Trinidad. Semi-domesticated tree ducks (*Dendrocygna viduata* and *D. bicolor*) were probably hunted, but their eggs would have been collected and hatched under adult ducks kept in the villages.[209] The black vulture or corbeau (*Coragyps atratus*), also a semi-domesticate, was probably introduced into Trinidad by man.[210]

Collecting

The collection of wild fruits and tubers added to the food obtained from agriculture, hunting and fishing, and other wild plant resources were exploited for dyes, resins, medicines, poisons, fibres and timber wood.

Tubers and the leaves of wild plants were probably only eaten in times of scarcity. Wild amaranths (*Amaranthus* spp.) were eaten by the Spanish in 1612 when food supplies were low[211] and zamia tubers (*Zamia* sp.) probably figured amongst the wild roots collected.[212] The leaf buds or "cabbages" of cabbage palm and gru-gru palm may have been eaten, as they are known to have been in Tobago.[213] Wild fruits commonly collected were probably the sea grape and coco plum (*Chrysobalanus icaco*) both found fringing sandy beaches.[214] The wild counterparts of cultivated fruit trees would also have been harvested: they would have included mamey, sweetsop and soursop, guava, hog plum and possibly pawpaw.[215]

Wood was needed for the construction of canoes and houses, for utensils and firewood. For the construction of canoes large trunks were needed, and they came from West Indian cedar, silk cotton, crappo, incense and galba.[216] The same species would have been used in the construction of houses with the addition of tapana (*Hieronyma caribaea*) and the fiddlewoods (*Citharexylum* sp. and *Vitex* sp.). The roofs would have been thatched with the leaves of palm trees—carat, timite and cocorite—and the grass leaves of white roseau. The leaves of cocorite would have also been used in basketry.

Fibres were extracted from a number of wild plants and trees; the most important was rope mangrove (*Pariti tiliaceum*), whose fibre was prized for cordage and hunting and fishing nets.[217] The fibrous stems and trunks of the West Indian elm, seaside mahoe (*Thespesia populnea*) and cousin mahoe (*Urena lobata*), and the fibre around the seeds of the silk cotton tree, would also have been used.[218] Dyes were mainly obtained from cultivated sources but a yellow dye was probably extracted from fustic (*Chlorophora tinctoria*)[219] and a red dye from logwood or "palo de tinta" (*Haematoxylon campechianum*). The oil from the seeds of crappo may have been used in the preparation of paint and to anoint the body.[220] Other tree species yielded gums, oils and resins which would have been used for lighting, caulking canoes, and for attaching points to arrows, stone chips to manioc graters and blades into handles. Resinous wood from the locust tree (*Hymenaea courbaril*) and the incense tree (*Protium guianense*) was burned to give light. Their resins together with that of balata were probably also used as glues. Balsam would have been obtained from the locust tree, incense tree, balsam (*Copaifera officinalis*) and lignum-vitae (*Guaiacum officinale*) and was used for medicinal purposes. Purgatives would have been made from the leaves of cassia (*Cassia occidentalis*) and oil from the seeds of physic nut (*Jatropha curcas*). Infusions of the leaves of Christmas bush (*Eupatorium odoratum*), garden balsam (*Justicia pectoralis*) verrani (*Stachytarpheta jamaicensis*) and mosquito bush, the plants themselves of shiny bush (*Ocimum* sp.) and the roots of minnie root (*Ruellia tuberosa*) would have all been used in curing colds and lowering feverish temperatures.[221] Lignum-vitae, which is now rare in Trinidad, was probably used as a stimulant before being adopted by the Spanish as a cure for syphilis. Narcotic snuffs were made from tobacco and cohoba (*Piptadenia peregrina*).[222]

The most important source of poison for use on arrowheads was probably the juice extracted from bitter manioc but others would have included lucky nut (*Thevetia peruviana*) and supple jack (*Paullina pinnata*).[223] From *Lonchocarpus latifolius* a fish stupefacient could have been extracted, whilst antidotes to poisons took the form of infusions of the bark of physic nut, verrani and *Byrsonima crassifolia*.

Two wild plants may have been used for cleansing purposes; from the soap berry (*Sapindus saponaria*) a kind of soap could have been obtained[224] and small branches of chaw stick (*Gouania lupuloides*) may have been used as a kind of toothbrush.[225]

Craft activities

The indians of Trinidad were skilled workers in clay, stone, wood and bone but the use of metals was probably unknown to them,[226] although it has been suggested that the indians knew how to work gold by hammering.[227] With the exception of stone local materials were used. Stone tools were imported in a manufactured state, except for a few knives that were hewn from poor quality chert and quartzite found in the Northern Range.[228] The only examples of wooden artefacts found are two zoomorphic stools, a shallow bowl, a canoe paddle and a mortar, which were accidentally preserved in the Pitch Lake.[229]

Pottery articles made were almost exclusively bowls, of various shapes and sizes, and cassava griddles. Bowls were made by the coil method and the surface smoothed with stone polishers:[230] the wheel was unknown. Cassava griddles were made of thick flat plates of clay. The articles would then have been fired in an open hearth. The type of pottery made by the indians when the Spanish arrived was poorer in quality than that of previous cultures that had existed in Trinidad. Vessels for holding water and food would have been made also from the fruits of the calabash tree and the bottle gourd.

The most common implements found in the middens were celts, probably used as hammerstones, pestles and polishers, for wood splitting and as weapons.[231] Most of the celts were of foreign origin but many had been reworked: this suggests that the indians lacked suitable stone rather than the knowledge to make them.[232] Blades were made of chert and quartzite and inserted into wooden handles to serve as knives. They would have been multipurpose. Mortars for grinding were made of stone[233] as well as shell and sometimes calcite, and their small size suggests that they were not used for grinding maize. Digging sticks made of wood would have been the most important agricultural tools but owing to their perishable nature there is no archaeological evidence of them. Most of the weapons would have been made of wood,[234] wooden arrows, spears and darts probably having fish bones as points. Clubs and shields would probably also have been wooden. Lovén noted that both round and rectangular shields were used in Trinidad, whilst shields were unknown in the Antilles.[235]

One of the most important manufacturing activities of the indians was the making of canoes for use in trading with the mainland and neighbouring islands. Canoes were made by the dugout method; plank construction was unknown in Trinidad.[236] Columbus noted that some of the canoes had a central section in which the *caciques* and their wives travelled.[237] Large trees[238] were felled and hollowed out by alternate hacking and burning. Pitch from La Brea and south-east Trinidad may have been used to caulk the canoes, especially those made from the silk cotton tree, whose wood is porous.[239] Pitch was also found on potsherds at Mayaro, which would indicate that it was melted in pots or used to mend them.[240]

Woven fibre garments, probably of cotton, were worn by the indians

of Trinidad whom Columbus met on his third journey in 1498[241] and
buttons and needles found in middens indicate that cloth was woven;
skin garments would not have been made because they would decay
rapidly in the humid climate. Several fibres from vegetable resources
would have been used in spinning and weaving but it is not known what
techniques were employed. Pelleprat relates that spindles and bobbins
were not used but that the fibre was rolled and twisted against the thigh
with the hand.[242] Coarser fibres would have been used for making fishing
lines, nets and cords. Hammocks may have been made locally or have
been imported from the Orinoco, where the Warrau indians made them
from the leaves of the moriche palm.[243] Baskets would have been made
from the leaves of palm trees,[244] particularly the cocorite palm.

Body ornaments in the form of rings, necklaces and bracelets have all
been found in the middens. Beads were made of coral, stone and bone[245]
and two necklaces have been found, one of a portion of a monkey skull
and another of Amazon stone.[246] Rings and bracelets would have been
made of wood and stone.[247] Castellanos noted that the indians wore gold
nose ornaments and feathers.[248]

Two types of houses were probably built in Trinidad. Smaller houses
would have been round in outline and built to house up to 100 people.[249]
They would have been bell-shaped in profile with the walls and roof as
one or with a conical roof placed on top of separate walls.[250] In both
cases large poles would have supported a roof made of palm or grass
leaves. Larger houses would have been similar in structure but rectangular in form, and used for village meetings and ceremonies.[251]

Trade

Trade within Trinidad was probably of little economic importance.
Trade would have been carried out by individuals and groups in an
informal manner; there were no established markets or other forms of
organised exchange. At all times of the year food from domesticated and
wild vegetable and animal resources would have been available in all
parts of the island. Local and seasonal variations in these resources may
have stimulated a certain amount of trade but midden evidence suggests
that it was limited in its extent. The most important traffic that occurred
would have been in marine fish and animals from the coast to inland
villages, such as St. Joseph, Siparia, Princes Town (Savanna Grande)

and Mayo, though it may not have involved trading. Goods traded would have included game animals but more often durable goods such as pottery, beads, feathers, knives and bones for specialised purposes.

Most of the intra-island trade would have been carried out by canoes, since nearly all settlements were located near the sea or with easy access to it by river transport. The south and east coasts, where most of the settlements were, were well supplied with landing places.[252] The water on the west coast was shallow but it could be approached in canoes, whereas the north coast was only accessible at Maracas, Las Cuevas and Toco. Where possible rivers would have been used to transport goods inland. St. Joseph was considered by the Spanish to be "the best [settlement] in the island because canoes can sail up the river to within half a league of the town".[253] Some sites were located some distance from navigable rivers so that goods would have had to be transported overland. Evidence of overland travel is seen in the numerous bivuoac sites, particularly in the south of the island. These sites may have been the temporary overnight camps of hunters but their distribution suggests that they followed definite routes linking settlements, and probably therefore were also used by traders. The trails followed watersheds in preference to low marshland and heavily wooded areas. Two main lines of bivuoac sites have been identified. One follows a watershed route from Devil's Hill and Trinidad Hill, north-east to Princes Town (Savanna Grande), thence almost due east through Rio Claro and Ecclesville to Radix Point.[254] From Princes Town another watershed route probably led north to Mayo.[255] A second major line of bivuoac sites has been identified in the Southern Watershed Reserve stretching along the coast from Erin to Mayaro Bay.[256] Runners would have taken messages between villages.[257]

Trade with other Antillean islands and the mainland was more significant. Although fishing was concentrated in inshore waters, the presence of offshore species in Trinidad middens suggests that the indians possessed sufficiently sophisticated maritime techniques to enable them to venture into deep waters, and for trading purposes possibly as far as Puerto Rico.[258]

Trade was most frequent between Trinidad, Venezuela, Guiana and Margarita in aboriginal times, and until recently indians from Guiana landed at Erin Bay and at rare intervals made their way to San Fernando via Siparia to trade.[259] The indians of Trinidad probably exchanged whale and fish oils, shells and possibly some salted fish for durable goods such as celts, hammocks, knives and possible some game animals not known in Trinidad.[260] Navigation between Margarita, Cubagua and Trinidad was easy[261] and pottery evidence indicates early contacts between these islands.[262]

Trade with the Antilles was probably vital to both parties involved. Stone implements were important items of trade, since Trinidad lacked suitable stone from which these could be made. Celts from Martinique, Dominica, Grenada, Tobago and Guyana are all represented in Trinidad middens, together with beads of foreign origin and shells from Barbados.[263] In exchange the indians of Trinidad could offer numerous game animals and vegetable products not found on the Antillean islands, but as yet insufficient work has been carried out on the middens of the Antillean islands to verify this pattern of exchange. In the immediate pre-conquest period trading with the islands and the mainland was made difficult by continuous Carib attacks, which Rouse has suggested may have been of sufficient intensity to isolate Trinidad from the cultural developments that were taking place on the mainland and neighbouring islands, making it a "cultural backwater".[264]

Aboriginal society and ideology

In the absence of direct archaeological and documentary evidence relating to the socio-political and religious life of the indians in Trinidad at the time of discovery, any account of these aspects of culture must rely on indirect and comparative evidence and hence involve speculation.

Without assuming any direct causal relationship between economy and society, the structure of the economy and the size and distribution of population may provide insights into an otherwise unknown field of culture.

It has been demonstrated that food production in aboriginal times was sufficient to support a relatively large population concentrated in villages of about 500 people. An extended family would only constitute a group of 50–100 people[265]—Steward suggests a maximum of 150[266]— so that villages were probably composed of a number of extended families, each of which would have occupied a single house as they did in Hispaniola.[267] Although extended families would have had separate houses, many individuals would have had consanguineal ties with members of other families. Each extended family was probably composed of members related through the female line, forming an extended matrilineal family.[268] The matrilineal nature of aboriginal society in Trinidad is suggested by the fact that it was the nephew of *cacique* Baucunar who was inheritor to his lands,[269] for in a matrilineal society a man's heirs are his sister's children, not his own.[270] The matrilineal nature of the families may have been related to the practice of matrilocal residence which required men to take up residence with the wife's family after marriage. The latter rule may have resulted from the role played by women in the sedentary life of the community. Women were responsible for the planting, weeding and harvesting of crops, so that in Trinidad, where agricultural products accounted for 60–70% of total food production, they were the major food producers. This role not only increased the status of a woman in society, but her greater ties to the land and to other female members of the extended family through co-operation in agricultural activities made her continued presence in her native group after marriage desirable. Men, conversely, were absent from the settlement for considerable periods, hunting, fishing and fighting, and the co-operation needed in such activities was less dependent on common residence.[271]

Probably all members of the village were employed in tasks appropriate to their age and sex; there is no evidence of a class of craftsmen being exempted from routine labour or of a class of slaves. Evidence for slavery in pre-Columbian times exists for Hispaniola, where slaves were called *naborías* by the Spanish,[272] and for Arawak indians of the Orinoco basin.[273] The only evidence of possible slavery in Trinidad is a report by Velasco, who in describing the Arawak indians "of the coast from Trinidad to the east of the mouth of the river Amazon", said that in summer they formed expeditions against the Caribs and, if they could, they captured them for use as slaves.[274] If such captures were made it is likely that captives were quickly assimilated into Trinidadian society rather than forming a distinct class of slaves. The only indians probably exempt from routine labour were the *cacique* and shaman.

The role and authority of the village headman or *cacique* is difficult to ascertain since titles accorded to people in authority by early observers were used inconsistently. The most commonly used title was *cacique*, which was taken from the Arawak for a village headman[275] and applied to any indian who showed any authority. Here it is used with its original meaning. The title *principal* was used more consistently to describe leaders with less authority, but it was sometimes used synonymously with *cacique*. Borde notes that the civil and military leaders in Trinidad were called *acarewanas* by the indians,[276] but they appear to have been renamed *capitanes* by the Spanish.[277] In no case has the specific authority designated by the title been defined.

The *caciques* were civil leaders but their role in society does not appear to have been very significant. Since most economic activities were probably carried out on a family rather than village basis, their economic role was probably small. In the Greater Antilles crimes were judged by the *caciques*, with stealing and adultery punishable by death[278] but it is not known whether *caciques* in Trinidad were empowered with judicial authority. Their primary function was probably as village spokesmen in matters involving contact with other indian groups. On the basis of this role they would have been ascribed a higher status than other members of a village.

The *cacique* does not appear to have fulfilled any religious role; that was left to the shaman. The principal functions of the shaman were to communicate with spirits and to heal the sick. He was not the village headman but his assumed position would have been sanctioned by society: there is no evidence that the shaman was invested with the position, or that the position was hereditary as it became in other Antillean islands. Tobacco and yopa—a snuff made from cahoba— were both used as stimulants.[279] Illnesses were treated with the aid of various herbs and infusions and objects with special curative powers. Dudley in his list of Trinidad indian words includes "Harova—a stone for the headache".[280] Whilst the shaman gained prestige through his activities he was subject to harsh treatment if he failed to carry out a cure.[281]

Whilst villages were largely independent in civil matters, in warfare they were joined together under military leaders. Unlike *caciques*, whose position was hereditary, military leaders appear to have been chosen on the basis of ability in war and it is possible that they were selected on the basis of trials of strength and courage.[282] It would appear, however, that only *caciques* could become military leaders. Above the provincial military leaders were two overall leaders between whom Trinidad was divided.[283] They co-ordinated the troops and worked out the plan of battle.

Although villages joined together to defend themselves from the

Caribs and the Spanish, they were often in a state of war or near-war with each other.[284] It has been suggested that the indians who inhabited Trinidad were naturally more warlike than the indians of other Arawak-inhabited Antillean islands,[285] but this has not been proved. A common reason given for continued warfare between groups is population pressure on resources, particularly favourable resources.[286] This would seem inapplicable to Trinidad, where there was plenty of land available even given that population pressure is felt before it is realised. The desire for favoured lands along the banks of rivers or secondary forest and, if village territory was well defined, access to areas for hunting and fishing may have stimulated some warfare, but not all. The state of chronic warfare in which Yanomamö villages of the borderland between Venezuela and Brazil exist has been attributed to the failure of Yanomamö political institutions to govern effectively conflicts arising within villages resulting in village fission and the establishment of mutually hostile, independent villages.[287] Given the weak political structure of aboriginal society in Trinidad, it is possible that inter-village warfare in the island had such an origin.

The aboriginal Trinidadian conception of the world, like that of the indians of Guiana,[288] would have been related to limits of communication. Disregarding the chance occurrence of indians being carried to distant lands by freak weather conditions, the limits of sea communication, attested by traded goods would have been the coast of the Tierra Firme, from Venezuela to Brazil, and the islands of the southern Caribbean. Contacts with the northern islands would have been infrequent, particularly at the time of discovery, when Carib raids made distant trading in the Caribbean difficult. Aboriginal mythology in the West Indies reflected the conception of a small world. In Hispaniola, for example, the indians believed that the sun and moon came from a local cave known as Giouocua, whilst women were believed to have originated in Martinique.[289] Beyond the world as it was conceived by the indians was a type of heaven, which was unattainable by natural means but could be reached under certain conditions. Members of indian groups who migrated and were never seen again were thought to have gone to heaven, whilst occasional visitors from distant parts would have been regarded as heavenly messengers.

Heaven was regarded as the residence of a supernatural power "who praises the good and punishes the evil and the souls of those who live well go to him".[290] The belief in an after-life, where the soul departed from the body and departed to a heaven where it lived a glorified version of earthly life,[291] is attested by the presence of mortuary offerings in the form of bowls of food, jars of water and celts found at burial sites.[292] Offerings have been found only with male bodies, but not with all, and they may be related to status achieved through dexterity in warfare or hunting. In the Greater Antilles the supreme being was thought to have given yuca (manioc) to mankind and was called Yocahu,[293] but Trinidad gods appear undefined. The indians would also have believed in the existence of spirits of ancestors and natural phenomena and that, if they could gain control of them, they would gain supernatural power. This was to be achieved by the construction of idols, or zemis, built of wood, stone, bone, shell, clay or cotton[294] in which the spirits of ancestors or nature then resided. The construction of zemis reached a high development in the Greater Antilles, where they were worshipped in caves or temples especially erected for the purpose. In Trinidad zemis never played such an important part in the life of the indians. No temples were built and despite an extensive search of all caves in Trinidad none appears to have been inhabited or used for religious purposes.[295] There is also a conspicuous absence of idols or zemis apart from two possible zemis taking the form of rock carvings or petroglyphs found at Caurita and Lagon Doux.[296] Modelled pottery handles found on vessels may, however, have performed a similar function. The handles usually take the form of animals but occasionally they resemble human beings.[297] It is thought that since most of the animals portrayed on handles were common components of the indian diet, they were not totemic but that the purpose was to appease the souls of animals hunted and to encourage them to breed. The same would have applied to human-form figurines, since little distinction between man and animal appears to have been made in aboriginal ideology.[298] As far as is known from midden evidence the indians do not appear to have had any food prejudices. Various other objects appear to have had some spiritual significance, including a piece of monkey skull found at Palo Seco[299] and water-worn pebbles from river gravels which may have been used as rain charms, as they were in Puerto Rico.[300] The design of a pottery stamp found at Erin by Fewkes is thought by Lovén to represent a frog,[301] which is often regarded as a fertility symbol and as a hunting charm in parts of Guiana.[302]

Little is known of the social activities of the indians of Trinidad but the scant evidence suggests that ceremonialism was poorly developed.[303]

No ball courts or dance plazas, such as occur in the Greater Antilles, have been found in Trinidad[304] and the lack of set-up idols and temples suggests that there were few religious ceremonies. The main amusements were probably singing and dancing and possibly some ball games, but group activities appear to have been largely unorganised.[305]

part three

Spanish discovery and conquest 1498-1592

4
Sixteenth-century Trinidad: A Military Base for El Dorado

Trinidad was discovered on 31st July 1498 by Columbus on his third voyage to the New World.[1] Although the Spanish did not obtain a permanent foothold on the island until 1592, during the sixteenth century indian culture was profoundly modified as an indirect result of discovery and subsequent attempts at settlement. Contact between the Spanish and indians occurred in three ways which may be distinguished chronologically as reconnoitring, enslaving and colonisation.

The earliest contacts between the Spanish and the indians were amicable: the Spanish only wanted to reconnoitre the island and the lands fringing the Gulf of Paria, for here it was thought that the claims of the Columbus family were most tenuous and could be effectively challenged.[2] Authorised expeditions that followed the course taken by Columbus in 1498 to the Gulf of Paria were numerous in the post-discovery years. They included the following: in 1499 Alonso de Ojeda, Alonso Niño and Amerigo Vespucci; in 1500 Diego de Lepe and Vincente Yánez Pinzón; in 1501 Cristobal Guerra and in 1502 a second expedition of Alonso de Ojeda.[3] Ojeda in 1499 is the only one known to have landed in Trinidad, though it is possible that the others renewed their supplies of water, food and wood in the island.

Once Trinidad was found to be highly populated it became the focus of Spanish enslaving raids. The general decline of indian population that occurred in the Greater Antilles in the early sixteenth century through contact, disease and excessive work—particularly on the sugar estates[4]—created a labour shortage at the same time as the rapidly

71

expanding pearl fishing industry established in Cubagua and Margarita was increasing its demands for labour. These demands could not be satisfied from Spain, however, and because in the early part of the century negroes were not thought of as an alternative labour source, the indians of the New World were the only source of supply. The Crown was intent on upholding the liberty of indians in the New World and only permitted their enslavement if they were found to be either warlike or Caribs, that is "cannibals". In 1510 it was said that there were no peaceful indians along the whole coast of the Tierra Firme, except in Trinidad,[5] but the following year the island also was declared Carib and the Crown gave permission for the enslavement of the indians, who could be taken to any part of the Indies and sold for profit.[6] There were vociferous complaints from Las Casas that Trinidad had been wrongly designated as Carib and in 1518 Figueroa was commissioned to ascertain which islands and parts of the Tierra Firme were in fact inhabited by Caribs. In 1520 he reported that the indians of Trinidad were "people of goodwill and friends of Christians"[7] and as such could not be legally enslaved. It was not that the *conquistadores* needed permission from the Crown to enslave the indians—they were far enough from Spain to make independent decisions—but Crown sanctions did release them from the surveillance of the missionaries and other religious personnel. In 1530, Sedeño in vain petitioned the Crown for permission to enslave the indians of Trinidad on the grounds that they were "carib and people who eat human flesh and have other rites and evil customs and are very warlike."[8] The Crown refused permission but the enslavement continued. In 1552 Navarrete wrote "it is not possible to find nor detail all the injustices, attacks, damages and ravages which the people of this coast [the pearl coast, of Paria and the island of Trinidad] have suffered from the Spaniards from the year 1510 to the present day".[9] Further attempts were made by the Crown in 1558 to prevent the enslavement of indians, when the citizens of Hispaniola were specifically instructed not to take indians from Trinidad since they were not Caribs.[10] In the same year the employment of indians in the pearl fisheries was forbidden,[11] but still the enslavement continued. The raiding of Trinidad for indians not only led to a rapid decline in the population but it caused the indians, also influenced by accounts of the activities of the Spanish in other islands, to resist any Spanish attempts to settle the island.

The rapid discovery and colonisation of the New World was hampered by Spain's lack of manpower and naval resources, so that only those areas which were considered to be economically profitable were colonised at an early date. In the early part of the sixteenth century Spanish activities in the Caribbean were focused on the pearl fisheries of Cubagua, Cumana and Margarita and it was not until 1521 that a contract was made with Rodrigo de Bastidas for the colonisation of Trinidad.[12] The island, however, officially belonged to the Columbus family, then headed by Diego Columbus, and Bastidas, not wishing to incur law suits, waived the claim.[13] In 1530 a second contract was made with Antonio Sedeño, who, stimulated by the legend of El Dorado and the number of slaves from Trinidad who were arriving in Puerto Rico where he was *contador*, had petitioned the Crown for permission to settle the island.[14] In 1532 Sedeño established the "pueblo de camucurabo" but was forced to withdraw to Margarita to re-equip and re-muster.[15] The following year he returned and rebuilt the settlement on the site of the suburb of Port of Spain at present known as Mucurapo, and called after the name of the indian province of Camucurabo, meaning in Carib the place of the silk cotton tree.[16] The site was chosen by Sedeño because that part of the island was "more peaceable, and densely populated and more abundant in provisions".[17] By the time Sedeño had succeeded in establishing a settlement on the island the interest of Spanish *conquistadores* had been diverted to Peru; in reply to Sedeño's plea for supplies from Cubagua he was told that he could not expect any provisions or other assistance since "all have gone to Peru to seek riches".[18] As a result he abandoned the island in 1534.

It was not until 1553 that another contract for the settlement of Trinidad was made with Juan Sedano,[19] but this was unfulfilled. The next attempt at colonisation was in 1569, by Juan Troche Ponce de León,[20] who was instructed in his contract to establish a settlement in Trinidad apart from the indians. Miguel Diosdado who accompanied Juan Troche Ponce de León on his colonising expeditions relates its foundation as follows: "We came finally and anchored and made port in the place where we are at present building a fort and huts, which we have called the town of the Circumcision because it was on that day [New Year's Day] we came and settled at this flat lowland place next to the water which is a strong point where there are great mountains and lands to cultivate and a great quantity of limestone with which we have already experimented". The precise site of the settlement has not been determined, although it is known to have been "very near the Caroni river".[21] It has been suggested that it was the precursor to St. Joseph, which was founded by de Berrío in 1592,[22] but the description given by Diosdado gives the impression that the "town of the Circumcision" was sited on the coast and near sources of limestone, neither of which describe the site of St. Joseph. The most likely place for the Spanish to have encountered limestone is in the vicinity of Port of Spain, possibly at Laventille. Wherever it was located the settlement was short-lived, for at the end of 1570, after only nine months, Juan Troche Ponce de León growing weary of life in Trinidad and lacking supplies abandoned the island.

Another contract for the settlement of Trinidad was made with Francisco de Vides in 1592,[23] but he was anticipated by Antonio de Berrío's campmaster Domingo de Vera y Ibargoyen in its actual colonisation. De Vides complained that the act of possession was illegal and the Crown ordered de Berrío to leave the island. He refused and there was nothing the Crown could do about it. A permanent base for expeditions attempting to find El Dorado had been established and with it an "urban" base from which Trinidad itself could be colonised.[24]

The discovery of the New World opened up new horizons for other seafaring nations, notably England, France and Holland, that were anxious to undermine Spanish power in Europe; Spanish America was the most vulnerable part of the Spanish Empire. Ships sailed to the New World from France and England with royal licences to disrupt Spanish trade routes and oust the Spanish from tenuously held islands in the Caribbean which could then be used as bases for attacking Spanish settlements and colonising the mainland. The French and English had no immediate interest in obtaining slave labour for economic activities either in the island or elsewhere, or of forcing their culture on the indian population. Accordingly they were more acceptable to the indians, who gladly received any visitors who could help them defend the island against attacks from both Caribs and the Spanish. By the end of the century the presence of the French and English[25] in Trinidad had become a serious threat to the Spanish, so much so that the contract made with de Vides in 1592 stated, as one of the aims of settling the island, that "English and French corsairs should not go to winter in Trinidad or make boats there or supply themselves with provisions or seek information or take canoes for the harmful incursions and sackings which they have carried out".[26] Dutch ships did not undertake regular voyages to the Caribbean until the 1590s[27] when they were primarily interested in the exploitation of the salt deposits at Araya and the smuggling of pearls from Cubagua and Margarita, but they would have replenished their supplies in Trinidad where they had commercial relations with the indians.

Although Carib raids on Trinidad began in the pre-Columbian period they continued with increased intensity during the sixteenth century. With their bases in Dominica, Martinique, St. Lucia, St. Vincent and Grenada, the Caribs attacked the indians of the island "in their homes and whilst they are hunting and fishing, and they carry them off and kill them to eat".[28] By 1592 Carib attacks were occurring every day and it is possible that by then they had established settlements, either temporary or permanent, in the island.[29]

5
The Initial Impact of Discovery and Conquest: Demographic Disaster

During the sixteenth century indian culture was mainly modified indirectly as a result of the decline in indian population and its movement inland. Most early visitors to Trinidad were impressed by the large number of indians there were in the island. Enciso described it as "highly-populated" and in 1570 Diosdado said that above all the island was "so highly populated that it is a thing worthy of admiration".[1] It was not until the end of the sixteenth century, as the Spanish saw their sources of manpower for expeditions to El Dorado dwindle, that there were vociferous complaints about the decline in Trinidad's population.

The actual decline in the indian population is difficult to estimate in the light of the unreliability of figures given by sixteenth century observers. Dobyns has suggested that by 1570 the Caribbean islands possessed only one twentieth of the population they had had at the time of discovery.[2] Since it has been estimated that the population of Trinidad at the time of conquest was between 20 000 and 30 000 and it is known that after three centuries of population decline the indian population was about 2000, the depopulation ratio is clearly inapplicable to Trinidad. Although the population of the island decreased considerably as a result of raiding attacks, as far as is known it was not ravaged by disease and many indians probably escaped to the densely forested hills. Given that the indian population of Trinidad in 1680 was about 5000[3] and that it suffered as great a decrease by raiding as it did in the early years of intense contact, it may be estimated that the population of the

76

island in 1592 was between 15 000 and 20 000;[4] that is half of what it had been prior to conquest.

The main causes of this decline in the indian population were the enslaving raids of the Spanish and the Caribs, and the indirect consequences of the Spanish occupation of the island.

Whilst the Crown was anxious to uphold the freedom of the indian as a subject of the King of Spain, it was faced with the problem of indians who refused to be incorporated into the Spanish Empire and who rejected the Roman Catholic faith. Was the Crown justified in waging war on the indians? While moral issues were debated in Europe, the *conquistadores* were faced with the more practical problem of obtaining labour for the development and further expansion of the Spanish Empire. By the time the Crown had decided that the indians could not be enslaved,[5] much of the damage had been done; no laws could change the pattern of activities that had existed for half a century and in any case the New World was remote and the needs of labour were pressing.

No sooner had Trinidad been discovered by Columbus than it became an important source of indians for labour in the developing enterprises in Santo Domingo, Puerto Rico, Cubagua and Margarita. In 1510 two Dominican fathers, Francisco de Córdova and Juan Garcés, went to Trinidad under the guise of instructing the indians in the Catholic faith, but having encouraged the indians on board their ship, they weighed anchor and sailed to Santo Domingo where they sold them as slaves.[6] A similar raid was effected by Juan Bono who in 1516 captured 185 Trinidad indians and sold them in Puerto Rico.[7] By 1521 there were many indians from Trinidad in the Greater Antilles and in that year Rodrigo de Bastidas was instructed to take "some slaves from the said island of Española and San Juan that are natives of the said island [Trinidad] and the coast of the Tierra Firme" for use as interpreters.[8] From 1520 it was illegal to enslave indians from Trinidad but as late as 1569 the Crown was repeating orders to the citizens of Hispañiola that they should not raid the island for slaves.[9] Although many indians were taken to the Greater Antilles, the majority were probably sold in Cubagua and Margarita, particularly during the first half of the century when the pearl fishing industry flourished.[10] Borde suggests that between 1505 and 1527 40 000 indians were taken to Cubagua and Margarita,[11] and although this number is probably exaggerated, it indicates the scale on which enslaving raids were occurring. Despite the ban on taking indians from Trinidad *residencias* on officials of the islands of

Cubagua and Margarita throughout the sixteenth century indicate that raids still occurred.[12] The enslavement of the indians and their carriage to other parts of the New World was probably the major cause of the drastic decline in the indian population in the sixteenth century; the Spanish, however, blamed it on the Caribs.

One of the advantages of settling Trinidad was seen by Domingo de Vera as preventing "the notable harm that the carib indians natives of dominica, granada, matalino [Martinique] and other islands do in killing and eating the natives of this island [Trinidad] and their Spanish neighbours".[13] By 1612 Caribs were attacking both the Spanish and the indians well inland in the foothills of the Northern Range. It seems likely that by that time the Caribs had settled on the northern coast and were conducting their raids from there. In 1637 Jacques Ousiel reported that there was a supply of plantains at Maracas "from the old plantations of the Caribs who were driven away from the aforesaid island [Trinidad] by the Spanish and still come there every year in their canoes to lay provisions".[14] Carib raids would have certainly led to a decrease in the indian population, such that one witness could testify in 1612, "it has been the fault of the Caribs that the island has been depopulated, having had many more inhabitants than at present";[15] nevertheless, the Caribs possessed far less effective means of capture than the Spanish who had sophisticated weapons and ships that could transport several hundred indians at a time. The Caribs were to blame but the Spanish even more so.

The clash between indians and Spaniards led in other ways to a decrease in the indian population. Since the indians rejected the Spanish they found themselves in a state of war. As a direct result a number of indians were killed in battles which were attempts to prevent the Spanish from settling in the island. Indirectly the effects were more serious. The indians could no longer devote their full attention to food production, neither could they exploit effectively the island's resources since considerations of defence demanded the movement of settlements inland. This meant that the level of food production declined and famines, such as that which occurred in 1533,[16] were not unknown. Consequently, as well as a direct decrease in the population there was a reduction in its ability to reproduce.

During the sixteenth century the village continued to be the characteristic form of indian settlement, although the indian population declined and was re-distributed in response to Carib raids. Of the 24 settlement sites known to have existed in pre-Columbian times only six—St. Joseph, Mayo, Princes Town, Siparia, Arima and Buenos Ayres—have yielded any evidence of Spanish contact. The Spanish artefacts found at those sites may not be regarded as exclusively sixteenth-century; indeed, with the exception of St. Joseph, it is likely that they were introduced in the late seventeenth and eighteenth centuries, when missions are known to have been established at Mayo, Princes Town, Siparia and Arima. The lack of Spanish and European artefacts at other sites may not, however, be regarded as evidence of the abandonment of those sites in the colonial period, for many of the settlements could have existed in isolation from, or with only casual and intermittent contact with, the Spanish and other Europeans.

In contrast to the concentration of settlement sites in the southern part of the island, documentary evidence from the sixteenth century indicates that the indian population was distributed throughout the island. Columbus noted in 1498 that there were many settlements in the south,[17] whereas Sedeño noticed that many *caciques* had their lands in the provinces of Chacomari and Camucurabo, in the foothills of the Northern Range, and commented that others living in higher parts of the Northern Range supplied him with food.[18] Martín López considered that the west coast of Trinidad was "unhealthy" but Sedeño thought it to be the most populated part of Trinidad.[19] In 1570 Diosdado sailed along the west coast "seeing lands, ports and communicating with the natives and entering in villages where they treated us well" and later in 1594-5 Dudley tried to settle near Paracowe (probably present-day San Fernando) "where manie people of the islands had theire habitation", including 7 or 8 *caciques* who swore allegiance to the English crown.[20] Raleigh noted that the "Nepoios" indians were living on the east coast,[21] but in view of the swampy conditions in Manzanilla Bay their settlements were probably limited to Mayaro and the north-eastern peninsula around Toco.

Although the indian settlements were distributed throughout the island, during the sixteenth century the indian population was forced to retreat inland as a result of the continual raids that occurred in the coastal areas. As early as 1500 Yánez Pinzón visited the Gulf of Paria "without seeing anything else but small villages destroyed".[22] The movement of the population inland was also a movement to higher land. In 1554 the *Escribano* of Margarita stated that the hills were highly populated and that many of the coastal villages had been partly destroyed by the Spanish,[23] and by 1612 it was reported that "the few indians that there are left of the infinite number there were in the island have hidden themselves and moved well inland".[24] The retreat of the indian population inland probably had important consequences for the indian economy. Although the availability of fresh water was little affected by the movement of the indian population inland, it would have been difficult for the indians to secure the protein from marine resources that was necessary to maintain a balanced diet. Also, communications with the coast were more time-consuming, involving greater travelling distances and more arduous conditions. All these factors would have led to stresses in the aboriginal economy.

There is no evidence, either archaeological or documentary, relating to the size of indian villages. The decline experienced by the indian population in the sixteenth century must have been manifest in the size of the villages, although somewhat obscured by the amalgamation of settlements. The villages as a whole must have suffered a differential decline in size, with the coastal villages sustaining the greatest losses. It seems likely, therefore, that the villages varied considerably in size with a maximum around 500. The form of the indian settlements is similarly undocumented but it is likely to have been very similar to that which existed in pre-Columbian times.

The indian economy under stress

The Carib and Spanish raids on Trinidad that continued throughout the sixteenth century had serious effects on the indian economy. The decline in the male population and its preoccupation with matters of defence rather than subsistence probably caused a decrease in labour inputs in hunting and fishing. This in turn led to a decrease in the amount of protein available to the population and increased its dependence on domesticated sources of food thereby upsetting the dietary balance that had been maintained in pre-Columbian times. The decrease in protein availability was in part compensated for by the introduction of new plants and animals from both the Old World and the New, and by the declining needs of the population. More directly, attacks on hunting and fishing parties and the ravaging of cultivation plots must have decreased the efficiency of food production and lessened the impact of newly introduced tools and techniques. The unreliability of food resources meant that both the indians and Spanish were at times driven to depend on the collection of wild vegetable products. Collecting also provided the raw materials for craft activities, which may have increased in importance in the sixteenth century as European demands for manufactured goods increased; trade with the Antilles probably continued, though lessened by the greater intensity of Carib raids. The increased dependence of the indian economy on less reliable sources of food and manufactured goods rendered it less stable and productive than it had been in pre-Columbian times.

Agricultural Production

The products of agriculture probably made a larger contribution to the economy in the sixteenth century than they had done in the pre-Columbian period, as a result of the drawing off of male labour from hunting and fishing. As far as is known agriculture continued to be practised under a system of shifting cultivation, but small plots may have been cleared for the cultivation of specialised crops that were demanded by foreign traders. Although domesticated livestock were introduced into Trinidad in the sixteenth century they did not give rise to ranching activities, which might have necessitated a restructuring of the agricultural system.

In the sixteenth century cultural factors played a more significant role in determining the location of cultivation plots or *conucos*. As in pre-Columbian times the indians preferred to locate their plots on low-lying but well drained land in the vicinity of rivers and within a few miles of the coast, but their susceptibility to attack by Caribs and the Spanish militated against their location in coastal areas. As early as 1500 Pinzón noted that villages along the coast of the Gulf of Paria were in ruins[25] and by 1554 it appears that the hills were densely populated with cultivators whilst the lowlands were battlefields.[26] The general movement of the indian population inland meant that more land was cultivated at higher altitudes and on steeper slopes where it would have been more susceptible to erosion. Also, upland soils were less fertile than those of the alluvial banks and plains formerly cultivated. There is no evidence that newly introduced crops extended the boundaries of cultivation within the limits set by defensive considerations.

Land clearance would still have been effected by ring-barking, cutting and firing. Although the indians continued to use stone axes and knives for cutting down the vegetation, they would also have had the use of metal tools brought by Europeans.[27] Although the efficiency of cutting down trees would have been raised by the employment of metal tools, the movement of the population into more remote areas would have necessitated the clearance of primary forest, which would have taken longer to clear than secondary forest.[28]

After burning, the *conucos* were planted with a variety of crops. Metal planting and weeding tools may have been obtained from Europeans but the adaptability of the digging stick to various types of terrain would have encouraged its persistence as the principal agricultural implement. Food crops would have been planted in the *conucos* but specialised products, such as cotton and tobacco, may have been grown in specially cleared plots. The cultivation of non-alimentary crops would have reduced the labour inputs in food production. The result would have been a rationalisation of the crops grown and the subsequent withdrawal of low-yielding species. This might account for the apparent loss of starchy varieties of sweet potato[29] whilst other low-yielding crops such as arrowroot would have been retained because of distinctive attributes. The loss in the variety of crops grown would have in part been compensated for by the introduction of new crops from both the Old and New Worlds. However, the overall decreased diversity of crops planted in the *conucos* would have meant that the diverse forest eco-system would have been replaced by a more specialised agricultural system where soil fertility decline, soil erosion and vegetation degradation would have received greater encouragement. By the sixteenth century the soils cultivated would have been inherently less fertile and their fertility may have declined further with the planting of certain protein-rich crops, such as maize, which make relatively greater demands on soil nutrients. Soil erosion would also have been encouraged by the cultivation of steeper slopes than had been cultivated in pre-Columbian times.

If the decreased availability of land for cultivation was not paralleled by the decrease in the indian population, there would have been a tendency to reduce the periods of time that the land lay fallow. If this was the case it would have led to a decrease in soil fertility and the more frequent exposure of the soil to sun and rain would have encouraged leaching and soil erosion. In addition short fallowing would have led to degradation of the vegetation cover and an extension of the areas of savanna. It is unlikely, however, that pressure on land was more than localised for a sixteenth-century observer noted that the indians of Trinidad "cultivate little land and they do not raise livestock and the land is extensive and it would appear that it is all fertile and suitable for cultivation."[30]

During the sixteenth century a number of new crops were introduced to Trinidad, despite the fact that the indigenous indians continued to be the only permanent inhabitants of the island. The Spanish introduced many crops to the Greater Antilles from the Old World and from there they were spread throughout the New World. In addition they carried many New World domesticates to the more remote parts of the Americas and the Caribbean, which had not received them in pre-Columbian times. Casual contacts with representatives of other European nations may have resulted in the diffusion of several Old World domesticates to the New World, though there would have been little stimulus for the indians to adopt them given the ephemeral character of the contact. The increased movement of indian groups between the mainland and the islands in the sixteenth century may also have resulted in the wide dissemination of crops.

Whilst the Spanish exploited indian food resources they were anxious to establish their own agricultural activities and introduced many crops formerly unknown in the New World. All contracts made by the Crown for the settlement of the island contained instructions for the introduction of Old World plants, particularly sugar cane, and also livestock. Although the plants introduced were intended to be grown on land owned by the Spanish but worked by the indians, many of them were adopted by the indians themselves. Not all the plants and animals that were introduced were suited to the tropical conditions of the islands and as a consequence many failed to become established. Those that were adapted to the conditions spread rapidly and diversified the already diverse assemblage of domesticates found in the New World.

During the sixteenth century manioc, maize and sweet potatoes remained the most important food crops. In 1533 Antonio Sedeño and his men were sustained by some *caciques* who provided them with "some maize, yuca, potatoes and other roots"[31] and in 1595 the French and English were reported as being supplied with "maize, cassava, potatoes, plantains and other fruits".[32] The Spanish adopted maize as a staple crop when Old World cereal crops failed. Sedeño in 1533 laid out maize fields within the palisaded settlement he had built.[33] Other seed crops that probably flourished in the sixteenth century included the common bean and the lima bean. The jack bean (*Canavalia ensiformis*), a Central American domesticate, may have been introduced to Trinidad in the sixteenth century though its low repute as a food crop may have delayed its spread to more distant parts of the Americas.[34] The squashes were probably introduced in the early colonial period; however, their pre-Columbian arrival in the island remains a possibility since they are commonly associated with maize which was certainly present at that time. A late pre-Columbian date for the introduction of squashes to Margarita has been favoured[35] but Oviedo only noted the presence of the calabash gourd in the West Indies in the sixteenth century.[36] Once they had been introduced, squashes would have become important sources of food owing to their high carbohydrate content and good keeping qualities.[37] The bottle gourd was probably also cultivated.

The eagerness of the Spanish to introduce to the New World crops with which they were familiar in the Iberian peninsula resulted in the early transference of wheat and barley. Wheat (*Triticum aestivum*) was taken to the Antilles by Columbus on his second voyage in 1493 but it did not prosper.[38] Undaunted, the Crown instructed Columbus to take 6000 *fanegas* (660 000 lb) of wheat and 600 *fanegas* of barley (*Hordeum sativum*) to the New World on his third voyage in 1498.[39] Since Trinidad was Columbus' first landfall on that voyage he may have introduced the indians to those crops but it is unlikely that they were planted; even if they had been they would have perished in the moist climatic conditions. In 1553 Sedano was instructed in his contract for the settlement of Trinidad and part of the Tierra Firme to take "tools and implements for sowing wheat and barley and all other plants that should be necessary"[40] but the contract was never fulfilled. Even if wheat was not grown in Trinidad some knowledge of the crop is indicated by Dudley's list of Arawak words used in Trinidad where wheat is called "maurisse"[41] and in 1607 a Spaniard, Lupercio Despés, was charged with having stolen four *fanegas* (440 lb) of wheat from an indian.[42] A small variety of rice (*Oryza sativa*) was introduced to Hispañiola in 1512 and it was adopted readily in hot wet lowlands where it grew well.[43] There is no evidence, however, that it was introduced to Trinidad at an early date. Two other protein-rich crops that may have been introduced to the island in the sixteenth century are pigeon peas (*Cajanus cajan*) and chick peas (*Cicer arietinum*). It has been suggested that pigeon peas were an early post-conquest introduction to the West Indies[44] but it seems more likely that, being African in origin, they were introduced at the time of the slave trade,[45] that is at the end of the seventeenth century. Chick peas are generally considered as new arrivals in the tropics[46] but it is known that they were important constituents of the diet of Spanish immigrants.[47]

The fruits that had been introduced into Trinidad in the pre-Columbian period continued to flourish. Pawpaw and cashew, if they had not been present at an earlier date, would have made their appearance in the island in the sixteenth century. Pawpaw may have reached Trinidad via the mainland from Central America or it may have been introduced to Santo Domingo by the Spanish and from thence to Trinidad.[48] It was growing in Trinidad in the early seventeenth century.[49] The cashew may have been introduced to Trinidad by the Caribs with whom it was associated[50] or it may have been introduced by the Spanish from Central America, possibly via the Greater Antilles. The avocado pear (*Persea americana*), a Central American domesticate, was probably introduced to the West Indies in the sixteenth century by the Spanish, although it has been suggested that it was first introduced to Jamaica in 1650[51] and from thence to other islands. It would have been suited to the poor but well drained soils of the Northern Range.[52]

The most important crops introduced into Trinidad in the sixteenth century by the Spanish were fruit trees. Although they were taken to the New World for the use of the Spanish, they were readily adopted by the indians. Juan Troche Ponce de León in his contract for the settlement of the island in 1569 was specifically instructed to introduce fruit trees.[53] Among these, citrus species would have figured significantly and would have included sweet orange (*Citrus sinensis*), sour orange (*C. aurantium*), lime (*C. aurantifolia*), lemon (*C. limon*) and citron (*C. medica*). The notable absentee from the citrus group would have been the grapefruit (*C. paradisi*), which is now considered to be a cross between the shaddock (*C. maxima*) and the sweet orange. Since the former was not introduced to the West Indies until the seventeenth century when it was taken to Barbados,[54] it could not have been present in Trinidad in the sixteenth century. Citrus trees were well suited to the ecological conditions of the Caribbean islands and they spread rapidly as escapes from cultivation.[55]

Three Asian fruits that may have been present in Trinidad in the sixteenth century are the sweet or musk melon (*Cucumis melo*), the pomegranate (*Punica granatum*) and the banana (*Musa paradisiaca*). The musk melon was introduced to the New World at an early date[56] and since it was growing in St. Kitts in 1630[57] it may have been present in Trinidad in the late sixteenth century. At that time Acosta also noted that there was a "great store of pomegranates" in the New World[58] and in 1631 they were growing in Barbados.[59] It is unlikely, however, that if pomegranates had been introduced to Trinidad in the sixteenth century, they would have spread as rapidly as they did in the drier Lesser Antilles. Whilst plantains were probably present in Trinidad in pre-Columbian times and were abundant in the sixteenth century,[60] the banana proper (*Musa paradisiaca* var. *sapientum*) was not introduced until the post-conquest period. Bananas were taken to Hispaniola from the Canaries in 1516[61] and subsequently introduced to the other West Indian islands in the sixteenth century. In addition to the fruits mentioned above, apples, pears, plums, peaches, apricots, quinces and mulberries were all introduced to the New World at an early date[62] but if they had been introduced to Trinidad they would not have flourished, being unsuited to the ecological conditions of the island. None of them is at present grown in Trinidad.[63]

Grapes (*Vitis vinifera*) for wine and olives (*Olea europea*) were important in the Spanish diet and the early settlers were eager to cultivate them in the New World. Shoots of vines were taken to the Antilles by Columbus on his second voyage in 1493[64] and a *cédula* of 31st August 1531 ordered that all sea captains should take olives and vines to the Indies.[65] In 1569 Juan Troche Ponce de León was instructed to take vine cuttings to Trinidad[66] but in 1590 Acosta reported that neither grapes nor olives grew well in the Antilles.[67]

In addition to fruits, a number of vegetables may have been introduced from the Old World. In 1533 Sedeño built a palisaded settlement in Trinidad and planted "maize fields and vegetables".[68] Although it is not known what vegetables were planted they may have included cabbages (*Brassica* sp.), onions (*Allium cepa*), carrots (*Daucus carota*), lettuces (*Lactuca sativa*), radishes (*Raphanus sativus*), garlic (*Allium sativum*) and aubergines (*Solanum melongena*) which were all introduced to the West Indies prior to 1600.[69] It is doubtful, however, if any of them were adopted by the indians.

Tobacco and cotton were important items of trade between the indians and Europeans in the sixteenth century. Tobacco in particular was sought after by the English[70] and by the beginning of the seventeenth century Espinosa noted that "the chief staple of this country is tobacco".[71] In 1532 Sedeño was given permission to trade with the indians of Trinidad for cotton[72] and in 1593 de Berrío reported that there was "a great quantity of cotton" in the island.[73] Although wild cacao was found growing in Trinidad in 1616[74] cultivated trees were probably introduced to the island in the sixteenth century. It has been suggested that cacao was introduced to Trinidad from Central America in 1525[75] although there is no documentary evidence to support this. However, it was probably present in the late sixteenth century, for it was present in Trinidad in the first decade of the seventeenth century.[76] Sugar cane may have been introduced into Trinidad in pre-Columbian times via a Pacific route but if not it was certainly introduced to the island by the Spanish in the sixteenth century. Sugar canes were taken to the New World by Columbus on his second and third voyages and on the latter he offered them to the indians of the Gulf of Paria.[77] These canes did not prosper, however, but the plant was reintroduced to Santo Domingo where the first sugar mill was built in 1509.[78] In 1530 Sedeño was given the privilege that "the first sugar mill which you should build in the island [Trinidad] shall be free of all constraints and duties and that for the said mill you can take from Spain and the Indies all iron tools that should be necessary without paying the duties of *almojarifazgo* or other duties and all other necessary items".[79] Although it is likely that sugar cane was taken to Trinidad at that time there is no mention of a sugar mill in the inventory of his estate.[80] Sugar cane was growing in Trinidad in 1570 and in 1593 Trinidad was described as "very abundant in sulphur, maize and sugar cane".[81]

Two South-East Asian domesticates, indigo (*Indigofera tinctoria*) and ginger (*Zingiber officinale*), which became important commercial crops from the mid-seventeenth century onwards, were probably introduced to Trinidad in the sixteenth century. *Indigofera suffructicosa*, from which the indians obtained a blue dye, was present in Trinidad in pre-Columbian times but it was not until the post-conquest period that *Indigofera tinctoria* was introduced to the Greater Antilles and from thence to other islands.[82] It was the latter species that was commercially grown at a later period. In 1593 de Berrío reported that Trinidad was "a very good land for ginger"[83] but whether it was grown there at that time is uncertain. It was growing in Trinidad in 1636[84] and its introduction in the sixteenth century therefore seems likely.

Several other species which were used for medicinal purposes made their appearance in the New World in the sixteenth century. *Cassia fistula*, a domesticate of South-East Asia was introduced in 1517 to Hispaniola,[85] where it was used mainly as a purgative but possibly also for skin diseases. It was probably an early arrival in Trinidad for in 1570 Diosdado noted that it was growing there.[86] The castor oil plant (*Ricinus communis*) may also have been introduced to the West Indies by the Spanish shortly after their discovery[87] though its probable African origin and its common association with negro populations in the seventeenth century[88] suggests that it reached the islands in slave ships. The oil extracted from the seeds had various uses, particularly a medicinal use as a purgative.

From the time of discovery the Spanish were anxious to introduce domesticated animals to the Antilles for both conquest and colonisation. A horse was considered to be worth more than a hundred men in conquest since the indians were terrified of them[89] and other domesticated animals were vital for the maintenance of the Spanish in the New World. Trinidad was considered suitable for the establishment of ranching activities because it possessed "great plains of savannas for the breeding of livestock".[90]

Columbus took horses, cattle, sheep, goats and pigs to Hispaniola on his second voyage in 1493,[91] but the sheep and goats did not prosper in the humid tropical climate. Horses, on the other hand, faired well and in 1500 a royal stud farm was established there. The enterprise was obviously successful for in 1507 the King ordered that no more horses were to be taken to the New World from Spain.[92] The earliest would-be colonisers of Trinidad were contracted to introduce domesticated animals into the island. In 1521 Rodrigo de Bastidas was instructed to take to Trinidad "200 cows and 300 pigs and 25 mares and any other animals".[93] Since the contract was not fulfilled, Sedeño was probably the first person to introduce livestock to Trinidad. In 1531 he collected "horses, mares, heifers and other livestock" in Puerto Rico[94] before attempting to colonise Trinidad. Many of the horses perished on the journey and those that arrived alive were killed by the indians. In the following year Sedeño returned to Trinidad from Margarita taking with him eleven horses. It is likely that other animals were taken as well but by the beginning of 1573 the indians had killed all the horses and livestock.[95] Undaunted, Sedeño having experienced casualties in the transfer of horses from Margarita to Trinidad, determined not to take a further eight horses by sea "because of the lack of fodder and the long distance of the journey and the difficult navigation because of the currents" but to "open a way through the mountains of the Tierra Firme at great cost and labour from the port which is called Bacunare until arriving at the province of Paria".[96] Although five of the eight horses were wounded in battle in 1533, the remaining three were entrusted by Sedeño to a friendly *cacique* when he abandoned the island in 1534.[97] Juan Troche Ponce de León in his contract to settle the island in 1569 was instructed to take to Trinidad within four years over 100 horses, 100 mares, 500 cows or calves, 1000 ewes and 200 pigs and goats from the islands of Hispaniola, Puerto Rico, Cuba, Margarita and the provinces of Venezuela, Santa Marta, Cartagena and Tierra Firme.[98] At the end of that year animals were landed in Trinidad[99] but it is not known what kind of animals they were or whether any of them survived after the island was abandoned in 1570. Certainly it would have been easy for cattle to survive in the savannas, although there is no evidence of feral cattle being present in the sixteenth century. In 1591 Domingo de Vera y Ibargoyen reported that "the state in which we find ourselves at the moment is that we are 300 and more armed men and there are 80 horses and cows and some pigs to support the city of St. Joseph which is in this island and that of Santo Thomé".[100] Although considerable numbers of domesticated animals had been taken to Trinidad during the sixteenth century they did not lead to the establishment of pastoralism. In 1638 Diego Ruíz Maldonado observed that "the island is fertile although there is a lack of cattle".[101] Even if a number of domesticated animals did outlive the expeditions that brought them and turn feral, they evidently did not multiply as they had done in the Greater Antilles.[102]

Minor domesticated animals introduced into Trinidad in the sixteenth century included dogs, chickens and turkeys. Dogs were important animals of conquest[103] but they were also kept as pets. They were taken by Sedeño from Puerto Rico to Trinidad in 1531.[104] The chicken (*Gallus gallus domesticus*), a South-East Asian domesticate, was an important source of protein for the Spanish, in the form of meat and eggs. Chickens were taken to Brazil in 1500[105] and they were being kept by the indians when Dudley visited Trinidad in 1594.[106] They may have been introduced to the island from Brazil but it is likely that they were taken there by the Spanish on a colonising expedition. In 1595 de Berrío sent Sparrey "a dozen hens, three deer and some fruits of the land".[107] The turkey (*Meleagris gallopavo*), a domesticate of Mexico, is thought to have been present in Venezuela in pre-Columbian times,[108] but there is no evidence of its presence in Trinidad. It is possible that it was introduced to the island in the sixteenth century either directly from Venezuela or indirectly from Central America via the Greater Antilles.

In addition to domesticated animals a number of undesirable wild species accompanied the Spanish in their journeys to the New World. The black rat, the roof rat and the brown rat were probably all introduced accidentally to Trinidad in the sixteenth century and they must have done considerable damage in the indian *conucos*. The house mouse was probably also introduced at that time.

Hunting and Fishing

During the sixteenth century hunting and fishing continued to make significant contributions to the indian economy, although labour inputs in the two activities were reduced as a result of the decline in the male population and the increased amount of time spent in defence. Though the exploitation of terrestrial and aquatic animal resources for indian consumption declined, the demands of both Spanish and other European visitors to the island probably maintained the overall level of utilisation. A spatial re-distribution in the exploitation of resources occurred, however. The movement of the indian population inland led to the hunting of more remote game animals, particularly those found in dense forest areas, and for defensive reasons fishing became concentrated inshore. The exposed coastal margins themselves no doubt suffered some decline in their animal populations as a direct result of the hunting activities of the Spanish and other casual visitors to the island.

The sixteenth century witnessed the continuing importance of the open-forest environment for hunting and of deer and peccaries in the indian diet.[109] Both deer and peccaries were also important sources of food for the Spanish who, once they had exhausted the ephemeral supplies they had brought with them, were dependent on wild food resources and on supplies from friendly *caciques*. It is interesting that the agouti which was another open-forest species hunted in the pre-Columbian period and which is still common in the island today, was not mentioned by early observers. It would almost certainly have been hunted and may have been included under the title of lapes, which were presented to the French and English by the indians in 1595.[110]

Closed-forest species hunted by the indians in the sixteenth century included the red howler monkey. In 1570 it was noted that there was "a great quantity of monkeys" in Trinidad and in 1594 Robert Dudley reported that he had passed through a wood "whereof munkies, babions and parats were in great abundance".[111] Other mammals hunted were probably the nine-banded armadillo, a dense forest inhabitant, an anteater (*Tamandua longicaudata*) and two species of opossum (*Didelphis marsupialis* and *Philander trinitatis*). Birds continued to be hunted for food and feathers and kept as pets. The variety of parrots impressed sixteenth century observers. Enciso noted that there were "tame green parrots and some have yellow fronts and learn to talk and speak a lot", whilst Columbus saw "parrots as large as chickens".[112] The former description probably refers to the Amazon parrot which would have been an important source of feathers, together with macaws (*Ara* spp.) and the scarlet ibis (*Eudocimus ruber*). Parrots were also described by the Spanish as "sweet to eat".[113] Pigeons and ground doves would have continued to be exploited.

Turtles, especially the green turtles (*Chelonia mydas*), were important sources of food for both the Spanish and the indians in the form of meat and eggs. They were particularly susceptible to exploitation due to their exposed littoral habitat and it is likely that the over-exploitation of turtles, which occurred in many West Indian islands,[114] began in Trinidad at that time. Probably the only other reptile hunted was the iguana.

During the sixteenth century sophisticated hunting techniques would still have been used by the indians but supplemented and modified by contact with the Spanish and other Europeans. Larger animals would still have been caught by pit-trapping and with the bow and arrow. Although the Spanish introduced metal tools, particularly those made of iron, to the indians,[115] there is no evidence that the latter made metal arrow heads. The indians continued to use fish bones as arrow heads: Enciso in 1519 wrote, "Here they use arrows as long as an arm made of rushes, which are found in that country, and at the bottom they insert bones of fish for points and the points are as strong as diamonds".[116] Castellanos noted that sharks' teeth were used for arrow points whilst other arrows were made by hardening the tips of rushes and reeds with fire.[117] Poisoned arrows were also used by the indians, but their use may have been restricted to battle. The reduced amount of time available for hunting and fishing may have led to the increased use of fire as a hunting device, although this is not mentioned in the documentary record.

FORSYTH LIBRARY
FORT HAYS STATE UNIVERSITY

Fishing probably provided the greater part of the proteins needed by the indian population. The Spanish also turned to fishing as an important source of food. Columbus was impressed by the "unlimited fish" there were in the island[118] and in 1533 Sedeño attempted to develop the fishing industry in Trinidad by capturing some indians and trying to sell them in Cubagua in order to use the proceeds to buy nets. Royal officials in Cubagua, however, forbade the selling of the indians and said that they could send no nets or other assistance since all efforts were focused on Peru.[119] In 1534 Sedeño again complained to the officials in Cubagua, saying that the boats they had in Trinidad had been damaged and there was no shipwright to mend them; also that the fishing nets were not strong enough and as a consequence they had no fish to eat.[120] In 1569 Juan Troche Ponce de León in his contract to settle Trinidad was instructed to establish two fisheries[121] but it is unlikely that he accomplished this during his short stay in the island.

Inshore demersal fish, particularly sea catfishes and weakfish, croakers and corvinas continued to be the most important fish caught. Offshore fishing on the continental shelf would have declined in importance, though couvalli and carite or Spanish mackerel were probably still important constituents of the indian diet. Marine mollusca, particularly chip-chip, were an important source of food for the indian population but the Spanish were more impressed by the oysters which grew on the roots of mangrove trees.[122] The Spanish were probably more interested in obtaining large amounts of food with the minimum expenditure of effort and had little consideration or even awareness of declining resources.

Large fish and aquatic mammals would have been caught with bows and arrows. In addition the indians may have used the harpoon and the trammel net, which were both introduced to the New World by the Spanish in the early colonial period.[123] Fish traps may also have been introduced for the capture of smaller fish. Hooks and lines would have continued to be used, with the hooks for the most part made of bone and shell. In addition metal fishing hooks were obtained from foreign visitors to the island.[124] Dugout canoes remained the most important means of water transport, being well adapted to the shallow approach waters around the coast of Trinidad. It is possible that formerly unknown nautical techniques such as the use of the sail may have been introduced to the island during the sixteenth century by the Spanish, either from the Old World or from the western coast of South America.[125]

Collecting

During the sixteenth century collecting made heavier demands on the vegetation cover. In addition to the use made by the indians of wild plants for food, medicines, poisons, dyes, resins and timber, the Spanish and other European visitors collected wild fruits and tubers and selectively felled many trees for the construction of houses and boats and for medicinal and dyeing purposes.

Throughout the sixteenth century the continual attacks by Caribs and the Spanish would have decreased the reliability of domestic food sources and occasionally caused the indians to be dependent on wild vegetable products as "famine foods". In 1535 it was reported that there had been a drought in June 1533 during which the indians could only get "roots and wild herbs" to eat for six months.[126] It is doubtful that the scarcity was caused by a drought; more likely it was the result of the disruption of the economy by continual raiding. In addition to roots and leaves, particularly wild amaranths (*Amaranthus* spp.), wild fruits would have also been collected. Littoral wild fruits were especially susceptible to exploitation by the numerous groups, both indian and European, that made temporary stops in Trinidad to replenish supplies. Francisco Durango testified that he had collected a great number of coco plums to eat in Trinidad.[127]

The largest tree species including the West Indian cedar, the silk cotton, crappo, incense and galba were all used by both the indians and the Spanish for house and boat construction. The settlement built by Sedeño in 1533 was palisaded with "many trees as large as barrels" and the whole was surrounded by a ditch and "spiny palms".[128] It contained 30 or more houses covered with straw—probably the grass leaves of white roseau.[129] Many other temporary settlements would have made similar demands on the vegetation.

Fibres were extracted from wild plants and trees by the indians but the Spanish appear to have relied on imports from Spain. Sedeño in 1534 appealed to the officials in Cubagua to send him "thread for fishing nets, and thread and needles to sew sails".[130] The Spanish did, however, use the indian vegetable dyes and they became important items of export to Spain. Rodrigo de Bastidas in his contract to settle the island in 1521 was allowed to sell and profit from "the brasil wood and lignum-vitae" of Trinidad and was only required to pay a 10% duty.[131] Brasil

wood was a term used by Europeans to describe dye woods, which for
Trinidad would have included logwood and fustic, which produce red
and yellow dyes respectively. Lignum-vitae was used by the indians for
general medicinal purposes in aboriginal times but it was not until the
post-Columbian period that it was adopted by the Spanish as a cure for
syphilis, which had been introduced to Spain from the Greater Antilles.[132]
It was probably not until the Spanish permanently occupied Trinidad
that the tree was systematically felled for commercial purposes. Gums,
oils and resins would have been extracted from the locust tree, incense
tree and balata. Medicinal preparations continued to be made by the
indians from various vegetable products and tobacco and yopa were
both used as stimulants.[133]

Craft Activities

Stone, wood, clay, bone and shell objects made by the indians were supplemented by metal goods introduced to the island by the Spanish and
other Europeans. The indians obtained precious metals by trade with
the indians of the Tierra Firme[134] but it is unlikely that they practised
smelting. Dudley, however, claimed that he met an indian "who was
well known in matters of smelting calcurie" and at Carowas on the west
coast he found some melting pots and some dross.[135] Although metal
goods were traded by the Spanish and other Europeans for provisions,
the visitors do not appear to have taught the indians the art of metal
working. A smithy was established in Trinidad by Sedeño in 1533 with
the express purpose of making metal goods for trade with the indians.[136]
Altogether the sixteenth century did not witness the exploitation of any
natural or mineral resources not exploited by the indians in pre-
Columbian times, although the exploitation of some of them at least was
probably more effective.

Most of the tools used by the indians continued to be made of stone,
wood and bone, though as metal tools brought by the Spanish became
more generally available they were readily adopted. Metal hatchets and
knives aided vegetation clearance and released the indians from their
dependence on foreign sources of stone for the manufacture of crude
stone celts. Metal fish hooks were also introduced by Europeans.

The weapons possessed by the indians were unsophisticated compared
with those of the Spanish. Martín López in 1550 noted that "the arms
of the indians are bows, arrows, clubs and darts"; the Spanish possessed

"harquebuses, guns, swords and shields".[137] As far as is known, the indians did not adopt any of the European weapons.

Pottery objects, particularly bowls, continued to be made of a fairly soft ware that was decorated with crude punctuations and appliqué work. Fine glazed European pottery was introduced to the island but not the techniques of its production. The spinning and weaving of cotton continued to be an important indian activity, stimulated by the demands of foreign visitors to the island. The Spanish imported coarser fibres, including cord and threads for making fishing lines and nets[138] but the indians continued to use fibres obtained from local sources.

The indians wore gold nose ornaments, crowns and breast plates, which were obtained from indian inhabitants of the Tierra Firme by trade, and headdresses of feathers.[139] During the sixteenth century they also obtained many beads of various shapes and sizes from Europeans.[140]

Canoes continued to be the most important means of water transport as they were well adapted to the shallow beaches and the strong currents that existed in the Gulf of Paria. Canoes were still made by the dug-out method, but their manufacture was aided by the introduction of more effective cutting tools. It is doubtful whether the European sail was adopted by the indians. The Spanish continued to make sailing vessels, sending to Cubagua for the materials to make sails.[141] Trinidad became an important centre for canoe making and boat building during the six-teenth century due to the abundance of suitable wood. The English and French called there to make boats and in 1593 de Berrío considered that one of the advantages of using Trinidad as a base for operations in Guiana was "its large supply of canoes so that as many people can be taken for a single journey as we would desire".[142]

Indian houses were built of local wood and leaves, in round and rectangular forms. Rectangular houses such as that constructed by Juan Bono for a village in Trinidad in 1516, were used for social occasions.[143] Even houses built by the Spanish during their temporary occupations of the island were constructed on similar lines to those built by the indians, despite the fact that Sedeño brought with him two masons and three carpenters.[144]

Trade

Intra-island trade declined in importance in the sixteenth century as a result of the disruption of trade links and the increased availability of goods from extra-island sources. Nevertheless, a certain amount of trade in food products continued with difficulty. Seasonal variations in food production from both terrestrial and aquatic sources continued to stimulate a certain amount of trade, particularly between the coastal and inland settlements. In addition items obtained from Europeans constituted important items of exchange between villages.

Most of the intra-island trade was carried in dugout canoes, though the continual attacks made by the Spanish and Caribs must have made such trading hazardous. The movement of the indian population inland for defensive purposes would have reduced its accessibility to the coast so that ridge-top trails may have been used more intensively for trading purposes.

A complex pattern of inter-island trade developed in Trinidad in the sixteenth century among the indians, Spanish and other Europeans, notably the French and English. As far as the Spanish were concerned, they alone were allowed to trade with the indians but they were forbidden to trade with foreigners. The latter law was, however, impracticable in the absence of supporting trade from Spain. The Europeans were opportunists, selling to the Spanish for material gain and to the indians for help in the form of supplies to enable them to attack Spanish trade routes and eventually to oust the Spanish from some parts of the New World. The indians were the gullible pawns. The indians traded with other indian groups on the mainland and in the islands and also with the Europeans who could offer help in preventing the Spanish from settling in Trinidad.

Trade between the indians of Trinidad and other West Indian islands and the mainland continued throughout the sixteenth century despite the attacks of Spanish and Carib enslavers. Trinidad continued to supply the islands with game animals, which were noticeably absent in those areas, and the mainland with fish products and other foods. In return they received durable goods, metals and stone. The indians of Trinidad obtained gold and pearls from the indians of the Tierra Firme and the island in fact became an important base for pearl trading.[145] The importance of Trinidad as a trading centre was noted by Sancho de Sotomayor who in 1573 observed: "By this river [the Orinoco] come indians for more than 300 leagues in their canoes to barter trumpets, pearls, salt and axes with those of Trinidad and even with the colonists of the island of Margarita, which they reach in their canoes under the care of other Aruac indians who are of the coast more to the windward of Trinidad".[146]

The Spanish system of trading, which from 1503 was regulated by the *Casa de Contratación* in Seville, was monopolistic. All goods destined for the New World and all colonial products intended for Spain were to be carried in Spanish vessels, and trading with foreigners was forbidden for both the indians and Spanish. The system functioned in the early sixteenth century but as new territories were discovered and their potential began to be developed, there were insufficient ships or sailors to maintain the required frequency of the visits. In addition, other European nations tried to break the Spanish monopoly by attacking merchant ships. The Spanish replied by developing a convoy system,[147] but even so many ships that left for the New World never returned to Spain. The infrequency with which Spanish ships visited all parts of the Indies forced the Spanish colonists to trade with foreign ships and to send their produce elsewhere for survival.

Although the ships that Spain sent on colonising expeditions were well supplied with plants, seeds, livestock and tools, they had limited amounts of food and once these had been exhausted the Spanish became dependent on the indians for provisions. It was not only that "the Spanish in extremity never planted; they depended on the indians for food. When the indians withdrew, when no crops were planted the Spanish starved"[148]; but also that the short periods during which the Spanish were present in the island did not permit the establishment of productive agriculture. At first the Spanish could only obtain food from the indians. As soon as Juan Troche Ponce de León's expedition arrived in Trinidad in 1569, the Spanish went to the indian villages "exchanging goods from Castille for provisions".[149] In 1563 it had been decreed that any boats embarking on colonising expeditions in the New World should take goods of small value, such as "scissors, combs, knives, axes, fish hooks, coloured bonnets, mirrors, bells, glass beads and other things of this kind"[150] for trade with the indians. All trade between the indians and the Spanish was theoretically governed by orders and laws from Spain. Sedeño was only allowed to trade with the indians of Trinidad "as free men, as they are, and exchange with them all gold, silver and precious stones and pearls and jewels and other necessities and cotton clothes and cotton and canoes and other kinds of things which they have, giving them for it that which they agree in such a way that it should be voluntary".[151] At a later date Juan Sedano was instructed to trade with the indians through the clergy and was under pain of death and loss of goods not to attack or illtreat them.[152]

It is doubtful, however, that much trade did occur between the indians of Trinidad and the Spanish. Certain *caciques* gave the Spanish supplies but most of the indians were intent on routing them from the island and remained hostile. The lack of supplies from Spain added to the precarious situation in which the Spanish lived during their short occupations of the island. During the sixteenth century only one ship, of 120 tons, was registered as leaving Andalucía for Trinidad,[153] despite vociferous appeals for supplies. In 1534 Sedeño complained that the Spanish in Trinidad were driven to drink sea water for salt and to eat unpalatable cassava cakes—*chacos*—that had been given to them by a friendly *cacique*.[154] The lack of support from Spain in the form of simple food necessities may be regarded as one of the principal reasons for the failure of the Spanish to establish a permanent settlement on the island until the end of the century.

Most of the indians who were enslaved were taken during attacks on the island but a certain number were obtained through trading with the indians, despite the fact that this was forbidden. After it had been decided that the indians of Trinidad were not Caribs, the Crown only permitted the enslavement of those indians kept by the indians themselves as slaves and in 1542 the New Laws of the Indies were passed stating that "for no cause of war nor any other whatsoever though it be under the title of rebellion, nor by ransom, nor by any other manner can an indian be made a slave".[155] Nevertheless, a clandestine trade in indians developed. In 1595 Raleigh noted that on the south side of the mouth of the Orinoco the Spanish bought "women and children from the cannibals which are of that barbarous nature, as they will for 3 or 4 hatchets sell the sonnes and daughters of their own brethren and sisters, and for somewhat more even their own daughters: hereof the Spaniards make great profit, for buying a maid of 12 or 13 yeeres for three or fower hatchets, they sell them again at Margarita in the West Indies for 50 and 100 pesoes, which is so many crownes".[156] It is likely that such a trade also developed in Trinidad.

Other Europeans, particularly the French and English and later the Dutch, had four main aims in the Caribbean: to weaken the Spanish Empire to breaking the Spanish monopoly of trade in the West Indies; to gain a foothold for settlement in the New World; to share in the riches that the New World had to offer; and to profit from the vulnerable position of the Spanish colonists by illegally selling them vital provisions. Instrumental in the achievement of the first three objectives was the establishment of Trinidad as a base of operations. This could only be brought about with indian co-operation. In return for small durable goods the indians were to supply the French and English with provisions and allow them to settle temporarily in the island; this was consistent with the indian aims of preventing the Spanish settling in Trinidad and trade flourished. Dudley, arriving in Trinidad in 1594, noted that the indians "did often resort to my ship and brought us hennes, hogs, plantains, potatoes, pinos, tobacco and manie other pretie commodities which they exchanged for hatchets, knives, hooks, belles and glasse buttons".[157] In 1570 Diosdado had reported to the Crown that "there is much danger from the French who come here each year and the indians are brought over by their gifts" and in 1592 de Berrío considered that one of the most important reasons for settling the island was to stop "the English ships trading with the indians".[158] The Europeans not only traded in Trinidad for local goods but also for those brought from other islands and the mainland. In 1596 it was noted that indians from the Orinoco took urapo—probably a hardwood species, *Bauhinia obtusifolia*, used for naval construction—to Trinidad to sell to the French.[159]

Not only did the Europeans trade with the indians but they sold provisions to the isolated Spanish colonists. Although the Spanish were forbidden to trade with foreigners they had little choice, given the high prices and infrequent deliveries of goods from Spain.[160] During the sixteenth century this trade was not well developed in Trinidad since the Spanish had not established a permanent settlement there, but it became very significant later.

Indian society and ideology

The relationship between the size of population and organisation of that population undermines the existing social organisation.[161] Although there is a mathematical relationship between the complexity of social organisation and population size,[162] the relationship is not casual and demography alone cannot explain a specific kind of social organisation.[163] Clearly societies with the same population do not necessarily have the same organisation; and those that have suffered a decline in population will not have the same social organisation as those societies that have reached that same population level for the first time.

In pre-Columbian times a village was composed of a group of extended matrilineal families, the organisation of which was based on the matri-local residence rule, which itself related to the importance of women as food producers. Although during the sixteenth century the role of women as food producers probably increased as a result of the withdrawal of men from subsistence activities, the matrilocal residence rule would not have been strengthened. This was for two reasons: first, although the continuance of women in their native villages after marriage for the more efficient production of crops would have become even more desir-able as the exploitation of other sources of food declined, their links with the land, like those of the men, would have been increasingly disrupted as the population retreated inland for defensive purposes and second, as villages lost population it would have been economically and defensively expedient for them to amalgamate. Such an amalgamation could not occur without a change in the marital residence rules, allowing men to remain in the villages after marriage and permitting immigrants to join the community. The result would have been a village where most of the members were related, but not necessarily through the female line. Service has described how a lineally structured group may change into a composite group through population decline, particularly as a result of culture contact.[164] Such a change in social organisation would not have been characteristic of all villages in Trinidad in the sixteenth century. The social organisation of villages located inland would have been less altered by population loss but it would have had to become more adapt-able and prepared to accept immigrants who would formerly have been excluded. In those villages the original members probably continued to adhere to the matrilocal residence rule whereas immigrants probably had no specific residence rule and would have moved as economic, social and defensive conditions changed.

The *caciques* continued to exercise some authority in their villages and were particularly important in contacts with the Spanish. Their offices probably continued to be inherited matrilineally, though some *caciques* must have lost the little authority they possessed as their villages were destroyed. The status of the *caciques* would have been undermined to some extent by the lack of consanguineal ties between them and immi-grant members of the village, who would have endowed older members with status regardless of kinship. The status of the shamans, based on their healing and prognostic abilities, may also have been in question as the frequency of calamities and their inability to cope with the con-sequences of them increased under a state of war. They continued to prognosticate and to heal the sick with the help of herbal medicines and objects of supposedly curative power. They also continued to take tobacco and yopa as stimulants. Castellanos noted that on the eve of a battle with the Spanish in 1533, "one took tobacco and the other yopa so that they could foretell what the future held, the squares, streets and roads were full of charmers and soothsayers".[165]

The weakened nature of the socio-political organisation of the indians and the declining status of civil leaders in Trinidad in the sixteenth century was in part compensated for by the development of links between villages and the emergence of military leaders based on the common interest of defence rather than kinship. During the sixteenth century energies that had formerly been expended in intervillage warfare were channelled into a form of "nationalism" and the defence of the island. Baucunar, leading an indian attack on the Spanish in 1553, said ". . . we go to war not for amusement of pleasure, but to die for our land, defending our sons and wives."[166]

This is not to suggest that intervillage rivalries disappeared completely but that they declined in significance as the need for a united opposition against the Spanish grew and a military organisation that cut across village loyalties developed to co-ordinate defence activities. The development of such an organisation would have been aided by the breakdown of the social structure in many villages.

The military leaders would have been elected from the *caciques* of a group of villages on the basis of ability in warfare. The military leaders Baucunar and Maruana were respectively described as "a brave man" and "a powerful *cacique*". These two leaders co-ordinated all military activities in Trinidad and were superior in authority to the provincial leaders. This two-tiered military organisation is indicated by Castellanos who relates that in 1533 Baucunar called on the provincial military leaders—*principales*—to supply men and arms to attack the Spanish, who, led by Sedeño, were attempting to settle the island. As a result Guyma brought 300 brave men, Pamacoa provided 400 men skilled in handling canoes, Amanatey, who had been instructed in military school, brought 100 and Paraguani another 100 men,[167] each probably drawing from several villages. The efficiency of the military organisation in Trinidad in part explains the late establishment of a permanent Spanish settlement in the island.

Apart from the emergence of military leaders indian society in Trinidad remained relatively undifferentiated. The Carib and Spanish practice of taking captive slaves was probably adopted by the indians of Trinidad, if it had not already occurred in pre-Columbian times, but there is no evidence of the emergence of a class of slaves: social stratification was not and did not become a characteristic of indian society. In 1530 Sedeño was given permission to trade with the indians of Trinidad for their slaves and in 1532 he was given a Carib indian by a friendly *cacique*.[168]

The indian conception of the world must have altered fundamentally with the arrival of the Spanish in Trinidad in 1498. The physical appearance of the Spanish and their material culture must have demonstrated to the indians that they had come from unknown lands. Whether this fact prompted the indians to believe that the Spanish were messengers from heaven is not known, but certainly they did not attribute divine powers to them as did the Incas and Aztecs.[169] The indians who Columbus met in 1498 thought he had come from the south and treated him amicably.[170] If the indians at first believed that the Spanish were heavenly messengers they would have been promptly disillusioned by the conduct of the Spanish in the early conquest years. The indians believed in a supernatural power that praised good and punished evil[171] and the Spanish were self-evidently not just in their judgement. The whole indian population could not be evil.

Once the indians had suffered at the hands of the Spanish and it had become apparent that their object was to enslave them, the indians felt justified in making war on the Spanish. Baucunar in 1533 said that the indians were going to war against the Spanish because ". . . truthfully they wish to make us their slaves and subjects so that we should sow their lands, and those to whom we should not be acceptable take us from our fertile banks, carrying us off in fetters and chains by sea to get to know foreign lands. In their estates and farms you will die of inhuman work, separated fathers from sons, brothers from beloved brothers."[172] The rejection of the Spanish meant the rejection of their religion. The conversion of the indians to the Holy Catholic faith was one of the principal aims of Spanish colonisation in the New World; although the Spanish could uphold the freedom of the indian they could not uphold his freedom to practise what was considered to be a "false" religion.[173] All five contracts made by the Crown for the establishment of a permanent settlement on the island included instructions that priests were to accompany the expeditions[174] but in view of the hostile reception of the indians it is unlikely that by the end of the century they had effected any conversions. The indian ideology must have remained basically unchanged; they would have continued to believe in the spirits of ancestors and in natural phenomena, as intermediaries in the attainment of supernatural power, without the support of temples and idols.

part four

Spanish colonisation
1592-1776

6
Institutions of Colonisation

Early voyagers to the New World fully expected to find mythical beings such as dragons, griffins and giants, which were common creatures of medieval legends,[1] and their first encounters with indians made them uncertain as to their nature and what their relationship with them should be. Gradually it became accepted through observers' reports and the debates they prompted that the indians possessed souls and as such were candidates for conversion and civilisation. The right of Spain to instruct the indians in the Catholic faith had been granted to the King of Spain by Pope Alexander VI in 1493 but it was not until the end of the sixteenth century, when the issue had been discussed in Europe and the New World, that Spanish sovereignty and the right to conquest was established;[2] no doubt this was partly because it was unrealistic to expect Spain to withdraw from parts of the Indies where colonisation had already begun. The Spanish Crown had two main aims in the New World: to christianise and civilise its native population and to exploit its resources to the benefit of the Crown and to the glory of Spain and Spaniards. To achieve these aims an elaborate secular and ecclesiastical bureaucracy was established with power centralised in the hands of the Crown. In this way all activities in the New World could be controlled and directed by the Crown and the power of other sections of the population, particularly the aristocracy, could be suppressed.

Secular and ecclesiastical bureaucracies

The most important administrative, judicial and ecclesiastical decisions were made in Spain through the Council of the Indies, a judicial and advisory body that was formally established in 1524; the *Casa de Contratación*, established in 1503 to deal with trade and commerce, and the *Consejo de Hacienda*, that dealt with financial matters. Although the King was theoretically the chief legislator most of the laws were drafted by the Council of the Indies and subsequently accepted or rejected by him. The most important administrative institution in the New World was the *audiencia*, which, although essentially a high judicial court, served as the King's mouthpiece and the guardian of his interests. In addition it had special responsibilities for the indians and for the conduct of *residencias* and *visitas*. All posts were filled by the Crown and a check was kept on the *audiencias* by the viceroys, who, as direct representatives of the Crown, could issue orders, except on judicial matters, to the *audiencias*. The *audiencias* in return were to keep the viceroys informed of the state of the territories within their jurisdiction. Initially Trinidad with Guyana formed one of the nine provinces under the jurisdiction of the *Audiencia* of Santo Domingo and the Viceroyalty of New Spain. However, during the seventeenth century the presence of foreigners in Trinidad waters made communications with other Caribbean islands difficult, so in 1662 the island was detached from the *Audiencia* of Santo Domingo and placed under the jurisdiction of the mainland *Audiencia* of Santa Fé,[3] and later transferred to the Viceroyalty of New Granada when it was created in 1717. When the latter Viceroyalty was temporarily abolished in 1723, Trinidad remained under the *Audiencia* of Santa Fé but returned to the Viceroyalty of New Spain. Then, when the Captaincy General of Venezuela was established in 1731, Guyana was detached from the province of Trinidad and Guyana and placed under the Captaincy General, while Trinidad remained under the *Audiencia* of Santa Fé. In 1742 the military and financial affairs of the island were transferred to the Captaincy General, which was under the *Audiencia* of Santo Domingo, since it was thought that this would result in greater administrative efficiency.[4]

At the head of each province within the *audiencia* was a governor, who was chosen by the King for a five year term of office. He was the chief administrator in his province and had supreme control of military affairs within his jurisdiction in the name of the King. During the first half of the seventeenth century he was also president of the highest court in the province. Although the Governor was always under the watchful eye of the *audiencia*, which could conduct a *residencia* on his behaviour, Trinidad was sufficiently far from Santo Domingo to allow the Governor a considerable degree of autonomy. As in all of Spanish America, the Governor also had the right to postpone the execution of laws and orders if he considered them prejudicial to the interests of the colony, replying to the Crown, "*obedezco pero no cumplo*" [I obey but I do not execute]. *Residencias* on governors throughout the colonial period indicate the latitude of their conduct. In 1617 the parish priest of St. Joseph complained that the Governor Diego Palomeque y Acuña had abused the rights of the *vecinos* and was calling himself, "Pope and King, and archbishop, bishop and vicar general".[5]

The ecclesiastical bureaucracy that the Spanish established in the New World was part of the political organisation that the Crown set up to administer the Empire. The King was in charge of ecclesiastical affairs, which he administered in consultation with the Council of the Indies. The ecclesiastical bureaucracy was divided into two sections: the secular clergy and the regular clergy. The insufficient numbers of secular clergy in the New World required that part of the Church's task, as an instructor in the Catholic faith and an arm of the State, should be entrusted to the missionary orders, otherwise known as the regular clergy: the missions were never intended to be permanent institutions but pioneering ones, which would be handed over to the secular clergy after 10 years.[6]

In practice, however, this seldom occurred, so that the secular clergy generally preached to the Spanish, and the indians in the *encomiendas*, while the regular clergy retained possession of the missions and preached to the unconverted. To a large extent the two clerical groups remained distinct from each other, although they were both under the jurisdiction of the Crown. All appointments were made by the head of the missionary order in Spain and the bishop of the diocese respectively. In the case of Trinidad the regular clergy were recommended by the head of the Catalonian Capuchins and the secular clergy by the Bishop of Puerto Rico, to whose diocese the island belonged during the greater part of the seventeenth and eighteenth centuries.

Trinidad at the beginning of the seventeenth century was under the jurisdiction of the Archbishop of Santa Fé but in 1625 it was encharged to the Bishop of Puerto Rico[7] because no representative from Santa Fé had visited the island.[8] The decision was reversed in 1662 when Trinidad was taken from the *Audiencia* of Santo Domingo and placed under the *Audiencia* of Santa Fé since it was said that the Bishop of Puerto Rico "would have to make the journey by sea at great cost and danger because the enemy have many settlements near the island and usually infest the coasts of it and, connected by land with the archbishopric and jurisdiction of Santa Fé, it is certain that it could be assisted with greater convenience".[9] There is some doubt that this transference in jurisdiction was made: in 1707 it was again suggested that Trinidad should be placed under the diocese of Santa Fé because it was considered that pastoral visits and salary payments could be made with greater ease from Bogotá.[10]

The Spanish secular and ecclesiastical bureaucracies were designed to gain and maintain control of the Empire, even at the expense of efficiency. The fact that many officials had spatially overlapping responsibilities did lead to jurisdictional conflicts, but it had the advantage of promoting tale-telling, which had a restraining effect on the activities of officials particularly in the more remote parts of the Empire.

Social stratification

Political control of the population in the New World was aided by the introduction of a stratified form of social organisation, which incorporated the indians as vassals of the King of Spain and the negroes as slaves. Social stratification was considered essential for the maintenance of political control for, as was stated by the Council of the Indies in 1806, "it is undeniable that the existence of various hierarchies and classes is of the greatest importance to the existence and stability of a monarchical state, since a graduated system of dependence and subordination sustains and insures the obedience and respect of the last vassal to the authority of the sovereign".[11] The strata in Spanish colonial society were determined by the nature of society in the Peninsula; and by the descent and culture of different groups, which were at first identified by their racial affinities. The indians of the New World had been entrusted to the King of Spain for protection and instruction in the Holy Catholic faith and, as his vassals, they theoretically had the same status as Spaniards. The indians were to be free: free from slavery, unless they rebelled; free to change their place of residence and occupation; free to own property; and with access to special tribunals and law courts. In return for these privileges they were forced to surrender their freedom to practise a "false religion" and they were obliged to contribute to society in the form of tribute and as hired labourers or *mitayos*.[12] Such a system supposedly upheld the rights of the indians and ensured their christianisation and civilisation, while it secured due rewards for the Spaniards, who had taken part in the discovery and colonisation of the New World.

Similar concern for the physical and spiritual welfare of negroes was not expressed by the Spanish Crown. Negroes could be enslaved and were not protected by laws as the indians were, although in practice the latter were little better than slaves. The ambivalence of the Crown's attitude to the two ethnic groups may be explained by the fact that, unlike the indians, the negroes were not vassals of the Crown and indeed had been used as slaves in the Peninsula prior to the discovery of the New World.[13]

Although the Spanish and indians theoretically had the same social status, it was inevitable that, as conquerors and "civilised" human beings, the Spanish should regard themselves as socially superior to the indians. Many of the Spaniards who went to the New World claimed to be of noble descent but others just assumed noble status on arrival. Their social status was, however, largely a state of mind and it was not enforced by legal privileges. The King as head of the social body was the ultimate source of legislation defining the status of groups and individuals, dispensing privileges and favours, such as *encomiendas*, land grants, offices and honours, and revoking them as it desired.[14] Their lack of permanent legal privileges meant that the Spanish in the New World never formed a political class.[15] Since their legal status was always liable to change, the Spanish tried to establish their social status through their wealth and claims to noble descent and *"limpieza de sangre"*. With the gradual mixing of races and the birth of American Spaniards or creoles these claims came to be of utmost importance in determining social status; colour was only significant in general terms. Social mobility did exist, however. Those members of the mixed races who showed enterprise or by some means received official favour were accepted as having higher social status despite their colour and lack of claims to noble descent. During the eighteenth century the racial basis of the social hierarchy was undermined by miscegenation, population increase, and an improvement in employment opportunities in the army and trades, and replaced by one based more on the economic role of the individual in society. While race continued largely to determine employment, racial divisions, particularly between the mixed races, became less marked and social advancement more easily attainable. The rigid social hierarchy based on claims to nobility and race had been shown to be not only socially unjust, but economically ludicrous.

The Spanish and indian republics

Although miscegenation meant that many parts of the New World very soon became characterised by people of mixed race, for administrative purposes the Crown upheld the basic distinction between Spaniards and indians that had been made in the sixteenth century. Experience of the early years of conquest had demonstrated that not all Spaniards could be entrusted with the important task of christianising and civilising the native population. It was in its desire to protect the indians from physical and spiritual abuse and to establish secular and ecclesiastical organisations appropriate to the distinct needs of the two populations, that at the end of the sixteenth century the Crown began to formulate laws that were destined to isolate the indians from the rest of the population.[16] Theoretically Spaniards and indians were to live in separate towns and villages, which had been assigned lands; they were to be administered by different royal officials and possess their own town councils; they were to be subject to distinct judicial systems; and they were to worship in separate churches under the guidance of different priests (Table VI). Thus the Crown envisaged the establishment of two republics, one Spanish and one indian. Since the motive behind segregation was the protection of the indian, the mixed races were regarded as part of the "Spanish republic" and legislation was passed forbidding them to reside in indian villages. As such the two republics that emerged may be better described as indian and non-indian.

Institutions of colonisation

Within the socio-political framework outlined above three institutions were instrumental in the christianisation and civilisation of the indians and the economic exploitation of the resources of the New World: the town, the *encomienda* and the mission. Their establishment also facilitated spatial and administrative segregation since the Spanish towns were to be inhabited by the non-indian population, whilst the indians were to be encharged to the care of *encomenderos* and missionaries.

Spanish colonisation in the New World was to be urban-based. Although spatially isolated, the cities and towns as administrative centres, the places of residence of Spanish officials and merchants, and the

TABLE VI

Spatial and administrative segregation of the Spanish and indian
populations in Trinidad

	"Spanish republic"	"Indian republic"
Residence	Spanish towns	Indian villages and missions
Land holdings	Private and communal lands around Spanish towns	Private and communal lands around indian villages and missions
Administration (a) Secular	(i) Royal officials Governor, magistrates (*alcades*), solicitors (*procuradores*), and accountants (*contadores*)	*Corregidores de indios* for missions and *encomiendas* under Crown control
	(ii) Elected officials Town council (*cabildo*)	Town council (*cabildo*)
(b) Judicial	*Audiencia* and special military and ecclesiastical courts	*Juzgado de Indios*
(c) Ecclesiastical	(i) Secular clergy Parish priests	*Curas doctrineros* in *encomiendas*
	(ii) Regular clergy Priests in monasteries and convents	Missionaries in missions

centres of ecclesiastical activity were to be the springboards of colonisation. The establishment of a town was followed by the allotment of lands and indians found in the vicinity of the town but the recipients of concessions remained urban dwellers and the town emerged as a centre of exploitation of the natural and human resources in the surrounding countryside.

The civilisation of the indians was to be effected largely by the means of the *encomienda*—a semi-feudal paternalistic institution, whereby grants of indians were given to eminent colonists as personal rewards for merits and services. In return for protection and instruction in the Catholic faith, the indians were obliged to pay the *encomendero* tribute in the form of money or goods. Although as a civilising institution the *encomienda* did achieve some success it was never economically viable owing to the Crown policy of granting lands in areas spatially separated from the *encomiendas* and of prohibiting the employment of indians in personal service, a custom which was designed to prevent the development of seigneurial estates that could be a potential threat to its power. The failure of the *encomienda* as an economic institution ultimately led to its disintegration and abolition.

Missions served the dual purpose of bringing the indians under the control of the Spanish and into the fold of the Catholic church. The independent nature of the missions and their jealous protection of the indian population in their care, however, conflicted with the wishes of the Crown and effectively reduced the potential labour force that was vital for economic development. In these circumstances the missions aroused considerable opposition and in Trinidad they were abolished. The abolition of these two institutions in the island clearly indicated the need for means of achieving Spain's imperial objectives; it was not, however, until the end of the eighteenth century that the Empire was reorganised on the basis of a centralised system of control.

The foreign threat

Exclusive Spanish control of the island was periodically threatened by the English and Dutch who at various times established temporary settlements there as bases for attacking Spanish shipping and settlements, and for trade. Trinidad was considered by Europeans to be too unhealthy for permanent settlement. In 1654 the English decided that once they had attacked St. Joseph they would leave it in the hands of the indians, "for it will be dangerous to leave any English there by reason of the unhealthiness of the soil for it is situated at the mouth of the Orinoco"[17], and the French never settled the island because "it was said to be a very unhealthy place for Europeans . . . and it was agreed that the island of Trinidad defended itself by its bad climate and the barrenness of its soils"[18]. The English and Dutch settlements that were established were short-lived and took the form of forts rather than civil settlements. The first English settlements were made by Robert Dudley in 1595 who for two months settled "in the name of the Queen of England in two places which are Paracoa [San Fernando] and Punta de Gallo"[19]. In 1631 the English under Henry Colt landed at Punta de la Galera but in the following year Colt was captured and the settlement destroyed by the Spanish.[20] In 1639 another group of Englishmen under Marsham temporarily settled in Trinidad, possibly at Toco, but were forced to retreat by Caribs, and in 1640 Jeremy Hartley established a settlement at Punta de la Galera where he remained for five years "without any considerable mortalities, as being the greater part planters from St. Christophers, and other islands in these parts, and had more judgement to make choice of a drier and fitter piece of land to build on than the other colonie . . . yet these people likewise settled on the Leeward side of the island, by the place which they call the Warwick river in ye chart and fixed on that place fearing ye Spaniards"[21]. They eventually withdrew, fearing disease and Spanish attack[22]. The other colony referred to was that formed at Moruga in 1644 whose population was decimated by disease and the survivors forced to retreat to Barbados within two years.[23] The Dutch were more active in attacking St. Joseph than they were in establishing settlements. At various times during the early part of the seventeenth century the Dutch established themselves at Punta de la Galera and Moruga but were driven away by the Spanish.[24] During the latter part of the century, when the foreign nations had obtained footholds on a number of the West Indian islands and in parts of the mainland,[25] trading expeditions were mounted from there and there were no further attempts to settle the island.

7
The Spanish Republic

The Spanish towns

In 1592 St. Joseph, or San José de Oruña as it was originally known, was founded as a symbol of Spanish possession and as the centre from which the colony could be administered by the Crown and Spanish culture disseminated. As a symbol of Spanish possession of the island it was essential that the town should be located on a defensive site; a town located on the coast would have been too vulnerable to attack and as a consequence the island too susceptible to loss. As a result St. Joseph, like most principal towns founded by the Spanish in the New World, was sited inland, Domingo de Vera y Ibargoyen chose the present-day site of St. Joseph because it was "abundant in provisions and there are many lands which can be sown, pastures, water and common lands and other things necessary to found a settlement and it has good ports and is near the sea and in communication with the native indians".[1] Contrary to the Ordinances for the establishment of new settlements, which stated that they should be made without harming the indians, St. Joseph was founded on the lands of the *cacique* Goanagoanare, who was forced to withdraw to another part of the island.[2] No sooner had the town been founded than it was sacked by Raleigh in 1595 and left deserted by Antonio de Berrío who went on an expedition up the Orinoco. During his absence Felipe de Santiago, in the name of Francisco de Vides, with whom the original contract for the settlement of the island had been made, landed in Trinidad and rebuilt the town, renaming it San Felipe de Montes.[3] In the following year Domingo de Vera returned and seized the town in the name of Fernando de Berrío, the son of Antonio de Berrío who had died in Guyana. From that time on the town was permanently occupied, although there were fluctuations in the number of inhabitants.

The form of St. Joseph followed that laid down in the Royal Ordinances of 1573 concerning the layout of new towns. The main plaza was designated and plots reserved for the church, called Nuestra Señora de la Concepción, the Governor's palace, town hall and prison.[4] Subsequently other plots were given to the Spanish settlers but it is doubtful if any were given to indians. All of the buildings were made of mud, wood and straw; in 1637 St. Joseph was described as consisting of about 30 houses, sometimes more, sometimes less, "made of earth stamped solid, which they call tapias, and roofed with thatch or other combustible material".[5] Similarly, in 1681 the parish priest complained to the Bishop of Puerto Rico that the church was "made of tapias covered with palms and all so rough and unadorned and indecent for the celebration of divine worship and moreover it is old and a threatened ruin and so narrow that on feast days the greater part of the people listen to mass outside."[6] The combustible nature of the material with which houses were built meant that they were often destroyed by fire[7] as well as being sacked and burnt by the Dutch and English, sometimes in alliance with the Caribs and native indians.[8] The rebuilding of many of the houses and public buildings often involved a change in their location such that in 1722 an inhabitant of St. Joseph complained that the houses had been dispersed by numerous fires.[9]

Port of Spain, known by the Spanish as Puerto de España, seems to have been used as a port and defensive outpost from the earliest years of colonisation. It was located on the site of the present-day port, possibly at Mucurapo, where the Spanish settled temporarily in the sixteenth century. Like St. Joseph the port was attacked and burnt several times, but on being rebuilt in 1678 it was resited near the mouth of the Caroni.[10] Throughout the seventeenth century the port does not appear to have been composed of more than ten houses plus a guard house and a church and it is doubtful if it formed more than an unorganised cluster of buildings.

During the first half of the eighteenth century the *vecinos* took to living on their estates[11] to the extent that in 1757 the Governor Pedro de Moneda reported that St. Joseph was totally abandoned because "the house that falls into ruins is not rebuilt in the town but in the hills where they [the *vecinos*] are found to be living so that in the town there are not more than 20 houses, most of them belonging to married women, widows, spinsters and commoners".[12] As a result in 1761 the *Cabildo* ordered all *vecinos* to take up residence in the towns and in the following year the Governor reported that "today in Port of Spain I count 30 houses rebuilt, although they are not yet finished, and the same in St. Joseph."[13] At this time Port of Spain did not extend further west that La Puntilla and consisted of only two streets—Calle de Infante (now Duncan Street) and Calle del Principe (now Nelson Street)—with the Governor's palace situated at the eastern end of the town at Piccadilly.[14] In 1766 an earthquake destroyed a large part of both towns[15] but in 1777 Roume St. Laurent observed that in Port of Spain there were "several canons on a battery, a church, and about 80 houses covered with straw and palisaded with roseau, and plastered with a mixture of mud and cut grass and whitewashed" and in St. Joseph "a church and about 90 houses of the same construction".[16]

Throughout the Spanish colonial period there were only two towns in the island. St. Joseph was given the title of *ciudad* or town on the basis of its administrative function carried out by the Governor in conjunction with other Spanish officials, mainly judicial, and by the *Cabildo* or town council. Although the jurisdiction of the Governor and other Spanish officials theoretically extended to the whole island, their influence was most strongly felt in the Spanish towns. Chosen for a five-year term of office by the Crown, the Governor could rule the island with a large degree of independence, being spatially isolated from the surveillance of the *Audiencia*. In such circumstances the Crown was dependent on its clergy and on the *Cabildo* to curb the Governor's power. In 1745 the *Cabildo* revolted against the actions of the Governor which they deemed as prejudicial to the island, and succeeded in having him replaced.[17] However, the *Cabildo* could not always be relied upon, since it possessed interests, generally economic, that were independent of and often in conflict with those of the Crown. In 1713 the Bishop of Puerto Rico suggested that the interim government of the island should be carried out by the Sargeant Major and not by the *Cabildo*, since experience had shown that members of the *Cabildo* were only concerned with augmenting their cacao estates.[18] The Crown agreed and it was partly against this ruling that the *Cabildo* revolted.

The *Cabildo* of St. Joseph was initially chosen by Domingo de Vera y Ibargoyen, when the town was founded in 1592. At that time two magistrates (*alcaldes ordinarios*), a chief constable (*alguacil mayor*), a standard bearer (*alférez*) and five other town councillors (*regidores*) were chosen. During the seventeenth century the *Cabildo* seems to have functioned with two *alcaldes ordinarios* and four *regidores*, of which one was an *alférez* and one an *alguacil*.[19] The offices were theoretically elective but there is doubt that with the shortage of "whites" to fill the required posts, many officials would have retained their positions for life and they may even have become hereditary. Positions falling vacant would probably have been sold by the Governor. In the 1680s Sebastián de Roteta petitioned the King to grant St. Joseph the title of *ciudad* so that "in the new year it should be possible to have elections of *alcaldes ordinarios*, *alférez mayor*, *alguacil mayor*, *procurador general* and other less important offices in conformity with the ancient customs of Spain in consideration of the great poverty they [the *vecinos*] suffer they cannot hope for any office of those referred to and they live extremely disconsolately desiring these positions".[20] When St. Joseph was given its official title of *ciudad* in 1691 it received the faculty to elect a *cabildo* composed of two *alcaldes ordinarios*, four *regidores*, an *alcade de hermandad*, a *procurador* and an *alguacil*. In 1702 the lack of suitable people to fill the offices reduced the number of *regidores* to three, but by 1777 four councillors were being elected once again.[21] Law and order was maintained in St. Joseph by the *Santa Hermandad*, which was essentially a royal police force, with police and judicial powers.[22] An *alcalde* of the *Santa Hermandad* was chosen by de Vera when he founded St. Joseph in 1592[23] but the institution does not appear to have received official status until 1644.[24]

During the seventeenth and early eighteenth centuries attacks from both Caribs and foreigners had required the capital to be located inland, but, with the increasing importance of trade in the New World as a whole and in the economy of Trinidad in particular, a coastal location became more desirable. Thus in 1735 Governor Don Estevan de Liñan y Vera decided to take up residence in Port of Spain.[25] It was not until 1757, however, that it became the Governor's permanent residence. Two years later the *Procurador* of Trinidad informed the King that St. Joseph was being abandoned so that, "not even the form of a town remains, only its title".[26] By 1777 the Governor and all the royal officials were living in Port of Spain, whilst the *Cabildo* remained in St. Joseph.[27] This meant that whilst commercial matters could be attended to with greater efficiency, the administration of the island was divided between the two towns.

The spread of the Christian faith to Trinidad was hampered both by the difficulty of securing the necessary personnel and the great distance of the island from the episcopal seats in San Juan and Bogotá. Throughout the seventeenth and eighteenth centuries the Bishop and Governor complained about the lack of secular clergy;[28] in 1706 Trinidad possessed only four secular clergy, compared with 21 in Cumaná and 18 in Margarita.[29] It was not that salaries were insufficient, for in the early part of the century they were higher than in the latter two places.[30] However later, following the cacao failure and the subsequent lack of tribute and tithe payments, they did become a problem.[31] The allocation of clergy by the Bishop of Puerto Rico was hampered by the self interest of other parts of his diocese; in 1713 the Governor of Margarita refused to allow a number of clergy to be taken from the island for employment in Trinidad.[32] Throughout the seventeenth century there appears to have been at least one parish priest in St. Joseph and one Franciscan father in the convent. In 1645 the parish priest was aided by a sacristan, who had not been ordained, and in addition there was a chaplain to the garrison.[33] In 1716 the *vecinos* of Port of Spain requested a parish priest because communication between the two Spanish towns was difficult.[34] The Crown agreed but it was not until 1774 that a sacristan was placed in the Port.[35] The difficulty of obtaining secular clergy meant that for much of the time the four positions remained vacant. The most regularly filled position was that of parish priest of St. Joseph, which was the most senior of the four.

Establishments of the regular clergy similarly remained unoccupied for much of the seventeenth century. A Franciscan convent was founded in Trinidad in 1592 under the title of San Antonio de Padua[36] and it functioned with a staff of one until it was abandoned in 1652 because of attack by foreigners.[37] In 1705 it was being maintained from the province of Caracas, but it did not possess a priest; even when it was occupied there was generally only one cleric.[38] In 1714 another convent called San Joachin and Santa Ana was erected by the Dominicans,[39] and in 1722 a hermitage was established in Port of Spain.[40] Nothing is known of the work of these orders.

The Inquisition was never introduced into Trinidad, although an attempt was made to do so by a French Jesuit while Martín Mendoza was Governor. He was despatched to Guyana by Mendoza who saw his presence in the island as a threat to his own power and as unnecessary in the light of the negligible influence of Protestantism there.[41]

Population

The original Spanish population of Trinidad consisted of settlers who remained in the island after taking part in expeditions to the Orinoco.

The actual number that remained must have been few, for of 2200 that participated in expeditions at the end of the sixteenth century only 60 survived.[42] In 1609 St. Joseph only contained 35–40 men.[43] The small Spanish population in Trinidad was the subject of considerable anxiety, particularly to the Spanish themselves, since neither agriculture nor trade could be developed and the island lay open to attack by Caribs and foreigners. In 1612 Governor Sancho de Alquiza complained that agriculture could not be developed unless 100 cultivators were sent from Spain.[44] and in 1617 the *Procurador* of Trinidad petitioned the Crown for 300 negroes, of which two-thirds should be men, to plant cacao because "the island is so lowly populated with natives and the Spanish are so few and those that there are spend most of their time with their arms in their hands against the said Caribs."[45] Although negro slaves were not forthcoming from Spain, the inhabitants obtained them illegally from foreigners and in fact carried out a lucrative trade in selling them to other parts of the Indies,[46] whilst a number of personal slaves were introduced under individual concessions.[47] The Spanish colonists also succeeded in obtaining indian slaves from villages along the Orinoco, Cumaná, Guyana and Santa Fé by trade.[48]

In addition to negro slaves, the inhabitants requested immigrants for the defence of the island and in 1615, of the 70–80 ordered by the King and the 100 requested, 50 men were sent from Puerto Rico.[49] In 1634 the Bishop of Puerto Rico asked for 25 families to be sent to Trinidad because, "there are 26 *vecinos* subject to 4000 warlike indians in the island",[50] but they never arrived. In 1685 the King conceded 30 families from the Canaries for the better defence of the island and in particular Port of Spain but there were delays in their transport[51] and there is no evidence that they ever arrived. The population of the Spanish settlements thus received little assistance from immigration. In 1688 St. Joseph and Port of Spain possessed 90–100 and 10–12 *vecinos* respectively, including whites, *mestizos* and *mulatos*, and an indian population of 292 composed of adults and children employed in the personal service of the *vecinos*.[52] To these may be added about 250 wives and children of the *vecinos* and an unknown number of slaves—probably about 100—giving a total population of about 750 for the two Spanish towns (see Table VII.)

The small permanent population of both towns throughout the eighteenth century continued to cause anxiety to many of Trinidad's Governors who repeatedly petitioned the Crown for immigrants, in the form of soldiers and settlers, to help in the defence of the island.[53] The need was particularly great at the end of the seventeenth century when the island, and Port of Spain especially, was attacked by French pirates and corsairs,[54] and when Guaroon indians from the Orinoco were inciting the indians in the missions to riot.[55] In 1700 the Council of War

TABLE VII

Population of St. Joseph 1592–1700

1592	Antonio de Berrío has "85 selected Spaniards" in Trinidad TTHS *14* 27.7.1592
1609	35–40 men at St. Joseph TTHS *81* 30.11.1609
1612	St Joseph has "up to 32 straw houses and 40 men" AGI CAR *971* 14.6.1612
1615	St. Joseph has 70 Spaniards TTHS *170* 29.7.1615
1616	"there are not 30 persons left to defend the island" AGI SD *25* 8.3.1616
1617	"there are not 50 men and of those most are ill or disabled" AGI SD *179–1–24* 28.8.1617
1622	St. Joseph contained 500 inhabitants Ponte, *Bolivar y Ensayos*, p. 28
1624	The Kings subjects do not add up to 40 AGI SD *179–1–47* 12.7.1624
1634	"26 *vecinos* subject to 4,000 indians" AGI SD *172–3–125* 23.2.1634
1636	Impossible to muster 40 men who belonged to the island TTHS *82* Nov. 1636
1637	28–30 *vecinos* resisted an attack from the Dutch AGI SD *179–2–51* 4.12.1637
1637	"30 houses and 40–50 men" TTHS *137* Dec. 1637
1640	Contains about 40 houses de Laet, *L'histoire du Nouveau Monde*, p. 604
1642	60 *vecinos* Espinosa, *Compendium and Description*, p. 56
1645	"it is a place of 45 *vecinos*" AGI SD *179–4–154* 1645
1646	60 *vecinos* Díaz de la Calle, *Memorial y Noticias Sacras*, p. 27
1654	St. Joseph garrisoned with 100 Spaniards TTHS *721* 1654
1655	St. Joseph composed of 200 inhabitants Pelleprat, *Relato de las misiones*, p. 51
1666	80–100 Spaniards CSP (AWI) *86* no.1368: 436 1666
1671	Island composed of 80 *vecinos* AGI SD *179–2–57* 4.2.1671
1678	104 men including old and ill AGI SF *218* 16.2.1678
1687	50 *vecinos* amongst whites, *mestizos*, and *mulatos* who can bear arms AGI SF *218* 2.1.1687
1688	St. Joseph possessed 90–100 *vecinos* AGI SD *179–3–85* 18.7.1688
1700	120 *vecinos*, whites, *mestizos* and creoles in the island, AGI SD *666* 1700

received a letter from the Governor of Trinidad stating, "This island is in a very poor state and there are not more than 120 *vecinos*, whites, *mestizos* and creoles, being only 80 capable of bearing arms . . . and in all the island not more than 30 soldiers with one captain".[56] Although the King resolved to send 50 men to Trinidad it is not known whether they arrived.[57] Nevertheless, despite the great loss in the indian population through their release from personal service, the two towns increased in total population during the first two decades of the eighteenth century, partly as a result of the economic expansion that the island experienced during that period. In 1716 the *vecinos* petitioned the Crown for a chaplain for Port of Spain, because the priest at St. Joseph had to attend over 300 souls in that town[58] and by 1722 there were 56 *vecinos* in Port of Spain and 126 in St. Joseph, including "whites, *mestizos*, negroes and *mulatos*".[59] Using a reasonable multiplication factor of five, the total populations were probably about 250 and 600 respectively. Following the cacao blast in 1725 the *vecinos* began to take up residence on their lands, so that in 1730 the Bishop of Puerto Rico on a visit to Trinidad found 341 souls "of confession and communion" in St. Joseph and another 367 in the valleys surrounding the town, excluding the population of the indian villages that were located there.[60] As well as the shortages of food that the inhabitants of the two towns experienced, they also suffered epidemics, the most notable of which was a smallpox epidemic in 1741. In that year the Governor reported, "no day passes without 3, 4, or 5 people dying . . . such that already no more dead will fit in the church . . . and in this town alone [St. Joseph] 70 have died, which is remarkable considering its small population."[61] In 1748 the island was described as depopulated,[62] but by the time the next census was taken it had risen above its former level: in 1763 the total populations of St. Joseph and Port of Spain were 786 and 440 respectively.[63] In about 1770 the inhabitants were still regarded as very poor. They were said to "cure each other with home-made remedies since they do not have medicine, a doctor or a surgeon".[64] Nevertheless the populations of the two towns continued to rise to 1053 and 632 respectively in 1777.[65]

Racial composition

Encouraged by the imbalance in the sex ratio, racial mixing was most common in the towns of St. Joseph and Port of Spain, where Spaniards, negroes and indians lived in close proximity. Mixed marriages, although legal from 1501, were not encouraged by the Crown.[66] As a result most of the relationships between people of different races were casual and most of the offspring illegitimate. Legitimate *mestizos* were probably absorbed into the community as Spaniards or creoles for they are not specifically mentioned until 1687.[67] Illegitimate *mestizo* children were probably brought up as indians. In Trinidad in 1688 there were 11 *mestizo* children of indians working in personal service, one fifth of the total number of children so employed, and none of them was legitimate. At the same time there were 13 free *mulatos*, the legitimate offspring of Spaniards and negroes, who themselves employed indians in their personal service.[68] Through the colonial period the number of Peninsular or creole Spaniards declined: in 1705 St. Joseph was registered as having 80 men who could bear arms "and of those very few Spanish, most of them *mestizos*, *mulatos* and free negroes, all poor people".[69] In 1713 the militia of St. Joseph was composed of 10 whites, 12 *mestizos*, 22 *mulatos*, 3 negroes and 3 *grifos*. These figures did not, however, include the members of the *Cabildo* and regular army, who would have been white.[70] With the cacao failure a number of *vecinos* left the island, leaving in 1733 only 162 non-indians adult inhabitants of whom only 28 were white and the majority of the rest were of mixed race.[71] In 1750 the *Cabildo* complained that they could not find a sufficient number of intelligent people to fill the required offices since, in referring to a revolt against the Governor in 1745, they observed that "the last troubles forced all the principal male inhabitants to leave the island".[72] Thus Port of Spain with a population of about 300 was composed of "a mixture of indianised Spaniards and half castes as well as some French and Corsican foreigners".[73] In 1763 whites, who probably included creoles and *mestizos*, since neither were specifically mentioned, constituted 21·5% and 54·3% of the populations of Port of Spain and St. Joseph respectively.[74] The higher percentage of whites in St. Joseph may be explained by the great number of government officials and members of the *Cabildo* who resided there. In Port of Spain negroes, euphemistically known as *pardos*, were dominant as a free class.[75] In both towns free *morenos* and *mulatos* formed the next most numerous group. By 1777 the percentage of whites in St. Joseph had dropped to 23·5% while that of Port of Spain had risen to 30%. This change in the racial composition of the two towns may in part be explained by the change in the residence of the Governor and other Spanish officials to Port of Spain. The overall decline in the percentage of whites from 32·7% in 1763 to 26·2% in 1777 may be explained mainly by the higher fertility rate of other racial groups expressed in the larger size of negro and *mulato* families—about 3·8 and 3·0 children per family respectively compared with 2·1 for white families.[76]

Social classes

Those persons classified as white would have included Peninsular Spaniards, creoles, and *mestizos*. Peninsular Spaniards had the highest social status, which was reinforced by their roles as government officials, ecclesiastics, *encomenderos* and landowners, whereas creoles generally had to be content with less important positions in the church and military and occasionally in the *Cabildo*. In Trinidad the church probably offered little prospect for social advancement, but a number of creoles would have entered the officer ranks of the five regular companies that were established in the island.[77] The social prestige of ecclesiastical and military positions was legally reinforced by the *"fuero eclesiastico"* and *"fuero militar"*, which exempted clerics and soldiers respectively from tithe payment and trial in civil courts. In Trinidad the distinction between Peninsular Spaniards and creoles does not appear to have been made until the late seventeenth century when in 1688, 10 of the 82 *vecinos* who had indians in their personal service were called *republicanos*.[78]

Most of the sexual relationships between Spaniards and indians would have been casual so that most *mestizos* would have been illegitimate and the association of *mestizos* with illegitimacy in part accounts for their inferior social position. During the seventeenth century in Trinidad legitimate *mestizos* appear to have been accepted in society as Spaniards for, in a list of *vecinos* who held indians in their personal service in 1688 *mestizos* are undefined although other racial groups are.[79] Although *mestizos* are mentioned in estimates of the population of the island at the beginning of the eighteenth century, they are not specifically identified in the latter part of the century and it is likely that despite the stigma of illegitimacy generally attached to *mestizos*, given the small size of the "white" population, they were considered as "white". Like the Spaniards, *mestizos* were exempt from tribute payment and from forced labour under the *mita*, but their socially inferior position was enforced by laws which prevented them from holding positions of authority in the government and church, and from joining the army.[80]

Mulatos and *zambos* assumed a more inferior status in society for in addition to the stigma of illegitimacy possessed by *mestizos* they also had the stigma of slavery, being born of negro slave women. Their inferior social status was confirmed by their payment of tribute and work under the *mita*, in addition to the restrictions that were placed on *mestizos*. Due to their military ability however they were eventually permitted to join the army and thereby exempted from tribute payment. During the eighteenth century in Trinidad miscegenation resulted in an increasing percentage of people of mixed race in the population, with distinctions between *mestizos*, *mulatos*, *zambos* and negroes becoming blurred. In the second half of the eighteenth they were known as *morenos* or *pardos* and social distinction was based on their legal status as slaves or freemen.[81]

Whilst the majority of negroes were slaves their social status was higher than that of indians. Associated with the Spaniards, they spoke the same language and although forbidden to dress as Spaniards they were culturally more akin to them than were the indians. Also, although the negroes were mainly slaves, they always had the chance of obtaining their freedom by special favour. In Trinidad in 1688 there were two free negroes who themselves had indians working in their personal service.[82] The gradual manumission of slaves created a landless group of negroes and people of mixed race. Some were absorbed into the army, while others were employed in domestic service and lesser mechanical trades. Attitudes towards slavery mellowed during the eighteenth century. In 1776 the King specifically ordered that 38 negroes taken from an English ship should be treated as paid servants and not as slaves.[83] With the increasing manumission of slaves, however, those that remained enslaved would have assumed an inferior social position.

Although the above social classes could be identified, the boundaries between them were never well defined, owing to marriages and casual relationships between people of different racial origins and social class, and the possibility of a rise in status through favour or enterprise. In 1777 the Trinidad census only distinguished between whites, free people of mixed racial origin, slaves and indians.[84]

The economy

The Spanish introduced into Trinidad a commercial system of agricultural production based on the permanent cultivation of selected crops which could be exported to Spain in return for vital provisions and manufactured goods. For its operation it was dependent on abundant labour resources and trading opportunities; unfortunately Trinidad lacked both. The lack of labour resources meant that agricultural production remained at a low level and ships were therefore not encouraged to stop at the island. As a result, when crops were produced they were often wasted and vital food crops and other provisions could not be imported. Thus the Spanish came to depend for supplies on contraband trading and trade with the indians in the *encomiendas*, the absence of which would probably have led to a collapse in commercial agricultural production.

Land holdings

Grants of land were given in perpetuity to nearly all Spanish settlers according to their merits and services. Individual grants were theoretically limited to 5 *peonías* or 3 *caballerías*, that is 500 or 1500 acres respectively, but they were sometimes larger.[85] Land grants were made in Trinidad as soon as the Spanish settled there. In 1595 Raleigh reported that Antonio de Berrío had "divided the island and given to every soldier a part".[86] Most of the land grants would have been located around St. Joseph, the site of which had been chosen partly on the basis of the agricultural potential of the area,[87] in the Maracas valley and around Port of Spain. The grants of land would have been made in one piece and were intended to be cultivated permanently, but it appears that as crops yields declined new lands were opened up, thus bringing about a reversion to a shifting mode of cultivation, which was inefficient in terms of commercial production. In 1717 it was reported that the lands were so infertile that, after harvesting maize for two years and cacao for six years, they had to be abandoned. Thus cacao estates in the valleys of Paraure, Tacarigua, Piarcules, Amana, Tunapuna, Curepe, and Aricagua, and along the banks of the Caroni, were deserted and areas of "virgin forest" opened up in the Arauca valley and the upper reaches of the Aricagua valley. Other lands, near Port of Spain, at Rio Seco, Cimaronero, Tragarete and St. Ann's had also been abandoned as infertile. The infertility of the land was probably exaggerated in a successful attempt to persuade the Crown to suspend a cadastral survey:[88] in a separate account one landowner maintained that her lands in the upper Aricagua valley could produce 100 *fanegas* of cacao a year employing only four slaves.[89] Similarly, at a much later date, the French coloniser Roume St. Laurent observed that around Port of Spain "several crops of maize are harvested every year without the use of manure and without impoverishing the soil which still appears in its first vigour".[90] Cultivation did, however, spread up the slopes of the valleys in the Northern Range where the *vecinos* took up residence.

Sources of Labour

A great obstacle to the agricultural development of estates was the shortage of labour about which the Spanish colonists made continual complaints, saying that they were forced to work "with their own hands" to provide for their families.[91] Indian labour was so scarce that in the early eighteenth century open conflict developed between landowners, *encomenderos* and missionaries over access to supplies of indian labour in the *encomiendas* and *missions*.

Although a number of eminent colonists were given grants of indians as *encomiendas* from whom they could collect tribute, they could not *legally* employ them in their personal service. They did, however, subject the indians to considerable abuse. In 1614 the Governor was charged with having given new *encomiendas* to *encomenderos* who had sold the indians they had originally been granted to landowners,[92] and there is no doubt that from the earliest years of colonisation indians were emloyed in the personal service of *encomenderos*. In 1657 due to the poverty of the island the Crown legalised the employment of indians by the *encomenderos* for three days a week but in 1682 the prohibition against the employment of indians in personal service was reconfirmed.[93] The *encomenderos* maintained, however, that since the indians could not pay their tribute in crops "it is necessary that they work in weeding the cacao trees and sow and harvest maize and manioc, which is our bread".[94] Also, they maintained that the indians preferred to pay tribute in the form of labour service. Hence in 1705 the indians were working 54 days a year on the *encomenderos'* estates instead of paying 54 *reales* in money or agricultural produce. In 1707 this was sanctioned by the *Alcaldes Ordinarios* who were governing the island, but the decision was reversed in 1714 when the Crown repeated the order that the indians were to pay their tribute in goods.[95] By that time the very existence of the *encomiendas* was in question.

In the New World all unemployed indians were bound by a decree of 1549 to present themselves in the central square for hire. This unenforced system of labour naturally failed to attract many indians so it was ruled in 1609 that every indian village was to make available one-seventh of its male population at a time to work for fixed wages on public works.[96] A wide variety of activities could be regarded as public services, as long as they were not obviously for private gain.[97] In Trinidad public service included "helping in the defence of Barbacoa, Maracas, and Curaguate every 8 days, moreover helping in attacks which present themselves and today they are in the service of Your Majesty 18 or 20 indians . . . cutting carat to cover the Government buildings".[98] "Public service", however, was loosely defined: indians could be employed in the service of landowners on the grounds that it was in the public interest to maintain agricultural production. During the seventeenth century in Trinidad, however, this system of forced labour called the *mita* would not have been an important source of labour, for indians in the *encomiendas* were generally assigned to their *encomenderos* and the greater part of the rest of the indian population had retreated to inaccessible parts of the island.

When missions were founded at the end of the eighteenth century, they drew from the hills and forests indians who had formerly been outside direct Spanish control and hence unavailable for work on Spanish estates. Although the *encomenderos* complained that their indians were leaving for the missions,[99] in the long term the landowners profited from their establishment, since they were later able to make use of their large labour force. As soon as the missions were founded the landowners requested that they should be allowed to employ mission indians, offering to give them pay, food and instruction in the Catholic faith. The missionaries agreed but the landowners failed to carry out their obligations so that "after six and eight months that they had them working on their *haciendas* they sent them back to the missions naked, dying of hunger, without instruction and without pay". The missionaries therefore, taking into account also the fact that the indians did not have time to work on their own land, decided not to allow any more indians to work on the cacao estates of the *vecinos*.[100] This led to conflict with the landowners, who succeeded in persuading the Crown that the missionaries could be more usefully employed in Guyana; in 1708 the King ordered the missionaries to leave the island and the missions to be placed under a *cura doctrinero* and a *corregidor*.[101] The order was not, however, put into effect until 1713 when the Bishop of Puerto Rico visited the island, because the new Governor was aware of the ulterior motives of the landowners and was concerned about the inability of the indians to pay tribute if they were employed for long periods by the landowners.[102]

The distribution of labour under the *mita* was made by the *corregidor* of the indian village and was subject to his personal whim. In 1705 the *cura doctrinero* complained that on four occasions when indians from the *encomiendas* had been available for hire "two or three have been given to *vecinos* and the rest to their *encomenderos* and *corregidor* because they are all of one house and family".[103] The *encomenderos*, therefore, either directly or indirectly, possessed almost exclusive control over the principal sources of labour in the island. This led to conflicts with other landowning groups who wished to employ indian labour, for there were many landowners and only four *encomenderos*. In 1711 Governor Don Félix de Guzmán suggested that there should be a free labour market because the indians of the *encomiendas* "only serve their *encomenderos* who are not the people with the largest estates but the most backward on account of which the indian labour is of little advantage to them".[104] As a result it was ordered that all *encomiendas* falling vacant should be administered by the Crown.[105] The *encomienda* of Aricagua had been administered by the Crown since 1689, when it was declared vacant on the death of the *encomendero* and the applicant failed to secure confirmation of his title.[106] By 1727 the *encomiendas* of Arauca and Aricagua were being administered by the Crown, the *encomendero* of the former having died in 1725, but the *encomienda* of Cuara was still in the hands of an *encomendero*, Don Manuel Coronado.[107]

As Fig. 7 shows, with the abolition of the *encomiendas* and missions the indian labour force was made more generally available to the *vecinos*, since, apart from the *corregidores*, there were no longer any bodies or officials who had preferential access to it. The conditions under which indians from the former missions could be employed were regularised, however: no indian could be employed for more than 16 days a year and landowners wishing to hire indians had first to obtain a licence from the government and the numbers hired had to be recorded by the *corregidor*.[108] Thus in the first half of the eighteenth century it was through the *mita* that the landowners would have obtained most of the labour they used, but the supply was insufficient.

If there were insufficient supplies of labour in the island then they had to be sought elsewhere. In 1637 it was thought that there were three hundred slaves in Trinidad of which two hundred were indian slaves and the other 100 negroes.[109] Indian slaves, mainly from the Orinoco, would have been cheaper and easier to obtain. Raleigh noted that young indians could be bought at the mouth of the Orinoco for three or four hatchets,[110] and an inventory of indians in the personal service of *vecinos* in 1688 indicates that most of them came from villages along the

Seventeenth and eighteenth centuries

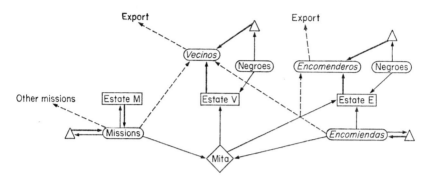

Later eighteenth century

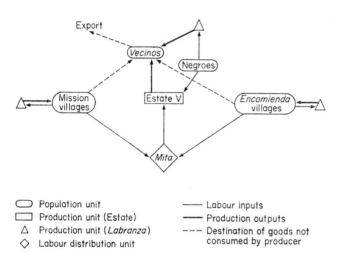

⬭ Population unit   —— Labour inputs
▭ Production unit (Estate)   ▬ Production outputs
△ Production unit (*Labranza*)   --- Destination of goods not
◇ Labour distribution unit   consumed by producer

FIG. 7. Sources of labour and production in Trinidad.

Orinoco and particularly from the village of Casanare. In that year, however, those indians that had been obtained from the mainland by trade and were employed in personal service were released.[111]

Negro labour in the area was scarce and consequently expensive throughout the colonial period.[112] In 1686 the Spanish in Trinidad were paying £100 for a negro slave.[113] During the seventeenth century there were few recorded landings of negro slaves in Trinidad and although during the eighteenth century the *asiento* made between the Spanish Crown and various slave trading companies ensured a regular supply of negroes for the New World, relatively few reached Trinidad and they did not constitute an important source of labour. In 1705 it was said that "although the island is very fertile there are no slaves to cultivate the land" and the *encomendero* of Arauca considered that the employment of indians in personal service was vital to the island's economy because "there are no slaves to cultivate cacao because negroes of the *asiento* do not come to this island and the few that there were died in 1704 with the general epidemic."[114] Part of the reason for the shortage of negro slave labour in the island was that the *vecinos* preferred quick profits from trading to uncertain profits from agricultural development, and hence resold slaves that were introduced into the island to other islands and parts of the mainland. Brito Figueroa estimates that of 70 000 negroes that entered Venezuela between 1700 and 1799 20% were introduced illegally, mainly from Trinidad and Curaçao.[115] Few negroes remained in the island: in 1777 of a total population of 3432 only 222 or $6\frac{1}{2}$% were slaves. It must be remembered, however, that by this time many negroes had obtained their freedom.[116]

Agricultural production

On the estates land was permanently cleared and a few selected crops were grown. The relatively complete land clearance exposed the soil to sun and rain, particularly during the growing period, thereby encouraging erosion and the loss of soil fertility. Also, the permanent cultivation of land, allowing no resting period for the soil or the regeneration of a vegetation cover which, once burnt, could return nutrients to the soil, probably accentuated the decline of soil fertility.

Most of the crops on the estates were commercial crops destined for Spanish markets. A few food crops were grown in small quantities but they did not account for a significant proportion of agricultural production, at least not in the seventeenth century. The most important crop grown in the early seventeenth century was tobacco but the emphasis of production later shifted to cacao. In 1614 a report to the Council of the Indies stated that "there is nothing in the island but tobacco", despite the fact that Governor Sancho de Alquiza had forbidden the planting of tobacco in an effort to prevent illegal trading with foreigners.[117] In that year 85 000 lb of tobacco left the island for Spain and by the 1630s the annual production had reached 100 000 lb.[118] Tobacco production had been encouraged by the suspension of duties of *alcabala* and *almojarifazzo* in 1616, which had been granted because "the land is new and much frequented by enemies and there are no other crops except tobacco".[119] In addition to tobacco produced within the island, about 50000 lb was brought annually to Trinidad from the Orinoco for loading into Spanish ships.[120] Tobacco was produced throughout the seventeenth century and in 1683 was described as "the best tobacco in the world";[121] but production was severely hit by the development of tobacco cultivation in Virginia and Carolina so that by mid-century its status as the island's principal commericial crop was being challenged by cacao. Cacao—probably wild cacao—was found in Trinidad in 1616 but its cultivation did not spread rapidly owing to the shortage of labour in the island.[122] However, in 1645 Scott reported that "cacao groweth here in great plenty and the best sort in all the Indies"[123] and Díaz de la Calle described it as one of the principal two crops of the island, the other being tobacco.[124]

Cacao production increased during the latter part of the eighteenth century to a peak in 1704 when 248600 lb were exported and cacao was reported to be the island's only item of trade.[125] The profitability of cacao production was, however, largely governed by prices which fluctuated considerably and depended on trading opportunities, which were often disrupted by wars, and on the state of the European market. Cacao production in Trinidad, for example, suffered a setback at the end of the seventeenth century when Mexican cacao flooded the European market.[126] As shown in Table VIII between 1683 and 1725 the prices paid for cacao in Caracas fluctuated between a high of 460 *reales* for a *fanega* and an all-time low of 56 *reales* in 1713.[127] In 1711 the

TABLE VIII

Exports of cacao from Trinidad 1683–1719

	lb	Prices paid for cacao in Caracas in *reales* per *fanega*[a]
1683	126 335	100/420/460
1684	64 460	80
1685	143 570	80
1686	50 105	80
to Oct 1687	71 280	100

TABLE VIII—contd.

	lb	Prices paid for cacao in Caracas in *reales* per *fanega*[a]
1688	no data	100
1689	85 580	104/136
1690	111 223	136
1691	34 747	144/160/176
1692	78 766	174/200
1693	91 962	184/200
1694	82 707	176
1695	100 200	132/160
1696	105 380	112
1697	34 210	112
1698	125 180	112/120
1699	6 930	120/152
1700	133 650	120/152
1701	110 880	128/133/136
1702	133 595	128
1703	206 360	100/112/120
1704	248 600	100
1705	102 520	100
1706	98 120	80/100/112
1712	88 772	56/64/96
1713	60 207	56
1714	89 024	56/60/61
1715	88 220	60
1716	87 465	62/74/80
1717	152 829	100/104/108
1718	71 060	84/90
1719	127 380	68/84/88

Sources: AGI CONTAD *1678* 1683–86
AGI EC *705B* 1686–1687, 1689–90
AGI EC *712B* 1690–1701
AGI CONTAD *1675* 1701–1705
AGI EC *715B* 1706
AGI CONTAD *1675* 1712–1719

[a] Prices paid for cacao in Caracas are taken from Arcila Farías, *Comercio entre Venezuela y México*, pp. 134–5

Governor of Trinidad reported that although the harvesters in Trinidad had set the price of cacao at 144 *reales*, they were having to sell it in Caracas at 72 *reales* and in Margarita and Cumana at 56 *reales*, otherwise it would have been wasted.[128] By the early 1720s cacao exports had fallen to about 130000 lb.[129] The lack of expansion in cacao production was blamed on the shortage of labour, but the uncertainty of markets must also have played a significant role.[130] However, the real setback in cacao production occurred in 1725 when the cacao estates were devastated by disease caused by the fungus *Ceratocystis*.[131] At the time it was variously considered as a punishment from heaven for the non-payment of tithes,[132] and as the result of a drought or strong north winds.[133] The disease virtually caused the collapse of the estates and it had repercussions on the demographic, social and political structures in the island. In 1737 the King ordered the Governor to urge the inhabitants to re-establish cacao cultivation but by the 1750s only very small quantities were being exported.[134] In 1756 a new hardier variety of cacao called *forastero* was introduced from Brazil and it was this variety that was planted on the newly established estates.[135] In the 1770s observers reported that about 10000 lb of good quality cacao were being produced annually and in 1776 Raynal commented that the cacao produced in Trinidad was "in such perfection that it was preferred to that of Caracas and the Spanish merchants sought to anticipate each other by paying for it in advance".[136] Nevertheless, cacao never assumed the importance in the Trinidad economy that it had held at the beginning of the century.

For the establishment of cacao estates it would have been necessary to clear the land completely, after which the trees would have been cultivated permanently or for at least 12 years on poor soils, counting 6 or 7 years before fruiting and 5 or 6 years of harvest before yields declined. In most cases cacao trees would have been cultivated for longer periods since they were generally planted on the most fertile soils.[137] The practice of growing cacao under larger immortelle trees (*Erythrina micropteryx*) may have been adopted at an early date but it was first noted in 1777.[138] The impossibility of clearing land without the provision of a vegetation cover was noted in 1713 when the *Cabildo* reported that "the strong sun which is experienced every summer is of such a degree that without the shade of trees which keeps them [maize plants] succulent they are at great risk and since it is not possible to remedy the situation plots are left uncultivated after two years".[139] Although the latter observation relates to *conucos* it is even more true of cacao estates where land clearance was more complete and trees were exposed to sun and rain. It is likely therefore that shade-casting trees would have been planted on cacao estates, thereby partially recreating the forest ecosystem that land clearance had destroyed.

Compared with cacao and tobacco other commercial crops were grown in very small quantities. Although cotton was produced on a small scale in the seventeenth and eighteenth centuries,[140] it was not until the 1770s, after duties on cotton had been suspended to promote the development of the cloth industry in Spain, that it began to be commercially produced.[141] The suitability of the island for cotton production was noted by Roume St. Laurent, who in 1777 observed that cotton grew better in Trinidad than any other island.[142] Coffee (*Coffea arabica*) was first introduced into the New World in 1714, when it was taken to Surinam by the Dutch, but it did not reach the Antilles until 1720 when it was introduced into Martinique.[143] It was probably introduced to Trinidad shortly after that date and the first recorded export of coffee, which it is presumed was grown in the island, was in 1764 when 38 lb were sent to Margarita.[144] In 1777 a visitor to the island claimed that in Trinidad "coffee yields better than in any other part of America."[145] Although sugar cane was grown for local consumption,[146] partly in the form of rum, it was not commercially produced until the latter part of the eighteenth century because it was stated that sugar production required high capital investment and "there is not one single inhabitant of Trinidad, Margarita, Puerto Rico, or Santo Domingo capable of the undertaking".[147] Sugar cane grew well, however, and it was said to ratoon ten years in succession without being replanted.[148]

Other commercial crops grown on a small scale included indigo,[149] ginger, vanilla and cinnamon. Vanilla was present in Tobago in the late seventeenth century and it was introduced into Martinique and Guadeloupe from South America in 1701.[150] It probably arrived in Trinidad about the same time for in 1777 it was growing wild in the island.[151] Although vanilla grew well in Trinidad, the limited markets for the crop and the low prices paid for it by the Compañía Guipuzcoana de Caracas, which monopolised its trade, no doubt discouraged its cultivation.[152] Cinnamon (*Cinnamomum zeylanicum*) was introduced to Barbados from the East Indies about the turn of the century and was growing in Tobago in 1763, so that it seems likely that it reached Trinidad in the first half of the eighteenth century.[153]

The over-emphasis on commercial production meant that food crops had to be imported. As a result, when trade was at a low level due to the failure of the cacao harvest or when the landowners received less income as a consequence of changes in trade or market conditions, imports declined and food shortages were experienced. Although some food could be obtained from the indians it was insufficient, so as a protection against food shortages during the eighteenth century the landowners began to cultivate food crops. In 1761 the *Cabildo* ordered all *vecinos* to plant "manioc, plantains, maize and other fruits" so that their families should be provided for in times of shortage. The plots were to be proportional to the size of the individual family and the *vecinos* were subject to a fine of 30 *reales* and 20 days imprisonment if the plots were of insufficient size.[154] By 1777 there were 230 *labranzas* in the vicinity of St. Joseph and 59 near Port of Spain.[155] The three most important food crops grown were manioc, maize and plantains, which were grown on *labranzas* and occasionally on estates.[156] In 1777 71% and 89·5% of the *labranzas* belonging to *vecinos* in St. Joseph and Port of Spain respectively grew only these three crops. Other crops grown included cacao, sugar and beans.[157] In addition to the beans already grown in the island, the tonka bean (*Dipteryx odorata*), a northern South American domesticate,[158] and the broad bean (*Vicia faba*) of Mediterranean or south-west Asian origin, which was growing in Barbados in 1750,[159] may have also been cultivated. Many of the other crops introduced into Trinidad during the eighteenth century were African in origin and their cultivation was associated with negro slaves. As such it is unlikely that many of them were adopted by Spanish landowners since they would have possessed the stigma of slavery. If grown at all they would probably have been grown on a small scale only. Altogether food crop production on the estates and on *labranzas* increased to the extent that by the middle of the eighteenth century cassava, plantains and maize were being exported to the nearby mainland and islands, and in the case of the latter crop as far as Puerto Rico.[160]

Introduced citrus species and indigenous fruits probably continued to be the most important fruits grown. The fruits most noticeable to Alcedo were oranges, lemons and citrons, though he also reported that vines grew well and produced good grapes.[161] Fruits introduced during the eighteenth century would have included the tomato (*Lycopersicon esculentum*), the avocado pear (*Persea americana*) and three Asian domesticates: the mango (*Mangifera indica*), the sweet or musk melon

(*Cucumis melo*) and the pomegranate (*Punica granatum*). The tomato, an Andean domesticate, was probably introduced to Trinidad via Spain but it may have come from Barbados where it was established in the early eighteenth century[162] and with which the indians, if not Spanish, had trading contacts. The avocado pear, a Central American domesticate, was probably introduced to the West Indies by the Spanish in the sixteenth century, although it has been suggested that it was first introduced to Jamaica in 1650[163] and from thence to other islands. It would have been suited to the poor but well drained soils of the Northern Range.[164] The mango was first introduced to Barbados from Brazil in 1742[165] but it was not harvested there until 1761.[166] It is unknown whether it reached Trinidad prior to 1776. The musk melon arrived in in the New World somewhat earlier and since it was growing in St. Kitts in 1630 it may have been growing in Trinidad in the late sixteenth century.[167] At that time Acosta noted that there was a "great store of pomegranates" in the New World[168] and in 1631 they were growing in Barbados.[169] It is unlikely, however, that if pomegranates had been introduced to Trinidad in the sixteenth century, they would have spread as rapidly as they did in the drier Lesser Antilles.

The greatest food shortage in the island throughout the colonial period was in animal protein. Domesticated animals did not form an integral part of agricultural production. Apart from a few domesticated animals kept on the estates for transport and agricultural work, no ranching industry developed despite the fact that Trinidad possessed "vast savannas to raise livestock of all kinds"[170] and animal products were in demand and the prices for them relatively stable.[171] In the middle of the eighteenth century small numbers of cattle and horses were introduced from Guyana, but it was not until 1777 that a *hato de ganado* was established in the vicinity of Port of Spain.[172] The illicit trade in mules in Trinidad and Margarita, that Spanish officials in Bogotá claimed they could not prevent, was certainly not based on animals bred in the island but on those obtained from the mainland.[173] Chickens were probably the most important animals kept by the Spanish for food, since they could be reared without affecting the broad structure of the economic system. Much of the meat consumed by the Spanish was imported, often at exorbitant prices.[174] In 1770 the Governor complained that because there was no livestock in the island the *vecinos* were forced to eat "salted plantain, some cassava and dried salted fish and meat which is brought from Cumaná."[175]

Hunting and Fishing

Since meat and fish were not always available from imported sources, the Spanish were sometimes forced to turn to hunting and fishing for their supplies of animal protein. However, the two activities played only minor roles in the economy of the estates. In 1757 the *Cabildo* complained that "for want of cattle and all sorts of provisions, the inhabitants feed themselves with what they can get personally in the woods and from the sea, but many days they return to their houses without anything to eat".[176] The most important animals hunted were probably deer, agouti, and lape, which with pigeons, ground doves, and water fowl, would have been considered the most palatable by the Spanish. It is possible that birds were more important constituents of the Spanish diet than of the indian diet, since the techniques of capture, notably the use of guns, possessed by the Spanish were more efficient. Pelleprat noticed that in the West Indies and the Tierra Firme "there were not so many ring doves or so many partridges as there were at the time of Discovery".[177] On the whole, however, wild faunal resources remained largely unexploited by the Spanish population; the same was true of aquatic resources. In 1760 the Governor observed that the coasts of Trinidad abounded in fish but "the poverty, laziness and small number of its inhabitants . . . means that the resource is lost.[178] Others blamed the failure of the fishing industry on the excessive licence and anchorage dues that fisherman had to pay unless they were fishing for the Governor.[179] The only aquatic animal that was exploited by the Spanish appears to have been the turtle, which formed the basis of a lucrative trade, particularly with foreigners, and of which the Governor had a monopoly.[180] A turtle-oil industry also developed in Port of Spain.[181]

The unreliability of domesticated sources of food drove the Spanish to exploit wild vegetable resources. In 1612 the *Procurador* of Trinidad reported that there was a lack of provisions in the island and "the colonists support themselves with what they hunt and the greater part of the year they eat a grass called pixa, which in Spain they call bledos."[182]

Other economic activities

The Spanish developed few other economic activities; most of the manufactured goods which they required were imported from Spain.

The major craft activities established were based on the island's timber resources. Throughout the seventeenth century the timber trees of Trinidad continued to impress visitors and settlers. In 1645 Scott noted, "The very mountains are covered with large cedars, whitewood and excellent timber for building or sheathing of ships, especially in those parts of the world where the worm eats both oak and fir, which in regard of the bitterness of this timber they forbear doing injury. Diverse years abundance of excellent timbers for joiners use, for cabinets and all other kinds of rare woods."[183] The largest trees were used in ship-building, canoe construction and fortifications.[184] In 1621 the Governor of Cartagena petitioned the King for permission to have two boats built in Trinidad for patrolling the coast of the Tierra Firme because of the abundant timber resources in the island.[185] The boats were probably propelled by rowers or sails whereas the principal vessels for voyaging between Trinidad and the mainland and neighbouring islands were canoes made by the indians. The greatest demands on the forest cover, however, were probably made for building purposes. Houses were built of mud, wood and palm leaves, primarily those of carat;[186] stone, particularly limestone, was not used in the seventeenth century even for churches and public buildings, although a certain amount was exported at great cost to Guyana for the construction of a fortress.[187] As such the establishment of St. Joseph and its continual reconstruction following its destruction by foreigners, fires or natural deterioration probably resulted in the selective felling of many trees, amongst which the most important were West Indian cedar, silk cotton, crappo, incense and galba.

Despite the extensive forest reserves in the island, a trade in timber did not develop until the eighteenth century. Foreigners who occupied the Antilles were more aware of the island's timber resources; in 1763 the Governor of Grenada observed that the timber in Trinidad was "the best in this part of the world for shipping; besides vast quantities of curious woods for the inside of houses and cabinets."[188] During the seventeenth and early eighteenth centuries foreigners from the Antilles made illegal inroads on the forest of the north and east coasts.[189] In the second half of the eighteenth century the Spanish exported small quantities of wood, mainly to the mainland, but also as far as Puerto Rico, Santo Domingo and Vera Cruz,[190] and they maintained a contraband trade in cedar and logwood with the Dutch at Curaçao.[191] At that time the Governor of the island was anxious to expand the timber trade by establishing free trade in wood with "friendly foreign nations" but he was severely reprimanded for making the suggestion;[192] the Crown had not yet adopted a liberal attitude towards trade.

Trade

The economy of the Spanish towns and surrounding estates was dependent on trade for its supply of food products and manufactured goods, which were obtained in exchange for commercial agricultural products. However, trading contacts with Spain were insufficient and irregular. This was in part a function of the general breakdown of the Spanish commercial system, and in part a product of local conditions. As a result, trade failed to secure for Spain the agricultural products of Trinidad and colonists were often left with ruined crops and in great need of both food and manufactured goods.[193] In response to this situation the colonists turned to contraband trading to find outlets for their crops and sources of vital provisions.

Legal trading with Spain was always intermittent. For 20 years following the settlement of the island in 1592 no Spanish ship visited Trinidad[194] but in 1613 the King, alarmed by the presence in the area of foreigners with whom the colonists could carry out contraband trading, agreed that one ship a year should go to the island in the Nueva España convoy.[195] In the subsequent eight years one ship a year visited Trinidad[196] but by 1621 its capacity was insufficient to cope with the volume of trade and more ships were not forthcoming.[197] In the following thirty years only 15 ships visited Trinidad.[198] Thus, trading contacts between Trinidad and Spain were never very regular but as the convoy system began to break down, as a result of the bankruptcy of Spanish colonialism and the infiltration of foreigners their irregularity increased. In 1687 Governor Sebastián de Roteta complained that no registered ship had visited Trinidad for four years[199] and although in the subsequent decade six registered ships stopped there, only three of them were from Spain.[200] In 1705 it was suggested that all registered ships going to Caracas should stop at the island,[201] but it was not until 1716, when the *Cabildo* complained that no registered ship had arrived in Trinidad since 1702,[202] that the Crown agreed.[203] Since the convoy system had ceased to operate, contraband trading had flourished. It was therefore decided in 1720 to resuscitate the system and to give to privileged trading companies monopolies of trade with particular areas in return for which they were to maintain coastguards in those areas to prevent illegal trading. Attempts to revive the convoy system were not very successful and after a final effort to regularise the Vera Cruz convoy in 1754, it was finally abandoned in 1789.[204] The founding of the Compañía Guipuzcoana de Caracas in 1728, with the monopoly of trade with Venezuela did, however, have some success in suppressing contraband trading. In 1765, in consideration of the poverty of the island, Trinidad, as well as Cuba, Puerto Rico, Hispaniola, and Margarita, was allowed to trade, without special licence from the Crown, with the Spanish towns of Cadíz, Sevilla, Alicante, Cartagena, Malaga, Barcelona, Santander, Coruña and Gijón;[205] Trinidad was too poor, however, to benefit from the privilege. In 1776 the Caracas Company had its privileges extended to Cumaná, Guyana, Margarita and Trinidad[206] and by 1779 an agent had established himself in the island[207] and the economy had expanded sufficiently to attract regular trade.

Three main reasons were given for the irregularity with which registered ships visited Trinidad: the presence of authorised pirates and unauthorised corsairs in Trinidad waters; the difficult sea passage particularly from the Caribbean coast of Venezuela; and the lack of incentive for ships to go there.

France and England, later joined by Holland, were anxious to break the Spanish monopoly of trade with her Empire. Attacks on Spanish ships in Trinidad waters and whilst anchored in Port of Spain were most frequent during the latter part of the seventeenth and early eighteenth centuries.[208] In 1707 the Bishop of Puerto Rico observed that ships going to Trinidad were always liable to be captured due to their poor defence and the multitude of English and Dutch corsairs from the islands of Curaçao and Barbados in the area;[209] whilst a missionary at Cumaná complained that French corsairs around Trinidad, Margarita and Cumaná were attacking the Spanish and indians both at sea and on land.[210] The intensity of attacks by both pirates and corsairs decreased, however, in the latter part of the eighteenth century as foreigners became more interested in developing trading contacts than carrying out attacks, and as the Caracas Company established coastguards to protect shipping and prevent smuggling.

The long and difficult sea passage to Trinidad also discouraged ships from stopping there. Navigation from Caracas, Cumaná, and Margarita to Trinidad was easier than the return, but both passages involved passing through the Bocas where many ships were lost. The passage was particularly dangerous because the ships that visited Trinidad were "small sloops which were very risky to sail".[211] The distance from ports normally visited by Spanish vessels also discouraged trade. In 1717 arms from Spain destined for Trinidad were left at Cartagena because of "the long distance of more than 400 leagues to Trinidad and because there is no commerce between the two."[212]

During the seventeenth century the low level of agricultural production also discouraged ships from calling at Trinidad. In 1640 it was reported that "those coasts are so infested with enemies that there is no one who dares to traffic from these parts [Spain] to those ports [Port of Spain and Santo Thomé] because the risks are so great and the interest so small".[213] The situation did not improve in the eighteenth century. Just prior to the failure of the cacao harvest it was considered that the products from Trinidad, Cumana, Margarita and Maracaibo together could not pay for the goods brought by one registered ship from Spain.[214] After the failure of the cacao harvest the situation became more serious; the inhabitants could not pay for the imported goods they required[215] and the salary of the Governor had to be provided from Caracas because the duties levied on imports and exports, from which he was usually paid, were insufficient;[216] any incentive for Spanish ships to visit Trinidad had disappeared. The absence of trading records until 1751 suggests a lack of commerce, especially since entries for the earliest dates are extremely low. It is likely that a few Spanish ships visited Trinidad from 1725 to 1750 but most of the island's trade was probably contraband in nature. With the introduction of a hardier variety of cacao its cultivation was resumed but it was not until 1775 that it was exported further afield than the mainland. Other exports at that time included tobacco, wood, salt, and provisions[217] (see Table IX). The salt was not produced in Trinidad but was obtained from Margarita and Cumana and resold, almost exclusively to Guyana, where it was used for salting meat and fish (see Table X).[218]

Although at the beginning of the seventeenth century various treaties concluding European wars recognised Spain's monopoly of trade with her colonies, contraband trading and privateering by the English, French and Dutch nevertheless continued in Trinidad waters. The great demand of the colonists for European goods and provisions, the cheap price of contraband goods compared with those imported from Spain, the distance of the island from any effective centre of government compared with its easy access to foreigners, who had established settlements in nearby islands and on the mainland, as well as the weakened nature of Spanish naval power, all contributed to the success of contraband trading.

From registered Spanish ships the colonists hoped to obtain European goods, particularly clothes and hardware. However, in 1716 the

TABLE IX

Selected registered exports from Trinidad 1751–1776

Goods	Unit	Total	M	C	G	TF	NB	PR/SD	Other
Cacao	lb	36 844	3281	1180	2023			29 700	660
Tobacco	lb	8400	3575	1500	2775		75		475
Cotton	lb	25	25						
Coffee	lb	88			88				
Sugar	lb	275			275				
Maize	lb	153 890	79 145	7315	4675	1155	17 930	41 800	1870
Cassava	lb	6050	6050						
Cassava cakes	no.	1195	500		575	120			
Cassava thirds	no.	30	20		10				
Plantains	no.	6900	1900	5000					
Rice	lb	550							
Planks of wood	no.	2950	574	835	588			748	205
Salt	lb	68 428	1100	2200	64 028				1100
Pitch	lb	2500	500						2000

M=Margarita
C=Cumana
G=Guyana
TF=Tierra Firme
NB=Neuva Barcelona
PR/SD=Puerto Rico or Santo Domingo

Sources: AGI CONTAD *1677* 1751–1774
         AGI CAR *734* 1775–1776

TABLE X

Selected registered imports 1751–1776

Goods	Unit	Total	M	C	G	TF	RC	PC	Other
Meat									
(general)	lb	26 000	150	6500	10 100	1850	500		7100
Jerked meat	lb	15 750		4750	11 000				
Beef	lb	31 750		10 750	24 500	750	2000		2750
Salted beef	lb	9500	2500	7000					
Jerked beef	lb	31 200	300	9150	12 250			7500	2000
Fish	lb	15 900	8250		1400				
Salted fish	lb	16 425	13 425	2500			500		
Deep water									
fish	lb	625		625					
Cattle	no.	50			9			41	
Cows	no.	2			2				
Calves	no.	264		6	258				
Bull Calves	no.	200			200				
Young bulls	no.	12			12				
Horses	no.	59		4	55				
Mares	no.	3			3				
Young mares	no.	32			32				
Mules	no.	337	72	92	129				44
Donkeys	no.	2	2						
Pigs	no.	17		17					
Hides	no.	6986	256	4734	1434				562
Fat	lb	750			750				
Turtle fat	flasks	635			625				10
Beef fat	flasks	100			88				12
Cheese	lb	8300	25		6650	1250			375
Tallow	lb	15 350		11 225	3875				250
Soap	lb	125	50		75				
Soap	pesos	426	34	135		5		2	
Salt	lb	129 561	85 850	20 901	660	12 210	5420	3520	

M = Margarita
C = Cumana
G = Guyana
TF = Tierra Firme
RC = Río Caribes
PC = Puerto Campano

Sources: AGI CONTAD *1677* 1751–1774
         AGI CAR *734* 1775–1776

Cabildo complained that because no registered ship had come from Spain, the inhabitants had no clothes to wear,[219] and even when they did arrive they did not always bring the goods that had been requested.[220] As a result they turned to contraband trading to supply their needs and find an outlet for their products. As additional incentive to trade with foreigners was provided by the high prices paid for goods produced in the island. The need for convoys to protect Spanish shipping from attack by foreigners raised the cost of transport, which was transferred to colonial products on which heavy duties were levied. The absence of such duties on goods sold to foreigners made illegal trading attractive. In 1686 it was observed, "We [the English] profit by what we transport six to one, which makes the Spaniard generally so poor in the Indies and we to flourish so much the more".[221]

The isolated position of Trinidad in the Spanish Empire enabled contraband trading to flourish. In 1612 the Governor Sancho de Alquiza reported that the Dutch and English went in and out of Port of Spain as if they were in the English Channel.[222] Nevertheless, foreign ships trading in Trinidad waters always ran the risk of being captured by coastguards and having their cargo confiscated.[223] Similarly, the attitude of Spanish officials towards contraband trading could not always be relied upon. Most foreign vessels, therefore, entered Port of Spain on the pretext of obtaining supplies but hoping to carry out some trade.[224] In most cases, however, the colonists were more than willing to trade; in 1729 the Governor of Cumaná reported that illegal trading in Trinidad was encouraged by all the inhabitants without the exception of the highest ecclesiastics.[225] In 1745 the Governor of Trinidad was said to be trading with the French and Caribs[226] and in 1764 another Governor was accused of buying coffee from the French and reselling it to the Dutch in Curaçao.[227] Raleigh's observation at the beginning of the seventeenth century thus applies equally to the early eighteenth century: "The situation in Trinidad and on the Lower Orinoco may therfore be summarised as an economic invasion by the English and Dutch, actively abetted by the ill-served Spanish colonists and opposed by the Spanish government by open warfare and no quarter."[228]

During the seventeenth century most contraband trading was carried out with the Dutch, but towards the end of the century the French and English played a more important role, rivalling each other for trade with the Spanish colonies. In 1689 it was reported that there were 22 French ships in the coastal waters of Trinidad, Margarita and

Cumaná,[229] and in 1727 the French Crown gave official licence to all French vessels to trade with the Spanish islands of Trinidad, Margarita and Puerto Rico.[230] Shortly after, four French ships, two from Martinique, arrived in Trinidad.[231] One ship was going along the coast selling "flour, wines, rum, and many other kinds of goods and merchandise which it had loaded in Martinique carrying out most of its trading with the island of Margarita" but in Trinidad "they could sell a little because of the poverty of its inhabitants".[232] The Assembly of Barbados in 1730 complained that they were unable to compete with the French since goods that they introduced from other parts of the New World were 20% dearer because they had to be carried to England first, whereas French goods could be traded direct.[233] For most of the eighteenth century, however, the English did have the advantage of possessing the *asiento** which meant that, whilst introducing slaves to the islands and mainland, they could avail themselves of the opportunity to introduce other items, and incur less risk of having their goods confiscated. Although the French and English took over the trading supremacy formerly held by the Dutch, during the eighteenth century the Dutch established in Curaçao and Surinam still carried out some trade with Trinidad. In 1700 the Dutch West India Company based on the Essequibo were trading in the Orinoco and Trinidad, exchanging saltfish for cacao[234] and in 1730 the *Armador de Corso* complained that the Governor of Trinidad was trading with the Dutch in Surinam.[235]

At the beginning of the seventeenth century the principal item of trade was tobacco.[236] In 1611 Thomas Roe reported his arrival in Port of Spain "where there are 15 sayle of ships freighting smoke, English, French and Dutch",[237] while another Englishman testified that about 30 English ships anchored annually at Punta de Gallo sailing to Port of Spain in mid-February to exchange "wine, tafetas, printed cloth, linen, English cloth, and many other goods" for tobacco.[238] Later cacao became the most important item sought after by foreigners but after its failure in 1725, timber and turtles, which were both relatively scarce in the Antilles became important items of exchange.[239] Situated at the south-eastern corner of the Caribbean sea, between the settlements of the French, English and Dutch on the mainland and in the Antilles, Trinidad would have also acted as an entrepôt where goods could be bought and sold by representatives of foreign nations.

Indians and negroes were also lucrative sources of trade. Both

* A formal contract for the exclusive right to introduce negroes.

Spaniards and foreigners profited from the illegal sale of indians, particularly in the island of Margarita, where they fetched 40 or 50 *pesos*.[240] Indians who were sold came from Trinidad and from villages along the Orinoco, particularly the village of Casanare.[241]

Although there was a shortage of labour in Trinidad the Spanish settlers preferred to make short-term profits by buying negroes from foreigners and selling them in other parts of the Indies rather than employing them on their estates. In 1605 Dutch merchants are known to have accepted an order from Trinidad colonists for 500 slaves to be delivered the following year.[242] In fulfilment of the contract 470 negroes were landed in Trinidad by Isaac Duverne in 1606.[243] However, in 1613 the Governor Sancho de Alquiza reported that the colonists had bought some negroes from foreigners but had resold them at 150 *pesos* each.[244] In 1627 a Portuguese arrived with five negroes and a number of rebel indians who were sold to the colonists but who were supposedly returned when the trade was declared illegal by the Governor.[245] Again in 1678 a number of negroes were taken to Trinidad by an Englishman, Daniel Boon.[246] These recorded landings of negroes in Trinidad must represent a small proportion of those that actually occurred. In addition the Spanish undertook to introduce negroes from Spain whom they had obtained from Portuguese traders in Africa. In 1674 an *asiento* was made with Antonio García and Sebastián Siliceo for the annual introduction of 4000 negroes for five years of whom 120 were to go to Trinidad, Margarita, and Cumaná.[247] The contract was rescinded two years later, however, because of the bankruptcy of the operators. There were therefore no legal introductions of negroes in the seventeenth century. Thus Spain, with no footholds on slave coasts in Africa, found herself unable to meet the requirements of her colonies; in contrast foreigners carried out a lucrative contraband trade in negroes, particularly in the islands and along the coasts of the Caribbean. Preferring an agreed monopoly with a foreign country to unauthorised contraband trading, the Crown decided to sell the *asiento*. The main competitors were the English and French, who had ousted the Dutch from the trading posts they had held in West Africa.[248] European politics determined that the *asiento* should go to the French and in 1702 a contract was made with the French Guinea Company. Its fulfilment, however, was hindered by wars and by 1705 at least, no negroes had arrived in Trinidad under the *asiento*.[249] By the Treaty of Utrecht in 1713 the *asiento* was transferred to the English South Seas Company, which undertook to introduce into

Spanish America 4800 negroes annually, selling them in Cumaná, Maracaibo, and the Windward Islands at 150 – 300 *pesos* each.[250] Between 1716 and 1718 about 40 negroes were introduced into Trinidad from Barbados in return for cacao,[251] but after the cacao failure it is unlikely that may slaves arrived for the colonists would not have been able to pay for them. In 1733 the South Seas Company sent its last annual ship and its supply ended in 1739 with the outbreak of war. The Company finally surrendered all claims to the *asiento* in 1750 receiving £100000 as compensation.[252] In 1764 an *asiento* was made with Miguel de Uriarte for the annual introduction of about 7000 negroes, of which only 500 or 600 were to be destined for Cumaná, Santo Domingo, Trinidad, Margarita, and Santa Marta "considering that they have few inhabitants who are poor", and the price was reduced from 290 to 275 *pesos* because of the poverty of the colonists in those areas.[253] The contract lasted until 1778 but it is unknown how many slaves were introduced under this *asiento*.[254]

Neither trade with Spain nor contraband trade was able to satisfy the food requirements of the Spanish inhabitants of Trinidad. Some food, particularly meat and fish, was imported from Cumaná and Margarita,[255] but most probably came from trade within the island. Trading links between the Spanish and the indians, both in the *encomiendas* and outside, probably developed soon after conquest. They would have been most regular with indians in the *encomienda*: the rest of the population had retired well inland and did not go to St. Joseph unless they were fetched,[256] so that trade would have been intermittent and on a small scale. Trading did not involve large travelling distances; the greatest distance that goods would have had to travel was from Port of Spain, where Spanish goods were imported, to St. Joseph, either by way of the Caroni river or overland by a "rough path".[257] Imported goods formed the basis of Spanish trade with the indians, and the Governors who had preferential access to them established profitable businesses illegally selling wine and cloth at exorbitant prices.[258] In return the indians offered mainly food crops such as maize, manioc and beans, but also small quantities of commercial crops, particularly tobacco and later cacao. In 1705 an *alcalde ordinario* claimed that the *conucos* cultivated by the indians in the *encomiendas* supported St. Joseph, supplying its *vecinos* with maize and manioc.[259] Many of the goods would have been bought and sold in the market place of St. Joseph but others were probably exchanged on a personal basis. Most goods were probably bartered, partly because of the personal nature of trading and partly due to the absence of a metallic currency. Where necessary certain mediums of exchange were used. In 1602 axes, knives and cutlasses were being used as money, but later tobacco and cacao beans were used as units of exchange.[260]

8
The Indian Republic

Encomiendas were granted to eminent settlers when St. Joseph was founded in 1592, though the number of grants made and the number of indians involved is uncertain. Throughout the greater part of the seventeenth century, however, most indians remained outside direct Spanish control and it was not until 1687 that missions were founded in the southern part of the island. Even then a substantial proportion of the indian population remained outside the sphere of direct Spanish influence. The missions and the *encomiendas* were officially abolished in 1708 and 1716 respectively but they persisted as distinct socio-economic entities until the end of the eighteenth century.

The *encomiendas*

During the early colonial period the *encomienda* was regarded as the most important institution for the civilisation and christianisation of the indian population and for ensuring due rewards for those who had taken part in discovery and conquest. In return for protection and instruction in the Catholic faith, indians were under obligation to pay the *encomendero* tribute in the form of money or goods. Because of the Crown's policy of separate development only a few Spanish officials, either secular or ecclesiastical, ever visited the villages that had been granted as *encomiendas* and political control of the indian population was achieved indirectly by changes in its social organisation and population decline, rather than by powerful Spanish officials.

The political power of the *caciques* was assumed by the Spaniards, to whom the *encomiendas* had been granted. Although the noble status of *caciques* was officially recognised, they became little more than instruments

151

for the collection of tribute and organisation of labour under the *mita*. This undermined the confidence of the indians in their leaders, as did the intermarriage of the latter with the Spanish. Although the *encomiendas* granted to individuals bestowed status and power on their recipients, it was limited because the indians could not be used to develop seigneurial estates and because a check was kept on their power by officials of the Spanish bureaucracy—*curas doctrineros* and *corregidores de indios*. It was to these officials that the indian villages were entrusted when the *encomiendas* were abolished in 1716.[1]

Corregidores de indios were appointed by the viceroy for three years as administrative and judicial officials, whose most important tasks were the regulation of indian labour under the *mita* and the supervision of trade between Spaniards and indians. It is not known whether any *corregidores* were appointed to the *encomiendas* in Trinidad in the seventeenth century but they were present in the island in 1705,[2] and in 1711 the Governor was given the faculty to appoint them.[3] The *corregidor* was supposed to protect the indians from exploitation by the *encomenderos*, but in practice his position gave him personal access to indian labour and if, as was the case in 1705, the *corregidor* and the *encomendero* were "all of one house and family",[4] the indians received little protection. The position of the *corregidor* was quite powerful. When the *cura doctrinero* complained that the *encomenderos* were employing indians in their personal service he was told not to meddle in the affairs of the *encomiendas* but "only in the fulfilment of your obligation and office looking after the education and teaching of those indians encharged to you",[5] and in 1716 the *corregidor* succeeded in having one of the *curas doctrineros* suspended.[6] With the abolition of the *encomiendas* the role of the *corregidores* would have become more important since they assumed the responsibilities of the *encomenderos* and were sole dispensers of indian labour in the island.

The incorporation of the indians in the *encomiendas* into the Spanish Empire was to be accompanied and aided by their christianisation, which was to be effected by *curas doctrineros* who the *encomenderos* were obliged to provide. However, after 40 years of contact with the Spanish the parish priest of St. Joseph reported that most of the indians were "living like barbarians using their false idolatries and their shamans speaking with the devils".[7] Most indian conversions were effected by members of a lay brotherhood, known as the Cofradía del Glorioso San Pablo, who in 1645 claimed that they had converted 250 indians from the *encomiendas*.[8] Many indians, however, died without baptism, including the Arawak *cacique* Aramaya,[9] and even fewer were confirmed because episcopal visits were so rare. In 1688 the Governor Sebastián de Roteta complained that there had been no *cura doctrinero* in the *encomiendas* for 12 years because of the general lack of secular clergy in the diocese. Aricagua did, however, possess a chaplain in the hermitage of San Juan Baptista.[10] Governor Félix de Guzmán placed the blame at the feet of the *encomenderos*, who refused to pay the *curas* or provide them with wine, bread, oil and ornaments.[11] The failure of the *encomenderos* to provide the necessary Catholic instruction contributed to the abolition of the *encomiendas* in 1716.[12] The provision of clergy for the indian villages did not improve, however, because of the lack of secular clergy in the diocese and the lack of indian tribute from which their salaries were paid.[13] They were, however, more consistently provided for than the indians in the former mission villages, probably because they played a more vital role in the island's economy and their commitment to both Church and State was therefore more desirable. Also, they were nearer the centres of Spanish administration.

In the indian villages granted as *encomiendas* the indians had their own elected officials, who formed a *cabildo*. The *cabildo* varied in its composition throughout the century but at a minimum it was composed of two *alcades*, two *regidores*, and two *aguaciles*.[14] Since indians elected to the *cabildo* had to be approved by the *corregidor* and *cura doctrinero*, it was more an instrument of Spanish control than a potential threat to Spanish authority.

Political control of the indians in the *encomiendas* was aided by the breakdown in the social organisation of their communities, brought about by exogamous marriages and a decline in their populations. The matrilocal residence rule was impossible to adhere to since non-indian exogamous marriage partners were forbidden to take up residence in indian villages. This plus the fact that the male assumed a more significant role in the family probably led to a change in the matrilineal rule where extended families were related through the female line. Similarly, with an increased number of marriages between people of different villages and non-indians, the consanguineal links between village members would have been increasingly broken, so that single family living units probably began to supersede extended family units as the basic social components of villages;[15] but marriage seems to have held little significance for them. At the beginning of the eighteenth century the *Procurador* of the missions complained that the indians in the *encomiendas* were living barbarically "mixing each one with a great number of women which he chooses freely for all kinds of vice and without more control than his inclinations".[16]

It is not known how many indians were granted in *encomiendas* but altogether they probably did not exceed 1000. Antonio de Berrío is said to have granted 70 *encomiendas*[17] but most of them were probably small, consisting of only a few or even individual indians; only four were recorded consistently throughout the seventeenth and early eighteenth centuries. Of the four villages two were located in the Tacarigua valley and one each in the Arauca and Aricagua valleys (Fig. 8) probably on

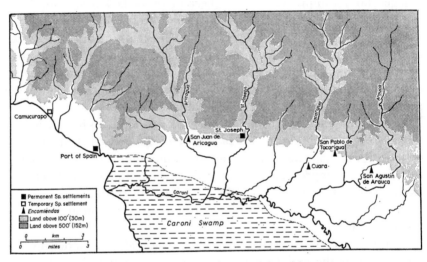

FIG. 8. Location of *encomiendas* and Spanish towns.

the sites they occupied in pre-Columbian times, but they have not been identified with any certainty.[18] One of the *encomiendas* in the Tacarigua valley may have been located near the Roman Catholic church where indian potsherds have been found,[19] in which case the other *encomienda* in that valley must, according to eighteenth century maps, have been located at Orange Grove, although as yet no archaeological remains have been found there. The *encomienda* at Arauca must have been located near the present-day village of Arauca but similarly no remains have been found there. The indian village of Aricagua was probably located at San Juan in the Aricagua valley, particularly since it was formerly known as San Juan de Aricagua.[21] The name is located on eighteenth century maps at that site,[22] although the village had ceased to exist before mid-century. So far only non-ceramic remains have been found there.[23] All four possible sites are located on the banks of rivers in the foothills of the Northern Range about 50 ft (15 m) above the Caroni Plain. After the cacao failure the physical and social structure of the villages began to disintegrate as the indians left to live in the surrounding hills, although they were forbidden by law to do so.[24] In 1732 the Governor Bartolomé de Aldunate observed that "the *encomiendas* have maintained themselves without formal villages . . . and they have lived in the hills as if they were heathen."[25]

During the early years of colonisation the population of the *encomiendas* declined. The hard work which the *encomenderos* forced the indians to do has often been regarded as a major decline of the indian population in the New World,[26] but it is unlikely that overwork was directly responsible for the majority of indian deaths; at worst the obligation of indians in Trinidad did not involve working for the *encomendero* for more than three days a week. This is not to say that whilst the indians were employed by the *encomenderos* they were not ill-treated. As early as 1595 Raleigh described how the Spanish had made "the ancient casui, which were Lordes of the country to be their slaves, that he [Antonio de Berrío] kept them in chains and dropped their naked bodies with burning bacon and other such torments".[27] In 1605 one *encomendera* herself related that in Trinidad in six years 1000 indians had died of ill-treatment.[28] Not only were the indians ill-treated but many of them were sold by their *encomenderos* as slaves in Margarita, Cumaná, and other parts of Venezuela; one eye witness testified that he had seen 10–12 canoe loads of indians from the *encomiendas* in Trinidad going to Margarita.[29] The *encomenderos*, however, blamed the Caribs for the loss in indian population. In 1612 it was reported that "there is no *encomienda* of those that have been granted that has thirty indians because each day the Caribs carry them off from their houses and cultivation plots" and one *encomendero* complained that the Caribs had seized 24 of his indians.[30] A less dramatic reduction in the indian population of the *encomiendas* would have occurred as a result of the break-up of families and the consequent decline in the fertility rate. In 1605 an *encomendera* observed that the indians "are divided between many soldiers whom they serve separated some from others, twenty serving one and ten another, separated from their wives and sons and taken from their *principales*, which is one of the things they resent most."[31] During the seventeenth century only four *encomiendas* were consistently recorded.

In 1612 it was stated that the number of indians in the *encomiendas* did not exceed 100, but since the number probably included only tributary indians the total number was probably between 400 and 500.[32] In 1645 the largest of the four *encomiendas* had less than 20 tributary indians and the smallest had five,[33] but by 1678 the total number of tributary indians counted between the ages of 14 and 60 had risen to 117.[34] This increase may represent a recovery in the birth rate after the devastating impact of the early years of colonisation or the success of the *encomenderos* in persuading indians outside the *encomiendas* to work for them initially for gifts and then including their names in the lists of indians in their *encomiendas*.[35] In 1688 the population of three of the *encomiendas* appears to have been increasing slightly, with families consisting of between three and five persons and in fact one had increased from a total population of 78 in 1683 to 114 in 1688.[36] Conversely, the other appears to have been declining, with only five children under the age of 18 out of a total population of 26. The causes for these differential growth rates are unknown. The total population of the *encomiendas* in 1688 was 301 of which 30% were males over the age of 18, a figure which, discounting the anomalous decline of the *encomienda* in the Aricagua valley, is not dissimilar to that estimated at the beginning of the century. Rather than cause a decline in the indian population, after the initial impact of the early years of colonisation, therefore, the *encomiendas* in Trinidad tended to conserve it.

During the early part of the eighteenth century the population of the *encomiendas* continued to increase (see Table XI), despite complaints from the *encomenderos* that their indians had been enticed into the missions; one *encomendero* complained that 53 families had left his *encomienda* for the missions.[37] The only *encomienda* that declined in population during that period was that of Aricagua, which in 1712 had only seven tributary indians.[38] After the effective abolition of the missions in 1713 a certain number of indians may have taken up residence in the *encomiendas* to avoid having to make long journeys to the Spanish estates in the foothills of the Northern Range, where they were employed under the *mita*. Later with the abolition of the *encomiendas* themselves, the indian villages may have attracted indians formerly outside the influence of Spanish culture. A small number of indians from the mainland, particularly Chaimas and Guaranos, took up residence in the former *encomiend-villages*,[39] but they were probably forced to do so having been brought from the Orinoco, where the *encomenderos* had previously obtained them through illegal trade. By 1721 the total population of the villages had more than doubled to 650 from 301 in 1688.[40] In 1732, however, the Governor observed that "because of the failure of the cacao harvest the indians are seen in their ultimate extermination suffering from illnesses made worse by the lack of food, medicine and a doctor".[41] The smallpox epidemic of 1741 which caused a considerable decline in the population of St. Joseph must also have affected the indians in the neighbouring villages, but by 1763 when the first comprehensive census of the population of the former *encomiendas* since the cacao failure was taken, their

TABLE XI

Total population of the encomiendas and missions 1683–1777

	1683	1688	1691	1700	1712	1715	1721	1722	1727	1763	1777
Encomiendas											
Arauca	78	114	172	255	298		317			272	317
Tacarigua		101	78	139	197		207			213	198
Cuara		60	49	68	70		86			192	196
Aricagua		26	25	28	32		40				
TOTAL	78	301	324	490	597		650			677	711
Missions											
Guayria				222	240	230		227	238	51	62
Savaneta				209	226	234		212	210	133	112
Savana Grande				429	401	366		385	422	235	291
Montserrate					304	297		324	359	125	184
TOTAL				860	1171	1127		1148	1229	554	649

Sources: 1683 AGI SD *179–3–95* 16.3.1683
　　　　　1688 AGI SD *179–3–84* 27.1.1688
　　　　　1691 AGI SD *179–3–93* 18.9.1691
　　　　　1700 AGI SD *588* 22.9.1700 (*Encomiendas*)
　　　　　1700 AGI SD *582* 22.9.1700 (Missions)
　　　　　1712 AGI SD *627* 16.6.1712, 18.7.1712
　　　　　1715 AGI SD *627* 6.3.1715
　　　　　1721 AGI SD *583* 1.9.1721
　　　　　1722 AGI SD *583* 27.2.1722
　　　　　1727 AGI SD 583 14.3.1727
　　　　　1763 AGI CAR *198* 19.11.1763
　　　　　1777 AGI CAR *260* 8.6.1777

population had increased to 677 (see Fig. 9),[42] even though by that time the village of Aricagua had ceased to exist. Most of the rise in the population would have resulted from natural increase; small numbers

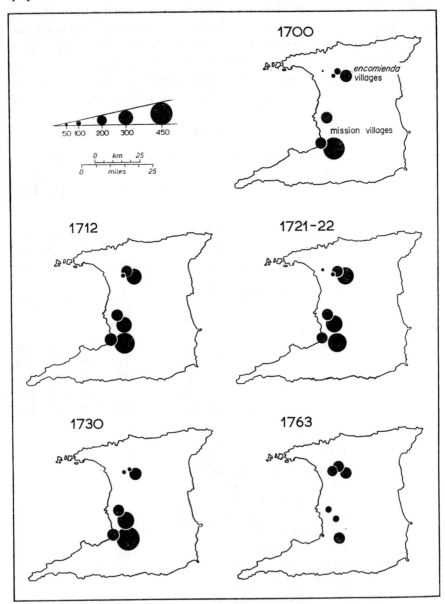

FIG. 9. Indian population under Spanish control.

of indians from the mainland did settle in the island but they mainly formed distinct villages.[43] By 1777 the total population of the three former *encomiendas* had risen to 711.[44]

The economy of the indians of the *encomiendas* was an agricultural one based on the production of the food crops, with trade playing a relatively minor role in contrast to the economy of the estates. Food crops were grown for consumption by the indian population, for tribute payment and for sale to the *vecinos* of St. Joseph and Port of Spain. The reliance of the Spanish population on food from the latter two sources was indicated by the *encomendero* of Arauca who in 1705 stated "from my *encomienda* the greater part of this town is supported by buying cassava and other provisions to maintain itself".[45] In effect the produce from the land cultivated by the indians in the *encomiendas* supported the whole of the Spanish and indian population in and around St. Joseph. Through this trade the indians were able to obtain durable goods and protein provisions.

Land in the vicinity of the indian villages was cultivated under a modified system of shifting cultivation, where food crops were the most important products but specialised crops found a subordinate place or were cultivated in small separate exclusive plots. The extensive nature of cultivation was indicated in 1785 when, as a result of increasing land values due to colonisation schemes, it was suggested that "the extensive lands which are assigned to these small villages [*encomienda* villages] which they have maintained and maintain always uncultivated" should be taken over by the Crown.[46]

To meet the demands for provisions from its own population and from the *vecinos* high labour inputs were required. Much of the indians' time was devoted to paying tribute, either in the form of personal service or in the production of crops. In 1711 Governor Don Félix de Guzmán complained that they had little time to cultivate their own lands.[47] Even after tribute had been made payable to the Crown and not to the *encomenderos* the indians were obliged to work under the *mita* and if such work coincided with the time they needed to cultivate their own lands so much the worse: "the winter comes with heavy rains and the indian with his children and wife remains deprived of all sustenance for he will not have been able to sow to harvest".[48] The situation became even more critical in times of low cacao prices because, as tribute was often paid in cacao, they had to work "all year" to provide it[49] and after the cacao failure work for tribute payment became "excessive".[50] Thus the inability of the indians to produce food for their own consumption often led to food shortages.[51]

As a result of the drawing off of male labour to work in the personal service of *encomenderos* or under the *mita*, labour inputs on their own lands declined. Not only did this lead to a diminution in the variety of crops grown in the *conucos* but it led to a shift in emphasis from the cultivation of root crops to seed crops. The most important food crops grown were maize, beans and manioc[52] which were all said to abound in the island.[53] Maize in particular assumed an important place in the *conucos*. In 1643 four or five varieties of maize were known on the adjacent mainland in Nueva Barcelona and it was estimated that half a *fanega* could support one man for a month.[54] The concentration on the cultivation of a more limited number of crops meant that the assemblage of plants grown was biologically less productive than either the former forest cover or the assemblage commonly associated with *conuco* cultivation[55], whilst the shift in emphasis from root crops to protein-rich seed crops, which are more demanding on soil nutrients, probably caused soil fertility to decline more rapidly.

Non-essential and relatively unproductive crops were probably withdrawn from cultivation but in part they were compensated for by the introduction of new species. Newly introduced crops would have been more readily adopted into this system of agriculture than on the estates because of the more diverse nature of the ecosystem. Certain Old World crops such as pigeon pea, Guinea corn (*Sorghum vulgare*) and species of yams (*Dioscorea alata* and *D. bulbifera*), which were all present in the West Indies by mid-century,[56] may have been cultivated on a small scale. It is also possible that rice (*Oryza sativa*) reached the island in the seventeenth century for it was being cultivated in Tobago in 1667.[57] The potato (*Solanum tuberosum*), an Andean domesticate, may have been experimented with in the seventeenth century but it would have produced only moderate yields, being unsuited to the ecological conditions of the island.[58] It was cultivated in Barbados in 1640.[59] Probably the most important fruits grown were plantains, pawpaws, and pineapples.[60] In 1680 the plantain was described as "the most important fruit of the land" and three varieties were distinguished including the introduced banana and two non-sweet varieties.[61] By the end of the seventeenth century citrus fruits had become well established in Cumaná[62] and Guyana,[63] while in Trinidad in 1680 a missionary described wild lemons and oranges as the most impressive fruits of the island.[64] The water melon (*Citrullus lanatus*), an African domesticate, was probably introduced at this time since it was present in the outer Leeward islands in the mid-seventeenth century[65] and was grown in the Tacarigua valley in Trinidad in 1711.[66] Newly introduced fruit trees may have included the date palm (*Phoenix dactylifera*), the oil palm (*Elaeis guineensis*), an African domesticate, and the coconut, which were all found in Barbados in the seventeenth century.[67]

During the eighteenth century with the development of the slave trade additional crops may have been introduced from Africa. Although the residential segregation of negroes and indians would have militated against the diffusion of crops introduced as a result of the slave trade, they may have been obtained through contacts on the estates and in the markets. Their adoption by the indians in the *encomiendas* probably occurred more readily than on the estates, due to the greater diversity of plants grown in the *conucos* and the relative lack of social prejudice against their adoption. Crops which probably arrived in the New World with the slave trade included the eddo, taro, or dasheen (*Colocasia esculenta*), okra or ladies' fingers (*Hibiscus esculentus*), eggplant or aubergine (*Solanum melongena*), the lablab, hyacinth or bonavist bean (*Lablab niger*) and other varieties of yam (*Dioscorea* spp.). "Eddies" were present in Tobago in 1683[68] and they arrived in Barbados in the first half of the eighteenth century.[69] Okra, a tropical African domesticate, was established in Barbados in 1695 while the hyacinth bean was growing in that island in 1647;[70] however it may not have spread to other Antillean islands until the eighteenth century.[71] It is unlikely that it was introduced to Trinidad at an early date since there were few negroes in the island at that time. The eggplant was introduced at a much later date; although identified by Acosta in the West Indies in the sixteenth century[72] it does not appear to have been cultivated widely, if at all. It was probably reintroduced with the slave trade in the eighteenth century, being first identified in Barbados in 1750.[73] In addition to food crops, small quantities of commercial crops including cacao, cotton, and tobacco were grown for tribute payment and sale, but they probably accounted for only a small proportion of total agricultural production.

Sources of animal protein were not readily available to the indians in the *encomienda* villages; they lacked domesticated animals and had insufficient time to exploit wild resources. The most important domesticated animal raised for food was the chicken, which was also used in payment of tribute.[74] Pigs and goats were probably kept in small numbers and in 1717 an inhabitant of St. Joseph observed that they also had "horses and mares", although by law indians were forbidden to ride them.[75] Labour inputs by the indians were largely absorbed by work on the estates and their own lands, leaving little time for hunting and fishing. The hunting of open-forest species, such as deer and agouti, in the foothills of the Northern Range may have continued on a small scale, possibly using improved weapons such as metal arrow and lance heads that had been introduced by the Spanish. The inland location of the indian villages would have militated against the exploitation of marine resources, but freshwater resources, although scarce, were used: in 1717 the indians complained that their *encomenderos* only gave them plantains to eat, so to get "some small fish they went and looked for some in the streams".[76] Some imported meat and fish were probably also available through trading with the Spanish, but only at high prices.

While the Spanish in the towns and on the estates were almost wholly dependent on the *encomiendas* for supplies of food, the indians in the *encomiendas* were largely self-sufficient. The distance of the villages from the sea made it difficult for them to trade with other indian groups and foreigners. Most trading with the Spanish was on a small scale although the indians were dependent on trade with them to obtain vital goods such as tools. The Spanish government officials who had preferential access to most imported goods monopolised them and sold them at exorbitant prices.[77] Although imported goods were important in the indian economy they were of less significance to the indians than to the *vecinos* who depended on them almost exclusively.

The missions

Missions in the New World not only christianised the indians but extended the political control of the State by bringing them into the sphere of Spanish influence.[78] The missions were jointly administered by the missionaries and *corregidores de indios* who effectively restrained each other from attaining too much power or autonomy in areas which were often at the limits of "civilisation". Theoretically, after 10 years the missions were to be handed over to the secular clergy, who were considered to be politically more reliable. In Trinidad this transference occurred after 21 years, not as a result of general policy but rather as the outcome of conflicts between the missionaries, landowners, and *encomenderos* over supplies of indian labour.

Appointments of regular clergy in the New World had to be approved by the King. Missionaries for particular tasks were selected by the head of the religious order in Spain, but from 1692 the heads of the missions or prefects of particular areas were chosen by the missionaries themselves.[79] Once approved by the Crown, and given permission to leave the area to which they had been assigned, the missionaries were largely independent, though from 1696 they received financial support from the Crown in the form of an annual allowance of 50 *pesos*, which was increased to 150 *pesos* in 1738.[80]

In 1687 the Catalonian Capuchins assumed responsibility for the conversion of the indians of Trinidad and Guyana and, from then until 1708 when the missions were abolished in Trinidad, 24 missionaries entered the island.[81] They were insufficient, however, to enable the efficient functioning of the missions; not only was there lack of suitable missionaries in Catalonia but there were also delays in obtaining permits for missionaries to leave Spain.[82] When the missions were handed over to the secular clergy in 1713, the bishop of Puerto Rico was faced with the problem of finding additional personnel from a diocese that was already lacking in clergy, and the problem was increased by the fact that the clergy needed to be able to speak the languages of the indians in the former missions.[83] So, despite the fact that the Crown had specifically ordered that the positions of the *curas doctrineros* should be filled by secular clergy, the suitability of the missionaries for the task and the lack of any other clergy to fill the offices meant that in 1719 two were temporarily placed in the former missions,[84] and in spite of complaints to the Council of the Indies they continued to fill the posts, primarily because they knew the indian languages.[85] Later in the century missionary effort was again directed at Trinidad. In 1733 it was decided that 12 Catalonian Capuchins should go to Trinidad and Guyana, but because of rivalries between missionary orders on the mainland their remission was suspended.[86] In 1744 further missionaries were ordered for the province and in 1749 they succeeded in establishing the mission of Los Santos Reyes at Mucurapo.[87] However, they were forced to leave the island by the lack of financial support from the Governor, who refused to pay them their annual allowance.[88] Meanwhile, the indians in the former missions remained without Christian instruction. In 1764 the former mission villages had been without a *cura doctrinero* for nine years.[89]

Corregidores de indios were appointed as administrative and judicial officials, with the intended purpose of preventing the missions from becoming too powerful and independent. There is no evidence, however, that such posts were established in the missions prior to their abolition in 1708.[90] As in the *encomiendas*, the *corregidor* maintained control of the indian population with the co-operation of the *caciques* and the elected indian *cabildo*. In 1755 Alvarado, conducting a survey of the missions in Guyana, reported, "so that there should be regular subordination in the villages and civility amongst individuals, they elect from the most diligent and reasonable indians a certain number of officials and ministers of justice . . . so that the indians should obey them and be ruled by them".[91] Although elected by the indians, the officials, as in the *encomiendas*, were little more than instruments of the missionaries and "legal fiction to cover the missions' absolutism".[92] As soon as the missions were founded in Trinidad indian officials were elected[93] but their numbers fluctuated throughout the century; in 1712 the missions had two *alcaldes*, four *regidores* and two *alguaciles*, but generally they only had two *regidores*.[94]

Between 1687 and 1700 several missions were founded in Trinidad, of which four survived as indian villages throughout the eighteenth century. The missions were primarily located according to the distribution of the indian population, but their actual sites took into consideration supplies of fresh water, the agricultural potential of the surrounding lands, and ease of access to the sea. In Trinidad the greater part of the indian population was located in the southern part of the island to which it had retreated during the seventeenth century and so missions were founded there. To maintain political control of the missions the Crown considered it desirable for them to have good communications with the centres of Spanish population, but in Trinidad land communications between the missions and Spanish towns were by difficult indian trails, or by longer, though easier, sea routes. Communications between the missions themselves were also difficult; in 1735 the former mission of Monserrate was described as being "three leagues of inpenetrable paths and deep rivers" from Savana Grande.[95]

The first mission founded was that of Savana Grande, present-day Princes Town, which was located "on a large savanna more than four leagues east of from Mount Naparima",[96] where it was estimated that there were about 1000 indians[97] and 150 indian chiefs.[98] At the same time a mission was founded under the name of "Purísima Concepción de María Santísima", more commonly known as Guayria "on the mount

which is called Naparima".[99] Four leagues to the north-east of Guayria
the mission of Santa Ana de Savaneta was founded [100] "on the banks of a
river whose crystal waters produced an abundance of fish of a delightful
flavour".[101] The mission of Nuestra Señora de Montserrate appears to
have been established at a slightly later date, being unmentioned in the
list of missions given in 1700.[102] By 1705, however, it possessed 51
indians who could bear arms.[103] All other missions were short-lived.
San Francisco de los Arenales was founded in 1687 "on the Arena river
which flows into the river Tumpuna, one of the tributaries of the Caroni,
in a sandy area half way between this river and the Tamanaques
mountain".[104] In 1699 the indians of the mission revolted, killing the
Governor and a number of missionaries, and as a result it was abandoned.[105] Other missions founded were abandoned because of attacks
by the Guaranos indians of the Orinoco. In 1699 the mission of San
Francisco de Careiro, founded in that year, was attacked and the remaining indians were transferred to the mission of San Joseph de
Mayaro, which was also founded in 1691. In 1692 some of the indians in
the mission fled and in 1697 the remainder revolted; the mission was
abandoned and the few indians captured were taken to Guayria.[106]
Although the missionaries wanted to establish three more missions at
Moruga, Los Cocos, and between Punta del Gallo and Punta de Cedro,
where there were large indian populations,[107] it is unknown whether
they were ever founded. In 1689 a priest was living at Los Cocos, and
Borde states that both missions at Mayaro and Moruga were devastated
by Guaranos indians,[108] though he may have mistaken the mission of
San Francisco Careiro at Guayaguayare for that at Moruga. Apart from
a short-lived mission that was founded at Mucurapo in 1749 under the
title of Los Santos Reyes[109] only four of the mission villages founded survived throughout the eighteenth century: Guayria, Savaneta, Savana
Grande, and Montserrate.

The mission villages were miniature versions of Spanish towns. Houses
were aligned on the north, south and west sides of a central square, and
on the east side were located the church, the presbytery and other
communal buildings.[110] In 1714 all four missions also possessed a *casa de
cabildo*, which was used for village meetings.[111] The houses appear to
have been occupied by more than one family or family groups: the
average number of indians per house about that time was 9·5, whereas
the average family size was only four, including husband, wife and two
children.[112]

In 1694 a missionary claimed that since 1687, 2000 souls had been collected in four missions, of which 1636 had been baptised, but by that date 250 of the baptised adults and one third of the children had died.[113] By 1707 the total population of the missions had been reduced to 919.[114] This decline in the mission population may be attributed to four factors. First, all the missions would have suffered population losses through desertion in the first few years following their foundation,[115] a process which would have been accelerated by revolts in the missions. Second, the missions themselves were attacked by indians from the mainland. The mission of Guayria in particular suffered considerable losses amongst indians and missionaries from attacks by Guaranos indians from the Orinoco.[116] Third, at the turn of the century indians in the mission of Savaneta were striken by "vómitos de sangre" which by the 1700 had claimed 10 victims.[117] Fourth, the total effect of these losses in population would have been to reduce the fertility rate, making it difficult for the indian population to maintain itself. However, by the time the royal order, that the missions should be placed under the care of the secular clergy, was brought into effect in 1713, the total indian population in the missions had risen to 1201[118] and although in the following year the missionaries complained that the indians were leaving the missions for the forests, by 1722 the indian population had dropped only slightly to 1148.[119] The general decline in the island's population following the cacao failure was reflected in the population of the former mission villages, whose total number of tributary indians fell by 30%, from 265 in 1727 to 189 in 1735.[120] It was a decline from which the mission villages never recovered, despite the fact that they attracted a number of indians from the mainland. In 1735 it was said that one Capuchin missionary, who had been temporarily employed in the former missions of Guayria and Savaneta had collected 66 "heathen indians" into the former missions, whilst in 1739 150 pagan Chaima indians from the mainland were living in the four missions.[121] Nevertheless by 1763 the total population of the former missions had fallen to 554, the greatest decline occurring at Guayria where the population was less than one quarter of what it had been in 1727.[122] The reason for the differential decline in the populations may be related to their location (see Fig. 9); the coastal location of Guayria would have made it easy for indians to escape from the former mission villages and for diseases to be introduced from both the mainland and the Spanish settlements. Work by indians under the *mita*, which took them to Spanish settlements, would have also aided miscegenation and the spread of disease.[123] The slight increase that occurred in the population of the former mission villages to 649 at the end of the period was a reflection of the general economic expansion in the island.

The missions founded in Trinidad established within their jurisdiction a distinctive form of agriculture. The missions were intended to be economically self-sufficient,[124] producing and selling commerical crops, such as cacao, which were exported to Caracas,[125] and growing food crops for themselves and other missions in need. The nature of cultivation after the effective abolition of the missions in 1713 is unknown, but it was probably like the modified system of shifting cultivation practised by the indians in the *encomiendas*. It appears, however, that even after the missions were abolished, trading links with other missions were retained; in 1724 provisions, in the form of "rice, plantains, cassava, molasses and cacao" were sent to the missions in Guyana.[126]

Given that the missions were established in densely populated areas, their actual location was probably determined on the basis of freshwater availability and agricultural potential. Although it has been suggested that missionaries in the New World had little agricultural experience.[127] In Trinidad the missions were located in the foothills of the Central Range with the mission settlements placed on slightly rising ground, and the communal *hacienda* and the *labranzas* of the indians occupying the surrounding lowlands.[128]

Although the missions should have had at their disposal sufficient labour at no cost, external demands were made on their labour resources. Soon after the missions were founded the landowners requested that the indians should be made available for hire, and the missionaries agreed. However, the landowners failed to comply with the conditions of hire, so the missionaries refused to allow their further employment. For several years, therefore, the missions had exclusive use of indian labour but when they were abolished the indians were obliged to work under the *mita* for 16 days a year.[129]

Both commercial and food crops were grown in the missions. Cacao was probably grown communally on a *hacienda* belonging to the missions, while food crops were grown mainly on *labranzas* belonging to the indians.[130] The indians were bound to work on the *hacienda* for two days and on their own lands for four days; commercial crops were sold in St. Joseph and on the mainland, while food crops sustained the population of the missions and any products left over entered the "community chest" which the Crown ordered to be erected in each mission in 1689 to safeguard against food shortages.[131] After the cacao failure commercial crops probably declined in significance and in 1777 an inventory of the lands of the former missions indicated that all the *labranzas* were cultivated with manioc and plantains.[132] Domesticated animals do not appear to have figured as significantly in the economy of Trinidad missions as they did on the mainland, where ranching activities were developed on a large scale under mission auspices. However, a small number of horses and mares were probably kept for transport and chickens, pigs and goats raised for consumption.

The missionaries were aware of the abundant wild life in the areas in which they established missions and it is likely that the indians who had formerly relied on hunting and fishing for their supplies of animal protein, continued to carry out these activities. Hunting and fishing would have been encouraged by the proximity of the missions to the foothills of the Central Range and to the coast. Archaeological evidence from Mayo, where the mission of Montserrate was located, suggests that the most important animals hunted were the collared peccary, the nine-banded armadillo and lape, which would have been common inhabitants of the rather dense forest surrounding the mission.[133] The other three missions were established in more open-forest areas, with Savana Grande on the edge of a savanna, where deer and agouti would have been more commonly hunted.

Because the missions were intended to be self-sufficient, it is unlikely that trade played an important role in the economy, except as an outlet for commercial crops and a source of selected European goods. Commercial products were sent to Port of Spain from whence they were exported either to Spain or to other parts of the New World. The most important European goods required by the missions were wine, oil, vestments, ornaments, together with agricultural implements, for which they were dependent on the arrival of registered ships from Spain and to a lesser degree on contraband trading. A certain amount of exchange may also have occurred between mission indians and other indian groups in the island or on the adjacent mainland.

Indian outsiders

Those indians outside the *encomiendas* and missions did not escape the dramatic cultural changes experienced by indians who came into direct contact with the Spanish. Although the intensity of contact was lower, the indirect effects of contact on the indian population were no less disastrous.

In 1612 it was estimated that of the 40000 indians there had been in the island there were not 4000 left.[134] The figure of 40000 probably refers to the late sixteenth century and to the estimates of de Berrío and de Vera y Ibargoyen in particular, which have been judged as exaggerated, a more likely estimate being 15000–20000.[135] The actual number of indians in the island in 1612 probably exceeded 4000 although the latter figure is consistent with reports that together account for the loss of 23000 indians, through Carib raids, emigration and harsh treatment,[136] without considering the effects of a decreased fertility rate, disease and famines. In 1633 an Englishman reported that there were 4000 indians in Trinidad, who had retreated to distant parts of the island,[137] but in 1678 the Governor Tiburcio de Axpe y Zuñiga claimed that he called together 500 *principales*,[138] which would suggest that the total indian population was much higher, Similarly in 1694 the missionaries claimed that in six years they had gathered together more than 2000 indians in four missions.[139] It is estimated, therefore, that at the time the missionaries arrived in Trinidad there were about 5000 indians in the island, one third of the 15000–20000 estimated for the end of the sixteenth century. Numerical and general estimates of the size of the native population outside the former *encomiendas* and missions in the eighteenth century are lacking, but it may be assumed that, given the low population at the end of the century when more comprehensive surveys and censuses were undertaken, the century as a whole saw a gradual decline in the native population.

Early observers blamed the decline of the indian population on the presence of the Spanish and Caribs in Trinidad waters. Many indians, fearing direct contact with the Spanish, fled to the mainland, particularly "to the port which they call Paria"[140]; others were the victims of Carib attacks. In 1612 a witness claimed that the Caribs had eaten more than 12000 indians in Trinidad,[141] while the Governor of Guyana estimated that as a result "the injuries and crimes which the Caribs effect in the island of Trinidad", 10000 indians had emigrated and settled in Guyana.[142] This was confirmed by the *Procurador* of Trinidad who in 1612 observed that "most of the indians have withdrawn at a great distance for fear of the said Caribs abandoning this island and passing to the Tierra Firme".[143] The intensity of Carib raids appears to have declined in the latter part of the seventeenth century, when fewer complaints were made by the islands inhabitants.

The Caribs could be blamed in part for the decline in the native population but here were other causes. Those that remained declined slowly in number as a consequence of malnutrition, disease, decreased fertility and migration. Their system of food production was not only disrupted by the withdrawal inland but also by the reduced extent of the exploitable environment and the time that could be spent in subsistence activities. The result was probably local and seasonal food shortages, which were probably in part overcome by trading with foreigners, but may have led to malnutrition and occasional famines. Diseases, notably smallpox, measles and syphilis, may also have had decimating effects on some indian villages, although there is no documentary record of their occurrence during the seventeenth century. During the eighteenth century noted epidemics included the following: in 1700 "vómitos de sangre"; in 1704 a general epidemic; an unknown epidemic in 1720, and two smallpox epidemics in 1741 and 1771–2.[144] Migration both to the mainland and to missions and *encomiendas*, also caused a direct decline in the native population outside the control of the Spanish. The death and emigration of individuals would have caused the breakdown of family structures, resulting in a decrease in the birth rate, thereby making it difficult for the population to maintain itself. Also, population losses probably caused marriage residence rules to become more flexible, with the couple joining whichever group considerations of economy and defence demanded. This would have resulted in the establishment of indian groups, whose dominant social unit was the nuclear family and only some of whose members were related; group cohesion was largely expedient rather than being based on kinship ties. Since the latter had formed the basis of the authority of *caciques*, their status was undermined and any prestige accorded to them was probably based on their military or organisational ability. They continued to be distinguished by insignia.[145]

The overall decline in the indian population outside Spanish control occurred despite the addition of indians, who had been brought to the island as slaves and were later released, or who were voluntary immigrants. In 1688 the Governor Sebastián de Roteta ordered that all indians who had been obtained by illegal trade from the Orinoco, and had been kept in the personal service of *vecinos*, should be freed. Those indians who had belonged to the inhabitants of Port of Spain were settled in that town and those from St. Joseph were established in a newly founded village called Santa Cruz de Buenavista. The village was located "a quarter of a league from this town [St. Joseph] in a suitable place, healthy, abundant in freshwater, forests and agricultural land".[146] It originally contained 37 houses around which *labranzas* and grazing lands were granted. No sooner had the village been founded, however, than the indians began to leave, so that by 1735 the indians were "so dispersed and in so many different places" that it was impossible to instruct them in the faith.[147] The Governor at the outset was worried that the population of Buenavista would not increase because of the lack of married couples and the predominance of women and children.[148] Although 302 indians were released from the personal service of *vecinos* by 1705 there were only 20 men in Buenavista who could bear arms[149] and in 1730 there were only 53 indians living around the village.[150] Apart from the low birth rate the village probably lost a large proportion of its population through desertion because there was no form of political control within the settlement.

During the eighteenth century a number of indians from the mainland voluntarily migrated to Trinidad. A certain number of them, particularly Chaimas, were incorporated in the former missions and *encomiendas*, but most formed distinct villages. The majority of the indians arrived in the second half of the eighteenth century and migrated as a result of efforts made by Aragonese Capuchin missionaries in the province of Cumaná to settle them in missions.[151] Chaima indians established themselves at Toco and Punta de Cumana, whilst flat-nosed Caribs settled at Punta de Arrecifes.[152] The actual location of their settlements is not known but they must have been generally located in the vicinity of the present-day Toco and Cumana.[153] The French settled amongst the indians located at the north-east corner of the island, where they exploited turtles and coconuts at Manzanilla.[154] It was the presence of the French which prompted the Governor to suggest that the villages of Toco and Punta de la Galera should be moved to the centre of the island, where they could not communicate with foreigners.[155] However, the suggestion was never taken up. In addition, Arawak indians, presumably from the mainland, established themselves at Siparia, Erin and Mucurapo.[156]

The retreat of the indian population inland, which began in the sixteenth century as a result of Carib attacks, continued in the seventeenth century as the Spanish colonised the island. In 1612 the Governor

Sancho de Alquiza complained that he was unable to find any indian rowers to take him to the mainland because "they have retired inland and do not come to this town [St. Joseph] unless they are fetched.[157] Governor Juan de Eulate in 1633 noted that the indians were settled along the south coast, particularly at Moruga and Punta de la Galera,[158] an observation that was confirmed by the Dutch in 1637: "on the east side of the island named Punta Galera dwell two nations, the one called nipuyos and the other arawak, over six hundred able men".[159] The withdrawal of the indian population was in part reversed during the latter part of the century when Governor Tiburcio de Axpe y Zúñiga called together 500 indian leaders and proposed to them that they should settle in the coastal area, where they could defend the island, and be more easily assimilated into Spanish society.[160] Although the indian leaders agreed and the Governor reported that some indians had already gone to live in the coastal areas, it is doubtful whether a radical change occurred in the distribution of indian settlements. When the missionaries arrived in Trinidad in 1687 they found the area around Naparima "the most highly populated with indians in the island" with "a village called Los Cocos highly populated with indians situated on the east of the island half way between the two points of Galera and Blanquizales" and other indians living at Moruga and Punta de Gallo.[161] The large number of indians incorporated into the missions and the desire of missionaries to found further missions in that part of the island underlined the uneven distribution of the native population; a distribution that was not significantly altered in the eighteenth century. It is likely, however, that local changes occurred in the location of settlements. The precise location of the indian villages is unkown but they were probably sited somewhat inland though with good access to the coast for trade and the exploitation of marine resources on which they were still partially dependent. For a short period during the early eighteenth century Guaranos indians from the Orinoco carried out enslaving raids on indian villages in Trinidad,[162] but Carib attacks diminished and, after 1720, Trinidad coasts became relatively safe for settlement. They may have resulted in the gradual re-location of many of the indian villages near the coast, where fishing and trading would have been facilitated.

Away from the estates, *encomiendas* and missions, the nature and relative importance of cultivation, hunting and fishing in the economy changed as a result of Carib raids and population decline. During the seventeenth century Carib raids discouraged the indians from living in coastal areas. This forced retreat inland meant that the indians had to cultivate more elevated and generally poorer soils, which would have produced lower yields and could not have been cultivated for such long periods. Also, defence requirements and the cultivation of certain commercial crops for trade with foreigners would have caused a decline in labour inputs, and probably led to the selective cultivation of high-yielding crops and the withdrawal of lower-yielding ones. Thus the assemblage of plants grown in the *conucos* would have become less diverse and it is unlikely that, when labour inputs in defence decreased at the end of the seventeenth century and food demands declined in parallel with the indian population, those crops that had formerly been withdrawn were readopted.

The decreased availability of labour, the movement of the population inland and the presence of hostile Carib indians in Trinidad waters in the seventeenth century probably led to a decline in the importance of fishing in the economy and an increase in the contribution made by hunting. However, the presence of small harbours along the coast and a report that near La Brea "a great number of fish are caught"[163] suggests that fishing still played an important role in the economy. Fishing during the seventeenth century probably concentrated on the inshore environment with shellfish accounting for a very large proportion of the marine fauna exploited. During the eighteenth century Trinidad coasts became safe for settlement, and this may have resulted in an extension of fishing to the offshore environment, although it appears that a large proportion of animal protein obtained by the indians on the north and east coasts came from turtles, which they caught with nets.[164]

Trade between indian groups in the island probably continued throughout the seventeenth century, but with difficulty. The presence of Caribs in Trinidad waters rendered cabotage hazardous, and the re-distribution of the indian population following the settlement of the Spanish in the island and Carib attacks disrupted existing trade routes. Most of the goods traded were probably food products, though trinkets obtained from trading with foreigners were probably exchanged. Trade between the indians and foreigners was more vital to the latter: the English, French and Dutch were concerned with obtaining a foothold on the island and in replenishing supplies, whereas the indians were only interested in obtaining non-essential European curiosities. Many foreigners visited the island to trade and it has been suggested that they established themselves as middlemen in indian villages, where they regulated the exchange of goods between the indians and Europeans.[165] In 1689 it was said that indians living at Amacuro and Chacachacare could speak French[166] and at a later date indians were in constant contact with the French who had settled at Toco and Cumana. The indians themselves also ventured to other West Indian islands, particularly Barbados and Tobago, in search of trade;[167] in 1702 Captain Poyntz reported that "the King of the Caribbees who lives in Trinidad and Tobago is very desirous of trade with the English.[168]

part five

Spanish colonial reorganisation 1776-1797

9
The Advent of Liberalisation

The political and economic stagnation into which Trinidad slipped in the early eighteenth century was symptomatic of the decreasing effectiveness of the Spanish colonial system in maintaining exclusive control of its territories and developing their resources. Within the Empire political control was beginning to be challenged by secular and ecclesiastical officials, while from the outside foreign nations were making more concerted efforts to acquire trade openings in Spanish territories. Economic production was stagnating and an increasing proportion of royal revenue was being lost in contraband trading, which increased as the monopolistic trading system collapsed. If Spain was to retain her Empire and reap the benefits of its resources, the Spanish colonial system had to be reorganised.

The period of political and economic reorganisation of the Empire coincided with the spread of egalitarian doctrines in Europe and it was inevitable that the principles of equality of opportunity and non-restriction which they embodied should be incorporated in new policies.[1] The exclusive attitude of the Crown had proved to be unrealistic since it could not be supported by the financial and human resources available, so new ideas were adopted as much as a practical solution to the problems of Empire as from any belief in their intrinsic merit. The reorganisation of the Empire thus involved centralisation of administration together with the liberalisation of restrictive attitudes towards land division, trade, and foreigners.

Bureaucratic reorganisation

Despite the administrative reforms of the early eighteenth century the Spanish bureaucratic system failed to retain exclusive political control of the Spanish colonies and to secure for Spain the full rewards of Empire. The revitalisation of the Spanish Empire under the Bourbons thus involved the centralisation of administration which was intended to eliminate pockets of independence and to place political control in the hands of the Crown and a few politically reliable individuals, who were under its immediate authority. It was to this end that the intendant system was created. The intendants assumed many of the administrative, judicial and financial functions of the governors and *corregidores*. Appointed by the King they were answerable to him alone. They thus combined the advantages of efficient local government with complete subordination to the Spanish Crown.[2] In 1776 the Intendancy of Venezuela was created, incorporating the provinces of Venezuela, Maracaibo, Cumaná, Guyana, Margarita and Trinidad,[3] which themselves formed smaller administrative units called *partidos* at the head of which was a *subdelegado*.[4] In 1791 Trinidad was made a separate Intendancy and the Governor of the island was appointed Intendant,[5] thereby increasing his authority.

The integration of areas under the jurisdiction of the Intendant of Venezuela was aided by the separation of Trinidad, Margarita, Cumaná Guyana and Maracaibo from the Viceroyalty of Nueva Granada and their attachment to the Captaincy-General of Venezuela, which was under the jurisdiction of the *Audiencia* of Santo Domingo.[6] Trinidad thus came closer to its administrative centre and its government was rendered potentially more efficient.

Within the island the Governor remained the most powerful administrator. From 1779 to 1783 the Governorship was divided into civil and military positions,[7] but the experiment was apparently unsuccessful because the two posts were amalgamated in 1783 when José María Chacón was appointed as political and military Governor of the island.[8] Before 1791 the authority of the Governor was probably undermined in part by the *subdelegado* who took over some of the Governor's judicial and administrative responsibilities, particulary with regard to economic development; nevertheless the success of Chacón as Governor led to the extension of his period of office and to his appointment as Intendant. His position thus embraced wide powers, which could only be questioned with any authority by the Crown.

The Governor was aided in his administration by a number of judicial and financial officials who, apart from the lieutenant and the *asesor*, were all nominated by him[9] and the only independent body, the *Cabildo*, which in the past had acted as a check on the conduct of the Governor, had its powers curtailed. In 1777 the *Cabildo* was composed of two *alcaldes ordinarios* and four *regidores*[10] but its numbers were later increased to eleven, incorporating some of the municipal officers of Port of Spain.[11] This increase in its membership did not reflect its increasing importance. Its jurisdiction was limited to Port of Spain and in 1791 when the Intendancy was created with the Governor as chairman, and with vast powers over agriculture, commerce and finance in the island, the *Cabildo* was virtually relegated to an advisory position.[12]

The ecclesiastical bureaucracy did not experience similar changes in its organisation at the end of the eighteenth century. The Crown had begun to place less emphasis on the Church as an instrument of royal control and support for its civil administration, and more on the armies that had gradually become established in the New World.[13] Although the Crown did not make any parallel changes in the structure of the ecclesiastical bureaucracy, it did centralise administration by claiming the right of the *Patronato*, which it assumed as a direct consequence of sovereignty rather than as a papal concession, and which it used to limit the rights and privilges of the clergy.[14] Certain minor modifications in organisation did improve administrative efficiency: in 1790 the ecclesiastical affairs of Trinidad were placed under the Bishop of Guyana.[15]

Immigration policies

Within this centralised administration liberal policies towards immigration and trade were adopted. The preceding centuries of Spanish settlement in Trinidad had indicated that its small Spanish and indian populations were insufficient for the economic development of the island. If agriculture and trade were to be developed immigration was necessary. The lack of potential immigrants in the Iberian Peninsula or in Spanish colonies obliged the Crown to open Trinidad's doors to foreign settlers. In 1776 the Crown granted to French Catholics the first of many concessions aimed at encouraging foreign immigration. Governor Fàlquez was instructed to encourage the immigration of French Catholics from the Antilles, particularly from those islands that remained under the control of the British as a result of the Treaty of Paris of 1763, which included Dominica, St. Vincent, Grenada and Tobago.[16] As an incentive foreigners were given land grants according to the "quality and wealth of each one", a concession that was particularly attractive to them since many of their own estates had been destroyed by sugar ants.[17] As a result in the following two years nearly 2000 immigrants arrived, of whom 1500 were slaves, and in 1777 Roume St. Laurent estimated that 383 families, including 286 from Martinique, 40 from Dominica, and 57 from Grenada, were on the point of leaving for Trinidad with about 33000 slaves.[18] In 1779 the same concessions were made to the Irish Catholics in the Danish colony of Santa Cruz.[19] The state of war between France and England in 1778, which Spain joined on the side of the French in 1779, tended to slow down immigration in the early 1780s[20] but by the time war was concluded by the Treaty of Versailles, which gave to Britain Grenada, St. Vincent, St. Kitts, Montserrat, Nevis and Dominica, Roume St. Laurent had managed to secure fuller concessions for immigrants under the *Cédula* for the Population of Trinidad of 1783.[21] The concessions granted to French and Irish Catholics were extended to include all Catholics. Immigration increased and amongst the new colonists were fugitive slaves from nearby islands who obtained concessions as freemen on arrival in Trinidad. There was some anxiety as to the presumed criminal nature of some of the former slaves.[22] In order to prevent the island from becoming a refuge for "robbers, fraudulent bankrupts, criminals or men lost in vice", it was resolved that all slaves who had fled from other islands should pay their price plus 6% for every year they had absented themselves, whilst those unable to pay were to be returned.[23] In this way the Governor aimed at retaining the enterprising refugee slaves and at the same time dispense with the criminal elements.

Immigration, miscegenation, and the spread of egalitarian ideas in Europe accelerated the breakdown of the old social order based on race and claims to nobility and replaced it by one based on enterprise and ability, reflected in the economic role of the individual in society. Although distinctions were still made in censuses between whites, coloureds, slaves and indians, it was a group's economic position which determined its actual status. The new form of social organisation effectively removed from the Crown an important means of political control—a social hierarchy based on criteria determined by the Crown and incapable of being changed by the individual.

To maintain control of the island's population, which as a result of immigration had not only increased but contained a number of immigrants of dubious political and criminal inclinations, new instruments of political control were called for. In 1785 three positions with the title of Commissioner of Population were created to deal primarily with land distribution and conflicts, but it was hoped that they would also encourage the new colonists "to obey and love our laws".[24] Each Commissioner was responsible for a department of the island, divided into north, central and southern sections. The first Commissioner of Population was Roume St. Laurent, whose temporary appointment was approved in 1786.[25] In 1787 the duties of the Commissioners were extended to include the registration of population changes, including internal migrations, agricultural production and land sales, while the first Commissioner, who received twice the salary of the other two, also had to see to the maintenance of roads and the preservation of slaves. The Commissioners were also responsible for the policing of the rural areas and so were regarded as *alcaldes de monte*.[26] The departments of the Commissioners were together divided into 28 quarters with a Commandant at the head of each who helped the Commissioners maintain civil law and order.[27] The Commandants, chosen from eminent local colonists, resided in their quarters and were visited by the Commissioners rather than vice versa.[28] In this way remote parts of the island were kept under careful surveillance. The maintenance of law and order in Port of Spain was in the hands of the *alcaldes de barrio*, who had no jurisdiction outside the Port.[29] In 1786 Port of Spain was divided into four or five *barrios*[30] and two *alcaldes* were appointed to each.

During the later part of the eighteenth century efforts were made to build up the military strength of the island in anticipation of an enemy invasion. Additional troops were sent from Cumaná and companies of militia, divided into whites, *pardos* and *morenos* were established with privileges under the *fuero militar* in Port of Spain and St. Joseph.[31] Control of politically unreliable elements in the population was, however, maintained by civil officials rather than the army. Under Article 13 of the *Cédula* of 1783 new colonists were ineligible for service in the regular militia and thus prevented from establishing a formal power base that might have been a threat to Spanish authority.

The state of the two republics

For ideological and practical reasons, towards the end of the eighteenth century the concept of the two republics was re-examined. The policy of segregating the indian and non-indian populations for protection and administration had resulted in the social and economic degradation of the natives. While the condition of the indians was of concern to the authorities, the policy of segregation was opposed to prevailing ideas in Europe, which envisaged the existence of a unified society in which all members worked together for the common good. In New-World terms it was considered that the education of the indians would not only improve their material welfare, but would enable them to be integrated into the social and economic life of the colonies. Although efforts were made at the end of the eighteenth century to establish schools to instruct the indians in the Spanish language and culture, some considered that the indians could be civilised with greater speed and at a lower cost by allowing greater contact between the natives and non-indians, particularly Spaniards. Others were more sceptical; they justified the enforcement of the laws of separation on the same grounds that their original proponents had done, maintaining that the indians needed to be protected from the "bad influence" of the non-indians, and particularly the mixed races.

If the Crown was convinced that the integration of the indian and non-indian populations was justified on ideological and moral grounds, there were economic factors that had to be taken into consideration. Indian tribute still formed an important source of revenue to the Crown, and both agriculture and mining were almost wholly dependent on indian labour. It was therefore felt to be imperative, particularly at this time when the Crown hoped to revitalise the American economy, that the indian population should be clearly defined and miscegenation minimised to prevent a decline in the tributary population and labour resources. Thus while the segregation or integration of the indian population was debated, the Crown remained silent.

In the absence of any directive from the Crown, the decisions were made at the local level whether to enforce or suspend the laws of residential segregation.[32] Some officials attempted to enforce the laws, with varying degrees of success, while others maintained that since the conditions which had prompted the introduction of the laws had ceased to exist, they were no longer disposed to enforce them. This argument was often used to violate the rights and privileges of the indians that were embodied in the laws, such as the usurping of their lands in favour of non-indian residents. Whether the laws of residential segregation were enforced or not, for administrative purposes the two populations still remained distinct.

There is no evidence to suggest that the segregation or integration of the indian population was the subject of hot debate in Trinidad; the condition of the declining indian population was eclipsed by the furore that followed the arrival of thousands of immigrants in the island. Nevertheless, it may be inferred from the history of the indian population during the later years of the eighteenth century that the administration was marginally in favour of integration. Although the indians were aggregated into distinct villages, the concentration was effected to gain access to the lands assigned to the former declining villages, rather than to segregate the indian population. Indeed, when Arima was founded a small number of non-indian settlers were established in the village to set a good example to the indians. Nevertheless, the indian villages remained administratively distinct and for this reason it is still possible to identify an indian republic and a non-indian republic in Trinidad at the end of the eighteenth century. It should be remembered, however, that by that time the non-indian republic consisted of predominantly French people of mixed race, and negro slaves.

10
Trinidad Rediscovered: The Impact of New Colonisation Schemes

The nature of immigration

The liberalisation of official attitudes towards immigration and the provision of incentives to attract colonists resulted in an influx of foreign immigrants who irrevocably changed the social and economic life of Trinidad. Between 1777 and 1797 the population of the island increased five-fold from 3432 to 17 718,[1] primarily as a result of immigration. In the two years following the granting of concessions to French Catholics in 1776 nearly 2500 immigrants arrived in Trinidad, of whom 1500 were slaves.[2] The period of highest immigration, however, followed the publication of the *Cédula* for the Population of Trinidad in 1783. By 1790 the total population of the island reached 13 247 of whom nearly 50% were slaves.[3] For the first time Trinidad became a slave colony. During the 1790s, however, Trinidad lost some of its negro immigrants, who left to aid their compatriots in the revolutions of Martinique, Guadeloupe and St. Lucia. These losses were more than compensated for in 1791 and 1793, when the island received many refugees fleeing from the same islands and Santo Domingo; republicans arrived from St. Lucia and Martinique, and royalists came from Guadeloupe and Santo Domingo.[4] Although the Governor was concerned that revolution might spread to the island he considered their arrival to be beneficial since "the greater part of them who come are extremely profitable subjects; not only themselves but the number of slaves which they bring, who are already acclimatised and experienced agricultural workers".[5]

The increase in the island's population was almost exclusively the result of immigration, as shown in Table XII: from 1786 to 1790 natural increase only accounted for about 10% of the total increase. The birth rate was between 15 and 20 per 1000 but the death rate was high, as was population loss by emigration. The high death rate was due to both "the normal losses of a new establishment"[6] and disease, accompanied by poor medical care and overwork. During the latter part of the century there were several outbreaks of smallpox, which caused a number of deaths but which were for the most part checked by vaccination.[7] Medical care in the form of a hospital was not provided until a provisional one was built in the late 1780s and even then it was inadequate.[8] The death rate among slaves was higher than that of freemen and was no doubt partly the result of overwork; in 1784 it was estimated that an estate owner would lose one third of his slaves in land clearance.[9] The *Code Noir* introduced in 1789 probably had some effect in reducing the burden of the slaves[10] but the lack of medical care and poor food given to them maintained the death rate at a high level.

The Spanish towns

During the latter part of the eighteenth century the population of Port of Spain increased as a result of immigration and its growing importance as an administrative and commercial centre, while that of St. Joseph declined. In 1777 the population of St. Joseph exceeded that of Port of Spain by about 400, but by 1797 Port of Spain possessed six times the population of the former.[11] Port of Spain succeeded in attracting a large proportion of immigrants. From 632 in 1777 its population rose to 1025 in 1784, of whom 602, including 191 slaves, were described as "new colonists": 18% of the total number of "new colonists" in Trinidad at that time.[12] By the following year the number of "new colonists" in Port of Spain had nearly doubled to 1019[13] and in 1788 Capt. Ricketts, a British observer, reported that its population was increasing daily.[14] By 1797 it had a population of 4525 of whom 938 were white, 1671 coloured and 1916 slaves. Most of the new colonists were French so that it soon became a predominatly French town. In 1802 when the British took over the island, 60% of the total number of freemen were French, the rest being Spanish and British (see Table XIII).

The decline in the population of St. Joseph reflected its declining

TABLE XII

Population change 1784–1795

	1784	1785	1786	1787	1788	1789	1790	1791	1792	1793	1793	1794	1797
Freemen													
Immigrants			540	994	420	488	333						
Births			43	65	71	65	75						
Emigrants & deaths			123	114	301	190	135						
TOTAL	2550	2741	3201	4110	3807	5170	5170	4695	5047	5212	5642	5257	6627
% of total population	38·4	36·8	35·4	35·6	32·4	39·6	41·0	39·0	36·0	35·4	36·3	34·4	37·6
Slaves													
Immigrants			1746	1876	830	154	46						
Births			68	61	72	101	109						
Emigrants & deaths			475	506	21	285	210						
TOTAL	2462	3300	4430	6009	6481	6451	6396	5916	7767	8264	8733	8944	10009
% of total population	37·8	44·3	49·1	52·1	55·3	49·4	48·2	49·2	55·4	56·0	56·2	58·5	56·4
Indians													
Births			56	42	35	41	26						
Deaths			70	19	21	37	50						
TOTAL	1491	1405	1391	1414	1428	1432	1408	1398	1198	1268	1114	1078	1082
% of total population	22·9	18·8	15·4	12·2	12·1	10·9	10·6	11·6	8·5	8·6	7·1	7·0	6·0
TOTAL	6503	7446	9022	11 533	11 716	13 053	13 247	12 009	14 012	14 744	15 519	15 279	17 718

Sources: AGI CAR *152* 1784, 1786
       AGI CAR *153* 1788, 1789, 1790, 1791, 1793, 1794, 1795
       AGI CAR *444* 1786, 1787, 1790, 1791, 1792, 1795
       AGI CAR *975* 1785
       AGI EST *66* 1794
       Mallet *Descriptive account of the island of Trinidad*, 1797

TABLE XIII

Distribution of free men by nationality in 1802

	WHITE			COLOURED		
	English	Spanish	French	English	Spanish	French
Santa Anna	18	9	34	48	48	135
Tragarete	5		32			
Mucurapo	14		20	1	18	60
Maraval	2	6	6		89	109
Diego Martin	20	5	66	14	69	210
Carenero	14		62	8	5	173
Las Bocas	2	7	13	1	14	33
La Ventilla	2	4	17	51	26	98
Cimaronero	4		3	7	25	35
Santa Cruz		26	5		361	1
Aricagua	11	4	34	1	182	30
Maracas		57	7		150	7
Tacarigua & Aruca	47	3	14	17	2	15
Arima & Guanapo		17	2	2	29	5
Toco & Salibea	6	14	11		29	25
Mayaro	1	2	27	6	6	74
Guayaguayare	3	7	25	1	10	28
Hicacos & Gallos	4		16	16	16	42
Los Cedros	7		8		9	11
La Brea	14	4	24	10	130	13
Oropuche	5		2	9	9	10
South Naparima	34	5	41	16	5	17
North Naparima	31	18	44	5	20	200
Punta de Piedra	4	7	35	1	58	15
Cuva & Savaneta	51	4	4	21	8	7
Chaguanas & Caroni		7	2		2	3
Las Cuevas & Maracas			2			
Port of Spain	350	207	530	348	219	1444
St. Joseph	14	92	7	16	212	4
TOTAL	663	505	1093	599	1751	2925[a]

Source: CO *295/6* 1802

[a]This total is an error in the document: it should read 2834.

status and functions. In 1782 it was reported that "the best families" were leaving for Port of Spain[15] and since it only succeeded in attracting 29 new colonists, by 1785 its population had fallen to 575, just over half of what it had been in 1777. During the 1790s the population of St. Joseph was increased slightly by the garrisoning of the town,[16] but in 1797 it had only 728 inhabitants, of whom 142 were white, 177 coloured and 409 slaves. In contrast to Port of Spain, however, it remained predominantly Spanish, over 80% of the total being Spanish in 1802.

Although the population of Port of Spain increased, most of the immigrants took up residence on lands they had been granted under the 1783 *Cédula*. As early as 1787 Governor Chacón reported that there were no agriculturalists, who formed "the true population", living in Port of Spain.[17] While the old Spanish inhabitants remained concentrated in the valleys surrounding St. Joseph and at La Brea, the French colonists settled along the western coast, particularly at Naparima, in the foothills of the Northern Range as far east as St. Joseph and on the east coast at Mayaro and Guayaguayare.[18] As shown in Table XIV, the percentage of "whites" in the rural areas was lower than in Port of Spain and St. Joseph; only at Maracas did it exceed 15% of the total population. The slave population in all areas excluding those with indian villages exceeded 50% of the total population, rising to over 80% at Tragarete, Las Cuevas and Cimaronero, the reason for which is unknown. The free coloured population was evenly distributed throughout the island, except for a curiously high concentration at Erin.

The determination of the Spanish Crown to develop the island's economy though immigration accelerated the change that was already occurring in the status of both Port of Spain and St. Joseph. The Governor and royal officials took up residence in Port of Spain in 1757 and with the movement of the *Cabildo* there in 1783, St. Joseph more or less ceased to function as an administrative centre though ecclesiastical affairs continued, into the British period, to be admininstered from there.[19] It had never functioned as an economic or social centre and its complete decline was only arrested by the establishment of a garrison, which was located there because St. Joseph was considered more healthy and strategic than Port of Spain.[20] Port of Spain not only assumed the administrative functions of St. Joseph but it developed as an important commercial centre, since goods could be obtained there more cheaply than in any other colony.[21] Most of the trade was handled by foreign merchants, including transient traders.[22] The success of Port of

Spain as a commercial centre was confirmed by the establishment of the foundation of the Freemasons' Lodge of United Brothers in 1795.[23] The town also served as a market for the internal sale of provisions and meat.[24] The increase in the permanent and transient population of Port of Spain led to its development as a social centre. In 1787 it was suggested that a theatre should be built but there were insufficient funds available.[25] More informal amusement centres sprang up, however, to the extent that the *Cabildo* limited the number of billiard saloons to nine and restricted the sale of certain local drinks.[26]

The rapid expansion in the population of Port of Spain necessitated the regulation of its layout and the provision of public services. In 1782 a plan was instigated which realigned the streets but maintained the same basic grid pattern. The aims of the plan were to clear houses from the shore for commercial purposes and to make way for public buildings, such as a customs house, a government house and a barracks.[27] The building of private houses also proceeded rapidly but it could not keep pace with immigration. In 1787 it was necessary to pay for a house 12 months in advance.[28] To allow the further expansion of the town westward and to make it more healthy, an engineer, José del Pozo y Sucre, was employed in 1787 to divert the St. Ann's river from its course—it formerly ran along Chacon Street—to the foot of the Laventille hills, to the present-day site of the Dry River (see Fig. 11).[29] The same engineer had in 1786 been commissioned to make plans for a barracks, hospital, prison and town hall. In 1787 these plans were sent to Spain and the result was that the Crown made an annual allowance of 200 000 *pesos* from Mexico and made available 400 infantrymen to carry out the work, which included the provisional building of a barracks, hospital, chapel, warehouses, government house, treasury and customs house.[30] All the buildings were constructed of wood and it was not long before they needed repairing. At the same time essential fortifications, including two batteries, one in Port of Spain and the other two leagues to the west, a magazine and a guard post in the Port were all completed,[31] but attempts to fortify Chaguaramas were hindered by losses in the workforce through overwork[32] and yellow fever[33] and did not succeed before the British captured the island.

The Church in Trinidad failed to keep pace with the increase in the island's population in the provision of clergy and in the building of churches. This was due to the decreasing emphasis placed by the Crown on the Church as an instrument of royal control, to the increasing

Table XIV

Population of Trinidad in 1797

Quarters[a]	White	Coloured	Slaves	Indian	Total	% White	% Coloured	% Slaves	% Indian
1. Las Bocas	31	29	153		213	14·5	13·6	71·8	
2. La Carenage	64	131	607		802	7·9	16·3	75·6	
3. Diego Martin	141	259	734		1134	12·4	22·8	64·7	
4. Macurapo	23	63	222		309	7·4	20·3	71·8	
5. Tragarete	20	16	240		276	7·2	5·7	86·9	
6. St. Anne	48	187	409		644	7·4	29·0	63·5	
7. Maraval	36	141	434		611	5·8	23·0	71·0	
8. Santa Cruz	30	211	133		374	8·0	56·4	35·5	
9. La Ventille	17	134	268		419	4·0	31·9	63·9	
10. Simaronero	6	51	266		323	1·8	15·7	82·3	
11. Acarigua	45	164	380		589	7·6	27·8	64·5	
12. St. Joseph	142	177	409		728	19·5	24·3	56·1	
13. Maracal	46	74	128		248	18·5	29·8	51·6	
14. Las Coivas	2	4	58		64	3·1	6·2	90·6	
15. Tacarigua and Arouca	35	164	603		802	4·3	20·4	75·1	
16. Arima and Guanapo	29	47	146	495	717	4·0	6·5	20·3	69·0
17. Toco, Salibea, Cumana	28	62	154	155	399	7·0	15·5	38·5	38·8
18. Mayaro	48	44	311		401	11·9	10·9	77·5	
19. Guayaguayare	61	46	301		410	14·8	11·2	73·4	
20. Erin	5	61	13		79	6·3	77·2	16·4	
21. Icaque and Gallos	55	105	214		375	14·6	28·0	57·0	
22. La Brea	58	102	395		555	10·4	18·3	71·1	
23. Siparia	1	0	0	139	140	·7	—	—	99·2
24. Naparima	165	346	868		1379	11·9	25·0	62·9	
25. Monserrat and Savana Grande	0	0	0	293	293	—	—	—	100·0
26. Pointe-à-Pierre	41	46	205		292	14·0	15·7	70·2	
27. Savaneta, Cuva, Cascajal	35	141	441		617	5·6	22·8	71·4	
28. Port of Spain	938	1671	1916		4525	20·7	36·9	42·3	
TOTAL	2151	4476	10 009	1082	17 718				

emphasis on economic development rather than spiritual enlightenment, and to the general lack of clergy. In 1777 there was a parish priest and sacristan in Port of Spain and St. Joseph and although the non-indian population had increased to over 10 000 by 1791 only two new parishes had been created at San Juan and San Fernando.[34] When they were

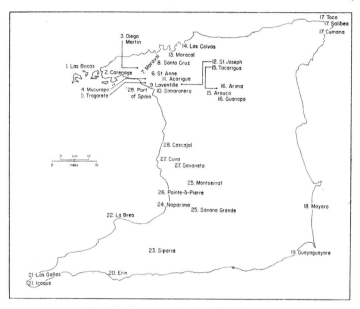

FIG. 10. Quarters for the 1797 Census.

established the Governor requested permission to look for clergy in foreign islands, in view of the lack of priests, but he was refused and instructed to look among the regular clergy and in particular the Capuchins of Andalucía, from whom two who spoke French were finally chosen.[35] The regular clergy in fact fulfilled their ecclesiastical role very often in secular positions. In addition the Franciscan convent in St. Joseph was at times occupied by a cleric but by 1790 the building had so deteriorated that it was impossible to celebrate mass in it.[36] In 1796 the convent was rebuilt, but in the same year the last member of the order died and from then on it was used as a convalescent hospital.[37]

Social classes

New colonists were to be treated as Spaniards and vassals of the King. Their immigrant status was not recognised in law, except that they had

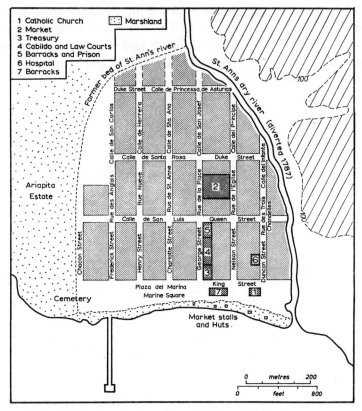

Fig. 11. Port of Spain at the end of the eighteenth century.

to be resident in the island for five years before they could be admitted to "all honourable public employments and posts in the militia according to their respectable capacities and circumstances".[38] Attitudes towards the new colonists were, however, hostile. The old Spanish inhabitants claimed that many of the immigrants were poor, possessing only a few slaves, while others were bankrupts from Martinique and Grenada[39] and some "untrustworthy fugitives from whom it is not possible to expect anything worthwhile".[40] They could not deny, however, that many immigrants came from respectable families, who possessed considerable captial and a large number of slaves[41] and among whom were a number who had held public office in their countries of origin.[42] All immigrants were automatically regarded as politically suspect, although they had to take an oath of allegiance to the Spanish Crown on arrival in the island. In 1778 it was suggested that the new colonists who had established themselves on the north coast should be moved inland to prevent them communicating with the enemy and carrying out contraband trade.[43] Political anxieties were greatest during the early 1790s when it was feared that, with the large French population in the island, the uprisings in Martinique, Guadeloupe, St. Lucia and Santo Domingo would spread to Trinidad.[44] An inhabitant at that time wrote, "the population is mostly composed of refugees and desperate characters, who had been implicated in all the rebellions and massacres in the neighbouring islands. Their principles are incompatible with regular government".[45] Despite these reservations the new colonists were absorbed into Trinidadian society. Until 1789 fugitive slaves had been accepted in Trinidad as freemen, but after that time all immigrants retained the same status they had held in their former place of residence.[46]

Immigration, together with miscegenation and increasing employment opportunities in the army and trades undermined the racial basis of the social hierarchy, replacing it by one based more on the economic role of the individual in society. Although employment was to a large degree still determined by race, racial divisions, particularly those between the mixed races, became less marked and a rise in social status more easily achieved. Most official positions in the island continued to be filled by "whites" and the most prestigious by Spaniards, both *peninsulares* and creoles. The positions of Governor and Intendant were filled by peninsular Spaniards,[47] but all creoles could aspire to lesser positions. Many of the new colonists came to the island with considerable capital resources and entered into agricultural and commercial activities. In 1788 Aymerich observed that all businesses in Port of Spain were French, English, North American or Antillean,[48] while the new colonists were renowned for their agricultural knowledge and enterprise.[49] From their economically advantageous positions they soon assumed posts in the municipal administration of Port of Spain and became Commandants of quarters in the rural areas.[50] As early as 1782 three positions on the *Cabildo* were filled by new colonists.[51] The influx of wealthy and enterprising colonists tended to displace the original Spanish inhabitants down the social scale. Emerging from a period of economic depression the Spanish lacked the financial resources of the French colonists[52] and a great part of their lands, their only source of potential wealth, which they had held since "time immemorial", was taken from them under the Proclamation of 1785.[53] While many held small estates around St. Joseph those that lived in Port of Spain were reduced to being "traders of singing birds and 'papelones'".[54] Some Spaniards probably entered the officer ranks of the army which was established in Trinidad in anticipation of further conflicts with England,[55] but in 1802 Governor Picton observed that there were only six or seven Spaniards of "any respectability" in Trinidad.[56]

Beneath those whose higher social status was recognised on the basis either of official positions or of wealth in agricultural or commerical activities was a class of small landowners and artisans, mainly French people of mixed racial origin but including a number of negroes, who had obtained their freedom by favour or enterprise and who owned small holdings.[57] The number of artisans in the island increased considerably at the end of the eighteenth century: "in 1777 the Island did not possess ten craftsmen of any denomination whatever and at present in 1781 there are upward of two hundred of approved merit in their different professions such as caulkers, carpenters, blacksmiths, masons and all foreigners".[58] As a landless class with republican sympathies they were considered to be politically unreliable and in 1802 the British Governor Picton described them as "a dangerous class which must be generally got rid of".[59]

At the bottom of the social scale were slaves. The spread of egalitarian ideas in Europe and the increasing belief in a free labour market, meant that slaves could obtain their freedom more easily.[60] Those that remained in servitude were treated more humanely under the *Code Noir*, which improved their material and social welfare but their social position did not alter substantially.

The economy

During the latter part of the eighteenth century the problems of labour shortages and lack of trade that had characterised the earlier part of the century were resolved by a change in the political attitude of the Crown. Foreigners, who were formerly excluded from Spanish territories, were welcomed and granted considerable concessions, particularly in the form of land grants. Such concessions succeeded in attracting a large number of immigrants, who came with their slaves and established estates producing commercial crops. The development of agriculture, with the trading concessions simultaneously granted to colonists, encouraged trade and enabled the inhabitants to export their products and to import some vital provisions. The lessons of overdependence on commercial crops had been learnt, however, and although the estates continued to concentrate on production of goods for export, at no time did products for internal consumption account for less than one quarter of the island's total agricultural production.

Land grants

Unlike many other islands of the Antilles, Trinidad still possessed extensive forest areas, which, although modified by centuries of shifting cultivation, were largely unoccupied as a result of the decline in the indian population. These areas could be cleared to form estates on which commercial agriculture production could be established. The success that the colonisation schemes achieved in attracting immigrants was largely due to the availability of unsettled land. The first concessions offered to French and Irish Catholics in 1776 and 1779 respectively included the granting of lands to colonists according to their "quality and wealth".[61] The number of land grants made under this scheme is unknown, but given that between 1776 and 1783 the number of freemen in the island increased from 1383 to 2550, including women and children, it seems likely that between 250 and 300 were granted.[62] In 1783 the concessions granted to French and Irish Catholics were extended to all Catholics in the *Cédula* for the Population of Trinidad and under Articles 3 and 4 white immigrants of either sex were to be granted 32 acres of land plus 16 acres for each negro or coloured slave they introduced. Free negroes and coloureds were to receive 16 acres of land and the same for each slave they introduced.[63] All grants made had first to be petitioned and surveyed and, after being granted, registered in the *Libro Becerro*. It would appear, however, that not all grants were registered; it is thought that eminent colonists and those who had received land in remuneration for services were exempt from registration, while poorer colonists could not afford the surveys and legislation involved in registration.[64] Thus, of about 2000 land grants made by the Spanish Government, only 137 were entered in the *Libro Becerro*.[65]

During the early years of immigration conflicts over land arose between the new colonists and the old Spanish inhabitants. Many of the Spaniards claimed large tracts of land, which they maintained uncultivated and hoped to sell to new colonists at exorbitant prices. The Governor thus reported in 1785 that "scarce is there a spot remaining that can be granted to new colonists, which is not claimed as property of the aforesaid Spaniards".[66] It was to ameliorate this situation that the Proclamation respecting land grants was issued in 1785. Under the Proclamation "immemorial possession" was regarded as an insufficient claim to land. Inhabitants who had held land for long periods in a state of cultivation were to be given priority over other claimants in respect of grants, provided that they made a claim to the government within three months. Other inhabitants who held land uncultivated were to choose the area they wished to receive as a land grant and the remaining land was to pass to the Crown. In this way it was intended that lands should not accumulate in the hands of those who lacked the means to cultivate them.[67] How strictly the Proclamation was imposed is unknown. Conducting a survey of the island two years later Matheo Pérez still complained that new colonists were forced to settle inland, often in the forest, since the old inhabitants had seized most of the land and were only willing to sell it to the new colonists at excessive prices,[68] despite the fact that from 1787 the sale of lands was regulated by the newly created Commissioners of Population.[69] The demand for rich agricultural land was such that indians from the former *encomiendas* were united and moved to Arima, to free land suitable for cacao in the valley of Tacarigua, which they had been assigned but, owing to their declining population, had been unable to cultivate for some time.[70] Despite the pressure on good agricultural land, many of the lands granted remained uncultivated or were abandoned after only a few years of cultivation.

Although it has been estimated that about 2000 land grants were conceded by the Spanish government,[71] the most comprehensive list of land grants, which was made by the British government when it seized control of the island, includes only 612 grants. Given the lack of other information relating to land grants these must be considered as representative of the total number granted. During the 1780s the majority of lands granted were located in valleys on the slopes of the Northern Range, particularly at Maraval, St. Ann's, Santa Cruz, Maracas and Aricagua, and also in Naparima. During the 1790s, however, land grants were more generally distributed and included parts of the east coast at Mayaro and Guayaguayare (see Fig. 12).[72] The area of land granted increased to a peak in 1789 when 5653·4 *quarrées* (18 092·5 acres) were conceded but levelled off with immigration in the 1790s to between 1000 and 2000 *quarrées* (3200 and 6400 acres) a year. While the size of the land grants varied according to the size and wealth of the immigrant families, it also appears to have varied according to location. The average size of land grants in the Northern Range did not exceed 50 *quarrées* (160 acres), whereas in more remote areas, such as Guanapo, Las Cuevas and Point Chupara, the average size of grants reached several hundred *quarrées* (see Table XV).

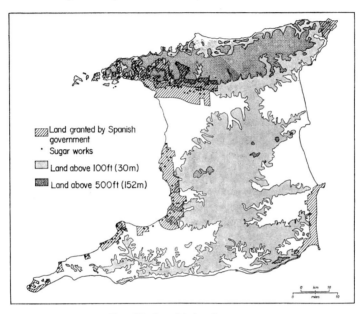

FIG. 12. Spanish land grants.

Sources of labour

During the latter part of the eighteenth century labour resources increased. In the 1770s indians formed the basis of the island's labour supply but as their numbers diminished and slaves became more generally available they became an insignificant source of labour. In 1784 it was estimated that 400 000 slaves were required for the commercial agricultural development of the island, estimating that one *fanega* of land cultivated in sugar, cotton, coffee and cacao would require 3, 2, 2½ and 1½ slaves, respectively.[73] Although lands were granted partly according to the number of slaves introduced by colonists, thereby in part ensuring that the size of land grants were not in excess of the

TABLE XV

Distribution and size of land grants in *quarrées* granted 1781–1797 and the percentage of land granted in each area cultivated in selected crops.

A	Location	Sugar	Cacao	Coffee	Cotton	Pasture and Provisions	Total number of grants	Average size of grants
	Gaspar Grande				100·0		1	170
37·2	Point Gorda				62·7		2	92·5
	Chaguaramas	32·5		67·4			4	151·2
18·1	Carenage	66·9	1·0			13·5	22	59
	Cuesse	43·5		56·4			4	186·3
2·1	Diego Martin	78·3		3·8		14·4	41	42·3
33·5	Mucurapo	52·8				13·3	11	20·7
24·0	Maraval	32·3	8·4	24·3		10·9	38	44·8
5·9	St. Ann's	10·5		35·0		48·3	43	29·5
	Tragarete	95·5				4·3	7	20
25·3	Santa Cruz	10·9	21·6	15·0		15·7	36	31
24·0	Maracas Valley		70.8				29·5	45·5
	Aricagua	60·2	23·2	1·9		9·6	25	43·2
15·1	La Ventilla	9·8		11·5	22·7	40·6	24	14·9
4·6	St. Joseph	35·0	35·9	4·9		15·5	55	17·8
20·4	Caura		96·5				5	25·5
61·6	Point Chupara					38·3	2	386·5
46·9	Aruca	50·9					12	173·5
23·8	Tacarigua	56·2					8	164·6
25·2	Arima		74·7			3·9	5	240
53·7	Guanapo		100·0				4	555·5
40·8	Las Cuevas						1·5	180
38·5	Toco	20·4			14·4	5·5	14	58·3
	Oropuche	51·5				8·0	7	159·1
51·5	Mayaro	33·2	2·1		9·0	3·8	14	105·2
43·8	Guayaguayare	·5			23·4	27·8	19	79
100·0	Erin						1	39·5
12·4	Hicacos	54·9			12·1	20·3	28	24·2
10·9	Cedros	59·9				29·1	9	94
59·0	Iroas	2·9				37·8	9	84·3
27·8	Guapo	56·8				15·3	5	161·4
5·7	La Brai	78·1				16·0	19	91·7
	South Naparima	100·0					4	112·3
	North Naparima	100·0					4	50·7
57·1	Naparima	91·1				3·0	45	92·1
	Pointe-à-Pierre	42·2					15	109·5
10·0	Cuva and Savaneta	83·2					21	189·3

TABLE XV—contd.

A	Location	Sugar	Cacao	Coffee	Cotton	Pasture and Provisions	Total number of grants	Average size of grants
48·5	Cascajal	51·3					3	63·3
71·7	Caroni	28·2					6	129·3
20·3	Cimaronero	38·0	0·9	5·0			8	59·3
	Carapachaima	100·0					1	47·5

Source: CO 295/35   1 quarrée = 3·2 acres = 0·49 fanega

A = either no account of cultivation, or abandoned, or never cultivated.
The nature of cultivation or abandonment refers to the period 1797–1815 when Spanish land grants were registered by the British.
The percentages of land either cultivated or abandoned do not sum to 100% for each area. The remaining area was cultivated in minor crops.
Most of the estates producing commercial crops also cultivated small quantities of provisions.

means possessed by the colonists to cultivate them, there were never enough slaves in the island. Thus, after 15 years of encouraged immigration the Governor still found he had to petition for a loan of a million *pesos*, to be made available over three years and repayable over ten with 6% interest if necessary to enable the colonists to buy 20 000 negro slaves.[74] The loan was granted in 1790, but from that date until 1797 the total slave population only increased from 6396 to 10 009.

Negro slaves arrived in Trinidad by four means: in the company of free colonists; by flight from other Antillean islands; by purchase from African slave traders; and by purchase direct from other parts of the New World. Most slaves entered Trinidad with free colonists. The fact that the size of land grants depended in part on the number of slaves introduced encouraged colonists to bring them to the island, even to the extent of first stealing them from other islands.[75] Many complaints were made from surrounding islands and Grenada passed special laws to prevent slave stealing.[76] The introduction of slaves was also encouraged by the abolition of both the import duty and the capitation tax on slaves. The latter was abolished for ten years under the *Cédula*, and perpetually in 1786.[77] In addition, many slaves fled independently from the Antilles to Trinidad, where, until 1789, they could obtain concessions as freemen. In that year, the practice was stopped and all immigrants were accepted at the rank they had held in their former place of residence.[78] Since most of these slaves arriving in Trinidad would have been accepted as freemen they would have made only a small contribution to the labour force of estates. Other slaves were made available for purchase in the island under slave trading contracts, but they were few in number. When the slave trade was declared open in 1789 the number of slaves introduced into the island increased; in 1791 Governor Chacón maintained that since the freeing of the slave trade 3307 slaves had been introduced to Trinidad but that there was still a great need for them in the island.[79] In subsequent years only a few slaves entered the island and their numbers never approached the 90% of total population which was considered normal in other Antillean islands:[80] in 1797 they formed less than 60% of the population. A number of colonists resorted to the Antilles for the purchase of slaves, obtaining licences to export crops and animals from Trinidad and the mainland for their payment, but the number of slaves that were introduced by such means is unknown.[81]

The number of slaves increased despite the high death rate in that section of the population. Some of the slaves introduced under the contract with the Baker and Dawson Company were of poor quality and included many who were old and ill and died within a few years of being introduced.[82] Some died of overwork on the estates but others managed to escape to the hills. In 1784 there were about 300 slaves living in the wooded areas around Port of Spain who had fled from the estates.[83] Working conditions improved slightly after 1789 when the *Code Noir* was published, which insisted on the employment of individuals in tasks appropriate to their age and sex and forbade their employment under the age of 17 or over the age of 60. Even so many slaves continued to suffer the effects of overwork, insufficient food and poor housing, and it was suggested that the large number of slaves on the west coast was a direct result of a better diet made possible by the availability of fish in the Gulf of Paria.[84]

Indians in small numbers were also available for hire on the estates and they were particularly desirable for land clearance work in which they were considered adept.[85] Applications for the use of indian labour had to be made to the *corregidor* who dispensed with it as he wished. The system was open to abuse. In 1782 one of the inhabitants complained that the *corregidores* were being bribed by the wealthy colonists to supply them with indians, while less influential and less wealthy colonists found it almost impossible to obtain them. It appears that the regularised *mita* system in the indian villages had broken down, for indians were being overemployed to such an extent that they had insufficient time to attend to their own *labranzas*.[86] The problem was that demands for indian labour, which was considered more desirable than slave labour because the indians were regarded as more sober and peaceable,[87] far exceeded the small supplies available.

In addition to indian and slave labour, a small number of landless people of mixed racial origin, who had obtained their freedom by favour or enterprise, were probably also available for hire as agricultural labourers[88] but most of these were probably absorbed into the rapidly expanding trade and craft industries and domestic service in Port of Spain.

Implements and animals, particularly mules and horses, were also required for commercial agricultural production. Implements had to be supplied from Spain and colonists were expressly forbidden to obtain them from the Antilles.[89] Under the *Cédula* for Population of Trinidad tools were to be provided from the factories of Biscay at wholesale prices for ten years.[90] This arrangement worked fairly well with implements, particularly hoes and cutting tools, which were supplied from Spain within a year of being requested,[91] but other agricultural equipment, particularly for sugar mills and rum distillaries, was more difficult to obtain:[92] in 1782 de Lapeyrouse, an inhabitant of Trinidad, was forced to exchange nine cattle for boilers and other sugar mill equipment with an inhabitant of Tobago.[93] Draught animals were also required for agricultural labour on the estates. From 1784 cattle and horses could be taken from Cumaná to Trinidad free of duty[94] and in that year 100 mules were sent to the island where they were shared out among the colonists.[95] Supplies of draught animals were, however, erratic and they failed to meet the demands of colonists, which during the 1790s increased with the expansion of sugar cultivation. Animal powered mills were favoured since they were cheap to establish—2000 *pesos* compared with 6000 and 6500 *pesos* for wind and water mills respectively.[96] In 1792, 582 mules were distributed to the colonists, who paid for them with the products of the subsequent harvest.[97] In 1793 a contract was made with Josef Antonio Garmendía for the annual introduction of 400–500 mules and 100 oxen for carts and sugar mills and in the following two years 832 mules entered the island.[98] Most of the mules went to the sugar-producing areas of Naparima and the valleys to the west of Port of Spain.[99] The shortage of animals was aggravated by two factors. First, about 15% of the animals on estates died every year from overwork and undernourishment.[100] Second, although mules were relatively cheap in Trinidad—30 *duros* as compared with 150 in other Antillean islands[101]—the colonists lacked large capital resources and had to rely on future harvests to pay for the animals purchased.[102]

Agricultural production

In 1776 Fálquez was instructed to promote the establishment of "plantations of cacao, coffee, sugar, vanilla, cotton, maize and other fruits suited to the climate".[103] Despite immigration in the late 1770s however, Intendant Abalos in 1780 reported that "the land remains more or less in the same state as nature produces"[104] and when Chacón assumed office as Governor he found that agricultural production was limited to cacao, maize, plantains, manioc and other root crops.[105] Chacón was similarly instructed to promote agricultural production[106] but his task was made easier by land and trading concessions granted under the *Cédula* for the Population of Trinidad. From 1777 to 1795 the value of commercial agricultural production increased from 3000 *pesos* to 1 588 000 *pesos* whilst the value of food products nearly doubled.[107]

The nature of commercial production was essentially similar to that practised in the early part of the century. Land was completely cleared, generally by indians,[108] and crops were grown until yields declined and the land was abandoned. Attempts to check losses of soil fertility and soil erosion were made by growing commercial crops beneath a specially planted canopy layer. Cacao trees were grown under immortelle trees (*Erythrina micropteryx*) for protection from the sun and coffee bushes were shaded by fruit trees and immortelle, generally planted about 24 – 30 ft apart.[109]

For historical reasons cacao continued to be the most important crop grown in the late 1770s but the production advantages of cotton, which required less investment and labour and provided quicker returns, soon contributed to the latter's rapid expansion. Cacao was grown almost exclusively by Spaniards[110] in valleys on the southern slopes of the Northern Range to the east of Port of Spain; it was almost entirely absent from other parts of the island (see Table XV). The cacao grown in Trinidad was of good quality and it could command high prices.[111] It had the advantage that once planted it required little attention apart from the collection of the fruit which was produced for nine months of the year and only required replanting after 100 years.[112] Its cultivation thus necessitated only half of the labour that sugar required.[113] It did, however, have two main disadvantages: first, it was expensive to establish and second, since no returns were forthcoming for at least five years, it required larger capital resources.[114] Because of its slow maturation, the period of exemption of duties to be paid on exported goods was extended for seven years for cacao so that cultivators would reap the same benefits from the *Cédula* as producers of other crops.[115] Throughout the latter part of the eighteenth century, however, cacao never accounted for more than 10% of commercial agricultural production by value (see Table XVI).

In the late eighteenth century four species of cotton were present in Trinidad—*Gossypium herbaceum, G. hirsutum, G. barbadense* and *G. arboreum*—but it was the last species that was cultivated most extensively.[116] The most important areas for cotton cutlivation were in the Bocas and on the east coast (see Table XV).[117] Cotton cultivation was established on a large scale soon after the beginning of immigration.[118] Its quick maturation and the low capital investment required to start its cultivation made it a natural choice for the new colonists.[119] In addition the Crown was anxious to establish its cultivation to supply the textile factories of Spain and, as an incentive released its cultivators from service in the militia.[120] In 1784 cotton was described as the only medium of exchange in Trinidad and in 1788 it was worth nearly half a million *pesos* and accounted for nearly 70% of the value of commercial production.[121] The main disadvantage of cotton was its susceptibility to attack by insects, notably the *chenilla* which devoured the leaves and boll of the plants.[122] This insect attacked cotton plants in Trinidad in 1789 and as it spread in the island[123] the inhabitants turned to the cultivation of sugar. The decline in the importance of cotton was seen as beneficial to the colony for two reasons: first, cotton was susceptible to drought and heavy rains so that its cultivation was precarious and its prices variable;[124] Second, it made heavy demands on soil fertility.[125] Nevertheless, after the failure of the cotton crop in 1789 its cultivation still continued, particularly in the drier areas of the Bocas and east coast.[126] Good quality cotton was produced, which was said to command 10% higher prices than cotton produced in other islands,[127] and it continued to make a substantial contribution to the island's economy reaching a maximum value of over half a million *pesos* in 1794.

TABLE XVI

Value of commercial crops produced in *pesos* 1786–1795

Crop	1786	1787	1788	1789	1790	1791	1792	1793	1794	1795
Cacao	8400	8400	18 913	26 975	31 200	32 200	38 468	40 420	113 600	113 600
%	2·43	1·59	2·86	4·28	4·60	4·16	4·20	3·75	7·59	7·15
Coffee	3000	6000	97 970	167 500	208 050	200 000	193 550	197 470	249 600	310 000
%	0·87	1·13	14·8	26·58	30·72	26·04	21·14	18·35	16·69	19·52
Cotton	300 120	424 260	459 270	326 430	251 370	190 880	225 855	196 020	601 000	522 000
%	87·16	80·5	69·46	51·80	37·12	24·85	24·67	18·21	40·20	32·87
Sugar	32 200	65 360	70 000	92 400	179 300	323 000	445 500	642 000	524 800	642 400
%	9·35	12·01	10·58	14·66	26·47	42·06	48·66	59·67	35·05	40·45
Vanilla	600	22 800	15 000	16 800	7200	12 000	12 000		6000	
%	0·17	4·32	2·26	2·66	1·06	1·56	1·31		0·4	
TOTAL	344 320	526 820	661 153	630 105	677 120	767 880	915 373	1 075 910	1 495 000	1 588 000

% = value of crop as a percentage of the total value of commercial crop production

Sources: AGI CAR *152* 1786
AGI CAR *153* 1788, 1789, 1790, 1791, 1794, 1795
AGI CAR *444* 1786, 1787, 1790, 1791, 1792, 1795
AGI EST *66* 1794

Although sugar was made locally throughout the eighteenth century, its commercial production did not commence until the 1780s and it was almost exclusively associated with French colonists.[128] The first sugar estate was established at Tragarete by de Lapeyrouse in 1787 and within the next decade over 150 sugar estates entered commercial production[129] with over 130 mills, mostly mule-driven, in operation.[130] The sugar estates were concentrated in valleys around and to the west of Port of Spain and along the coast of the Gulf of Paria (see Table XV).[131] Sugar cultivation was stimulated by the cotton failure in 1789. Its cultivation was considered preferable to cotton since yields were high and regular, particularly compared with other islands of the Antilles, where sugar had been cultivated continuously for some years and yields were declining.[132] Also, far from impoverishing the soil as cotton had done, it returned nutrients to the soil in the form of leaves and shoots.[133] Its production was encouraged by two factors in the 1790s: first the higher yielding Otaheite cane was introduced into Trinidad in the early 1790s, possibly in 1792;[134] second, the revolutions in Martinique, Guadeloupe and Santo Domingo created sugar shortages in England and France so that the price of sugar increased from 32 shillings a hundredweight in 1793 to 87 shillings in 1798.[135] Not all colonists turned to the cultivation of sugar; cotton cultivators persisted at Guayaguayare partly because it was said they lacked the capital resources necessary to establish sugar.[136]

Coffee, vanilla and tobacco were also grown in small quantities. Coffee cultivation became important about 1790. The coffee produced in Trinidad was of good quality, being able to command a 25% higher price than that cultivated in Martinique and Puerto Rico,[137] but it possessed most of the disadvantages of the other crops: like sugar it required large labour inputs, like cotton it was susceptible to attack by insects, and like cacao it took several years to mature.[138] It had the additional disadvantage that the bushes had to be replaced after 12 years.[139] It was mainly cultivated in the foothills of the Northern Range, particularly around and to the west of Port of Spain, but it does not seem to have been cultivated in the valleys of the Central Range, which were later considered to be the most suitable.[140] Vanilla never assumed a very significant position in the island's economy. It was said that the fortunate inhabitant who cultivated vanilla got rich quickly but the unfortunate one was ruined more quickly.[141] Its disadvantages were that it required large expanses of land, because it rendered the soil infertile after three years, and during cultivation it was susceptible to attack by insects and easily ruined by heavy rains.[142] The Compañía Guipuzcoana paid only a low price for the crop but its high value in relation to its small volume made it an important item of contraband trade.[143] The persistence of contraband trading also enabled the cultivation of tobacco to continue on a small scale, even though it had been forbidden in 1781.[144] Although good quality tobacco was produced it could not compete with that of Cuba[145] and its cultivation thus remained "more of a curiosity than a branch of agriculture" (see Table XVII).[146]

Although emphasis was on the production of commercial crops a large proportion of the estates also produced food crops, while some particularly on the east and south-west coasts, grew only provisions. Food crops were also grown on the smaller estates "the masters of which being poor but active, occupied themselves in the cultivation of bananas [plantains], manioc, yams, sweet potatoes, and maize for the consumption of the country".[147] The most important food crops grown were plantains, maize and manioc, but potatoes, tanias, eddoes, cassias and rice were probably also cultivated. The production of food crops was sufficient to support a small export trade with the mainland, particularly in maize and rice.[148] During the latter part of the eighteenth century the relaxation of trading laws allowed the wider dissemination of plants throughout the West Indies from all parts of the world. Amongst those introduced into Trinidad were breadfruit (*Artocarpus communis*), jack fruit (*Artocarpus heterophyllus*), nutmeg (*Myristica fragrans*) and East Indian almond (*Terminalia catappa*). The breadfruit, of Polynesian origin, was first successfully introduced to the New World in 1793 when it was taken to St. Vincent by Capt. Bligh.[149] It must have been introduced into Trinidad soon after that date and by 1804 it was reported to be growing well.[150] The jack fruit was introduced to St. Vincent at the same time and was probably introduced into Trinidad from there. It was growing in the island in 1806.[151] The nutmeg, also an Asian domesticate, was said to be growing in Tobago in 1786 though it is generally considered to be a nineteenth-century introduction to Trinidad.[152] The earliest documentary evidence for its presence in the island is in 1806, when it was introduced directly from India.[153] The East Indian almond was introduced into Jamaica from the East Indies in 1790,[154] and it probably reached Trinidad soon after that date. In addition many European garden crops were introduced and added variety to the diet of the inhabitants. They were grown on a small scale and probably only by European and other white colonists.

TABLE XVII

Value of food crops and products of savanna in *pesos*, 1786–1795

Crop	1786	1787	1788	1789	1790	1791	1792	1793	1794	1795
Plantains	100 600	122 600	118 200	166 600	164 800	176 000	222 000	182 000		
	62·83	60·12	57·61	63·95	64·74	69·84	70·88	59·05		
Manioc	43 800	48 600	70 387	67 050	61 950	51 300	60 000	93 300		
	27·35	23·83	34·30	25·73	24·33	20·35	19·15	30·27		
Maize	4450	6750	5925	11 850	8700	3700	8700	6800		
	2·77	3·31	2·88	4·54	3·41	1·46	2·77	2·20		
Others	11 250	25 950	10 650	15 000	18 900	21 000	22 500	26 100		
	7·02	12·72	5·19	5·75	7·42	8·33	7·18	8·46		
TOTAL	160 100	203 900	205 162	260 500	254 550	252 000	313 200	308 200	282 000	272 400
Savanna	25 100	28 900	29 600	38 900	37 800	48 400	80 000	81 000	114 000	124 000

% = value of crop as a percentage of the total value of food production

Sources: AGI CAR *152* 1786
     AGI CAR *153* 1788, 1789, 1790, 1791, 1794, 1795
     AGI CAR *444* 1786, 1787, 1790, 1791, 1792, 1795
     AGI EST *66* 1794

While abundant edible vegetables were produced, there was a great shortage of meat and fish in the island. Such as there was came from hunting, fishing and imported sources. The general disinterest shown in the development of ranching may probably be blamed on the over-emphasis on the commercial production of crops. Governor Fálquez was specifically instructed to develop livestock raising on the island's savannas but by the early 1780s one of the chief breeders had only 50 cattle.[155] Most of the island's meat came from the mainland but shipments were not regular and the inhabitants often lacked the means to pay for it.[156] Thus in 1782 St. Laurent complained that the troops were dying of hunger and an inhabitant reported that the colonists had to resort to contraband trading to obtain adequate supplies of meat.[157] The unsatisfactory nature of the situation was realised in 1784, when it was suggested that breeding ranches should be established and that for the purpose animals could be imported from Cumaná free of duty.[158] Many of the animals taken from Cumaná, however, went to the Antilles where they were exchanged for slaves. Contracts were made for the introduction of breeding cattle, such as that made with Marcos de Ribas in 1786 for the introduction of 800 calves and 200 cows from three to four years old,[159] but many animals were lost in transport and from the corral in Port of Spain, where conditions were poor and from which many cattle were stolen. Others escaped and became feral, but they were few in number.[160] Nevertheless efforts continued and small numbers entered the island, particularly in the 1790s when they became more generally available. In 1796 Charruca observed that cattle, mules and horses were cheap in Trinidad because they could easily be transported from the mainland—one cow cost only 20 *duros* in Trinidad compared with 100 *duros* elsewhere[161]—and at the time of conquest of the island by the British it was (exaggeratedly) claimed that there were over 2000 cattle in the Grand Savannah.[162] Other animals kept included sheep, goats, pigs, mules and horses. All animals appear to have been distributed throughout the island, as also was land given over to pasture.[163] The increasing importance of animals in the economy may be judged from the rising productivity of savanna land, which rose from 25 100 *pesos* in 1786 to 124 000 *pesos* in 1795 (see Table XVII).[164] Whether the savannas were improved with introduced grass species is unknown, though Guinea grass (*Panicum maximum*) was being grown in 1802 and it is likely that the inhabitants made its acquaintance some years before.

A certain amount of animal protein would have been obtained by hunting and fishing. Animals relished probably included deer, agouti, lape, peccary, and tatou while other species, such as monkeys, iguanas and manicou were probably eaten only by the lower social classes.[165] Waterfowl and other birds would also have been hunted and it is likely that their numbers decreased considerably with the increase in the population. Fishing activities pass unmentioned in the documentary record apart from turtle-catching. Turtle populations on the north and east coasts were probably severely depleted by demands made upon them by both local and foreign groups for consumption and for the extraction of oil,[166] though in 1837 they were still described as plentiful.[167]

Other economic activities

Nearly all other economic activities revolved around commercial agricultural production and included sugar, cotton and coffee milling and rum distilling. These activities only made their appearance in the island in the last two decades of the eighteenth century and they were located in the areas of crop production: sugar mills were concentrated around Port of Spain and along the coast of the Gulf of Paria; cotton mills in the Bocas and on the east coast; and coffee mills in the foothills of the Northern Range (see Table XVIII). From those areas their products were shipped to Port of Spain before being exported. From the inauguration of plans to colonise the island in 1776 it was hoped that a timber industry would develop involving ship building. Both Fálquez and Chacón were instructed to survey the island's timber resources and to select a suitable place for a dockyard. Previously the Co. Guipuzcoana had partially investigated the possibilities of developing Trinidad's timber trade but had not thought it worthwhile.[168] It was not until the 1780s that Chacón carried out his instructions to survey the island fully.[169] By that time much of the forest had been cleared to establish plantations and consequently much timber had been destroyed,[170] although some was exported to the treeless Antilles. Although the *Cédula* for Population of Trinidad allowed free access to the island's timber resources for shipbuilding, little advantage was taken of this concession. A few small boats were built but work was just beginning on a naval dockyard at Chaguaramas when the British took over the island.[171]

TABLE XVIII

Agricultural works established in Trinidad by 1797

Location	Sugar mills	Coffee mills	Cotton mills	Rum distillers
Las Bocas		1	42	
La Carenage	10	5	18	5
Diego Martin	19	12	4	9
Mucurapo	8	2		3
Tragarete	3			2
St. Anne	6	24	16	2
Maraval	3	7	1	4
Santa Cruz		5		
La Ventille	1	16	25	
Cimaronero	5	5	1	3
Acarigua	6	7		2
St. Joseph	13	7	4	2
Maracal	3	4		1
Las Coivas	1			
Tacarigua and Arouca	14	2		8
Arima and Guanapo		5		
Toco, Salibea and Cumana	1		59	
Mayaro	1		65	
Guayaguayare	1		74	
Erin			1	
Icaque and Gallos	5		3	
La Brea	20	3		6
Siparia				
Naparima	20	25	28	8
Montserrat and Savana Grande				
Pointe-à-Pierre	6		3	1
Savaneta, Cuva and Cascajal	13			3
Port of Spain				
TOTAL	159	130	344	60

Source: Mallet, *Descriptive account of the island of Trinidad*, 1797

Pitch had been used by the inhabitants of Trinidad since before the conquest for caulking small boats and canoes,[172] and during the eighteenth century small quantities were exported to Spain. In 1790 the Crown requested that a number of barrels of pitch be sent to Spain for testing. They were duly remitted and in the mid-1790s a pitch-refining works was established about one mile from Pitch Lake at La Brea. By 1797 about 1500 barrels were being exported annually.[173]

Trade

The concessions of free trade with nine Spanish ports granted to Trinidad, Cuba, Puerto Rico, Hispaniola and Margarita in 1765 were symptomatic of the general change in the Crown's attitude towards trading, brought about primarily by the failure of the convoy system and the monopoly companies to secure for Spain the greater portion of the products of her Empire and to cope with contraband trading.[174] The liberalisation of trade was intended to make legal trade attractive to both producers and traders and in particular to stimulate Trinidad's economy.

In 1776 two steps were taken towards liberalisation of the island's trade. In September Governor Fálquez was given permission to grant licences to inhabitants to trade with other Spanish ports, particularly on the mainland, and in November the activities of the Compañía Guipuzcoana were extended to include Trinidad, Margarita, Cumaná and Guyana.[175] The Company was given the non-exclusive privilege of the island's trade for 10 years, paying only a 2% duty on goods imported or exported, in return for maintaining coastguards to prevent contraband trading. In 1779 a Company agent was established in the island[176] but the amount of trade handled by the Company was never great; the days of the monopoly company were at an end. The Company ran into financial difficulties and in 1785 it was dissolved and incorporated into the Compañía de Filipinas.[177] By that time Trinidad had received special trading concessions under the *Cédula* for Population of Trinidad, which suspended for 10 years the payment of the tithe and the *alcabala* on all goods produced in the island, after which a 5% tithe and *alcabala* was to be paid, except on goods embarked for Spain in Spanish vessels, which were to be perpetually exempt from duty. Goods exported to and imported from French colonies were to be subject to a 5% duty, but slaves introduced from Spanish or foreign colonies were to be free of duty for 10 years, while goods exported to pay for them were also subject to a 5% duty. Slaves subsequently exported from Trinidad, however, were liable to a 6% duty.[178] The concessions were considerable but as early as 1784 Governor Chacón anticipated that trade would decline when the 10 years expired because duties payable in other Antillean islands amounted to only 6% and would thus undercut the 10% that would be payable after that time. He therefore petitioned the Crown for further concessions and in 1786 they were granted. The *Cédula* was modified so that after 10 years, counted from 1785, only a 2% tithe and sales tax was to be paid on goods produced in the island. All duties on slaves introduced into the island were abolished and the duty levied on goods exported to foreign colonies for the purchase of slaves was reduced from 5% to 3%, as was that on goods destined for French ports.[179] In the same year the period for which cacao was to be free of duty was extended for seven years, to compensate for the slow-maturing nature of the crop.[180] The effect of the concessions was immediate. In 1788 the Minister of Tobago reported that in 1783 Trinidad had been "a place of horrible misery" but had since become "one of the richest islands in the Antilles, a change due entirely to having a free Port and an open market".[181] The impressive results of allowing free trade persuaded the Crown to extend the duration of the concessions to 1800.[182] The only additional tax imposed during the last decade of the eighteenth century was a $\frac{1}{4}$% tax imposed on all imports and exports for the construction of a wharf in Port of Spain.[183]

In 1776 the island's trade was essentially provincial. Trinidad exchanged some commercial crops, such as cacao and tobacco, and natural products, such as timber, turtles and salt, for fish and meat (see Table XIX). Durable goods were obtained from registered ships but more often by contraband trading, which at that time included all trade with foreigners. The concessions granted in 1783 changed the pattern of trading, and immigration and agricultural expansion changed its nature. While in the late 1770s most of the island's trade was with neighbouring Spanish islands and the mainland, in the 1780s the greater part of Trinidad's exports went to the Antilles, particularly to Martinique and Grenada. The most important item of export to the Antilles was cotton; cacao was mainly sent to Spain via the mainland or Greater Antilles (see Figs 13 and 14). The rapprochement between France and Spain for the defence of the Caribbean against England was

TABLE XIX

Destination of selected exports, January 1777 to August 1784

	lb Cotton	lb Cacao	lb Coffee	lb Maize	lb Rice	no. Coconuts	no. Turtles	planks Timber
Margarita	5900	25 190		199 760	1100			338
Cumaná		14 520		17 520				
Barcelona	200	440		14 960	880			
Angostura		3960	400			600		40
Guarapiche	2375			7590				
Guyana	900	15 235	665	5500		2780	4	615
La Guaira				3300				316
Vera Cruz		55 000						
Santo Domingo		15 400						
Puerto Rico		49 720		1980				55
"Friendly colonies"	42 563	6600		56 710	18 402	33 510	88	310
"French colonies"	68 243	26 015	100	153 450	5860	23 420	151	60
"Foreign colonies"	6875	2640		229 570	460	5700		201
"Colonies" (unspecified)	34 956			770		1000	14	
Martinique	102 991	54 900		191 785	660	14 700	29	
Grenada	15 801	3850		12 100		3200		
St. Thomas	200	1100						
St. Lucia	6500							
St. Eustatius	34 956							
Curação		330						
TOTAL	322 460	274 900	1165	894 995	27 362	84 910	286	1935

Source: AGI CAR 734, 735 1777–1784

reflected in closer trading links between French and Spanish colonies in the New World. Although from 1783 Grenada was held by the English, trading links that had been established under the French were maintained. Thus, while trade with Martinique was said to be worth £1 200 000 a year in 1787,[184] Capt. Ricketts, conducting a survey of Trinidad in 1788, observed that its trade was mainly with Grenada "which from its vicinity will always command a preference to all other islands."[185] Exports to the Antilles, which are designated as "foreign colonies" in lists of the destinations of exports, consisted primarily of cotton, sugar and coffee (Table XX). In the 1780s cotton exports to the Antilles, which made their way to the cotton mills in England and France, were

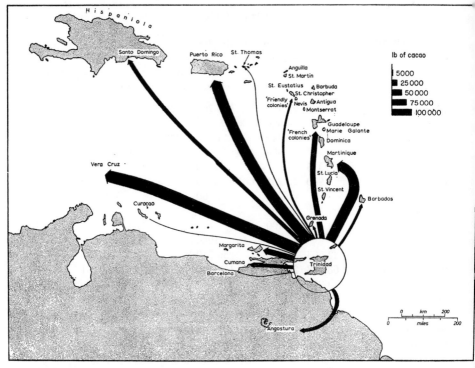

FIG. 13. Volume and destination of cacao exports 1777 to August 1784.

the most valuable item, but after the failure of cotton in 1789 sugar and coffee assumed more significant positions in the table of exports. Other goods exported included maize, rice, coconuts, turtles and timber. In return for these products Trinidad received durable goods and specialised food products from Europe in addition to slaves. Not all goods imported were consumed within the island—many were re-exported. The low duties payable on goods imported meant that "everything can be got in Trinidad at very fair prices and cheaper than in other colonies".[186] The island thus acted as a warehouse for goods passing from Spanish to French and English colonies and vice versa.

Trade with Spain increased in the latter part of the eighteenth century but it was of little value compared with the Antillean trade. Up to 1785 trade with Spain was handled by the Co. Guipuzcoana but in that year Trinidad despatched its first ship to Spain since its discovery. Under the *Cédula* for the Population of Trinidad the Crown granted two years in which foreign ships could be bought and registered in the island:

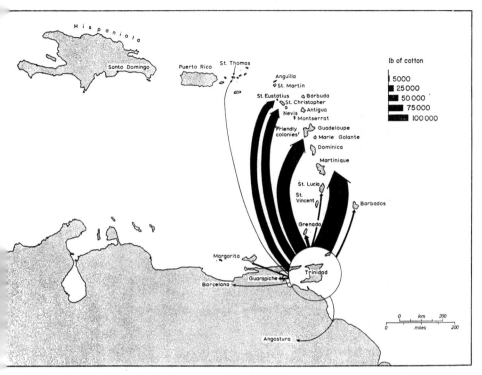

FIG. 14. Volume and destination of cotton exports 1777 to August 1784.

formerly all goods had to be carried in Spanish vessels. In 1786 the period in which ships could be registered was extended.[187] Under this concession several ships were purchased and it was these vessels that transported Trinidad's products to Spain in the latter part of the eighteenth century. By 1796 four ships were leaving for Spain annually.[188] Goods exported to Spain included mainly cacao and coffee, though some timber, rum and coconuts were also sent;[189] little cotton or sugar went to Spain (see Fig. 14). Imports from Spain consisted of only a few articles, the greater part of the ships' capacity being filled with goods which could be re-exported from the island to other parts of the New World.[190] Governor Picton in 1802 observed that there had been few trading contacts with Spain under the Spanish "except now and then a small cargo of cacao in return for writing paper, earthenware, Canary birds, Catalonia, Malaga and Tenerife wines, dried fruits, rosaries and besgay [Biscay] ironmongery".[191]

Trade with the mainland and neighbouring Spanish islands continued.

TABLE XX

Commercial crops exported to "foreign colonies", 1777–1796

	Cacao lb	Cotton lb	Sugar lb	Coffee lb
1777				
1778				
1779		6875		
1780		1550		
1781	4620	17 187		
1782	19 140	20 063		100
1783	30 635	119 570		
1784	42 392	194 471	1410	
1785	46 272[a]	113 386		3034
1786	35 255	178 987	1000	5448
1787	17 270	371 185	2237	2000
1788	45 809	314 534	1200	2100
1789	33 000	598 433[a]	37 839	1795
1790	19 832	299 577	19 076	14 177
1791	4 649	477 414	153 576	169 137
1792	9 543	444 916	260 488	92 740
1793	4306	346 762	614 488	262 619
1794	4070	301 887	2 064 098	517 212[a]
1795		354 002	2 333 989	178 094
1796	378	247 331	2 547 661[a]	257 504

[a] Peak year of export

Sources: Sales tax (*Alcabala*) records
　　　　 1777–1780 AGI CAR *734*
　　　　 1781–1785 AGI CAR *735*
　　　　 1786　　　ACI CAR *736*
　　　　 1787　　　AGI CAR *737*
　　　　 1788　　　AGI CAR *738*
　　　　 1789　　　AGI CAR *739*
　　　　 1790　　　AGI CAR *740*
　　　　 1791　　　AGI CAR *741*
　　　　 1792　　　AGI CAR *744*
　　　　 1793　　　AGI CAR *746*
　　　　 1794　　　AGI CAR *748*
　　　　 1795　　　AGI CAR *752*
　　　　 1796　　　AGI CAR *753*

In exchange for commercial and food crops, Venezuela provided Trinidad with most of its meat and fish. In 1786 all duties on provisions and animals imported from the Tierra Firme for the support of the island's population were abolished.[192] Such trade, although vital for the island's maintenance, was of little commercial value compared with the Antillean trade.

The continued introduction of slaves was considered essential for the economic development of the island. Most slaves were introduced by colonists but others entered Trinidad under contracts made with slave-trading companies. In 1784 a contract was made with Edward Barry on behalf of the Baker and Dawson Company of Liverpool for the provision of 4000 negro slaves. Trinidad was to be used as a base from which the islands and fringing mainland of the Caribbean were to be supplied.[193] In October 1784 the first batch of 640 slaves arrived, but, owing to the lack of facilities and food for their maintenance in the island until buyers should arrive, most were sent on to La Guaira, only 51 being sold in Trinidad.[194] The second batch that arrived was not unloaded but sent directly to La Guaira. Thus early in 1785 two ships arrived from Havana in search of slaves but found none available and therefore had to wait in Trinidad for several months until the Company could collect together slaves from other islands; finally they left with 643.[195] It became clear that Trinidad could not be conveniently used as a slave-trading centre: it was too far east, so that navigation from other islands was long and difficult; it was ill-equipped, having neither the facilities nor the food to maintain the slaves in the island until ships arrived to transport them to other parts of the New World; and it was claimed that the climate of Trinidad was unhealthy so that many slaves died before they were sold.[196] The great losses sustained among the slaves introduced by the Company were, however, largely a result of their poor condition, most of them having been obtained "second-hand" from various parts of the New World rather than direct from Africa.[197] In 1786 another contract was made with the Baker and Dawson Company for the introduction into Trinidad of slaves at 150 *pesos* per head. Although several ship loads arrived most slaves were transported to the mainland.[198] In 1787 the Governor Chacón advocated a contract with a Portuguese, Manuel Antonio Matos, who had settled in Trinidad and wanted to introduce 3000 slaves from the coast of Africa,[199] but by that time another contract had been made with the Baker and Dawson Company for the introduction of a further 100 slaves who were to be paid for with agricultural products.[200] In an effort to make slaves more generally available in the New World the Crown declared the slave trade free for two years, allowing Spaniards and foreigners to introduce slaves into Spanish colonies free of duty with a 4 *peso* bonus for good quality slaves.[201] As a result, from 1789 to 1791, 3307 slaves were introduced into Trinidad and in 1791 the period of free trade was extended for another two years and subsequently for another six years.[202] In 1790 the island had been granted permission to seek a loan of a million *pesos* for the purchase of slaves[203] but it is not known whether or from whom it was obtained, or how many slaves were introduced as a result.

The Spanish Crown continued to order the Governor of Trinidad to prevent contraband trading[204] but it was through trading concessions rather than through such prohibitive orders that the Crown succeeded in eliminating illegal trade. During the late 1780s fewer boats were seized in Spanish waters and in 1790 Governor Chacón reported that trading concessions had led to a decrease in contraband trading. However, because there had been a change from the cultivation of cotton to coffee and vanilla (both crops of small volume and high value and hence suitable for contraband trading), he considered it worthwhile to maintain a coastguard.[205] Blatant contraband trading thus apparently diminished, but there were more subtle ways available for the introduction of goods and the avoidance of the small duties payable on them. Most illegal trade probably occurred in Port of Spain. Spaniards from neighbouring areas were able to export goods to foreign nations duty-free through Trinidad and to obtain European goods at a low price. In 1782 the inhabitants of Port of Spain complained that the practice of transferring goods from Spanish to foreign vessels and vice versa brought in no revenue,[206] but Governor Chacón more perceptively saw that to impose a duty on the transference of goods would cut the advantage that Trinidad had over other ports;[207] the island had more to gain by allowing such trade than by levying duties. The freeing of the slave trade must also have increased contraband trading in Port of Spain because it gave foreign vessels the opportunity of stopping in the island, if only for 24 hours.[208]

Most of the island's trade was handled by foreign merchants who had become naturalised and who formed a large proportion of the population of Port of Spain.[209] These merchants bought produce from the estates and arranged for its embarkation: in 1790 a ship leaving for Cádiz was loaded with cacao and coffee which had been collected from 27 estates around Port of Spain by six merchants.[210] The movement of goods within the island was hampered by the lack of good roads, although in 1787 a 4% tax was imposed on the sale of rum to pay for public works, including roads.[211] In 1787 Aymerich reported that the new colonists had established themselves along the coast and he implied that the inland expansion of agricultural development would be difficult in view of the poor means of overland communication.[212] In 1793 the inhabitants in the northern part of the island complained that the paths from St. Joseph to Port of Spain were only meant for animals and not carts and that with the recent development of agriculture they were scarcely sufficient to handle one tenth of what was harvested. So they petitioned the Crown for a loan of 4000 *pesos* for the construction of a suitable road, which was granted in 1797.[213] The port itself was also poorly developed but with the expansion of trade a wharf was constructed in 1791.[214] By 1794, however, there was still no customs house and a lot of revenue was lost because transactions were made in private houses.[215] The efficiency of trading was also decreased by the insufficiency of vessels. In 1784 Chacón estimated that once the island had been developed it would require 742 ships of 500 tons to transport its products.[216] Although many small craft were foreign ships registered under the concession granted in the *Cédula* for the Population of Trinidad,[217] in the first six months of 1790 only 107 vessels left for foreign colonies and 116 for other parts of the New World, many of which were small boats and canoes.[218] In 1794 Chacón complained that one quarter of that year's harvest remained in warehouses where it was wasting because there were not enough ships to export it.[219]

The indians

While attention was focused on the social and economic changes brought about by foreign immigration, in the background Trinidad's native population continued its silent decline. Between 1777 and 1797 the indian population was nearly halved, from 1824 to 1082,[220] excluding a small number of indians who were still living in the forests outside Spanish control.[221] Part of the decline in the indian population may be attributed to increased miscegenation resulting from the establishment of colonists inland, and the high death rate and low birth rate. Diseases, notably smallpox and measles, maintained the death rate at a high level, although the effects of smallpox were reduced by inoculation at the end of the century.[222] The onerous work meted out to the indians by the *corregidores* and *capitanes* directly contributed to the high death rate and forced other indians to migrate.[223] Although the indians formed only a small proportion of the island's labour resources, they were in great demand and as they declined in number the work burden fell on those that remained. This had the effect of withdrawing indians from their own agricultural activities thereby causing them to suffer food shortages,[224] which, combined with their absence from their villages, contributed to the decline in the birth rate.[225]

The slowly declining population of the villages that were formerly *encomiendas* and missions (see Table XXI) persuaded Governor Chacón that it would be beneficial for the indian communities to be amalgamated. The villages of Tacarigua, Arauca and Cuara, which in 1783 possessed collectively 632 inhabitants, were to be aggregated at Arima, and the inhabitants of Savanna Grande, Savaneta and Guayria moved to Montserrate. Each new village was to be assigned four leagues of land. The clergy's house and prison were to be communally built while private houses were to be the responsibility of individuals. In the case of Arima the settlement was to be located on one bank of the river Arauca and the cultivation plots on the opposite bank, but at Montserrate lands granted were to be over 400 paces from the centre of the settlement.[226] In 1785 Chacón reported that the indians of Tacarigua, Arauca and Cuara had been moved to Arima, and that 16 indians who had been living in the "pueblo de Mendoza" near St. Joseph had also been taken there.[227] The village was laid out in the traditional manner around a large square with the church of Santa Rosa de Arima located on one side and the indian houses along the other sides.[228] By 1794 houses had been built but the population had declined from 626 in 1786 to 411 in 1794.[229] It is likely that much of the decline in the population can be accounted for by the uncertainty of food supplies and migration in the early years of foundation. Although Europeans were originally forbidden to take up residence in indian villages, when Arima was founded it was thought that a number of Spanish settlers would be a good example to the indians and in 1798 there were six non-indian families living in the village.[230] The relaxation of the policy of residential segregation must have encouraged miscegenation.

The amalgamation of the mission villages was never formally effected, but a degree of natural integration occurred. Guayria ceased to exist

TABLE XXI

Total populations of indian villages under Spanish control

	1777	1778	Jan. 1784	Dec. 1784	1785		1797
Former *encomiendas*							
Arauca	290	306	280	281	248 ⎫		
Tacarigua	211	229	200	200	193 ⎬ Arima	495
Cuara	185	199	182	182	185 ⎭		
Former missions							
Savana Grande	292	281	247	248	230 ⎫		
Montserrate	169	171	102	97	91 ⎭		293
Savaneta	115	123	96	98	91		
Guayria	64	61	18	18			
Non-native villages							
Siparia	139	91	76	76			139
Toco	81	84	72	72	⎫		
Cumana	118	165	190	193	⎬		155
Salibia or Arrecifes	37		26	26	⎭		
Matura	28	30					
Pititru		44					

Sources: 1777 AGI CAR *150*
1778 AGI CAR *150*
Jan. 1784 AGI CAR *444*
Dec. 1784 AGI CAR *152*
1785 AGI CAR *733, 152*
1797 Mallet, *Descriptive account of the island of Trinidad*

after 1784 when its population was registered as 18, and by 1794 the indians from Savaneta had moved to Montserrate.[231] Although at that time Chacón considered that the difficulty of obtaining priests for both groups justified the amalgamation of the remaining two villages of Montserrate and Savanna Grande, they remained distinct. By 1797 their population had decreased to 293, less than half of their population in 1777.[232]

The population of the four non-native indian villages located on the north-east coast of the island showed a similar decline. From 1778 no inhabitants were recorded for Matura and the total population of Toco, Cumana and Salibia decreased from 291 in December 1784 to 155 in 1797. Of the non-native indian villages only Siparia succeeded in maintaining the same population in 1797 as it had done in 1777, despite its decline to 76 in 1784. It is possible that Siparia incorporated some of the losses of other indian villages, particularly when they were amalgamated. Nothing is known of the form of these villages during this period. In 1790 Chacón reported that he had granted lands on the east coast to a group of Caribs, who although originally inhabitants of Trinidad had resided some years in St. Vincent.[233] This was the only new indian village established during the period and of 13 villages that existed in 1777 only six remained 20 years later.

Political control of the indian population, which became spatially and socially isolated from the rest of the population, became easier as the number of indians declined and the remaining villages were amalgamated into larger units. The two *corregidores de indios*, one in Tacarigua, Arauca and Cuara and the other in Savanna Grande, Savaneta, Montserrate and Guayria, continued to function administratively and judicially throughout the late eighteenth century. They exercised almost exclusive control over indian labour, which they disposed of as they wished.[234] The life of the indians, it was reported, was "more miserable than slaves being forced to work the greater part of the year in the service of the same subjects entrusted with their protection and help".[235] The non-native indian villages possessed *capitanes pobladores* who performed similar functions to the *corregidores* including the distribution of indian labour, and who were similarly charged with overworking the indians.[236] The *capitanes* were originally instituted as government officials in the early 1770s.[237]

The spiritual welfare of the indians continued to be in the charge of the *curas doctrineros*. In 1777 there were three *curas doctrineros* in the island, one at Tacarigua, Arauca and Cuara, another at Savanna Grande and Montserrate, and another at Guayria and Savaneta.[238] By 1791 they were reduced to two, the villages of Guayria and Savaneta having disappeared. The non-native indian villages remained without spiritual guidance although they asked for a priest, and specifically a Capuchin father, who would instruct them in the faith.[239] The villages of the northeast coast, however, remained without a priest although a *cura* was placed in Siparia.[240] How far the secular and regular clergy succeeded in converting the indians is unknown. In 1788 an English observer believed that they were in "the same savage state as they were at the first settlement of the island".[241]

The social organisation in the indian villages was well defined, with the *corregidores* and *capitanes* in their official positions possessing the highest social status. The indians were regarded as "docile and lazy"[242] and in need of being treated as children.[243] The decline of the indian population probably increased the significance of the nuclear family instead of the extended family and hence confirmed the decline in the status of indian *caciques* whose position had been based on kinship ties. Women still played an important role in indian society, however. An English observer in 1803 described how the men spent most of their time "swinging in hammocks, which slavery of their wives enables them to do, as all the work is done by women, planting the bananas, getting shellfish from the rocks and cooking for their lazy husbands".[244]

The economic activities in those indian villages that were formerly *encomiendas* and missions, and in those of indians who had recently arrived from the Tierra Firme and settled on the north-east coast, were integrated when the indian villages were amalgamated and the form of land tenure and cultivation was regularised. Outside Spanish control a small number of indians continued to subsist on *conuco* agriculture, but by this time they were numerically insignificant, and their economy therefore does not warrant separate discussion.

When the Intendancy of Venezuela was established in 1776, the Intendant was instructed to ensure that each indian head of family possessed a plot of land according to the size of his family and that it was maintained in cultivation. The land was to pass from father to son and uncultivated land was to revert to the community for reapportionment.[245] In 1777 Governor Fálquez inspected the 12 villages[246] to ensure that the indians possessed sufficient lands and again in 1783 Chacón stipulated that every indian over 16 years of age should have three *fanegas* of land (22 acres), which would be sufficient to supply the needs of a family of six. In addition they were to cultivate communally two plots of land, one in "plantains, maize, manioc, beans and rice" and another in cotton, for the needs of the community, with any surplus being sold by the *corregidor* for the benefit of the village.[247] Most of the indian villages failed to cultivate effectively the extensive lands they had been assigned in the late sixteenth century because of the decline in their populations,[248] and to make the lands available to colonists the indians from Tacarigua, Arauca and Cuara were moved to Arima in

1785. In compensation for the lands they had lost, they received 320 *fanegas* (2368 acres) on the banks of the river Arauca, but, because the lands were less fertile than those they had possessed previously, they received compensation in the form of a sum of money which was placed in the community chest.[249]

Indians in the villages under Spanish control were still eligible for hire, but the *mita* as a system of regularised labour appears to have disintegrated, leaving the *corregidores* to dispose of indian labour as they wished. As already indicated, the work was often so onerous as to cause the indians to flee and to render them unable to cultivate their own land to support their own families.

The most important crops grown by the indians on their *labranzas* and on community plots were plantains, manioc and maize.[250] Plots of commercial crops, particularly cacao and cotton, were also grown but they probably made only a minor contribution to the economy.[251] Governor Chacón hoped to promote the spread of pastoralism and in 1783 he suggested that each head of an indian family should be given at least one cow.[252] In view of the general lack of livestock in the island it is unlikely that such a distribution was ever effected. Smaller domesticated animals such as chickens and pigs were kept, but no larger domesticates were present in the indian villages in 1802. The indians probably obtained most of their protein by hunting because apart from the non-native indian villages located on the north-east coast they were poorly situated for the exploitation of marine resources. The indians on the north-east coast effectively exploited the aquatic environment, to such a degree that in the 1780s it was reported that they had completely exhausted the resources of the rivers near Cumana.

The indian villages that came under the control of the Spanish were intended to be largely self-sufficient in food, relying on surpluses they stored in granaries in times of shortage.[253] Since the European population no longer depended on the indians for food, trade was probably limited. Certain European goods such as wine, oil, clothes and tools would have been obtained in exchange for the small quantities of commercial crops produced by the indians. The opportunities for trade with foreigners were probably also diminished by the inland location of most of the villages, though it is likely that those who lived on the north-east coast would have had more regular contacts, allowing foreigners to take turtles, coconuts and wood in return for European goods.

part six

Conclusion

11
The Culture-contact Process: Local and Imperial Perspectives

Culture contact is the means by which cultural forms are introduced to a culture or produced within it under the stimulus of contact. No two cultures can co-exist without contact and the tendency for one to dominate the other, and the nature and consequences of culture contact are largely dependent on the dominant role played by one of them. Sahlins and Service have proposed the Law of Cultural Dominance, to predict which culture will dominate in a culture-contact situation. The Law states: "that cultural system which most effectively exploits the energy resources of a given environment will tend to spread in that environment at the expense of less effective systems".[1] A culture's degree of organisational complexity may also be used as a criterion for determining which culture will come to dominate in a given environment, since it is indirectly related to its ability to exploit an environment effectively, in that it is related to population size,[2] which is dependent on the available food supply. No one culture, however, can be effective in all environments. A specialised culture by being highly adapted to a specific environment may be more effective in that environment than a more advanced culture and thus resist for a time the encroachment of the latter. The adaptive potential of a more advanced culture is high, however, and as it moves into and adapts to a new environment, it is likely that a new culture will emerge which will be more effective in that environment. Only in very difficult environments, where cultures are highly specialised, may less advanced cultures persist. The spread of a dominant culture generally involves pressure being exerted on the subordinate culture, because as a culture becomes more adapted to its environment it becomes less likely to engender internal changes in the form of innovations or adopt new techniques and ideas introduced by diffusion and culture contact. It is then said to have become stabilised and only those changes that do not threaten its basic adaptation will be accommodated. The tendency for cultures to become stabilised and resistant to change has been called the Principle of Stabilisation.[3] For more fundamental changes to be made some motivating force, either mental or physical, is required. In a culture-contact situation pressure to change exerted by the dominant culture often takes the form of military conquest, sometimes involving cultural extinction, and/or colonisation.

In Trinidad the Spanish encountered an aboriginal culture that lived in relative harmony with nature. This was reflected in the size of the population which, estimated at between 20 000 and 30 000, was high considering the available technology and the island's resources. The economy, which was based on shifting cultivation, fishing, hunting and the collection of wild vegetable products, effectively drew on the re-sources of the environment without over-exploiting them. The socio-political organisation was relatively simple and essentially egalitarian. The effective residence unit was the village, which was composed of a number of extended families integrated by kinship ties. Groups of villages were only held together by a loose military organisation in which military leaders possessed limited powers that enabled them to mobilise forces in the event of a Carib attack. The ideology focused on the regulation of natural phenomena: gods were undefined; there were no special religious centres or ceremonies; and the priesthood was not institutionalised.

Aboriginal culture appears to have existed in this form without major change for over 1500 years and its resistance to change was most clearly demonstrated by the opposition of the indians to both Carib and Spanish settlement in the island. In Trinidad Spanish pressure on indian culture was exerted in two ways: first, by military conquest establishing military control of the island, and second, by colonisation involving the introduction of institutions to control the native population and change its culture.

The resistance of the indians to the Spanish occupation of the island was strong and despite the fact that considerable military effort was expended in attempting to settle the island, in order to use it as a base from which expeditions in search of El Dorado could be mounted, it took the Spanish nearly 100 years to obtain a secure military foothold. This was eventually achieved as an indirect result of the "demographic disaster" that profoundly modified the indians' way of life and weakened their resistance.

Military control of the island brought about the incorporation of Trinidad into the Spanish Empire and established a base from which colonisation could proceed and the indian population be integrated into Spanish society. The Crown, however, was anxious to protect the indians from abuse. It therefore chose the path of segregation rather than of integration and established institutions, such as the *encomienda* and the mission, which theoretically brought the indians under the care and influence of politically and spiritually reliable Spaniards. The protection of the indians was not, however, the only aim of the Crown with respect to the native population of the New World; indian populations were also required as sources of labour for the economic development of the Empire. It was as a result of labour service that indians and Spaniards came into sustained contact. Throughout the Spanish Empire each indian village was obliged, under the *mita*, to make available for hire at fixed wages a quota of its male population for work in public service. In addition, in Trinidad, as in other outlying parts of the Empire,[4] the inadequacy of indian agricultural production resulted in the substitution of tribute payment by labour services, which brought the indians into more constant contact with the Spanish in the towns and on the surrounding estates where they were ordered to work. Contact was less intense in the indian villages that were granted as *encomiendas*, since only a handful of Spaniards ever visited them. They thus remained distinct socio-economic units, although they were under the effective control of the Spanish and were forced to modify their way of life to meet Spanish requirements.

In the indian villages that were granted as *encomiendas* the Spanish assumed the political power of the indian leaders, who became instruments of the Spanish administration, collecting tribute and organising labour services. The native social organisation broke down with the decline in the indian population and, under Spanish pressure, the nuclear family began to replace the extended family as the basic social unit. As a direct result of Spanish demands for tribute and labour services, the indians began to concentrate more on the cultivation of seed crops, particularly maize, and their inputs into the exploitation of wild food resources declined. The total effect was a decline in the population of the indian villages granted as *encomiendas*. By the middle of the seventeenth century the indians had adjusted their way of life to meet Spanish demands and the population began to increase, despite losses through miscegenation that resulted in the emergence of mixed races in St. Joseph and Port of Spain. It was only at the end of the eighteenth century, when attitudes to racial mixing became more liberal and large numbers of immigrants of diverse racial backgrounds arrived in the island, that the indian fertility rate was outpaced by miscegenation and the number of indians of the former *encomiendas*, by then grouped at Arima, continued the decline that had been arrested for 100 years. The *encomienda*, therefore, having survived the dramatic cultural changes that occurred in the early years of colonisation, did ensure the survival of distinct indian villages until the end of the eighteenth century to a greater degree than other institutions that were introduced, even though in Trinidad it resulted in the more rapid assimilation of the indians than in other parts of the Empire. It is worth noting that the sole remaining descendants of the indian population in Trinidad today live in Arima. The cultural changes experienced by the indian villages that were granted as *encomiendas* are summarised in Fig. 15.

In Trinidad a large proportion of the indian population did not come into contact with non-indians until the end of the seventeenth century, when Capuchin missionaries establised missions in the southern part of the island. Although it was the Crown's intention that the missions should prepare the indians to take their place in Spanish society, in practice they formed spatially isolated independent communities, preventing the indians in their charge from coming into contact with other members of society; in Trinidad this extended to prohibiting their employment under the *mita*. Although the missionaries regulated all indian activities they did not profoundly modify their culture but merely added a cultural overlay, which was even more limited in Trinidad than elsewhere in the Empire, owing to the small number of missionaries involved and the short life of the missions. As a result, when the missionaries were expelled and the Spanish authorities failed to provide similarly effective administration, the mission villages began to disintegrate. Throughout the eighteenth century the population of the former missions declined initially as a result of disease and desertions, and later because of the racial mixing, which occurred more commonly as the colonisation of the southern and western parts of the island by foreign

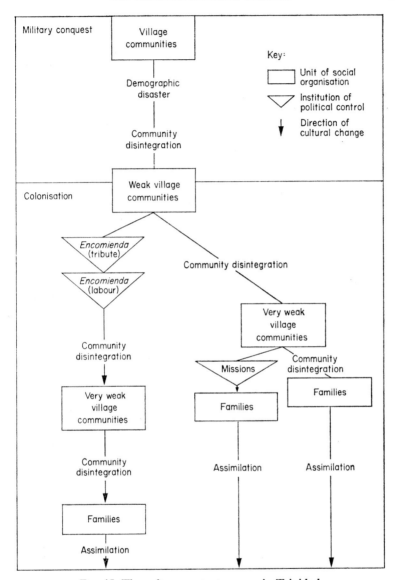

FIG. 15. The culture-contact process in Trinidad.

immigrants proceeded. Nevertheless, the existence of the missions had helped to retard the racial and cultural assimilation of a section of the indian population, with the result that two of the former missions still remained as indian villages at the end of the Spanish period.

The indians who remained outside Spanish control never recovered from the demographic disaster of the sixteenth century, which undermined the social organisation of villages and put strains on the economy at the same time that their area of economic activity became more limited. As the population continued its decline and Spanish control penetrated the island, individuals and small groups of indians were more easily drawn from their weakly integrated villages into Spanish-controlled communities, with or without being racially assimilated. This process was accelerated at the end of the eighteenth century when estates were carved out of the forest the indians inhabited, and the indians were employed on them as workers. Although at the end of the Spanish period no indians were recorded in the census as living outside Spanish-controlled communities, probably a small number still existed in the interior forest areas.

The fate of various indian groups within the island varied with the nature and intensity of contact, which was a function of the type of institution introduced to control the indian population, and with the viability of the indian culture itself. At the end of the Spanish period indian survival was greatest in the villages that had been granted as *encomiendas* followed by those that had formerly been missions. The Crown policy of racial segregation did encourage the survival of the indian population in that it minimised its contact with other racial groups. Even where the *encomienda* operated imperfectly and brought the indians into greater contact with non-indians than the Crown desired, the residential segregation of indians in distinct villages appears to have encouraged their survival. It might be supposed that indian survival would be greater in the missions, which were spatially and culturally more isolated than the villages that were granted as *encomiendas*. However, although the integrity of indian culture was preserved during the period when the missions existed, the viability of the missions depended on the presence of missionaries, who closely supervised all aspects of indian life. When the missionaries were expelled the indians found it difficult to adapt themselves to an independent existence. This was made more difficult by the fact that the missionaries had not managed to integrate the remnants of the disintegrated indian communities they had gathered together, but had substituted for them; indian dependence on the missionaries was encouraged at the expense of community integration. As a result, when the missionaries left, the missions disintegrated and individual families were rapidly assimilated into other more viable communities.

It may be argued that in general the *encomienda* as an institution had a greater chance of success with respect to ensuring indian survival than the mission, because it was introduced to areas where more highly developed cultures existed, whereas the mission operated in areas where indian culture was less well developed. The significance of the level of cultural development of native indian groups for an understanding of the culture-contact process has been indicated by Steward.[5] He suggests that the chance of indian survival was greater where their cultures were more highly developed because cultural institutions may act as a barrier to acculturation; in the highland states of the Andes and Middle America, the Spanish could control the indian population by modifying the indigenous state institutions that already existed without directly affecting the indian communities and individual families. For the Spanish to control less highly organised indian communities changes had to be brought about in the indian communities themselves, and once their village organisation had been undermined, the assimilation of individual families was rapid. As Fig. 16 shows, variations in the speed of acculturation and hence of indian survival in different parts of the Empire may thus be seen to be partially dependent on the level of cultural development of the indian groups at the time of conquest. Equally, decreasing levels of cultural development may be regarded as a sequence through which indian groups pass before assimilation takes place at the family level and the acculturation process is complete. In Trinidad few organisational structures existed to act as barriers to acculturation which, although it was slowed down by the introduction of the *encomienda* and the mission, occurred quite rapidly. It occurred less rapidly in the villages that were granted as *encomiendas* because they were probably initially the most viable indian communities in Trinidad at the time of discovery; indeed this was the reason they were granted as *encomiendas*, alongside the fact that their community organisation persisted longer into the colonial period. The mission villages, (see Fig. 16), however, were created out of the remnants of disintegrated indian communities and when the community organisation imposed by the missionaries was removed, no institutional barrier existed to prevent the acculturation of individual families.

The Spanish conquest and colonisation of Trinidad profoundly modified not only its culture but also its ecology. During the pre-Columbian period the economic activities of the indians did not result in the over-exploitation of plant and animal resources. The indians

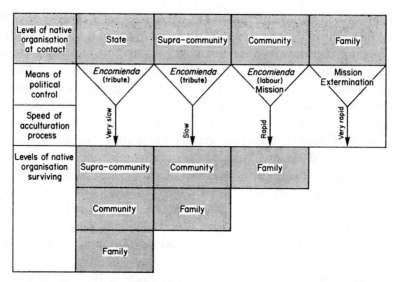

FIG. 16. The effect of the level of native organisation and means of political control on the culture-contact process.

practised a form of mixed-crop shifting cultivation which minimised demands on soil fertility, soil erosion, and vegetation degradation, because the variety of plants grown in the *conucos* simulated the structure and dynamics of the natural forest ecosystem.[6] Although indian land clearance for cultivation probably modified the structure and composition of the vegetation in many parts of the island, there are likely to have been only a few areas, such as the foothills of the Northern Range, where continued clearance and burning resulted in the establishment or increase in size of savannas. Similarly, there is no evidence that hunting and fishing resulted in faunal extinction.

During the sixteenth century the retreat of the indian population inland resulted in the clearance of areas of "virgin" forest, and a corresponding decline in the numbers of forest-loving animals such as the lape and nine-banded armadillo. The most profound modifications to the island's ecology probably occurred in the coastal areas, where visitors to the island selectively felled trees for boat building and reconstruction, and exploited wild food resources; both deer and turtles suffered a severe decline in numbers from which they never recovered.

Major changes in the natural environment occurred with the establishment of towns and estates in the foothills of the Northern Range, and later with the founding of missions in the southern part of the island, which all necessitated land clearance and the felling of trees for building purposes. The type of agriculture established on the estates involved the permanent destruction of the forest cover and the emphasis on a selection of nutrient-demanding crops increased demands on soil fertility and increased the susceptibility of the soil to erosion. Land clearance and accelerated hunting also resulted in some decline in animal populations, although this was in part compensated for by the introduction of domesticated animals from both the Old World and the New.

The most dramatic changes in the island's natural environment occurred at the end of the eighteenth century when, as a result of the granting of lands under the *Cédula* of 1783, particularly in the southern and central parts of Trinidad, large areas were permanently cleared of forest for the first time in the island's history. However, many estates were subsequently abandoned and revegetated by secondary forest so that in 1802 one observer estimated that only one hundredth of the island was cultivated.[7] Other observers acquainted with the lack of wild animals in the Antilles were enthusiastic about the island's wild faunal resources. An inhabitant in 1802 wrote, "the woods abound with game: wild hogs, deer, lapes, agoutis and armadillos".[8] Apart from turtles, which were heavily exploited throughout the colonial period, other marine resources remained virtually untapped and the island's rivers were said to swarm with fish.[9] Thus by the beginning of the British period the island's ecology had been substantially modified but, compared to other Caribbean islands, Trinidad was regarded as fertile and rich in natural resources.

The nature of Spanish colonisation and its impact on the culture and ecology of Trinidad was directly influenced by its location: not only was the island marginally located at the south-eastern corner of the Caribbean, but it was remote from the socio-economic centres of the Spanish Empire. It possessed no stores of precious metals or large groups of sedentary indians to attract would-be *conquistadores*; its most significant role in the Empire was in the early years of conquest and colonisation when it was sought after as a military base from which expeditions in search of El Dorado could be mounted. Little incentive existed in the island to encourage the Crown to invest financial and human resources there, and as these dwindled, the reality of Trinidad fell further behind the colonial vision.

Despite Trinidad's remoteness and comparative lack of resources the Spanish attempted to achieve the same goals by establishing the same institutions as in other parts of the Empire. They introduced into Trinidad a system of commercial agricultural production, the successful operation of which required adequate supplies of both labour and trading opportunities; unfortunately Trinidad lacked both. The shortage of labour in the island meant that production remained at a low level and as a result ships were discouraged from calling there. Also, the Spanish monopolistic trading system was unrealistic because Spain lacked the financial and human resources to support it throughout the Empire. This meant that contacts between Trinidad and the Peninsula were intermittent and the colonists were often left in great need of supplies and sometimes with their crops ruined. The success of contraband trading reflected the inadequacy of the Spanish trading system. Similarly the political organisation that the Spanish established in the New World operated imperfectly in Trinidad; as a result of insufficient personnel in Spain administrative posts in the island remained unfilled and because of the island's isolated position officials that were appointed acted with a considerable degree of independence. The work of the Church was hampered in a similar way. The hierarchy of social classes based on race that the Crown attempted to establish in all parts of the New World to aid the political control of the population was undermined in Trinidad by miscegenation. Thus in the early colonial period Spain failed to benefit from the island's resources or to maintain political control of its population. During the early seventeenth century Spanish control of the island was made possible by support from Spain in the form of immigration and trade, and by the breakdown of indian society. When the support from Spain failed, the colonists were forced to turn to the indians for vital supplies of food and during the early eighteenth century a symbiotic relationship developed between them, which the Spanish authorities were powerless to prevent.

The situation in Trinidad at that time was not unique in Spanish America. The desire of the Crown to revitalise its declining Empire involved the adoption of more flexible colonial policies that could be moulded to suit the requirements of different areas. Policies adopted for Trinidad involved the liberalisation of immigration and trade, within a framework of centralised adminstration. The centralisation of administration through the institution of the Intendancy and, in Trinidad the combination of the position of Intendant with that of Governor, increased administrative efficiency and brought the island under the more direct control of the Crown. The liberalisation of immigration and trade made possible the establishment of a productive commercial economy, even though it made heavy demands on the island's resources. While the rigid old colonial system had operated fairly well in the socio-economic centres of the Empire, the remoter colonies such as Trinidad flourished only with their new-found liberty.

appendices

appendices

Appendix 1
Selected references to names of indian groups in Trinidad

Primary sources, abbreviated in this Appendix and printed in small capitals, are given in full on pp. 314–319.

Araucas; Arawaques; Arawagoes; Aruacas; Arawacas CODIN 10 p. 49 1540, **21** p. 229 no date; Velasco, *Geografía y Descripción*, p. 136 1571–4; AGI SD **168–3–96** 1.3.1573; Harlow, *The Discoverie of Guiana* p. 12 1595; Purchas, *Hakluytus Posthumus*, vol. 16 p. 301 1602; AHNC **11–32** no. 6 f.20 1605; AGI SD **900–6–143** 16.8.1608; TTHS **137** Dec. 1637; Harlow, *Colonising expeditions*, p. 120 1645; Borde, *Historie de l'île de la Trinidad*, vol. 1 p. 38; Fraser, *History of Trinidad*, p. 1

Caribes; Caraibes; Carrebees AGI PAT **18–3–9** 1532; CODIN **21** p. 229 no date; de Laet, *L'histoire du Nouveau Monde*, p. 604 1640; Harlow, *Colonising expeditions*, p. 120 1645; Velasco, *Geografía y Descripción*, p. 136 1571–4; Borde, *Historie de lîle de la Trinidad*, vol. 1 p. 38

Carinepagotos Harlow, *The Discoverie of Guiana*, p. 12 1595; Purchas, *Hakluytus Posthumus*, vol. 16 p. 301 1602; de Laet, *L'histoire du Nouveau Monde*, p. 604 1640; Borde, *Histoire de l'île de la Trinidad*, vol. 1 p. 38; Fraser, *History of Trinidad*, p. 1

Chaguanes Borde, *Histoire de l'île de la Trinidad*, vol. 1 p. 38

Chaimas; Chaymas Borde, *Histoire de l'île de la Trinidad*, vol. 1 p. 38; Fraser, *History of Trinidad*, p. 1

Cumanagotos Borde, *Histoire de l'île de la Trinidad*, vol. 1 p. 38

Guaiquiri AGI PAT **18–6–9** 13.4.1554

Guayanes Espinosa, *Compendium and Description*, p. 75 1628–9

241

Iaio; Iaos; Jaios; Yaios   Harlow, *The Discoverie of Guiana*, p. 12
1595; Purchas, *Hakluytus Posthumus*, vol. 16 p. 301, 1602; de Laet,
L'histoire du Nouveau Monde, p. 604 1640; Borde, *Histoire de l'île de la
Trinidad*, vol. 1 p. 38

Mabouyes   Pelleprat, *Relato de las misiones*, p. 51 1655

Nepeios; Nepoios; Nepoys; Nepuyos; Nipuyos   AGI SD **168–3–96**
1.3.1573; Harlow, *The Discoverie of Guiana*, p. 12 1595; Purchas,
Hakluytus Posthumus, vol. 16, p. 301 1602; AHNC **11–32** no. 6 f. 20 1605;
AGI SD **900–6–143** 16.8.1608; Espinosa, *Compendium and Description*, p.
37 1628–9; de Laet, *L'Histoire de l'île de la Trinidad*, vol. 1 p. 38

Pariagotos   Borde, *Histoire de l'île de la Trinidad*, vol. 1 p. 38

Quaques   Borde, *Histoire de l'île de la Trinidad*, vol. 1 p. 38

Salives   Borde, *Histoire de l'île de la Trinidad*, vol. 1 p. 38

Salvages; Salvais; Salvaios; Sebays   Harlow, *The Discoverie of
Guiana*, p. 12 1595; Purchas, *Hakluytus Posthumus*, vol. 16 p. 301 1602;
de Laet, *L'histoire du Nouveau Monde*, p. 604 1640

Sapoyes = Nepuyos   Harlow, *Colonising expeditions*, p. 211 1645

Tamanacos; Tamanaques   Borde, *Histoire de l'île de la Trinidad*,
vol. 1 p. 38

Appendix 2
A list of mammalian species found in Trinidad

from: Allen and Chapman, "On a collection of mammals from the Island of Trinidad" and "On a second collection of mammals from the Island of Trinidad"; Allen, "Mammals of the West Indies"; Vesey-Fitzgerald, "Trinidad Mammals"; and Beebe, "Introduction to the ecology of the Arima valley".

Order **PRIMATES**
Family CEBIDAE
Alouatta seniculus   Red howler monkey
Cebus sp.   Capuchin monkey

Order **CHIROPTERA**
Family VESPERTILIONIDAE
Myotis nigricans
Thyroptera tricolor
Family EMBALLONURIDAE
Furipterus horrens
Molossus obscurus
Molossus rufus
Noctilio leporinus
Rhynchonycteris naso
Saccopteryx bilineata
Saccopteryx canina
Saccopteryx leptura
Family PHYLLOSTOMATIDAE
Anoura geoffroyii
Artibeus palmarum

Artibeus planirostris
Artibeus quadrivittatus
Chilonycteris parnelli
Chiroderma villosum
Choeronycteris intermedia
Desmodus rufus   Blood-sucking bat
Enchisthenes hartii
Glossophaga soricina
Hermiderma brevicaudum
Lonchorhina aurita
Mycronycteris megalotis
Phyllostomus hastatus
Pteronotus megalophylla
Sturnia lilium
Vampyrops caraccioli

Order **CARNIVORA**
Family FELIDAE
Felis pardalis   Ocelot, Tiger cat
Family MUSTELIDAE
Eira barbara   Tayra, Wood dog
Lutra sp.   Otter
Family PROCYONIDAE
Cercoleptes caudivolvus   Kinkajou
Procyon cancrivorous   Crab-eating raccoon
Family VIVERRIDAE
Herpestes auropunctatus   Mongoose

Order **RODENTIA**
Family DASYPROCTIDAE
Agouti paca   Lape
Dasyprocta aguti   Agouti
Family HETEROMYIDAE
Heteromys anomalus   Pouched rat
Family HISTRICIDAE
Coendu/Synetheres prehensilis   Prehensile porcupine
Family MURIDAE
Akodon urichi

Holochilus squamipes	
Mus musculus	House mouse
Nectomys squamipes	Bank rat
Oryzomys brevicaudatus	Rice rat
Oryzomys delicatus	Rice rat
Oryzomys speciosus	Rice rat
Oryzomys trinitatis	Rice rat
Oryzomys velutinus	Rice rat
Rhipidomys couessi	Arboreal rat
Rattus norvegicus	Brown rat
Rattus rattus	Black rat
Rattus rattus alexandrinus	Roof rat
Family OCTODONTIDAE	
Echimys armatus	Spiny rat
Proechimys guyannensis	Bristle rat
Family SCIURIDAE	
Sciurus aestuans hoffmani	Squirrel

Order **UNGULATA**
Family CERVIDAE
Mazama americana   Small brocket deer
Family DICOTYLIDAE
Tayassu pecari   White-lipped peccary
Tayassu tajacu   Collared peccary

Order **EDENTATA**
Family BRADYPODIDAE
Bradypus didactylus*   Two-toed sloth
Family DASYPODIDAE
Dasypus novemcinctus   Nine-banded armadillo
Family MYRMECOPHAGIDAE
Cyclopes didactylus   Silky ant eater
Tamandua longicaudata   Tamandua

Order **MARSUPIALIA**
Family DIDELPHIDAE
Didephis marsupialis   Large opossum

*Probably extinct in Trinidad.

Marmosa carri	Carr's mouse opossum
Marmosa chapmani	Mouse opossum
Philander trinitatis	Woolly opossum

Order **SIRENIA**
Family TRICHECHIDAE

| *Trichechus manatus* | Manatee |

Appendix 3
Plant Species

from: Grisebach, *Flora of the British West Indian Islands*; Prestoe, *Catalogue of plants*; Williams and Cheesman, *The Flora of Trinidad and Tobago*; Bailey, *Manual of Cultivated Plants*; Beard, "The natural vegetation of Trinidad"; Williams, *The Useful and Ornamental Plants*; Gooding, Loveless and Proctor, *Flora of Barbados*; Purseglove, *Tropical Crops*.

a. Systematic list of plants mentioned in the text

Family ACANTHACEAE

Justicia pectoralis Jacq.	Garden balsam
Ruellia tuberosa L.	Minnie root

Family AMARANTHACEAE

Amaranthus sp.	Amaranth

Family ANACARDIACEAE

Anacardium occidentale L.	Cashew
Mangifera indica L.	Mango
Spondias mombin L.	Hog plum

Family ANNONACEAE

Annona muricata L.	Soursop
Annona squamosa L.	Sweetsop

Family APOCYNACEAE

Thevetia peruviana (Pers.) K. Schum	Lucky nut

Family ARACEAE

Colocasia esculenta (L.) Schott	Taro, eddo, dasheen
Montrichardia arborescens (L.)Schott	Elephants' ear
Xanthosoma sp.	Tania, yautia, ocumo

Family BIGNONIACEAE

Crescentia cujete L.	Calabash gourd

Family BIXACEAE
Bixa orellana L.
Family BROMELIACEAE
Ananas comosus (L.) Merr.   Pineapple
Family BURSERACEAE
Bursera simaruba (L.) Sarg.   Naked Indian
Protium guianense (Aubl.) March   Incense
Family CACTACEAE
Acanthocereus pentagonus (L.) Britt. & Rose
Cephalocereus smithianus Britt. & Rose
Family CANNACEAE
Canna sp.
Family CARICACEAE
Carica papaya L.   Pawpaw
Family COMPOSITAE
Eupatorium odoratum L.   Christmas bush
Lactuca sativa L.   Lettuce
Family CONVOLVULACEAE
Ipomoea batatas (L.) Lam.   Sweet potato
Family CRUCIFERAE
Brassica sp.   Cabbage
Raphanus sativus L.   Radish
Family CUCURBITACEAE
Citrullus lanatus (Thunb.) Matsum. &
    Nakai   Water melon
Cucumis melo L.   Sweet melon, musk melon
Cucurbita maxima Duchesne ex. Lam.   Squash
Cucurbita moschata (Duchesne ex. Lam.)
    Duchesne ex. Poir.   Squash
Lagenaria siceraria (Molina) Standl.   Bottle gourd
Family CYCADACEAE
Zamia sp.   Zamia
Family CYPERACEAE
Cyperus giganteus Vahl   Mota grass
Family DILLENIACEAE
Curatella americana L.   Rough leaf, chaparo
Family DIOSCOREACEAE
Dioscorea alata L.   Yam

Dioscorea bulbifera L.	Yam
Dioscorea trifida L.	Yam

Family EUPHORBIACEAE

Hieronyma caribaea Urb.	Tapana
Hippomane mancinella L.	Manchineel
Jatropha curcas L.	Physic nut
Manihot esculenta Crantz	Manioc
Ricinus communis L.	Castor oil

Family GRAMINEAE

Gynerium sagittatum (Aubl.) Beauv. (syn. *Arundo saccharoides* (Humb. & Bonpl.) Poir.)	White roseau
Hordeum vulgare L.	Barley
Leptocoryphium lanatum H.B.K.	
Oryza sativa L.	Rice
Panicum maximum Jacq.	Guinea grass
Paspalum pulchellum H.B.K.	
Saccharum officinarum L.	Sugar cane
Sorghum vulgare Pers.	Sorghum
Triticum aestivum L.	Wheat
Zea mays L.	Maize

Family GUTTIFERAE

Clusia intertexta Britton	
Mammea americana L.	Mamey

Family LABIATAE

Ocimum sp.	Shiny bush

Family LAURACEAE

Cinnamomum zeylanicum Breyn.	Cinnamon
Persea americana Mill.	Avocado pear

Family LECYTHIDACEAE

Eschweilera subglandulosa (Steud.) Miers	Guatecare

Family LEGUMINOSAE

Arachis hypogaea L.	Peanut
Cajanus cajan (L.) Millsp.	Pigeon pea
Canavalia ensiformis (L.) DC.	Jack bean, Horse bean
Cassia fistula L.	Cassia fistula
Cicer arietinum L.	Chickpea
Copaifera officinalis L.	Balsam

Crudia glaberrima (Steud.) Macbride	Water locust
Dipteryx odorata (Aubl.) Willd.	Tonka bean
Erythrina micropteryx Poepp.	Immortelle
Haemotoxylon campechianum L.	Logwood
Hymenaea courbaril L.	Locust
Indigofera suffructicosa Mill.	
Indigofera tinctoria L.	Indigo
Lablab niger Medik.	Hyacinth, Bonavist bean
Lonchocarpus latifolius (Willd.) H.B.K.	Dogwood, Yellow savonette
Macherinam robinifolium (DC.) Vogel	Saltfishwood
Mora excelsa Benth.	Mora
Peltogyne porphyrocardia Griseb.	Purpleheart
Pentaclethra macroloba (Willd.) Kuntze	Bois mulatre
Phaseolus lunatus L.	Lima bean
Phaseolus vulgaris L.	Common bean
Piptadenia peregrina (L.) Benth.	Cohoba
Pithocellobium unguis-cati (L.) Mart.	Bread and cheese
Pterocarpus rohrii Vahl.	Bloodwood
Tamarindus indica L.	Tamarind
Vicia faba L.	Broad bean

Family LILIACEAE

Allium cepa L.	Onion
Allium sativum L.	Garlic
Aloe barbadensis Mill.	Barbados aloe

Family MALPIGHIACEAE

Byrsonima coriacea var. *spicata* (Cav.) Nied.	Locust berry
Byrsonima crassifolia (L.) H.B.K.	

Family MALVACEAE

Gossypium arboreum L.	Cotton
Gossypium barbadense L.	Cotton
Gossypium herbaceum L.	Cotton
Gossypium hirsutum L.	Cotton
Hibiscus esculentus L.	Okra or Lady's fingers
Pariti tiliaceum (L.) Juss.	Rope mangrove
Thespesia populnea (L.) Soland.	Seaside mahoe
Urena lobata L.	Cousin mahoe

Family MARANTACEAE

Calathea alluia Lindl.	Llerén or alluia

Maranta arundinacea L.	Arrowroot

Family MELIACEAE

Carapa guianensis Aubl.	Crappo
Cedrela mexicana M.J. Roem.	Cedar
Trichilia smithii C. DC.	Acurel

Family MORACEAE

Artocarpus communis J.R. & G. Forst.	Breadfruit
Artocarpus heterophyllus Lam.	Jack fruit
Brosimum alicastrum Sw.	Moussara
Chlorophora tinctoria (L.) Gaudich.	Fustic

Family MUSACEAE

Musa paradisiaca L.	Plantain, banana

Family MYRISTICACEAE

Myristica fragrans Houtt.	Nutmeg

Family MYRTACEAE

Psidium guajava L.	Guava

Family OLEACEAE

Olea europaea L.	Olive

Family ORCHIDACEAE

Vanilla planifolia Andr.	Vanilla

Family PALMAE

Acrocomia ierensis Bailey	Acrocomia palm
Bactris major Jacq.	Roseau
Cocos nucifera L.	Coconut
Elaeis guineensis Jacq.	Oil palm
Mauritia setigera Griseb. & Wendl.	Moriche palm
Maximiliana elegans Karst.	Cocorite
Phoenix dactylifera L.	Date palm
Roystonea oleracea (Jacq.) Cook	Palmiste or Cabbage palm
Sabal sp.	

Family PLANTAGINACEAE

Coffea arabica L.	Coffee

Family POLYGONACEAE

Coccoloba uvifera (L.) L.	Sea grape

Family PUNICACEAE

Punica granatum L.	Pomegranate

Family RHAMNACEAE

Gouania lupuloides (L.) Urb.	Chaw-stick

Family RHIZOPHORACEAE
Rhizophora mangle L.   Red mangrove

Family ROSACEAE
Chrysobalanus icaco L.   Fat pork, Coco plum
Hirtella racemosa Lam.   Coco chat
Licania biglandulosa Griseb.   Wild debasse
Licania ternatensis Hook. f.   Bois gris

Family RUBIACEAE
Genipa americana L.   Juniper

Family RUTACEAE
Citrus aurantifolia (Christm.) Swingle   Lime
Citrus aurantium L.   Sour orange
Citrus limon (L.) Burm. f.   Lemon
Citrus maxima (Burm.) Merr.   Shaddock
Citrus medica L.   Citron
Citrus paradisi Macf.   Grapefruit
Citrus sinensis (L.) Osbeck   Sweet orange

Family SAPINDACEAE
Paullinia pinnata L.   Supple jack
Sapindus saponaria L.   Soap-berry

Family SAPOTACEAE
Achras zapota L.   Sapodilla
Manilkara bidentata (A.DC.) A. Chev.   Balata

Family SOLANACEAE
Capsicum annuum L.   Annual pepper
Lycopersicon esculentum Mill.   Tomato
Nicotiana tabacum L.   Tobacco
Solanum melongena L.   Aubergine
Solanum tuberosum L.   English potato

Family STERCULIACEAE
Sterculia caribaea R. Br.   Mahoe
Theobroma cacao L.   Cacao

Family UMBELLIFERAE
Daucus carota L.   Carrot

Family VERBENACEAE
Cytharexylum sp.   Fiddlewood
Stachytarpheta jamaicensis (L.) Vahl   Verrani

Family VITACEAE
Vitis vinifera L.   Vine
Family ZINGIBERACEAE
Zingiber officinale Rosc.   Ginger
Family ZYGOPHYLLACEAE
Guaiacum officinale L.   Lignum-vitae

b. Index to common names of plants mentioned in the text

Cashew	*Anacardium occidentale* L.
Cassia	*Cassia fistula* L.
Castor oil	*Ricinis communis* L.
Cedar	*Cedrela mexicana* M.J. Roem.
Chawstick	*Gouania lupuloides* (L.) Urb.
Chick pea	*Cicer arietinum* L.
Christmas bush	*Eupatorium odoratum* L.
Cinnamon	*Cinnamomum zeylanicum* Breyn.
Citron	*Citrus medica* L.
Coco chat	*Hirtella racemosa* Lam.
Coco plum	*Chrysobalanus icaco* L.
Coconut	*Cocos nucifera* L.
Cocorite	*Maximiliana elegans* Karst.
Coffee	*Coffee arabica* L.
Cohoba	*Piptadenia peregrina* (L.) Benth.
Common bean	*Phaseolus vulgaris* L.
Cotton	*Gossypium arboreum* L.
Cotton	*Gossypium barbadense* L.
Cotton	*Gossypium herbaceum* L.
Cotton	*Gossypium hirsutum* L.
Cousin mahoe	*Urena lobata* L.
Crappo	*Carapa guianensis* Aubl.
Dasheen	*Colocasia esculenta* (L.) Schott
Date palm	*Phoenix dactylifera* L.
East Indian almond	*Terminalia catappa* L.
Eddo	*Colocasia esculenta* (L.) Schott
Egg plant	*Solanum melongena* L.
Elephant's ear	*Montrichardia arborescens* (L.) Schott
English potato	*Solanum tuberosum* L.
Fiddlewood	*Cytharexylum* spp. and *Vitex* spp.
Fustic	*Chlorophora tinctoria* (L.) Gaudich.
Garden balsam	*Justicia pectoralis* Jacq.
Garlic	*Allium sativum* L.
Ginger	*Zingiber officinale* Rosc.
Grapefruit	*Citrus paradisi* Macf.

Guatecare	*Eschweilera subglandulosa* (Steud.) Miers.
Guava	*Psidium guajava* L.
Guinea corn	*Sorghum vulgare* Pers.
Guinea grass	*Panicum maximum* Jacq.
Hog plum	*Spondias mombin* L.
Hyacinth bean	*Lablab niger* Medik
Immortelle	*Erythrina microteryx* Poepp.
Incense	*Protium guianense* (Aubl.) March
Indigo	*Indigofera tinctoria* L.
Jack bean	*Canavalia ensiformis* (L.) DC.
Jack fruit	*Artocarpus heterophyllus* Lam.
Juniper	*Genipa americana* L.
Lablab	*Lablab niger* Medik
Lady's fingers	*Hibiscus esculentus* L.
Lemon	*Citrus limon* (L.) Burm. f.
Lettuce	*Lactuca sativa* L.
Lignum-vitae	*Guaiacum officinale* Rosc.
Lima bean	*Phaseolus lunatus* L.
Lime	*Citrus aurantifolia* (Christm.) Swingle
Llerén	*Calathea alluia* Lindl.
Locust	*Hymenaea courbaril* L.
Locust berry	*Byrsonima coriacea* var. *spicata* (Cav) Nied
Logwood	*Haemotoxylon campehianum* L.
Lucky nut	*Thevetia peruviana* (Pers.) K. Schum
Mahoe	*Sterculia caribaea* R. Br.
Maize	*Zea mays* L.
Mamey	*Mammea americana* L.
Manchineel	*Hippomane mancinella* L.
Mango	*Mangifera indica* L.
Manioc	*Manihot esculenta* Crantz
Minnie root	*Ruellia tuberosa* L.
Mora	*Mora excelsa* Benth.
Moriche palm	*Mauritia setigera* Griseb. & Wendl.
Mota grass	*Cyperus giganteus* Vahl

Moussara	*Brosimum alicastrum* Sw.
Musk melon	*Cucumis melo* L.
Naked Indian	*Bursera simaruba* (L.) Sarg.
Nutmeg	*Myristica fragrans* Houtt.
Ocumo	*Xanthosoma* sp.
Oil palm	*Elaeis guineensis* Jacq.
Olive	*Olea europaea* L.
Onion	*Allium cepa* L.
Okra	*Hibiscus esculentus* L.
Palmiste	*Roystonea oleracea* (Jacq.) Cook
Pawpaw	*Carica papaya* L.
Peanut	*Arachis hypogaea* L.
Physic nut	*Jatropha curcas* L.
Pigeon pea	*Cajanus cajan* (L.) Millsp.
Pineapple	*Ananas comosus* (L.) Merr.
Plantain	*Musa paradisiaca* L.
Pomegranate	*Punica granatum* L.
Purpleheart	*Peltogyne porphyrocardia* Griseb.
Radish	*Raphanus sativus* I.
Rice	*Oryza sativa* L.
Rope mangrove	*Pariti tiliaceum* (L.) Juss.
Roseau	*Bactris major* Jacq.
Rough leaf	*Curatella americana* L.
Saltfishwood	*Machaerium robinifolium* (DC.) Vogel
Sapodilla	*Achras zapota* L.
Sea grape	*Coccoloba uvifera* (L.) L.
Seaside mahoe	*Thespesia populnea* (L.) Soland
Serrette	*Byrsonima coriacea* var. *spicata* (Cav.) Nied.
Shaddock	*Citrus maxima* (Burm.) Merr.
Shiny bush	*Ocimum* sp.
Soap berry	*Sapindus saponaria* L.
Sorghum	*Sorghum vulgare* Pers.
Sour orange	*Citrus aurantium* L.
Soursop	*Annona muricata* L.

Squash	*Cucurbita maxima* Duchesne ex Lam.
Squash	*Cucurbita moschata* (Duchesne ex Lam.) Duchesne ex Poir.
Sugar cane	*Saccharum officinarum* L.
Supple jack	*Paullina pinnata* L.
Sweet melon	*Cucumis melo* L.
Sweet orange	*Citrus sinensis* (L.) Osbeck
Sweet potato	*Ipomoea batatas* (L.) Lam.
Sweetsop	*Annona squamosa* L.
Tamarind	*Tamarindus indica* L.
Tania	*Xanthosoma* sp.
Tapana	*Hieronyma caribaea* Urb.
Taro	*Colocasia esculenta* (L.) Schott
Tobacco	*Nicotiana tabacum* L.
Tomato	*Lycopersicon esculentum* Mill.
Tonka bean	*Dipteryx odorata* (Aubl.) Willd.
Vanilla	*Vanilla planifolia* Andr.
Verrani	*Stachytarpheta jamaicensis* (L.) Vahl.
Water melon	*Colocynthis citrullus* (L.) Kuntze
West Indian cedar	*Cedrela mexicana* M.J. Roem
Wheat	*Triticum aestivum* L.
White roseau	*Gynerium sagittatum* (Aubl.) Beauv. (syn. *Arundo saccharoides* (Humb. & Bonpl.) Poir.)
Wild debasse	*Licania biglandulosa* Griseb.
Vine	*Vitis vinifera* L.
Yam	*Dioscorea alata* L.
Yam	*Dioscorea bulbifera* L.
Yam	*Dioscorea trifida* L.
Yautia	*Xanthosoma* sp.
Yellow savonette	*Lonchocarpus latifolius* (Willd.) H.B.K.
Zamia	*Zamia* sp.

Appendix 4
Sites of missions found in Trinidad

La Anuncíata de Nazaret de Savana Grande

This mission is generally considered to have been on the site of present-day Princes Town, which was formerly known as Savana Grande and whose position roughly corresponds with the site of the mission marked on eighteenth-century maps (AGI MP **185**, MNM Trinidad). Searching in Princes Town it was only possible to find indian pottery under the Roman Catholic church, sited on top of a bluff on the north-east side of the town, though its position is consistent with a description of the site given in 1687 and published in Armellada, *Por la Venezuela indígena*, p. 98.

La Purísima Concepción de María Santísima de Guayria

This mission was founded on "the mount which they call Naparima" (AGI SD **641** 14.3.1688) and is considered to be on the site of San Fernando, although two eighteenth-century maps place the mission farther north on the right bank of the river Guaracara, near Pointe-à-Pierre (AGI MP **185**). Its location was described as "on the skirt of a mountain, moderately chosen, whose eminence can serve as a viewpoint from which to guard the village overlooking from there a large part of the sea" (Armellada, *Por la Venezuela indígena*, p. 99). According to Bullbrook and Rouse, "On the excavation of a shell mound", p. 100, excavations at Point Bontour on Naparima Hill have so far only yielded indian and nineteenth-century artefacts but it is possible that the actual site was destroyed when the town was built.

Santa Ana de Savaneta

This mission was founded four leagues to the north-east of Guayria.
Borde in *Histoire de l'île de la Trinidad*, vol. 2, p. 43, indicates that it was
located on the left bank of the river Savaneta, a tributary of the river
Couva. An indian trial passes through the adjacent Rivulet valley and
it is possible that the mission was located on the watershed between the
two valleys near present-day Milton. A search in the area failed to un-
earth any evidence of a mission settlement but the land was highly
cultivated in sugar cane. The same place is indicated as the site of the
mission of Guayria by Crame, who locates the mission of Savaneta
slightly north of Cangrejos Point, north-east of Couva (AGI MP **185**
1777). The latter site coincides with a description of the mission about
1780, which says that "the mission of the indians of Savaneta is established in the valley of the river Floxo" (AHS SG **7326** *c.* 1780) but the
description may have been based on Crame's map. Crame clearly mis-
places the mission of Guayria and it seems likely that the site he indicates
for Guayria was in fact that of the mission of Savaneta.

Nuestra Señora de Montserrate

Reports of the location of the mission coincide to place it at Mayo. A
late eighteenth-century account says "passing from Pointe-à-Pierre and
from there to the River Guaracaro, the place of the indian mission of
Montserrate" (AHS SG **7236** *c.* 1780), which is consistent with Crame's
map of 1777 (AGI MP **185** 1777) and Rodríguez's map of 1785 (MNM
Trinidad). Since indian and Spanish artefacts have also been found in
Mayo under the Roman Catholic Church it is concluded that this was
the site of the mission.

San Francisco de los Arenales

Borde in *Historie de l'île de la Trinidad*, vol. 2, pp. 44–5, indicates that this
mission was founded "on the Arena river which flows into the river
Tumpuna, one of the tributaries of the Caroni, in a sandy area half-way
between this river and the Tamanaques mountain". San Rafael is

traditionally thought to be the site of the mission but no archaeological evidence has been found there, though this may be a reflection of the short duration of the mission. Descriptions of the site, however, would seem to suggest a location farther south along the Arena river, but no direct evidence could be found there.

San Francisco de Careiro

The site of this mission was described as "eight days by sea passing the punta del gallo and that of la galera" (AGI SD **179–3–102** 16.8.1693) which seems to suggest that it was on the east coast. It seems likely that it was located at Guayaguayare since Caulín in *Historia corográfica*, p. 83, equates the name Careiro with it. The short duration of the mission would explain the lack of artefacts found there.

San Joseph de Mayaro

The name of the mission suggests that it was located at Mayaro Bay, possibly at St. Joseph. Indian artefacts have been found all along the coast, though there is no direct evidence of the mission.

Los Santos Reyes de Mucurapo

Founded in 1749, this mission was of short duration (BNM **3851** 1780) and nothing is known of its actual site.

Santa Rosa de Arima

The indians from Tacarigua and Arauca were moved to Arima in 1789 and it is considered that the site of the mission was where the Roman Catholic school of Arima is now located, and where indian and nine-teenth-century artefacts have been found. See Bullbrook and Rouse, "On the excavation of a shell mound", p. 99.

Appendix 5
Non-native indian settlement sites in Trinidad

Toco

This settlement of Chaima indians was probably located within the village presently known as Toco. Its actual site is unknown although some indian potsherds have been found on a hill slightly to the east of the Catholic Church. See Bullbrook and Rouse, "On the excavation of a shell mound", p. 108.

Arrecifes or Salibia

All late eighteenth-century maps except that of Capt. Mallet place Salibia and Arrecifes slightly east of Toco. Since the names are not found together either in documents or on maps, and since one account mentions that Salibia was located in "the river Arrecife" (AHS SG **7236** *c.* 1780) it is assumed that both names refer to the same place. The actual site of the village is unknown.

Punta de Cumana

Although located in the vicinity of present day Cumana Point and Bay, according to late eighteenth-century maps, its actual site varies. Mallet's map places Cumana at present day Redhead, at the southern end of Cumana Bay near Tompire Bay, whilst Rodríguez's map of 1785 places it at Cumana Point and that of Crame just south of it in Cumana Bay (MNM Trinidad 1785, AGI MP **185** 1777). Some indian artefacts have been found on high ground backing the beach at Cumana but it is not known whether this was the site of the former indian village.

Matura

Matura was said to be located "$\frac{3}{4}$ of a league from the sea" (AGI CAR **150** 1.7.1760), probably just south of Matura point, at present-day Matura. So far no evidence of it has been found in that village.

Siparia

This settlement of Arawak indians was located in the village of Siparia. Since considerable numbers of indian potsherds have been found together with nineteenth-century artefacts under the Catholic church in that village it is assumed that it was the site of the Arawak settlement.

Pititru

Nothing is known of this indian settlement apart from its population in 1778. It is possible that Pititru is yet another name for Arrecifes because the latter is not included in the 1778 census although it is known to have existed at that time and is recorded consistently in the late eighteenth-century documents.

Notes

Chapter 1, pages 3–9

1. Lists of aboriginal and Spanish place names appear in Thompson, "Pre-British place-names".
2. Naipaul, *The Loss of El Dorado*, p. 318.
3. Social Science Research Council, "Acculturation", p. 974.
4. Comment in Beals, "Acculturation", p. 628.
5. Foster, "Culture and Conquest". Foster concurs with Drucker who in the "The native brotherhoods" p. 4 defines culture contact as, "The processes and results of situations of diffusion of culture in which materials and concepts are transmitted from one culture to another, when some degree of compulsion towards acceptance is exerted by the contributing culture on the recipient one".
6. Fortes, "Culture contact as a dynamic process", p. 53.
7. Hunter, "Methods of study of culture contact"; Mair, "The village census in the study of culture contact".
8. Social Science Research Council, "Acculturation", p. 973.
9. For example, Watson, "Cayuá culture change"; Drucker, "The native brotherhoods"; Spicer, *Cycles of Conquest*.
10. Albrecht, "Indian–French relations at Natchez"; Service, *Spanish–Guarani Relations in Early Colonial Paraguay*; and Geertz, *Agricultural Involution*.
11. Miranda, "Importancia de los cambios experimentados por los pueblos indígenas", p. 147.
12. Eggan, "Some aspects of culture change in the Northern Philippines".
13. La Farge, "Maya Ethnology"; Kubler, "The Quechua"; Service, *Spanish–Guarani relations*.
14. Elkin, "Reaction and interaction"; and Murphy and Steward, "Tappers and Trappers". The methodology employed in the latter study has also been used by Gould, Fowler and Fowler in "Diggers and Doggers".
15. Service, "Indian–European relations".
16. Social Science Research Council, "Acculturation", p. 975–79.
17. For example, La Farge, "Maya Ethnology"; Kubler, "The Quechua"; Rowe, "Inca culture"; and Gibson, *The Aztecs*.

18. Service, *Spanish–Guaraní relations*.

19. Bullbrook, "The Aborgines of Trinidad", *The Ierian Race*, Letter to W. Fred Taylor, "The Aboriginal Remains", and "The aborigines of Trinidad"; Bullbrook and Rouse, "On the excavation of a shell mound"; Rouse, "Prehistory of Trinidad", "The West Indies", "Pre-historic culture contact", "The entry of man", and Final Technical Report, Radio-carbon dates; Wing, Succession of Mammalian Faunas, and "Aboriginal fishing".

20. Las Casas, *Historia de las Indias, Tratados*; Castellanos, *Elegías de varones ilustres*; Enciso, *Descripción de las Indias Occidentales*; Velasco, *Geografía y Descripción*; Aguado *Recopilación Historial*.

21. Díaz de la Calle, *Memorial y Noticias Sacras*; Simón, *Noticias Historiales*; Espinosa, *Compendium and Description*; Linage, *Norte de la Contratación*; Caulín, *Historia corográfica*; Alcedo, *Diccionario geográfico-histórico*.

22. Harlow, *The Discoverie of Guiana*; Warner, *The voyage of Sir Robert Dudley*.

23. de Laet, *L'histoire du Nouveau Monde*; Raynal, *A philosophical and political history*.

24. Joseph, *A History of Trinidad*; Borde, *Histoire de l'île de la Trinidad*.

25. Fraser, *History of Trinidad*.

26. de Verteuil, *Trinidad*. Recent histories of Trinidad that cover the Spanish period include: Hollis, *A brief history of Trinidad under the Spanish Crown*; Carmichael, *A history of the West Indian islands of Trinidad and Tobago*; Williams, *History of the People of Trinidad and Tobago*; Naipaul, *The Loss of El Dorado*. Two articles by Morales Padron entitled, "Descubrimiento y Papel de Trinidad" and "Trinidad en el siglo XVII" are concerned with the early colonial period and are based on archival sources. Two books dealing with the change from Spanish to British rule are: Millette, *The Genesis of Crown Colony Government*; and Noel, *Trinidad, Provincia de Venezuela*.

Chapter 2, pages 13–19

1. Rouse and Cruxent, *Venezuelan Archaeology*, p. p.27.

2. Rouse and Cruxent, *Venezuelan Archaeology*, 34.

3. The terms Paleo-indian, Meso-indian, Neo-indian and Indo-Hispanic have been adopted by Rouse and Cruxent to identify four epochs in the indian occupation of the New World. The Paleo-indian epoch is identified by the presence of indian economies based on the hunting of large land animals. The Meso-indian epoch is characterised by the declining importance of hunting and the increasing significance of other means of subsistence, such as fishing and the gathering of wild food products. During the Neo-indian epoch agriculture replaces hunting, fishing, and gathering as the main means of subsistence. The Indo-Hispanic epoch is identified

by indian contact with the Spanish. For a more detailed definition of the above terms, see Rouse and Cruxent, *Venezuelan Archaeology*, pp. 1–3.

4. Cruxent and Rouse have recently suggested that the Paleo-indians were using rafts both for river crossings and for coastwise travel in very early times. See Cruxent and Rouse, "Early Man in the West Indies", p. 52.

5. Rouse, Final Technical Report.

6. Bullbrook and Rouse, "On the excavation of a shell mound", p. 108.

7. Rouse, radiocarbon dates from Trinidad. Cedros, the earliest known agricultural site in Trinidad, has yielded radiocarbon dates of 190 ± 70 BC and 100 AD ±80 but the actual arrival of the Neo-indians must have been some years earlier, indeed Olsen, in "On the trail of the Arawaks", p. 191, states that he would not be surprised if the earliest date for Cedros was pushed back to 400–500 BC.

8. Lathrap, *The Upper Amazon*, pp. 74–75.

9. The terms Saladoid and Barrancoid are derived from the pottery styles associated with the sites of Saladero and Barrancas. The home of Saladoid people in Venezuela has been the subject of controversy, Rouse (personal communication, 1970) favours the lower Orinoco, whereas Sanoja and Vargas at the Universidad Central Venezuela (personal communication, 1970) maintain that Saladoid pottery is difficult to find in the lower Orinoco, including the site of Saladero itself, but is well developed at sites on the coast of eastern Venezuela. Here Saladoid pottery seems to have reached its fullest development and acquired characteristic Antillean traits; indeed, according to Rouse and Cruxent, *Venezuelan Archaeology*, p. 284, the pottery found at El Mayal, in the Paria Peninsula, is almost identical to that at Cedros, Trinidad. An alternative explanation of the similarities of the two pottery styles has been proposed by Olsen in "On the trail of the Arawaks", p. 188. He suggests that Saladoid people migrated from Trinidad to the Paria Peninsula as a response to the movement of Barrancoid people to the island. It is not without significance that the latest date for the occupation of Cedros is 100 AD, which is precisely the same date as that for the earliest occupation of El Mayal.

10. For a fuller description of the succession of pottery styles found in Trinidad see Rouse, "Pre-history of Trinidad", p. 93–7, Rouse, "The West Indies", p. 310, and Bullbrook and Rouse, "On the excavation of a shell mound", pp. 94–98.

11. Rouse and Cruxent, *Venezuelan Archaeology*, p. 89.

12. Rouse, "Pre-history of Trinidad", p. 96.

13. Rouse and Cruxent, *Venezuelan Archaeology*, p. 127.

14. Bullbrook, "The aborigines of Trinidad", p. 34.

15. Rouse, personal communication 1970.

16. Rouse and Cruxent, *Venezuelan Archaeology*, pp. 15, 150.
17. Rouse, personal communication 1970.
18. Rouse, Final Technical Report; Rouse and Cruxent, *Venezuelan Archaeology*, p. 115; Rouse, "Prehistory of the West Indies", pp. 508–9.
19. Rouse, "The West Indies", p. 547.
20. Bullen, personal communication 1970.
21. Rouse and Cruxent, *Venezuelan Archaeology*, p. 150.
22. Lathrap, *The Upper Amazon*, p. 170.
23. Fewkes, "Prehistoric objects from a shell heap", p. 220; Bullbrook, "The aborigines of Trinidad", p. 72.
24. Bullen, personal communication 1970.
25. Bullbrook, "The Aborigines of Trinidad", p. 66, *The Ierian Race*, p. 40.
26. CODIN, **21** p. 229 no date; Velasco, *Geografía y Descripción*, p. 136 1571–1574.
27. Cortéz Sevilla, "Los indios caribes", p. 727.
28. Selected references to names of indian groups in Trinidad are given in Appendix 1.
29. ANHC **II–32** no. 6 f. 20 1605; TTHS **137** 1637.
30. AGI SD **900–6–143** 16.8.1608.
31. Harlow, *The Discoverie of Guiana*, p. 12.
32. Borde, *Histoire de l'île de la Trinidad*, Vol. 1 p. **41.**
33. Rouse, "The West Indies", p. 546.
34. AGI SD **168–3–96** 1.3.1573.
35. Espinosa, *Compendium and description*, p. 75.
36. Castellanos, *Elegías de varones ilustres*, vol. 1 p. 361.
37. Lovén, *Origins of the Tainan Culture*, p. 28.
38. CODIN **32** p. 90 15.6.15, **10** p. 308 23.12.1511.
39. Las Casas, *Historia de las Indias*, vol. 3 p. 185
40. CODIN **1** p. 380 1520.
41. AGI PAT **18–3–9** 1532.
42. See Appendix 1.
43. AGI PAT **18–3–9** 15.11.1532; ANHC **II–31** no. 16 12.10.1535; AGI SD **71–526** 15.1.1570; Warner, *The voyage of Sir Robert Dudley*, pp. 29, 70 1594–5; Hakluyt, *The Principal Navigations*, vol. 10 p. 4 1576; Harlow, *The Discoverie of Guiana*, pp. 118, 123 1595; D'Olwer, *Cronistas de las culturas precolumbinas*, p. 44 1500; Las Casas, *Tratados*, vol. 1 p. 125 1516.
44. Taylor and Rouse, "Linguistic and archaeological time depth", p. 114.
45. AGI CAR **971** 21.1.1612.
46. AGI PAT **18–6–9** 13.4.1554.
47. Simón, *Noticias Historiales*, vol. 2 p. 114.
48. Harlow, *Colonising expeditions*, p. 120 1645.
49. Rouse, personal communication 1970.

50. TTHS **166** 12.10.1535, Simón, *Noticias Historiales*, vol. 1 p. 153.
51. Coll y Toste, *Prehistoria de Puerto Rico*, p. 73.

Chapter 3, pages 20–67

1. D'Olwer, *Cronistas de las culturas precolumbinas*, p. 29.
2. TTHS **22** 1595.
3. For detailed descriptions of Trinidad's vegetation see Beard, "The natural vegetation of Trinidad", and Marshall, "The physiography and vegetation of Trinidad and Tobago". Beard classifies the vegetation of Trinidad into fifteen formations, eight of which he describes as "climatic" and seven "edaphic", although he states, "there is no valid or satisfactory distinction between these groups, they are arbitrary and made for convenience" (p. 36). The formations are distinguished on a physiognomic basis and within them floristic associations are identified. Whilst the physiognomic divisions are sound, he assumes that they are a reflection of climatic and edaphic conditions, the biotic influence being negligible. Whilst drier microclimatic conditions will affect the type of vegetation cover, the conditions themselves may reflect biotic interference. For this reason, in this study, the "climatic" and "edaphic" formation groups have been dropped and the vegetation types are distinguished on physiognomy alone. The main changes to Beard's classification concern coastal and lowland vegetation types, which have been amalgamated to form more extensive physiognomic units. These correspond more closely to Marshall's classification. The three montane formations have been amalgamated to form one vegetation type— montane forest.

	Formations identified by:	
Vegetation type	Marshall	Beard
Evergreen forest		Evergreen seasonal forest
Semi-evergreen forest	Tropical rain forest	Semi-evergreen seasonal forest
Deciduous forest		Deciduous forest
Montane forest	Montane forest	Lower montane forest Montane forest Elfin woodland
Littoral woodland	Beach forest	Littoral woodland
Mangrove swamp	Mangrove swamp	Mangrove woodland
Herbaceous swamp	Herbaceous swamp	Herbaceous swamp
Palm stands	Palm stands	Palm marsh, Palm swamp

| Vegetation type | Formations identified by: | |
	Marshall	Beard
Swamp forest	Freshwater swamp	Swamp forest, Marsh forest
Savanna	Savanna	Savanna

The most important zooarchaeological investigations in Trinidad have been carried out by Dr Elizabeth Wing at the University of Florida, Gainesville. The results of her investigations are to be found in her Ph.D. thesis—Succession of Mammalian Faunas on Trinidad, and an article entitled "Aboriginal fishing in the Windward Islands". The author is grateful to Dr Wing for further unpublished results of archaeological work carried out in the island.

4. For more detailed descriptions of the climate of Trinidad see Bain, *The rainfall of Trinidad*, and James, "The climate of Trinidad". The climate of the Caribbean is discussed in Twist, "Weather of the eastern Caribbean", and Kendrew, *Climates of the Continents*.

5. The major works discussing the geology of the island are: Kugler, *Trinidad, Handbook of South American Geology*; Liddle, *The geology of Venezuela and Trinidad*; Suter, *The general and economic geology of Trinidad*; Wall and Sawkins, *Report on the Geology of Trinidad*.

6. Columbus noted that, "all along the coast trees came down to the sea". Las Casas, *Historia de las Indias*, vol. 2 p. 9.

7. Beard, *The natural vegetation of Trinidad*, p. 86.

8. Beard, *The natural vegetation of Trinidad*, p. 93.

9. Beebe, "Introduction to the ecology of the Arima valley", p. 182; Vesey-Fitzgerald, "Trinidad mammals", p. 163.

10. Marshall, in discussing the occurrence of mora forest, concluded that the mora came to Trinidad in the late-Pleistocene to sub-Recent times from Guyana since when it invaded the crappo-guatecare forest already established there. Beard concurs with the opinion that mora is an invading species but maintains that, although a late arrival, it probably came to Trinidad before it was separated from the mainland in late-Pleistocene times. For a full discussion of the origin and presence of mora forest in Trinidad see Brooks, "Trinidad Mora"; Marshall, *The physiography and vegetation of Trinidad and Tobago*, pp. 31–32; Beard, *Ecological relationships*; and Beard, "The Mora Forests of Trinidad", pp. 188–9.

11. Carlozzi and Carlozzi, *Conservation and Caribbean Regional Progress*, p. 80.

12. Las Casas, *Historia de las Indias*, vol. 2 p. 13.

13. de Verteuil, *Trinidad*, p. 119.
14. Parsons, *The green turtle and man*, p. 36. In *The Turtle*, p. 151, Carr lists five species that visit Trinidad: hawksbill (*Eretomochelys* sp.); loggerhead (*Caretta* sp.); leatherback (*Dermochelys* sp.); green turtle (*Chelonia mydas*) and occasionally the African ridley (*Lepodochelys* sp.).
15. Warner, *The voyage of Sir Robert Dudley*, p. 71 1594–5.
16. Suter, *The general and economic geology of Trinidad*, p. 10.
17. TTHS **137** Dec. 1637.
18. de Verteuil, *Trinidad*, p. 94.
19. Velasco, *Geografía y Descripción*, p. 136 1571–4.
20. AGI PAT **18–6–9** 13.5.1554.
21. Beard, *The natural vegetation of Trinidad*, p. 149–151.
22. de Verteuil, *Trinidad* p. 461; Marshall, *The physiography and vegetation of Trinidad and Tobago*, p. 40; Cater, "Deforestation and soil erosion in Trinidad", p. 230–232; Beard, "Land Use Survey of Trinidad", p. 187; Beard, "The savanna vegetation", p. 206; and Alison, "A report on the needs for conservation", p. 6.
23. "open savanna land" was sought after by the Spanish as the site for St. Joseph. AGI PAT **26–33** 3.10.1592.
24. Liddle, *The geology of Venezuela and Trinidad*, p. 428.
25. Beard, *The natural vegetation of Trinidad*, p. 100.
26. For a review of estimates of aboriginal population in South America see Dobyns, "Estimating aboriginal American population", pp. 395–449.
27. Sauer, *The Early Spanish Main*, p. 65.
28. CODIN **21** p. 229 no date; Enciso, *Descripción de las Indias Occidentales*, p. 17; Castellanos, *Elegías de varones ilustres*, vol. 1 p. 361; Simón, *Noticias Historiales*, vol. 1 p. 149; Arellano Moreno, *Relaciones geográficas*, p. 45 27.10.1550.
29. ANHC **II–31** no. 15 15.9.1534.
30. Throughout this book Guyana refers to the region bounded by the Orinoco, Casiquiare, Negro, and Amazon rivers, which at present is politically divided into Venezuelan Guyana, Guyana, Surinam, French Guiana, and Brazilian Guyana. To avoid confusion the term Guiana is used to refer to the politically independent state of Guyana.
31. AGI SD **71–1–526** 15.1.1570.
32. BM ADD **36, 315** ff.122–5 24.11.1589.
33. AGI EC **1011A** 1.1.1593, 1595.
34. Sturtevant, "Taino Agriculture", p. 69.
35. Steward, "South American cultures", p. 677.
36. Carneiro, "Slash-and-burn cultivation", p. 47.
37. Las Casas, *Tratados*, vol. 1 p. 127.
38. Steward, "South American Cultures", pp. 676–677.

39. Rouse, "Settlement Patterns", p. 169.

40. Sauer, *The Early Spanish Main*, p. 65, 202–4. Sauer accepts Licenciado Zuazo's report to the Spanish Crown that at the time of conquest there had been 1 130 000 indians in Hispaniola. Given the area of Hispaniola the population density would have been 1470 per 100 km².

41. For the distribution of Neo-indian settlement sites see also Fig. 3.

42. AGI SD **180–3–134** 7.9.1633; Warner, *The voyage of Sir Robert Dudley*, p. 33; Morison, *Christopher Columbus*, p. 535; Las Casas, *Historia de las Indias*, vol. 2 p. 11.

43. AGI PAT **18–3–9** 15.11.1532.

44. Fonaroff, "Man and Malaria", p. 532.

45. Rouse, "Settlement Patterns", pp. 168–172.

46. Bullbrook and Rouse, "On the excavation of a shell mound", p. 105.

47. Wing, personal communication, 1970.

48. See p. 37.

49. See p. 47 and 50.

50. Bullbrook, "The aborigines of Trinidad" p. 11.

51. See p. 32.

52. Sauer, *The Early Spanish Main*, p. 63.

53. Fewkes, "Prehistoric objects", p. 200; de Booy, "Certain archaeological investigations", p. 486; Fewkes, "A prehistoric island culture", p. 77; Bullbrook, "The aborigines of Trinidad", p. 69; Rouse, "Pre-historic Caribbean culture contact", pp. 345–6; Bullbrook and Rouse, "On the excavation of a shell mound", p. 74; and Bullbrook, "The aborigines of Trinidad", p. 47.

54. Bullbrook and Rouse, "On the excavation of a shell mound", p. 46.

55. Arellano Moreno, *Relaciones geográficas*, p. 45, 27.10.1550.

56. Carneiro, "Slash-and-burn cultivation", p. 47. Since he does not specify the contribution made to the economy by collecting and trading, it is assumed that it was relatively insignificant.

57. Fewkes, "Prehistoric objects", p. 200; de Booy, "Certain archaeological investigations", p. 475; Bullbrook, "The aborigines of Trinidad", p. 69; Bullbrook, *The Ierian Race*, p. 9; Bullbrook and Rouse, "On the excavation of a shell mound", p. 23; and Bullbrook, "The Aborigines of Trinidad", p. 12.

58. See Table II.

59. RAHM CM **A/106 79** f.200–206, 28.1.1533; AGI CAR **971** 21.1.1612.

60. Conklin, *Hanunóo Agriculture*, p. 31.

61. AGI PAT **18–6–9** 1554.

62. Morison, *Christopher Columbus*, p. 533; Las Casas, *Historia de las Indias*, vol. 2 p. 9–10; D'Olwer, *Cronistas de las culturas precolumbinas*, p. 29.

63. Sauer, *Land and Life*, p. 175.

64. Carneiro, "Slash-and-burn cultivation", p. 48, 50.
65. Conklin, *Hanunóo Agriculture*, p. 34.
66. Sahlins, *Moala*, p. 54.
67. Parry, "Plantation and Provision Ground", p. 5; de Schlippe, *Shifting cultivation in Africa*, p. 66; Renvoize, *Manioc*, p. 18.
68. Spencer, "Shifting cultivation in southeastern Asia", p. 138.
69. Joyce, *Central American and West Indian Archaeology*, p. 226; Sauer, *Land and Life*, p. 189; Harris, "Plants, animals and man", p. 77.
70. Sauer, *The Early Spanish Main*, p. 51. Land was probably not completely cleared; large stumps of trees and vegetation debris would have remained on the surface when the crops were planted.
71. Sauer, *Land and Life*, p. 142.
72. Conklin, *Hanunóo Agriculture*, p. 150.
73. Richards, *The Tropical Rain Forest*, p. 378; Ramdial, *Shifting cultivation*, p. 3; Spencer, "Shifting cultivation in southeastern Asia", p. 39.
74. Carneiro, "Slash and Burn Agriculture", pp. 231–33.
75. Leeds, "Yaruro Incipient Tropical Forest Horticulture", p. 20.
76. Nye and Greenland, "The soil under shifting cultivation", p. 67; Harris, "The ecology of swidden cultivation".
77. Nye and Greenland, "The soil under shifting cultivation", pp. 70, 73; Watters, "The nature of shifting cultivation", pp. 81–2.
78. Harris, "The ecology of swidden cultivation".
79. Beard, *Ecological relationships*, p. 20.
80. Lovén, *Origins of the Tainan Culture*, pp. 354–6; Sturtevant, "Taino Agriculture", p. 73; Sauer, *The Early Spanish Main*, p. 51.
81. Sturtevant, "Taino Agriculture", p. 73.
82. Conklin, *Hanunóo Agriculture*, pp. 75–84; Sahlins, *Moala*, p. 54.
83. Sauer, *The Early Spanish Main*, p. 56. For a description of the cultivation of tobacco in Trinidad see Espinosa, *Compendium and Description*, pp. 56–7.
84. Sauer, *The Early Spanish Main*, pp. 56–9; Anderson, *Plants, man and life*, p. 137.
85. Clark and Haswell, *The economics of subsistence agriculture*, p. 37.
86. Conklin, *Hanunóo Agriculture*, p. 150.
87. Carneiro, "Slash-and-burn cultivation", p. 57; Harris, "The ecology of swidden cultivation".
88. For a list of cultivated plants and their harvesting periods see Williams and Williams, *The Useful and Ornamental Plants*.
89. Harris, "The ecology of swidden cultivation".
90. Espinosa, *Compendium and Description*, pp. 56–7.
91. Lathrap, "The 'Hunting' Economies", p. 27.
92. Harris, "Agricultural systems", p. 57.

93. The lack of land pressure in the Southern Range is indicated in an account of the island in 1554 which states that it would be possible to found a village of 200 people with agricultural lands without affecting the villages and lands of indians who were living there. AGI PAT **18–6–9** 13.4.1554.

94. Nye and Greenland, "The soil under shifting cultivation", pp. 73–126; Carneiro, "Slash-and-burn cultivation", pp. 55–7; Popenoe, "The pre-industrial cultivator", p. 70.

95. Carneiro, "Slash and Burn Agriculture", p. 233.

96. Harris, "Swidden systems and settlement".

97. Rogers, "Some botanical and ethnological considerations of *Manihot esculenta*, pp. 369–77.

98. See p. 37.

99. AGI SD **179–1–526** 15.1.1570; EC **1011** 1.1.1593; BM ADD **36, 315** f.264 *et seq.* 1595; Castellanos, *Elegías de varones ilustres*, vol. 1 p. 380; Arellano Moreno, *Relaciones geográficas*, p. 45 27.10.1550.

100. Sturtevant, "Taino agriculture", p. 70, quoting Las Casas and Benzoni; Sauer, *Early Spanish Main*, p. 53.

101. Parry, "Plantation and Provision Ground", p. 6; Sauer, *The Early Spanish Main*, p. 54.

102. AGI SD **179–1–526** 15.1.1570.

103. Sturtevant, "Taino Agriculture" p. 71, "The ethnography of some West Indian starches", pp. 184–9.

104. Friederichi, *Amerikanistiches Wörterbuch*, p. 662.

105. Espinosa, *Compendium and Description*, p. 85; Alvarado, "Glosario de voces indígenas", p. 184.

106. Joyce, *Central American and West Indian Archaeology*, p. 212; Lovén, *Origins of the Tainan Culture*, p. 368; Sauer, "Cultivated Plants", p. 511; Parry, "Plantation and Provision Ground", pp. 12–13.

107. Acosta, *Historia natural y moral*, p. 235; Joyce, *Central American and West Indian Archaeology*, p. 212; Heiser, "Cultivated plants", p. 938; Sauer, *The Early Spanish Main*, p. 54.

108. Joyce, *Central American and West Indian Archaeology*, p. 212; Sauer, *The Early Spanish Main*, p. 57.

109. Rouse, "The West Indies", p. 523.

110. Morison, *Christopher Columbus*, p. 544.

111. Rouse, "The West Indies", p. 523.

112. AGI SD **179–1–526** 15.1.1570, EC **1011** 1.1.1593; BM ADD **36, 317** f.385 Sep. 1595; Espinosa, *Compendium and Description*, p. 56; Simón *Noticias Historiales*, vol. 1, p. 152; Arellano Moreno, *Relaciones geográficas*, p. 45 27.10.1550.

113. Castellanos, *Elegías de varones ilustres*, vol. 1, p. 383.

114. Rouse and Cruxent, *Venezuelan Archaeology*, pp. 54, 143.
115. Meggers, "Environmental limitation on the development of culture", pp. 808–9.
116. Sauer, "Cultivated plants", p. 508
117. Harris, "The ecology of swidden cultivation".
118. Sauer, *The Early Spanish Main*, pp. 54–55.
119. Sturtevant, "The ethnography of some West Indian starches", p. 179.
120. Sauer, "Cultivated plants", pp. 504–6; *The Early Spanish Main*, p. 179.
121. Sturtevant, "The ethnography of some West Indian starches", p. 179.
122. Roumain, "Contribution a l'étude de l'ethnobotanique pré-columbienne", pp. 46–50, 68–70.
123. Warner, *The voyage of Sir Robert Dudley*, p. 70.
124. Harris, "Plants, animals, and man", p. 74.
125. Harris, "Plants, animals, and man", p. 74.
126. Espinosa, *Compendium and Description*, p. 56.
127. Hodge and Taylor, "The ethnobotany of the Island Caribs of Dominica", p. 520.
128. Purseglove, *Tropical Crops: Dicotyledons*, p. 647.
129. Roumain, "Contribution a l'étude de l'ethnobotanique pré-columbienne", pp. 27–9; Joyce, *Central American and West Indian Archaeology*, p. 236.
130. Castellanos, *Elegías de varones ilustres*, vol. 1, p. 390.
131. Espinosa, *Compendium and Description*, pp. 56–7.
132. Sauer, "Cultivated plants", p. 523.
133. Alvarado, *Datos etnográficos de Venezuela*, p. 186; Castellanos, *Elegías de varones ilustres*, vol. 1, p. 384.
134. Sauer, "Cultivated plants" pp. 533–5; Anderson, *Plants, man, and life*, p. 165.
135. D'Olwer, *Cronistas de las culturas precolumbinas*, p. 29; Las Casas, *Historia de las Indias*, vol. 2, p. 13; AGI PAT **18–3–9** 1532.
136. Merrill, "The Botany of Cook's Voyage", p. 279.
137. Sauer, "Cultivated plants", p. 527; Alexander, "The geography of Margarita", pp. 148–9.
138. Anderson, *Plants, man, and life*, p. 179.
139. Parry, "Plantation and Provision Ground", p. 10.
140. Watts, "Man's Influence on the Vegetation of Barbados", p. 50.
141. Patiño, *Plantas cultivadas y animales domesticos*, pp. 85–7.
142. Puente y Olea, *Los trabajos geográficos*, p. 400; Hendry, "The source literature for early plant introductions into Spanish America", p. 65; Mercadal, *Lo que España llevó a America*, pp. 71–2.
143. Merrill, "The Botany of Cook's voyage", p. 274.
144. AGI SD **179–1–526** 15.1.1570, EC **1011A** 1.1.1593.

145. AGI SD **179** 29.7.1616, 21.4.1617.
146. de Verteuil, *Trinidad*, p. 452.
147. Anglo-American Commission, *An experimental fishery survey*, p. 24.
148. de Verteuil, *Trinidad*, p. 451.
149. Bullbrook, "The aborigines of Trinidad", p. 20.
150. Bullbrook, *The Ierian Race*, p. 15; Castellanos, *Elegías de varones ilustres*, vol. 1 p. 391.
151. For a description of present-day fishing and partial check lists of fish found in Trinidad waters see de Verteuil, *Trinidad*, pp. 447–53; Brown, "The Sea Fisheries of Trinidad and Tobago"; Anglo-American Commission, *An experimental fishery survey*; Lowe, "The fishes of the British Guiana Continental Shelf"; Caldwell and Caldwell, "Fishes from the collection of the Southern Caribbean"; Wing, "Aboriginal fishing".
152. de Booy, "Certain archaeological investigations in Trinidad", pp. 474–5; Bullbrook, "The Aborigines of Trinidad", p. 67; Bullbrook and Rouse, "On the excavation of a shell mound", p. 23, 27.
153. Fewkes, "Prehistoric objects from a shell heap", p. 204; Bullbrook, "The Aboriginal Remains", p. 19; Espinet, "Life and Habits of the Arawak".
154. de Booy, "Certain archaeological investigations", p. 474; Bullbrook, "The Aborigines of Trinidad", p. 45. *Cyrena carolinensis* is equivalent to *Tivela mactroides* described by de Booy.
155. Fewkes, "Prehistoric objects from a shell heap", p. 209.
156. Brown, "The Sea Fisheries of Trinidad and Tobago", p. 19.
157. Parsons, *The green turtle and man*, p. 36. Huevo is the Spanish word for an egg.
158. de Verteuil, *Trinidad*, pp. 129, 447–53.
159. Méndez-Arocha, *La Pesca de Margarita*, p. 37.
160. Joyce, *Central American and West Indian Archaeology*, p. 215.
161. Rouse, "The entry of man" p. 11.
162. Bullbrook, "The aborigines of Trinidad", p. 69.
163. McKusick, "Aboriginal canoes", p. 9.
164. Bullbrook, "The aborigines of Trinidad", p. 20.
165. Wing, *Succession of Mammalian Faunas*, p. 47.
166. de Booy, "Certain archaeological investigations", p. 476.
167. Cárdenas, *Geografía física de Venezuela*, p. 243; Suárez, *Los Warao*, p. 81.
168. Bullbrook, "The Aborigines of Trinidad", p. 32.
169. Wing, *Succession of Mammalian Faunas*, p. 44.
170. AGI PAT **18–6–9** 13.5.1554.
171. Steward, "Causal factors and processes", p. 321.
172. Castellanos, *Elegías de varones ilustres*, vol. 1, p. 390. These would not have been tiger's claws since the tiger is not an inhabitant of the South

American sub-continent. They were probably from a puma (*Leo onca onca*) or possibly from a jaguar (*Felis concolor*).

173. Suárez, *Los Warao*, p. 81.
174. de Verteuil, *Trinidad*, pp. 419–20.
175. Beebe, "An introduction to the ecology of the Arima valley", p. 182.
176. Gilmore, "Fauna and Ethnozoology of South America", p. 383.
177. Bullbrook and Rouse, *Venezuelan Archaeology*, p. 84.
178. Harris, "Plants, animals, and man", p. 61.
179. Gilmore, "Fauna and Ethnozoology of South America", p. 371.
180. Fewkes, "Prehistoric objects from a shell heap", p. 209.
181. Gilmore, "Fauna and Ethnozoology of South America", p. 369.
182. Bullbrook and Rouse, *Venezuelan Archaeology*, p. 49.
183. Gilmore, "Fauna and Ethnozoology of South America", p. 376.
184. Beebe, "An introduction to the ecology of the Arima valley", p. 182.
185. Bullbrook, "The aborigines of Trinidad", p. 46.
186. TTHS **22** Sep. 1595.
187. Castellanos, *Elegías de varones ilustres*, vol. 1, pp. 383, 390.
188. Herklots, *The Birds of Trinidad and Tobago*, p. 70.
189. Wing, *Succession of Mammalian Faunas*, p. 42.
190. Roth, "An inquity into the animism and folklore of the Guiana indians", pp. 125, 138.
191. Zerries, "Primitive South America and the West Indies", p. 262.
192. Fewkes, "Prehistoric objects from a shell heap", p. 210.
193. Herklots, *The Birds of Trinidad and Tobago*, p. 4.
194. Harris, "Plants, animals, and man", p. 63.
195. de Verteuil, *Trinidad*, p. 119.
196. Gilmore, "Fauna and Ethnozoology of South America", p. 383.
197. de Verteuil, *Trinidad*, p. 126.
198. Gilmore, "Fauna and Ethnozoology of South America", pp. 373, 382, 406; Sauer, *The Early Spanish Main*, p. 244.
199. Bullbrook, "The aborigines of Trinidad", p. 20.
200. Bullbrook and Rouse, *Venezuelan Archaeology*, pp. 48, 52.
201. Coll y Toste, *Prehistoria de Puerto Rico*, p. 72; Bullbrook, "The Aborigines of Trinidad", p. 43; Rouse, "The West Indies", p. 546.
202. TTHS **166** 12.10.1535; Simón, *Noticias Historiales*, vol. 1, p. 153.
203. Bullbrook, "The aborigines of Trinidad", p. 21.
204. Gilmore, "Fauna and Ethnozoology of South America", pp. 364, 366, 369, 374, 404, 406; Sauer, *The Early Spanish Main*, p. 58.
205. Sauer, *The Early Spanish Main*, p. 273.
206. Sauer, *The Early Spanish Main*, p. 59.
207. Gilmore, "Fauna and Ethnozoology of South America", p. 460.
208. Harris, "Plants, animals, and man", p. 61.

209. Gilmore, "Fauna and Ethnozoology of South America", p. 389.
210. Gilmore, "Fauna and Ethnozoology of South America", p. 392.
211. AGI CAR **971** 21.1.1612.
212. Roumain, "Contribution a l'étude de l'ethnobotanique pré-colum-bienne", 51; Sturtevant, "The ethnography of some West Indian starches", pp. 190–2.
213. de Laet, *L'histoire du Nouveau Monde*, p. 605.
214. Roumain, "Contribution a l'étude de l'ethnobotanique pré-colum-bienne", pp. 52–3; Levi-Strauss, "The use of wild plants", p. 481.
215. Levi-Strauss, "The use of wild plants", p. 481; Pichardo Moya, *Los aborigenes de las Antilles*, p. 100; Sturtevant, "Taino Agriculture", p. 70.
216. Roumain, "Contribution a l'étude de l'ethnobotanique pré-colum-bienne", pp. 622–5; Levi-Strauss, "The use of wild plants", pp. 473–4; Williams and Williams, *The Useful and Ornamental Plants in Trinidad and Tobago*, pp. 11–12.
217. Sauer, *The Early Spanish Main*, p. 61.
218. Williams and Williams, *The Useful and Ornamental Plants in Trinidad and Tobago*, pp. 20–21.
219. Levi-Strauss, "The use of wild plants", p. 479; Williams and Williams, *The Useful and Ornamental Plants in Trinidad and Tobago*, p. 115.
220. Levi-Strauss, "The use of wild plants", p. 477.
221. Williams and Williams, *The Useful and Ornamental Plants in Trinidad and Tobago*, pp. 18–19.
222. Castellanos, *Elegías de varones ilustres*, vol. 1 p. 383; Friederichi, *Amerikanistiches Wörterbuch*, p. 452.
223. Williams and Williams, *The Useful and Ornamental Plants in Trinidad and Tobago*, p. 248.
224. Levi-Strauss, "The use of wild plants, p. 473.
225. Williams and Williams, *The Useful and Ornamental Plants in Trinidad and Tobago*, p. 176.
226. Bullbrook, *The Ierian Race*, p. 43, "The aborigines of Trinidad", p. 35.
227. Bullbrook, "The Aborigines of Trinidad", p. 70.
228. Bullbrook, "The Aborigines of Trinidad", p. 37.
229. Bullbrook, "The Aborigines of Trinidad", p. 22.
230. Bullbrook, "The Aborigines of Trinidad", p. 34, 39.
231. Bullbrook, *Letter to W. Fred Taylor*.
232. Bullbrook, "The Aborigines of Trinidad", p. 35.
233. Bullbrook and Rouse, *Venezuelan Archaeology*, p. 46.
234. Fewkes, "Prehistoric objects from a shell heap", pp. 201–2; Lovén, *Origins of the Tainan Culture*, p. 34.
235. Lovén, *Origins of the Tainan Culture*, pp. 36, 453.
236. McKusick, "Aboriginal canoes", p. 9.

237. Lovén, *Origins of the Tainan Culture*, pp. 37–8.
238. For species see p. 57.
239. Sauer, *The Early Spanish Main*, p. 60.
240. de Booy, "Certain archaeological investigations in Trinidad", p. 474.
241. D'Olwer, *Cronistas de culturas precolumbinas*, p. 29.
242. Pelleprat, *Relato de las misiones*, p. 76.
243. Bullbrook, *Letter to W. Fred Taylor*; Suárez, *Los Warao*, pp. 43–9.
244. Bullbrook and Rouse, *Venezuelan Archaeology*, p. 79.
245. Bullbrook and Rouse, *Venezuelan Archaeology*, p. 46; Bullbrook, "The Aborigines of Trinidad", p. 49.
246. Bullbrook and Rouse, *Venezuelan Archaeology*, p. 49.
247. Fewkes, "Prehistoric objects from a shell heap", p. 217.
248. Castellanos, *Elegías de varones ilustres*, vol. 1 pp. 383, 390.
249. Lovén, *Origins of the Tainan Culture*, pp. 344–5.
250. Sauer, *The Early Spanish Main*, p. 63; Joyce, *Central American and West Indian Archaeology*, pp. 219–224; Bullbrook, "The Aborigines of Trinidad", p. 69.
251. Sauer, *The Early Spanish Main*, p. 63.
252. de Verteuil, *Trinidad*, pp. 71–2.
253. BM ADD **36, 317** ff.61 *et seq.* 1596.
254. Bullbrook and Rouse, *Venezuelan Archaeology*, p. 109; Richardson, personal communication, 1970; Rouse, personal communication, 1970.
255. Richardson, personal communication, 1970.
256. Barr, personal communication, 1970.
257. Castellanos, *Elegías de varones illustres*, vol. 1 p. 382.
258. Bullbrook, "The Aboriginal Remains", p. 10–16.
259. TDD **3** 31.7.1817; Fewkes, "Prehistoric objects from a shell heap", p. 201.
260. Bullbrook, *Letter to W. Fred Taylor*, "The Aborigines of Trinidad", p. 32.
261. RAHM CM **A/107 80** 4.4.1535; Aguado, *Recopilación Historial de Venezuela*, p. 369.
262. Alexander, "The geography of Margarita", p. 116.
263. Bullbrook, *Letter to W. Fred Taylor*, and "The Aborigines of Trinidad", p. 27.
264. Rouse, personal communication, 1970.
265. Service, *Primitive Social Organisation*, p. 111; Fried, *The Evolution of Political Society*, pp. 66–9; Sanders and Price, *Mesoamerica*, p. 41.
266. Steward, *The theory of culture change*, p. 135.
267. Sauer, *The Early Spanish Main*, p. 63.
268. Steward, "South American Cultures", map 20 p. 684, 719.
269. Castellanos, *Elegías de varones ilustres*, vol. 1 p. 368.
270. Sahlins, *Moala*, p. 66.

271. White, *The Evolution of Culture*, pp. 153–4; Service, *Primitive Social Organisation*, p. 121.
272. Lovén, *Origins of the Tainan Culture*, p. 499.
273. Acosta Saignes, *Vida de los esclavos negros en Venezuela*, pp. 64–8.
274. Velasco, *Geografía y Descripción*, p. 153.
275. Lovén, *Origins of the Tainan Culture*, p. 504.
276. Borde, *Histoire de l'île de la Trinidad*, vol. 1 p. 301.
277. Purchas, *Hakluytus Posthumus*, vol. 16 p. 301.
278. Rouse, "The West Indies", p. 530.
279. Castellanos, *Elegías de varones ilustres*, vol. 1 p. 384.
280. Warner, *The voyage of Sir Robert Dudley*, p. 70.
281. Joyce, *Central American and West Indian Archaeology*, p. 198; Rouse, "The West Indies", p. 537–8.
282. Borde, *Histoire de l'île de la Trinidad*, vol. 1 p. 41.
283. Castellanos, *Elegías de varones ilustres*. vol. 1 p. 361.
284. Simón, *Noticias Historiales*, vol. 1 p. 153.
285. Taylor and Rouse, "Linguistic and Archaeological Time Depth in the West Indies", p. 114.
286. Newcomb, "Towards an understanding of war", p. 329; Vayda, 'Expansion and warfare amongst swidden agriculturalists", pp. 346–7; Fried, *The Evolution of Political Society*, p. 181.
287. Chagnon, "Yanomamö", p. 112.
288. ImThurn, *Among the indians of Guiana*, pp. 360-1.
289. Rouse, "The West Indies", p. 538.
290. Velasco, *Geografía y Descripción*, p. 153.
291. Bullbrook, "The Aborigines of Trinidad, p. 68; Bullbrook and Rouse, *Venezuelan Archaeology*, p. 79.
292. Lovén, *Origins of the Tainan Culture*, p. 563; Zerries, "Primitive South America and the West Indies", p. 250.
293. Rouse, "The West Indies", p. 535.
294. Bullbrook and Rouse, *Venezuelan Archaeology*, p. 111.
295. Hatt, "Had West Indian rock carvings a religious significance?", pp. 196–7.
296. Fewkes, "Prehistoric objects from a shell heap", pp. 210–2; de Booy, "Certain archaeological investigations", p. 478; Bullbrook and Rouse, *Venezuelan Archaeology*, pp. 34–40.
297. Bullbrook and Rouse, *Venezuelan Archaeology*, p. 79.
298. Bullbrook and Rouse, *Venezeulan Archaeology*, p. 49.
299. Bullbrook and Rouse, *Venezuelan Archaeology*, p. 44.
300. Lovén, *Origins of the Tainan Culture*, p. 652.
301. Roth, "An inquiry into the animism and folklore of the Guiana indians", p. 139; Zerries, "Primitive South America and the West Indies", p. 262.

302. Bullbrook and Rouse, *Venezuelan Archaeology*, p. 11.
303. Rouse, "The West Indies", pp. 533–4; Bullbrook and Rouse, *Venezuelan Archaeology*, p. 110; Rouse, "Prehistory of the West Indies" p. 510.
304. Bullbrook, "The Aborigines of Trinidad", p. 69. See Castellanos, *Elegías de varones ilustres*, vol. 1 p. 383.

Chapter 4, pages 71–75

1. Las Casas, *Historia de las Indias*, vol. 2 pp. 9–14; Morison, *Christopher Columbus*, pp. 527–537.
2. Sauer, *The Early Spanish Main*, p. 108.
3. Fernández de Navarrete, *Colección de viajes*, vol. 3 pp. 6, 233, and *Viajes de los españoles*, pp. 12, 23, 35; and Borde, *Histoire de l'île de la Trinidad*, vol. 1 pp. 69–70.
4. Córdova, "La encomienda", p. 23–49.
5. CODIN **32** p. 90 15.6.1510.
6. CODIN **32** p. 308 23.12.1511.
7. CODIN **1** p. 383 1520; Sauer, *The Early Spanish Main*, p. 195.
8. AGI PAT **18–3–9** 1532.
9. TTHS **93** 1552.
10. Ojer, *La formación del Oriente Venezolano*, p. 343.
11. Mosk, "Spanish pearl fishing operations", p. 399.
12. ANHC **II–31** no. 6 15.12.1521.
13. Carmichael, *The history of the West Indian islands*, pp. 17–8.
14. AGI PAT **18–9–1** 12.7.1530. El dorado, the gilded man, was chief of a tribe now thought to have inhabited Colombia. Once a year he covered his body with gold dust and rowed to the middle of a lake where he bathed and deposited offerings of gold. This legend was first heard of by the Spanish in 1535, who thought that if they found "El Dorado" they would find an empire of riches. The development and spread of the legend is discussed fully by Harlow in *The Discoverie of Guiana*, pp. xlv–xcvi.
15. AGI PAT **18–3–9** 15.11.1532.
16. Thompson, "Pre-British place-names", pp. 149–150; Carmichael, *The history of the West Indian islands*, p. 19.
17. Aguado, *Recopilación Historial*, p. 369.
18. TTHS **166** 12.10.1535.
19. AGI PAT **18–6–9** 26.10.1553.
20. AGI CAR **3** 15.1. 1569.
21. AGI SD **71–1–526** 15.1.1570.
22. Ojer, *La formación del Oriente Venezolano*, p. 272.
23. AGI CAR **2–2** 23.3.1592.
24. See p. 116. Towns and cities were integral parts of colonial expansion such that, as Kirkpatrick writes, "even if it [the city] only contained a

score of householders living in wooden huts, nevertheless, it had all the character of an organised civil community, claiming jurisdiction over the surrounding country". Kirkpatrick, *The Spanish Conquistadores*, p. 25.

25. English pirates and corsairs who visited Trinidad at the end of the sixteenth century included:

Andrew Baker	1576
John Chindley	December 1589 or January 1590
Benjamin Wood	1592
John Lancaster	June 1593
Jacob Whiddon	1593–4
John Burgh	1593–4
Robert Dudley	1594–5
Sir John Popham	1595
Sir Walter Raleigh	1595

See Warner, *The voyage of Sir Robert Dudley*; Hakluyt, *The principal navigations*, vol. 10 p. 84; Harlow, *The Discoverie of Guiana*; Andrews, *English Privateering Voyages*, pp. 62, 175; and Davis, *English colonies in Trinidad*.

26. AGI CAR **2–2** 23.3.1592.
27. Sluiter, "Dutch–Spanish rivalry", p. 171.
28. AGI PAT **18–6–9** 13.4.1554.
29. AGI PAT **26–33** 3.10.1592.

Chapter 5, pages 76–103

1. Enciso, *Descripción de las Indias Occidentales*, p. 17; AGI SD **71–1–526** 1570.
2. Dobyns, "Estimating aboriginal American population", p. 415.
3. See p. 169.
4. This figure of between 15 000 and 20 000 for the indian population at the end of the sixteenth century is consistent with de Berrío's estimate if the possible exaggeration of the latter is allowed for. He counted 7000 indians, from which he estimated that there must be 35 000 in the island. AGI EC **1011** 1.1.1593.
5. In 1542 the New Laws of the Indies were passed which forbade the future enslavement of indians and ordered the immediate release of women and children kept as slaves and of men who had not been enslaved for a lawful cause such as rebellion.
6. Borde, *Histoire de l'île de la Trinidad*, pp. 80–81; McArdle, *The Dominicans in the West Indies*.
7. Las Casas, *Historia de las Indias*, vol. 3 p. 138.
8. ANHC **II–31** no. 6 15.12.1521.
9. Ojer, *La formación del Oriente Venezolano*, p. 343.
10. Alexander, "The geography of Margarita", pp. 125–6.
11. Borde, *Histoire de l'île de la Trinidad*, vol. 1 p. 8.

12. Ojer, *La formación del Oriente Venezolano*, p. 158.
13. AGI PAT **26–33** 31.10.1592.
14. TTHS **137** December 1637. This compares with evidence of Caribs regularly visiting some of the unoccupied small islands of the Leeward group in order to hunt, fish, gather plants, and raise crops. See Harris, "Plants, animals and man", pp. 183–4.
15. AGI CAR **971** 21.1.1612.
16. See p. 93.
17. Las Casas, *Historia de las Indias*, vol. 2 p. 11.
18. AGI PAT **18–3–9** 15.11.1532; RAHM CM **A/106 79** ff.200–206 28.1.1532.
19. Arellano Moreno, *Relaciones geográficas*, p. 45 27.7.1550; Aguado, *Recopilación Historial*, p. 369.
20. AGI SD **71–1–526** 1.1.1570; Warner, *The voyage of Sir Robert Dudley* pp. 33, 44.
21. Harlow, *The Discoverie of Guiana*, p. 12.
22. Fernández de Navarrete, *Viajes de los españoles*, p. 23.
23. AGI PAT **18–6–9** 13.4.1554.
24. AGI CAR **971** 21.1.1612.
25. Fernández de Navarrete, *Viajes de los españoles*, p. 23.
26. AGI PAT **18–6–9** 13.4.1554.
27. ANHC **II–31** No. 15 15.9.1534 Sedeño claimed he had metal tools effective enough to cut down trees "as large as barrels".
28. See Conklin, *Hanunóo Agriculture*, p. 150.
29. Sauer, *The Early Spanish Main*, p. 54.
30. AGI PAT **18–6–9** 13.4.1554.
31. Simón, *Noticias Historiales*, p. 152.
32. TTHS **22** 1595.
33. ANHC **II–31** no. 15 15.9.1554.
34. Sauer, "Cultivated Plants", p. 500.
35. Alexander, "The geography of Margarita", p. 15.
36. Fernández de Oviedo y Valdés, *Natural History of the West Indies*, p. 87.
37. Sauer, "Cultivated Plants", p. 505.
38. Puente y Olea, *Los trabajos geográficos*, p. 381.
39. Mercadal, *Lo que España llevó a América*, 34.
40. AGI PAT **18–6–9** 26.10.1553.
41. Warner, *The voyage of Sir Robert Dudley*, p. 78.
42. AGI EC **1185** 1607.
43. Puente y Olea, *Los trabajos geográficos*, pp. 383–4; Mercadal, *Lo que España llevó a América*, pp. 44–46.
44. Purseglove, *Tropical Crops*, p. 237.
45. Harris, "Plants, animals and man", pp. 92–3.
46. Purseglove, *Tropical Crops*, p. 246.

47. Espinosa, *Compendium and Description*, p. 56; Arellano Moreno, *Relaciones geofráficas*, p. 255 27.10.1597.
48. Purseglove, *Tropical Crops*, p. 45.
49. Espinosa, *Compendium and Description*, p. 56.
50. Hodge and Taylor, "The ethnobotany of the island Caribs", p. 520.
51. Purseglove, *Tropical Crops*, p. 193.
52. Bulletin of the Department of Agriculture, "The avocado pear", p. 113.
53. AGI CAR 3 15.1.1569.
54. Purseglove, *Tropical Crops*, pp. 502, 506,
55. Acosta, *Historia natural y moral*, p. 410.
56. Mercadal, *Lo que España llevó a América*, p. 49.
57. Smith, *The true travels*, p. 55.
58. Acosta, *Historia natural y moral*, p. 411.
59. Watts, "Man's Influence on the Vegetation", p. 47.
60. AGI EC 1101A 1.1.1593.
61. Cheesman, *The history of the introduction of the more important West Indian staples*, p. 79; Tudela, *El llegado de España a América*, pp. 688–9; Parry, "Plantation and Provision Ground", pp. 9–10; Mercadal, *Lo que España llevó a América*, p. 86.
62. Robertson, "Some notes on the transfer by Spain of plants and animals", p. 18.
63. Williams and Williams, *The Useful and Ornamental Plants*, pp. 16–17.
64. Puente y Olea, *Los trabajos geográficos*, pp. 391–2.
65. Mercadal, *Lo que España llevó a América*, pp. 56, 65.
66. AGI CAR 3 15.1.1569.
67. Puente y Olea, *Los trabajos geográficos*, pp. 391–2, 396.
68. ANHC II–31 no. 15 15.9.1534.
69. Acosta, *Historia natural y moral*, p. 410.
70. Harlow, *The Discoverie of Guiana*, p. 126.
71. Espinosa, *Compendium and Description*, p. 56.
72. AGI PAT 18–3–9 1532.
73. AGI EC 1011 1.1.1593.
74. AGI SD 179 29.7.1616, 21.4.1617.
75. Purseglove, *Tropical Crops*, p. 572.
76. The Spaniard, Lupercio Despés, was also charged in 1607 with having stolen four *fanegas* of cacao from an indian. AGI EC 1185 1607.
77. Morison, *Christopher Columbus*, p. 543.
78. Cheesman, *The History of the introduction of the more important West Indian staples*, p. 71.
79. AGI SD 18–9–1 12.7.1530.
80. Deerr, *The History of Sugar*, p. 179.
81. AGI SD 71–1–526 15.1.1570, EC 1011 1.1.1593.

82. Harris, "Plants, animals, and man", p. 87.
83. AGI EC **1011** 1.1.1593.
84. TTHS **82** November 1636.
85. Puente y Olea, *Los trabajos geográficos*, pp. 400–1.
86. AGI SD **71–1–526** 15.1.1570.
87. Purseglove, *Tropical Crops*, p. 18.
88. Harris, "Plants, animals and man" p. 95.
89. ANHC **II–31** no. 15 15.9.1534.
90. AGI PAT **18–3–9** 13.4.1554.
91. Robertson, "Some notes on the transfer by Spain of plants and animals", p. 10; Johnson, "Introduction of the Horse", p. 590.
92. Tudela, *El llegado de España a América*, p. 733.
93. ANHC **II–31** no. 6 15.12.1521.
94. AGI SD **166–1–13** 15.7.1531.
95. RAHM CM **A/107 80** 4.4.1535, 28. 1.1533.
96. ANHC **II–31** no. 15 15.9.1534.
97. Aguado, *Recopilación Historial*, p. 459.
98. AGI CAR **3** 15.1.1569, 22.3.1569.
99. AGI SD **71–1–526** 15.1.1570.
100. AGI SD **179–1–2** 23.10.1591.
101. Arellano Moreno, *Relaciones geográficas*, p. 356.
102. Tudela, *El llegado de España a América*, pp. 706–19.
103. Aguado, *Recopilación Historial*, p. 371.
104. Simón, *Noticias Historiales*, p. 150.
105 Gilmore, "Fauna and Ethnozoology of South America", pp. 394–5.
106. Warner, *The voyage of Sir Robert Dudley*, p. 70.
107. AGI SD **179–3–104** 11.7.1595.
108. Gilmore, "Fauna and Ethnozoology of South America", p. 393.
109. AGI PAT **18–6–9** 13.4.1554 The *Escribano* of Margarita reported that in Trinidad "the meat which they eat is from the hunting of deer, pigs, tapirs and other kinds of animals which there are in the island".
110. TTHS **22** September 1595.
111. AGI SD **71–1–526** 15.1.1570; Warner, *The voyage of Sir Robert Dudley*, p. 71.
112. Enciso, *Descripción de las Indias Occidentales*, p. 17; Las Casas, *Historia de las Indias*, vol. 2 p. 14.
113. AGI SD **71–1–526** 15.1.1570.
114. Merrill, "The historical record of man", pp. 19–20.
115. ANHC **II–31** no. 15 15.9.1534.
116. Enciso, *Descripción de las Indias Occidentales*, p. 17.
117. Castellanos, *Elegías de varones ilustres*, vol. 1 pp. 389, 391.
118. Las Casas, *Historia de las Indias*, vol. 2 p. 14.
119. TTHS **166** 12.10.1535.

120. AGI SD **77–4–74** 24.1.1534.

121. AGI CAR **3** 15.1.1569.

122. Las Casas, *Historia de las Indias*, vol. 2 p. 13.

123. Méndez-Arocha, *La Pesca de Margarita*, p. 37.

124. Warner, *The voyage of Sir Robert Dudley*, p. 23.

125. Edwards, "Aboriginal watercraft", p. 107.

126. TTHS **166** 12.10.1535.

127. AGI PAT **18–6–9** 13.4.1554.

128. ANHC **II–31** no. 15 15.9.1554. The "spiny palms" referred to were probably *Acrocomia* or gru-gru palms.

129. Williams and Williams, *The Useful and Ornamental Plants*, p. 182.

130. AGI SD **77–4–74** 24.1.1534.

131. ANHC **II–31** no. 6 15.12.1521.

132. Harris, "Plants, animals and man" p. 81.

133. Castellanos, *Elegías de varones ilustres*, vol. 1 p. 383.

134. AGI PAT **18–6–9** 13.4.1554.

135. Warner, *The voyage of Sir Robert Dudley*, p. 47.

136. ANHC **II–31** no. 15 15.9.1534.

137. Arellano Moreno, *Relaciones geográficas*, p. 45 27.10.1550; ANHC **II–31** no. 15 15.9.1534.

138. AGI SD **77–4–74** 24.1.1534.

139. Castellanos, *Elegías de varones ilustres*, vol. 1 pp. 383, 390.

140. Simón, *Noticias Historiales*, p. 151, Warner, *The voyage of Sir Robert Dudley*, pp. 23, 70.

141. AGI SD **77–4–74** 24.1.1534.

142. BM ADD **36, 315** ff.251–4 27.7.1592; AGI EC **1011** 1.1.1593.

143. Las Casas, *Historia de las Indias*, vol. 3 p. 138.

144. ANHC **II–31** No. 15 15.9.1534.

145. AGI PAT **18–6–9** 13.4.1554; CODIN **32** p. 90 15.6.1510.

146. BM ADD **13, 964** quoted in Breton, "The Aruac Indians", p. 11.

147. Spanish merchant ships with their patrols sailed to the New World via the Canaries following the north-east trades and arriving in the Lesser Antilles where they replenished supplies before sailing on to the Greater Antilles and the mainland. Ships that followed a more southerly route may have stopped in Trinidad—see Chaunu, *Seville et l'Atlantique*, vol. VIII p. 601. For the return journey the ships reassembled in Cuba and sailed to Spain in convoy. The English and French pirates left Europe in March and April in time to attack the Spanish ships as they returned laden to Spain. Although the pirates failed to break the Spanish monopoly, the protection required of the Spanish authorities was costly in men, ships, and money. Parry, *The Spanish Seaborne Empire*, p. 258.

148. Naipaul, *The Loss of El Dorado*, p. 59.

149. AGI PAT **51–4** 2⁰ unico 1579. The date given on the document is 1579 but it is obviously wrong since it relates the events of Ponce de Leon's expedition which is known to have arrived in Trinidad in 1569.
150. CODIN **8** p. 489 15.7.1563.
151. ANHC **II–31** no. 1, no date.
152. AGI PAT **18–6–9** 13.4.1554.
153. Chaunu, *Seville et l'Atlantique*, vol. VIII p. 544.
154. AGI SD **77–4–74** 24.1.1534.
155. ANHC **II–31** no. 1, no date; Hanke, "The New Laws 1542", p. 146.
156. Harlow, *The Discoverie of Guiana*, p. 33.
157. Warner, *The voyage of Sir Robert Dudley*, p. 70.
158. AGI SD **71–1–526** 1.1.1570; BM ADD **36, 315** ff.251–4 27.7.1592.
159. Hakluyt, *The principal navigations*, vol. 10 p. 456, 1596.
160. Parry, *The Spanish Seaborne Empire*, p. 253.
161. Dumond, "Population growth", p. 319.
162. Carneiro, "On the relationship between size of population", p. 239.
163. Service, *Primitive Social Organisation*, pp. 72–3.
164. Service, *Primitive Social Organisation*, pp. 133–140.
165. Castellanos, *Elegías de varones ilustres*, vol. 1 p. 384.
166. Castellanos, *Elegías de varones ilustres*, vol. 1. p. 370.
167. Castellanos, *Elegías de varones ilustres*, vol. 1 pp. 361, 382–383.
168. ANHC **II–31** no. 1, no date, no. 9 15.11.1532.
169. Delgado, "El impacto cultural", pp. 324–340.
170. Las Casas, *Historia de las Indias*, vol. 2 p. 13.
171. Velasco, *Geografía y Descripción Universal*, p. 153.
172. Castellanos, *Elegías de varones ilustres*, vol. 1 p. 384.
173. Parry, *The Spanish Seaborne Empire*, pp. 174–5.
174. ANHC **II–31** no. 6 15.12.1521, AGI PAT **18–9–1** 12.7.1530, PAT **18–6–9** 26.10.1553, CAR **3** 15.1.1569, CAR **2–2** 23.3.1592.

Chapter 6, pages 107–115

1. Hanke, *Aristotle and the American Indian*, p. 3.
2. See Parry, *The Spanish Seaborne Empire*; Hanke, *The Spanish struggle for justice*, and *Aristotle and the American Indian*.
3. AGI SF **529** 25.10.1662, *Cédula* 22.10.1662.
4. Ponte, *Bolivar y Ensayos*, p. 30.
5. AGI SF **101** 12.7.1617.
6. Bolton, "The mission as a frontier institution", p. 46.
7. AGI SD **172–4–154**, *Cédula* 30.1.1625.
8. AGI SD **179–1–50** (*anejo*) 8.5.1629.
9. AGI SF **227** 15.7.1662.

10. AGI SD **575** 21.8.1707.
11. Quoted in MacAlister, "Social structure", p. 364.
12. Parry, *The Spanish Seaborne Empire*, pp. 174–5.
13. Mörner, *Race Mixture*, p. 112. Mason in *Patterns of Dominance* pp. 267–8 suggests that the common association of darkness with evil would have placed the negro at the bottom of the social scale.
14. MacAlister, "Social structure", pp. 357, 361.
15. Parra Pérez, *El régimen español en Venezuela*, p. 144.
16. Mörner, "Teoría y práctica de la segregación", pp. 278–80. The motives behind indian segregation and the legislation passed to achieve it are examined fully by Mörner in *La corona española y los foraneos* pp. 15–188. An ulterior motive behind the protection of the indian population may have been the maintenance of income from tribute; a decline in the indian population would have resulted in a loss of revenue.
17. TTHS **721** 1654.
18. BBV1A1 p. 59 1677.
19. AGI SD **179–3–104** 11.7.1595.
20. AGI SD **180–3–134** 7.9.1633 Punta de la Galera may refer to the southeast corner of Trinidad, which was so named by Columbus, or to the north-east point, which is at present known by that name and which is indicated as such on Dudley's map. Tradition relates that Colt landed at Toco rather than in the south-east but a map by Hack about 1680 calls the south-east corner of Trinidad Colt's point and documentary accounts give the impression that it was at that point that Colt landed.
21. Harlow, "Colonising expeditions," p. 130.
22. Carmichael, *The history of the West Indian islands*, p. 29.
23. Harlow, "Colonising expeditions", pp. 129–130; CO **1/20** no. 202 1666; CSP (AWI) **96** no. 1368 p. 436 1666.
24. BM AD **36, 324** ff.89–90 10.11.1637; BNM **2336** 1638; AGI SD **86–3** 8.7.1639, Davis, "English colonies in Trinidad", pp. 38–40; Goslinga, *The Dutch* p. 275.
25. The islands of the West Indies were occupied by foreign nations as follows:
    English— Barbados and St. Kitts (San Cristóbal) 1625, Nevis 1628, Antigua and Barbuda 1632, St. Lucia 1638/41, and Anguilla 1650;
    French— St. Kitts (San Cristóbal) 1625, Guadeloupe and Martinique 1635;
    Dutch— Curaçao 1634, San Martín, Saba, and San Eustaquio 1638
In addition the English, French and Dutch from the end of the sixteenth century attempted to found settlements to the Tierra Firme, particularly in Guyana, along the Essequibo, Berbice and Cayenne. These settlements were

used as trading bases and bases from which Spanish settlements and ships could be attacked.

Chapter 7, pages 116–150

1. AGI PAT **26–33** 3.10.1592.
2. AGI PAT **26–33** 3.10.1592; Harlow, *The Discoverie of Guiana*, p. 121 1596.
3. Harlow, *The Discoverie of Guiana*, pp. 123, 135 1596; Ojer, *La Formación del Oriente Venezolano*, p. 555.
4. Nuttall, "Royal Ordinances", pp. 249–254 The original form of St. Joseph is not known. The present-day savanna is presumed to have been the original site of the plaza delineated in 1592. The church is at present located one block away from the savanna which, if it was the original site of the church, would be consistent with the 1573 Ordinances for the laying out of New Towns, which stated that in inland towns "the church is not to be on the plaza but at a distance from it in a situation where it can stand by itself" (p. 251). During the seventeenth century the church was destroyed a number of times and on being rebuilt its site may have been changed, although grave stones dating from 1652 suggest that it was located at that site at least from the end of the seventeenth century. The remains of a fort have been found on the northern side of the savanna and it is thought that the barracks were located on the western side where according to de Verteuil (personal communication 1968, 1970) a certain amount of military regalia has been found. It seems likely therefore that the town hall (*Casa de Cabildo*) and the Governor's residence were located on the southern side of the savanna, between the savanna and the church, where the Royal Ordinances indicated that they should be located.
5. TTHS **137** Dec. 1637.
6. AGI SF **227** 10.5.1681.
7. AGI SD **179–3–113** 28.6.1696.
8. AGI CAR **971** 21.1.1612, SD **179–2–51** 4.12.1637, BNM **2326** 1638, TTHS **121** 20.3.1652.
9. AGI SD **627** 18.2.1722.
10. AGI SF **218** 11.1.1680 In 1680 Governor Tiburcio Axpe y Zúñiga reported that "the port was much lower down [presumably down the Caroni river] than where it is today, which is new land which has never been settled."
11. AGI SD **583** 24.12.1735.
12. AGI CAR **190** 1.12.1759.
13. AGI CAR **8** 7.1.1761, CAR **150** 30.3.1762.
14. Borde, *Historie de l'île de la Trinidad*, vol. 2 p. 114.
15. AGI CAR **946** 4.7.1767, SD **895** 19.11.1779.

16. AHNM **2845** no. 21 1777.
17. AGI CAR **422** 1745, Borde, *Histoire de l'île de la Trinidad*, vol. 2 pp. 99–103.
18. AGI SD **677** 17.5.1713, SD **627** 16.5.1715.
19. AGI SD **179–1–11** 14.1.1603, Díaz de la Calle, *Memorial y Noticias*, p. 27 1646.
20. AGI SF **13–2–173** no date.
21. AGI SD **582** 30.11.1700, SD **646** 6.12.1702, CAR **260** 1777.
22. Diffie, *Latin American civilisation*, p. 291.
23. AGI PAT **26–33** 3.10.1592.
24. Joseph, *A History of Trinidad*, p. 139, Hart, *Trinidad*, p. 195, Borde, *Histoire de l'île de la Trinidad*, vol. 1 p. 228.
25. AGI SD **583** 24.12.1735.
26. AGI CAR **190** 1.12.1759.
27. AGI CAR **150** 15.11.1777, AHNM **2845** no. 21 1777.
28. AGI SD **179–3–86** 1.8.1688, SD **677** 17.5.1700, SF **540–3–188** 15.8.1708, SD **646–168** 1713, SD **576** 13.4.1730, SD **583** 14.5.1736, SD **643** 26.5.1742, CAR **216** 28.9.1766.
29. AGI SD **575** 3.7.1706.
30. AGI SD **575** 3.10.1712.
31. AGI CAR **24** 21.12.1735, SD **381** 1.1.1741, CAR **57** 6.5.1763.
32. AGI SD **677** 17.5.1713.
33. AGI SD **172–4–154** 1645.
34. AGI SD **608** 6.9.1715, 19.5.1717.
35. AGI CAR **32** 28.4.1774.
36. Navarro, *Los Franciscanos*, p. 30, Harlow, *The Discoverie of Guiana*, p. 121.
37. TTHS **139** 10.5.1662.
38. AGI SD **666** 30.5.1705, SD **583** 19.3.1722, CAR **879** no date, *ca.* 1770.
39. AGI SD **627** 1714.
40. AGI SD **583** 19.3.1722.
41. Carmichael, *The History of the West Indian Islands*, p. 30.
42. TTHS **113** 1.5.1596, **132** 30.1.1599.
43. TTHS **81** 30.11.1609.
44. AGI CAR **971** 3.6.1612.
45. AGI SD **179–1–21** 21.4.1617.
46. AGI CAR **971** 20.4.1613.
47. For example AGI SD **24–2–98** 1600, SD **26** no date, *ca.* 1624, SD **27B** 22.12.1635.

    The origins of indians employed in the personal service of *vecinos* in 1688 were as follows:

ORINOCO		NUEVO REINO DE GRANADA	
Casanare	137	Pauto	2
Caura (Carib)	16	Jomo	1
Capure (Carib)	1	Santa Fé	4

ORINOCO		NEUVO REINO DE GRANADA	
Cuchibero (Carib)	1	Cabre	1
Meta	10	Unspecified	2
Jabana	1		
Roba	1	PROVINCE OF CUMANÁ	
Menjui	3	Mission of Piritu	3
Berbis—Dutch settlement	4	Guarapiche (Chaima)	1
GUIANA	20		
TRINIDAD	26	Source: AGI SD **179–3–85**	
		18.7.1688.	

In addition there were 56 children and 3 adults employed in personal service whose origin is unknown.

49. AGI SD **25** 10.10.1615, SD **156–1** 14.3.1618.
50. AGI SD **172–3–125** 23.4.1634.
51. AGI SF **218** 24.3.1685, 18.2.1686.
52. AGI SD **179–3–85** 18.7.1688, **179–3–87** 1.8.1688.
53. AGI SD **179–3–102** 16.8.1693, SD **677** 20.6.1694, SF **540–2–151** 31.12.1696, SD **582** 29.12.1699, SD **666** *ca.*1700, SF **423** 20.5.1706, SD **678**, **583** 16.4.1732, CAR **150** 15.12.1735, CAR **862** 7.7.1760.
54. AGI SF **216** 24.7.1689 (1684), SF **215** 3.7.1692 (1684), SD **179–3–98** 15.7.1693, SD **582** 25.1.1702 (1689), SF **13–2–173** no date.
55. See p. 164–165.
56. AGI SD **666** *ca.* 1700.
57. AGI SF **240–3–235** 18.6.1702.
58. AGI SD **608** 19.5.1717.
59. AGI SD **583** 19.3.1722.
60. AGI SD **678** 12.7.1730.
61. AGI SD **581** 20.3.1741.
62. AGI CAR **150** 9.7.1748.
63. AGI CAR **198** 19.11.1763.
64. AGI CAR **879** no date, *ca.* 1770.
65. AGI CAR **260** 8.6.1777.
66. Mörner, *Race Mixture*, p. 37.
67. AGI SF **218** 2.1.1687.
68. AGI SD **179–3–85** 18.7.1688.
69. AGI SD **666** 30.5.1705.
70. AGI SD **627** 17.4.1713. The term *grifo* was used to describe the offspring of a negro and an indian.
71. Joseph, *A History of Trinidad*, p. 146, Hart, *Trinidad*, p. 196, Borde *Histoire de l'île de la Trinidad*, vol. 2 p. 84, Fraser, *History of Trinidad*, p. 153.
72. Joseph, *A History of Trinidad*, p. 153.
73. Borde, *Histoire de l'île de la Trinidad*, vol. 2 p. 114.

74. AGI CAR **198** 19.11.1763.
75. The terms *pardo* and *moreno* translated literally mean dark-skinned and brown-skinned respectively.
76. The racial composition of the two Spanish towns in 1763 and 1777 is taken from AGI CAR **198** 19.11.1763 and CAR **150** 15.11.1777.
77. AGI CAR **878** 23.4.1762.
78. AGI SD **179–3–1688**. The term *republicano* was commonly used in Latin America to denote the American birth of a Spaniard. It was used synonymously with *criollo* in the early colonial period but it later came to possess political connotations.
79. AGI SD **179–3–85** 18.7.1688.
80. Mörner, *Race Mixture*, pp. 42–44.
81. AGI CAR **198** 19.11.1763.
82. AGI SD **179–3–85** 18.7.1688.
83. AGI CAR **203** 11.7.1766.
84. AGI CAR **260** 8.6.1777.
85. Diffie, *Latin American civilisation*, p. 72. *Peonías* were given to infantrymen and measured 100 acres each, whereas *caballerías* were given to cavalrymen and measured 500 acres each.
86. Harlow, *The Discoverie of Guiana*, p. 14.
87. AGI PAT **26–33** 3.10.1592.
88. AGI SD **627** 28.3.1713, SD **646** 29.4.1717.
89. AGI SD **627** 1714.
90. ANHM **2845** no. 21 1777. At this time Trinidad would have appeared fertile compared to other West Indian islands where sugar cane yields were falling and lands being abandoned.
91. AGI CAR **975** 1.6.1602, CAR **971** 21.1.1612, SD **179** 29.7.1616, SD **179–1–21** *anejo* 21.4.1617, SD **179–1–29** 31.1.1618, SD **179–1–38** 3.7.1619, SD **55–5** 26.10.1638.
92. AGI EC **1185** 1614.
93. AGI SD **179–3–83** 26.4.1688 *Cédula* 29.5.1682, SD **179–3–86** 1.8.1688.
94. AGI SD **582** 1705 and 13.10.1705, SD **666** 30.5.1705.
95. AGI SD **582** 31.3.1717, SD **647** 19.8.1718, *Cédula* 24.8.1714.
96. Parry, *The Spanish Seaborne Empire*, p. 187.
97. Simpson, *The Encomienda in New Spain*, pp. 104–5.
98. AGI SD **582** 1705.
99. AGI SD **582** 1705.
100. Rionegro, *Relaciones de las Misiones*, vol. 2, p. 307, Lodares, *Los franciscanos*, vol. 2 pp. 170–1.
101. AGI SD **646–128** 15.9.1708.
102. AGI SD **583** 25.4.1732.
103. AGI SD **582** 15.10.1705.

104. AGI SD **627** 14.8.1711.
105. AGI SD **647** 20.9.1716.
106. AGI SD **179–3–106** 3.5.1689.
107. AGI SD **583** 10.5.1725, 26.6.1727.
108. AGI SD **627** 6.3.1715.
109. TTHS **137** December 1637.
110. Harlow, *The Discoverie of Guiana*, p. 33.
111. See footnote 47, taken from AGI SD **179–3–85** 18.7.1688.
112. Brito Figueroa, *La estructura económica*, pp. 115–7.
113. TTHS **602** 1686.
114. AGI SD **582** 1705.
115. Brito Figueroa, *La estructura económica*, pp. 121, 137.
116. AGI CAR **150** 15.11.1777.
117. TTHS **169** 7.9.1614, AGI CAR **971** 3.6.1612.
118. AGI CONT **2617** 1614, TTHS **137** December 1637.
    Known shipments of tobacco to Spain in registered ships in the first half of the seventeenth century included the following:

July 1614	85 100 lb.
July 1620	60 500 lb.
August 1620	86 819 lb.
July 1622	60 400 lb.
November 1626	43 100 lb. Source: AGI CONT **2617**.

119. AGI SD **179–1–23A** 1.8.1617 *Cédula* 15.3.1616. The period of exemption was extended at intervals of several years. AGI SD **645** 26.10.1619, IG **473–3** 21.11.1625, 24.1.1631, SD **645** 17.6.1636 and its extension was recommended in 1640 (AGI SD **645** 30.4.1640).
120. TTHS **137** December 1637.
121. Poyntz, *The Present Prospect*, p. 42.
122. AGI SD **179** 29.7.1616. The *Cabildo* complained that "it is impossible to establish cacao estates because there is no one to plant the cacao and care for it, for it takes four years to bear".
123. Harlow, *Colonising expeditions*, p. 120.
124. Díaz de la Calle, *Memorial y Noticias*, p. 604.
125. See Table VIII AGI SD **666** 30.5.1705.
126. AGI SD **627** 14.6.1716, SD **179–3–103** 16.10.1693.
127. Arcila Farías, *Comercio entre Venezuela y México*, pp. 134–5.
128. AGI SD **627** 15.8.1711.
129. See Table VIII AGI SD **645** 10.2.1721.
130. AGI SD **583** 19.3.1722.
131. J.A.S.T.T., "A short history of cacao", p. 23.
132. Alcedo, *Diccionario geográfico-histórico*, p. 194.
133. Joseph, *A History of Trinidad*, p. 45.

134. AGI SD **649** 6.2.1737 See Table IX.
135. Borde, *Histoire de l'île de la Trinidad*, vol. 2 pp. 116–7.
136. AGI CONTAD **1677** 1751–1774, CAR **734** 1775–6, CAR **150** 15.11.1777; Raynal, *A philosophical and political history*, p. 179.
137. AGI SD **627** 28.3.1713.
138. AHMN **2845** no. 21 1777.
139. AGI SD **627** 28.3.1715.
140. TTHS **82** November 1636; Harlow, *Colonising expeditions*, p. 120.
141. AGI CAR **24** *Cédula* 24.10.1776.
142. AHNM **2845** no. 21 1777.
143. Cheesman, *The history of the introduction of the more important West Indian staples*, p. 81–4.
144. AGI CONTAD **1677** 1764.
145. TTHS **421** 11.1.1777.
146. Joseph, *A History of Trinidad*, p. 143.
147. Raynal, *A philosophical and political history*, p. 203.
148. TTHS **421** 11.1.1777.
149. TTHS **421** 11.1.1777.
150. Labat, *Nouveau voyage*, vol. 6 p. 465.
151. AHNM **2845** no. 21 1777; Alcedo, *Diccionario geográfico-histórico*, p. 194.
152. AGI CAR **150** 15.11.1777, CAR **934** 4.4.1777.
153. Watts, "Man's Influence on the Vegetation of Barbados", p. 53; Campbell, *Candid and impartial considerations*, p. 115.
154. AGI CAR **8** 7.1.1761.
155. AGI CAR **260** 8.6.1777.
156. AGI SD **627** 28.3.1713, SD **582** 31.3.1717. In 1717 indians from the *encomiendas* complained that the only food that had been given to them by the *encomenderos* was plantains.
157. AGI SD **260** 8.6.1777.
158. Purseglove, *Tropical Crops: Dicotyledons*, p. 260.
159. Watts, "Man's Influence on the Vegetation of Barbados", p. 54.
160. See Table IX.
161. Alcedo, *Diccionario geográfico-histórico*, p. 194.
162. Harris, "Plants, animals and man", p. 113.
163. Purseglove, *Tropical Crops: Dicotyledons*, p. 193.
164. Bulletin of the Department of Agriculture, "The avocado pear", p. 113.
165. Purseglove, *Tropical Crops: Dicotyledons*, p. 25.
166. Watts, "Man's Influence on the Vegetation of Barbados", p. 25.
167. Mercadal, *Lo que España llevó a América*, p. 49; Smith, *The true travels*, p. 55
168. Acosta, *Historia natural*, p. 411.
169. Watts, "Man's Influence on the Vegetation of Barbados", p. 47.
170. AGI CAR **150** 15.11.1777.

171. Córdova Bello, *Aspectos históricos de la ganadería*, p. 18. Small numbers of animals were kept by individual landowners; cattle and pigs figured amongst the goods offered in payment of tithes in 1629 AGI SD **179–1–50** *anejo* 8.5.1629.
172. AGI CAR **260** 8.6.1777.
173. TTHS **401** 1772 and see Table X.
174. AGI SD **627** 18.2.1722, CAR **879** no date *ca.* 1770, and Ramos Pérez, *El tratado de límites*, p. 152.
175. AGI CAR **879** no date, *ca.* 1770.
176. TTHS **804** 4.1.1757.
177. Pelleprat, *Relato de las misiones*, p. 12. The partridges described by Pelleprat were probably quail doves (*Geotrygon* sp.) since the former are not found in the island.
178. AGI CAR **862** 7.7.1760.
179. AGI CAR **443** 2.1.1778.
180. AGI CAR **537** 23.4.1775.
181. Borde, *Histoire de l'île de la Trinidad*, vol. 2 p. 114.
182. AGI CAR **971** 21.1.1612 Pixa or bledos were probably wild amaranths (*Amaranthus* spp.).
183. Harlow, *Colonising expeditions*, p. 120.
184. AGI SF **218** 16.2.1678, 1.10.1680.
185. AGI SD **900** 23.6.1621.
186. TTHS **137** 1637, AGI SD **179–3–113** 28.6.1696, SD **582** 1705, SD **583** 19.3.1722, SD **627** 18.2.1722, SD **678** 12.7.1730, CAR **150** 15.11.1777.
187. AGI SF **13–1–41** no date, SF **222** 1693.
188. TTHS **552** 19.1.1763.
189. AGI SD **582** 28.5.1701, AHS SE **6965** 23.4.1775.
190. See Table IX.
191. AGI CAR **24** 20.11.1764.
192. AGI CAR **946** 4.7.1767, CAR **32** 4.7.1774.
193. TTHS **137** 1637, AGI SD **645** 24.10.1653.
194. AGI SD **179–1–16** 8.1.1613.
195. AGI SD **25** 5.5.1613.
196. Chaunu, *Seville et l'Atlantique*, vol. VIII p. 544.
197. AGI SD **26** no date.
198. AGI SD **645** 30.4.1640.
199. AGI SF **218** 2.1.1687.
200. AGI EC **712B** 1690–1701.
201. AGI SD **666** 30.5.1705.
202. AGI SD **627** 14.8.1716.
203. AGI SD **582** 30.1.1719 *Cédula* 10.11.1717.
204. Haring, *The Spanish Empire*, pp. 336–7.

205. Haring, *The Spanish Empire*, p. 341.
206. AGI CAR **24** 16.11.1776.
207. AGI CAR **152–36** 24.3.1779.
208. AGI SD **650** 13.10.1690, SD **582** 20.2.1703; Hart, *Trinidad*, p. 196.
209. AGI SD **575** 21.6.1707.
210. AGI SD **641** no date *ca*. 1700.
211. AGI SD **575** 21.6.1707.
212. AGI SD **645** 15.1.1717.
213. AGI SD **645** 30.4.1640.
214. AGI SD **647** 3.10.1723.
215. AGI SD **583** 26.6.1727.
216. AGI SD **648** 8.7.1728.
217. See Table IX.
218. See Tables IX and X. Ramos Pérez, *El tratado de límites*, p. 155.
219. AGI SD **627** 14.8.1716.
220. For example in 1758 the Governor complained that a registered ship had brought "wine, oil, iron goods, nails and box of playing cards" but had not brought "cloth, particularly white cloth, hats, stockings or silk thread or other things that have been asked for and are very necessary" AGI CAR **150** 2.10.1758.
221. TTHS **602** 1686.
222. TTHS **57** 11.2.1612.
223. This was particularly true after the establishment of the Caracas Company in 1728, which maintained coastguards to prevent contraband trading. In 1766 38 negroes were seized from an English vessel at Guayaguayare (AGI CAR **10–1–35** 14.5.1766) and two years later several negroes were confiscated from another English ship proceeding from Grenada (AGI CAR **10–1–37** 14.9.1768).
224. AGI SD **179–2–58** 18.8.1678.
Dutch ships calling at Port of Spain between 1678 and 1681 included the following:

Date	From	To	Captain	Avowed purpose for stopping
18.8.1678	Amsterdam–Guinea	Margarita	Arnaldo Sombexo	Obtain supplies
14.12.1678	Curaçao		Guillermo Bec	To heal wounded man
14.1.1679	Amsterdam	Tobago	Diego Logroño	Trade
20.8.1679	Jesel	Margarita	Gerardo Juanes	Trade
22.8.1679	Visighe	Margarita	Juan Profeta	Trade
15.9.1679	Midelberg	Margarita	Pedro Banatem	Trade
14.4.1680	Amsterdam	Margarita	Pedro Brand	Trade and re- arm ship
4.5.1680			Elice Ballen	Trade
17.5.1680	Midelberg	Margarita	Juan Resmes and Juan Abran	Trade
29.1.1681	Holland–Santo Thomé	Curaçao	Pedro Bandenta	Trade—had 190 negroes
25.1.1681			Andrés Bronde	Trade

Sources: AGI SD **179–2–73** 10.5.1681, AGI SD **531–II–27** 15.7.1681, AGI SD **179–2–58–72** 1678–1681, AGI SD **874–2–41** 24.8.1679.

225. AGI SD **635, 881, 590** 16.4.1729.
226. AGI CAR **422** 1745.
227. AGI CAR **24** 20.11.1764.
228. Harlow, *The Discoverie of Guiana*, p. 15.
229. AGI SD **65** 18.8.1689.
230. CSP (AWI) **116** no. 24 p. 25 30.11.1727.
231. AGI SD **635** 16.4.1729, SD **583** 8.5.1730, SD **648** 29.12.1730, SD **615** 23.6.1730.
232. AGI SD **583** 8.5.1730, SD **648** 29.12.1730.
233. CSP (AWI) **117** no. 627 1.12.1730, **118** no. 386 p. 244 27.8.1731.
234. CSP (AWI) **98** no. 715 p. 481 9/20.8.1700.
235. AGI SD **582** 1.2.1730.
236. TTHS **22** September 1595, AGI **528–2** 1.6.1611, 6.8.1611, SD **179–1–147** 12.7.1624, SD **25** no date.
237. TTHS **98** 28.2.1611.
238. AGI SD **54–2** 26.6.1611.
239. AGI SD **179–2–80A** 18.2.1683, SF **216** 24.7.1689, Merrill, "An historical record of man", pp. 19- 20, AGI CAR **537** 23.4.1775.
240. ANHC **II–32** no. 6 1605, TTHS **81** 30.11.1609, AGI SF **528–2** 3.3.1611, SF 100 18.6.1614.
241. ANHC **II–32** no. 6 1605, AGI SD **179–3–85** 18.7.1688. See footnote 47.
242. Goslinga, *The Dutch*, p. 341.
243. Harlow, *Colonising expeditions*, p. 125.
244. AGI CAR **971** 20.4.1613. The negroes were sold for "pesos de cuchillos"— unit of weight measured in knives.
245. AGI SD **74–4–170** 9.3.1629.
246. TTHS **767** 1678.
247. TTHS **767** 1678, Brito Figueroa, *La estructura económica*, pp. 105–6.
248. Parry, *The Spanish Seaborne Empire*, p. 268.
249. AGI SD **582** 25.5.1705 *Cédula* 26.3.1702.
250. Brito Figueroa, *La estructura económica*, p. 108.
251. AGI CONTAD **1675** 1716–1718, SD **645** 25.6.1718.
252. Brito Figueroa, *La estructura económica*, p. 108, Parry, *The Spanish Seaborne Empire*, p. 300.
253. AGI CAR **23** 15.10.1765. The price in Trinidad was subsequently reduced by a further 10 *pesos* AGI CAR **23** 18.10.1766.
254. AGI CAR **32** 1.5.1773.
255. See Table X, AGI SD **666** 30.5.1705, SD **627** 15.8.1711, SD **645** 10.3.1721, SD **627** 18.2.1722, CONTAD **1677** 1751–1774.
256. TTHS **57** 11.2.1612.

257. AGI SD **179–3–104** 11.7.1595.

258. AGI SF **100** 18.6.1614, EC **701A** 1675.

259. AGI SD **666** 30.5.1705.

260. AGI CAR **975** 1.6.1602, TTHS **168** 20.4.1613, AGI SF **218** 7.1.1687.

Chapter 8, pages 151–174

1. AGI SD **647–46** 20.9.1716.

2. AGI SD **582** 1705.

3. AGI SD **646** 6.8.1713 *Cédula* 14.8.1711.

4. AGI SD **582** 15.10.1705.

5. AGI SD **646** 6.12.1707.

6. AGI SD **582** 16.12.1716.

7. AGI SD **179–1–50** 8.5.1629.

8. Díaz de la Calle, *Memorial y Noticias Sacras*, p. 27; AGI SD **172–4–154** 1645.

9. AGI SD **179–1–50** *anejo* 8.5.1629.

10. AGI SD **179–3–84** 25.1.1688, SD **179–3–86** 1.8.1688.

11. AGI SD **627** 14.8.1711.

12. AGI SD **647–46** 20.9.1716.

13. AGI CAR **24** 21.12.1735, CAR **190** 2.2.1757.

14. AGI SD **627** 18.7.1712, SD **583** 1.9.1721, SD **179–3–93** 18.9.1691, SD **260** 8.6.1777.

15. Service, "The Encomienda in Paraguay", p. 233.

16. AGI SD **677** no date, *ca.* 1700.

17. Arellano Moreno, *Relaciones geográficas*, p. 235, no date.

18. AGI SD **179–2–84** 27.1.1688.

19. Bullbrook and Rouse, "On the excavation of a shell mound", p. 99.

20. AGI MP **185**.

21. AGI SD **583** 1.9.1721.

22. AGI MP **185**.

23. AGI SD **627** 6.3.1715.

25. AGI SD **678** 16.4.1732.

26. For example, Córdova, "La encomienda", pp. 23–49.

27. Harlow, *The Discoverie of Guiana*, p. 14.

28. ANHC **II–32** no. 6 f.20 1605.

29. ANHC **II–32** no. 6 f.20 1605.

30. AGI CAR **971** 21.1.1612.

31. ANHC **II–32** no. 6 f.20 1605.

32. AGI CAR **971** 21.1.1612. Tribute was only payable by healthy male indians between the ages of 18 and 50. To arrive at a total population therefore it is usual to multiply the tributary population by a factor of 4 or 5.

33. AGI SD **172–4–154** 1645.

34. AGI SF **218** 16.2.1678.
35. AGI SD **677** 20.6.1694.
36. AGI SD **179–3–95** 16.3.1683, SD **179–3–84** 27.1.1688.

	Arauca	Tacarigua	Cuara	Aricagua
Men	40	29	20	13
Women	24	32	13	8
Children	50	40	27	5

37. AGI SD **582** 1705.
38. AGI SD **627** 18.7.1712.
39. AGI SD **627** 18.7.1712.
40. AGI SD **179–3–84** 27.1.1688, SD **583** 1.9.1721.
41. AGI SD **645** 6.3.1733.
42. AGI CAR **150** 9.7.1748, CAR **198** 19.11.1763.
43. See p. 171.
44. AGI CAR **260** 8.6.1777.
45. AGI SD **582** 30.5.1705.
46. AGI CAR **24** 22.2.1785.
47. AGI SD **627** 14.8.1711.
48. AGI SD **583** 25.4.1732.
49. AGI SD **575** 2.3.1713.
50. AGI SD **645** 6.2.1737.
51. AGI SD **583** 25.4.1732.
52. AGI SD **179–1–50** 11.4.1629.
53. de Laet, *L'histoire du Nouveau Monde*, p. 604.
54. AGI SD **623** 28.3.1653.
55. Geertz, *Agricultural Involution*, pp. 16–7; Harris, "Agricultural systems", pp. 5–6.
56. Harris, "Plants, animals, and man", p. 92.
57. CSP (AWI) **86** no. 1658 1667.
58. Williams and Williams, *The Useful and Ornamental Plants*, pp. 283–4.
59. Watts, "Man's Influence on the Vegetation", p. 47.
60. Espinosa, *Compendium and Description*, p. 56.
61. Armellada, *Por la Venezuela indígena*, p. 85.
62. BNM **18719**[31] 1673.
63. Pelleprat, *Relato de las misiones*, p. 61.
64. Armellada, *Por la Venezuela indígena*, p. 85.
65. Harris, "Plants, animals, and man", p. 92.
66. AGI SD **582** 22.2.1717.
67. Patiño, *Plantas cultivadas*, pp. 95–7; Watts, "Man's Influence on the Vegetation" pp. 49–50.
68. Poyntz, *The Present Prospect*, p. 17.
69. Watts, "Man's Influence on the Vegetation", p. 54.

70. Watts, "Man's Influence on the Vegetation", p. 52, 49.
71. Harris, "Plants, animals, and man", p. 114.
72. Acosta, *Historia natural y moral*, p. 410.
73. Watts, "Man's Influence on the Vegetation", p. 54.
74. AGI SD **677** 31.1.1711, SD **582** 22.2.1717.
75. Mörner, *Race Mixture*, p. 41.
76. AGI SD **582** 31.1.1717.
77. AGI CAR **422** 1745.
78. Bolton, "The mission as a frontier institution", pp. 45–47; Haring, *The Spanish Empire*, p. 188.
79. BNM **5361** *Cédula* 15.6.1692.
80. AGI SD **677** 20.5.1707 *Cédula* 21.7.1696; Rionegro, *Relaciones de las Misiones*, vol. 2 p. 241 *Cédula* 28.5.1738.
81. BNM **3561** 8.4.1687; AGI SF **540–3–188** 15.8.1708, SD **677** 20.5.1707.
82. AGI SF **255** 4.12.1689, SD **677** 20.9.1701, 25.10.1701.
83. AGI SD **646–168** 1713.
84. AGI SD **583** 19.3.1722.
85. AGI SD **576** 13.4.1730, SF **678** 13.11.1730, SD **678** 13.4.1732.
86. AGI SD **648** 10.10.1733; Lodares, *Los franciscanos capuchinos*, vol. 2 p. 202.
87. AGI SD **883** 6.4.1744.
88. BNM **3851** 1780.
89. AGI CAR **200** 28.7.1764.
90. AGI SD **646–122** 15.8.1708.
91. Lodares, *Los franciscanos capuchinos*, vol. 3 p. 220.
92. Diffie, *Latin American civilisation*, p. 622.
93. AGI SF **13–5–582** no date.
94. AGI SD **627** 6.6.1712, SD **260** 8.6.1777.
95. AGI SD **632** 15.12.1735.
96. AGI SD **641** 14.3.1688.
97. Armellada, *Por la Venezuela indígena*, p. 99.
98. Borde, *Histoire de l'île de la Trinidad*, vol. 2 p. 41.
99. AGI SD **641** 14.3.1688.
100. AGI SF **255** 13.3.1688, SD **641** 14.3.1688.
101. Armellada, *Por la Venezuela indígena*, p. 99.
102. AGI SD **582** 22.9.1700.
103. AGI SD **582** 1705.
104. BNM **18178** *libro* 3 1713; Borde, *Histoire de l'île de la Trinidad*, vol. 2 p. 44; Fraser, *History of Trinidad*, p. 3.
105. BNM **18178** libro 3 1713; Serrano y Sanz, *Relaciones históricas*, pp. 102–115.
106. AGI SD **677** 20.12.1703.
107. AGI SD **641** 14.3.1688.
108. AGI SF **255** 4.4.1689; Borde, *Histoire de l'île de la Trinidad*, vol. 2 p. 47.

109. BNM **3851** 1780; Rionegro, *Misiones de los Padres Capuchinos*, p. 191.
110. Borde, *Histoire de l'île de la Trinidad*, vol. 2 pp. 47–9.
111. AGI SD **627** 1714.
112. AGI SD **627** 6.6.1712, 1714.
113. AGI SD **677** 20.6.1694.
114. AGI SD **677** 20.6.1707.
115. AGI SD **677** no date *ca.* 1700.
116. AGI SD **677** no date.
117. AGI SD **582** 21.10.1700, 15.12.1700.
118. AGI SD **677** 17.5.1713.
119. Lodares, *Los franciscanos capuchinos*, vol. 2 p. 17; AGI SD **583** 27.3.1722.
120. AGI SD **582** 14.3.1727, CAR **24** 20.12.1735.
121. AGI CAR **150** 28.1.1739.
122. See Table XI.
123. Lodares, *Los franciscanos capuchinos*, vol. 2 p. 170.
124. Bolton, "The mission as a frontier institution", p. 48; Lodares, *Los franciscanos capuchinos*, vol. 2 p. 213.
125. Ponte, *Bolivar y Ensayos*, p. 29.
126. AGI SD **663** 15.10.1724.
127. Bolton, "The mission as a frontier institution", p. 57.
128. Borde, *Histoire de l'île de la Trinidad*, vol. 2 pp. 47–9.
129. AGI SF **540–3–249** 11.7.1713, SD **627** 6.3.1715.
130. Lodares, *Los franciscanos capuchinos*, vol. 3 p. 49.
131. AGI SF **531–12–38** 31.12.1689.
132. AGI CAR **260** 8.6.1777.
133. See Tables IV and V.
134. AGI CAR **971** 21.1.1612.
135. See pages 31 and 76.
136. ANHC **II–32** no. 6 f.20 1605; AGI CAR 971 21.1.1612.
137. AGI SD **180–3–140** 1633.
138. AGI **179–3–83A** 29.5.1682.
139. AGI SD **677** 20.6.1694.
140. ANHC **II–32** no. 6 f.20 1605.
141. AGI CAR **971** 21.1.1612.
142. ANHC **II–32** no. 4 f.13 4.1.1604.
143. AGI CAR **971** 21.1.1612.
144. AGI SD **582** 15.12.1700, SD **660** 17.10.1723, SD **581** 20.3.1741; Borde, *Histoire de l'île de la Trinidad*, vol. 2 p. 131.
145. Armellada, *Por la Venezuela indígena*, pp. 98–9.
146. AGI SD **179–3–85** 18.7.1688. The site of Buenavista is unknown but it may be the same as present-day Santa Cruz bearing the same name and located 6–7 miles from St. Joseph. The difficulty is that the document

relating the establishment of the settlement specifically mentions that the village was founded ¼ league from St. Joseph, that is less than a mile away (AGI SD **179–3–90** 8.4.1690), and in 1735 its site was described as being next to St. Joseph (AGI SD **583** 17.12.1735). In 1705, however, the *alcalde ordinario* complained that the indians of their own authority had moved more than ½ league from St. Joseph (AGI SD **666** 30.5.1705) but even this location does not correspond to present-day Santa Cruz. It is possible that the village has no expression in the present-day landscape.

147. AGI SD **583** 17.12.1735.
148. AGI SD **179–3–87** 1.8.1688.
149. AGI SD **666** 30.5.1705.
150. AGI SD **678** 12.7.1730.
151 BNM **3851** 1780.
152. AGI CAR **150** 1.7.1760, CAR **32** 1774–1784, CAR **260** 8.6.1777.
153. See Appendix 5.
154. AGI CAR **32** 1.8.1774, CAR **880** 2.11.1776, CAR **150** 13.6.1777.
155. AGI CAR **880** 2.11.1776.
156. AGI CAR **150** 1.7.1760, CAR **150** 15.11.1777.
157. TTHS **57** 11.2.1612.
158. AGI SD **180–3–140** 1633, SD **180–3–134** 7.9.1633.
159. TTHS **137** December 1637.
160. AGI SF **218** 16.2.1678.
161. AGI SD **641** 14.3.1688.
162. ANHC **II–32** no. 4 1717.
163. Linage, *Norte de la Contratación*, p. 646.
164. AGI CAR **150** 13.6.1777.
165. Borde, *Histoire de l'île de la Trinidad*, vol. 1 p. 213.
166. AGI SD **65** 21.7.1689.
167. CSP (AWI) **93** no. 1266 p. 339 30.8.1694, **97** no. 973 p. 528.
168. CO **28/6** no. 62 24.6.1702.

Chapter 9, pages 177–183

1. Lynch, *Spanish Colonial Administration*, p. 11.
2. Lynch, *Spanish Colonial Administration*, p. 46.
3. AGI CAR **253** 8.12.1776.
4. Haring, *The Spanish Empire*, p. 146.
5. AGI CAR **53** 20.1.1791.
6. AGI CAR **30** 8.9.1777.
7. Borde, *Histoire de l'île de la Trinidad*, vol. 2 pp. 14–1.
8. AGN RO **8** f.43 29.4.1783.
9. Borde, *Histoire de l'île de la Trinidad*, vol. 2 p. 288.

10. AGI CAR **260** 1777.
11. Noel, *Spanish Colonial Administration*, p. 218.
12. Borde, *Histoire de l'île de la Trinidad*, vol. 2 pp. 198–203.
13. Parry, *The Spanish Seaborne Empire*, p. 326.
14. Haring, *The Spanish Empire*, p. 169.
15. AGI CAR **947** no date; Watters, *A history of the Church*, p. 33.
16. AGI CAR **150** 3.9.1776.
17. AGI CAR **443** 14.9.1778.
18. AHNM **2845** no. 21 1777.
19. AGI CAR **443** 13.4.1779.
20. AGN IERH **20** ff.89–121 21.4.1782.
21. CO **295/56** 24.11.1783.
22. AGI CAR **87** 29.8.1784, CAR **394** 7.9.1784.
23. AGI CAR **20** 15.9.1786, CAR **152–95** 10.3.1787.
24. AGI CAR **132** 21.1.1788.
25. AGI CAR **24** 31.5.1786.
26. AGI CAR **444** 28.10.1787.
27. AGI CAR **444** 10.3.1787.
28. Anon, *A gentlemen of the island*, p. 8.
29. CO **295/8** July 1804.
30. Joseph, *A History of Trinidad*, p. 173 Halliday, *The West Indies*, p. 309.
31. AGI CAR **58** 31.7.1780; AGN IERH **20** f.82–3 1781–2; Pérez Aparicio, *Pérdida de la isla de Trinidad*, pp. 95–101.
32. Mörner, *La corona española y los foraneos*, p. 89. For an account of the reconsideration of the policy of residential segregation at the end of the eighteenth century see Part Six of the same book pp. 336–383.

Chapter 10, pages 184–224

1. AGI CAR **150** 15.11.1777; Mallet, *Descriptive account*, 1802.
2. AGI CAR **443** 1.3.1778, 14.5.1779.
3. AGI CAR **444, 153** 1790. The population of the island for the years 1784 to 1797 is given in Table XII.
4. Anon, *A gentleman of the island*, p. 60.
5. AGI EST **66** 28.6.1791.
6. AGI CAR **152–122** 30.6.1787.
7. AGI CAR **150** 1.3.1778, CAR **444** 28.10.1785.
8. AGI CAR **153** 2.5.1791, 3.11.1794.
9. AGI CAR **152** 22.11.1784.
10. A summary of the *Code Noir* is contained in Borde, *Histoire de l'île de la Trinidad*, vol. 2 pp. 170-7 and Williams, *History of the People of Trinidad*, pp. 46-7.
11. AGI CAR **260** 8.6.1777; Mallet, *Descriptive account*, 1802. The figures for

St. Joseph and Port of Spain in 1777 were 999 and 632 respectively, and in 1797 728 and 4,525.

12. AGI CAR **152** 31.12.1784.

13. AGI CAR **152** 31.12.1785.

14. TTHS **175** 20.1.1788.

15. AGN IERH **20** f.327–35 21.7.1782.

16. Borde, *Histoire de l'île de la Trinidad*, vol. 2 p. 295.

17. AGI CAR **152** 25.9.1787.

18. For the distribution of population according to race and nobility see Tables XIII and XIV.

19. CO **295/2** 22.3.1802; Joseph, *A History of Trinidad*, pp. 159–161; Hart, *Trinidad*, p. 197.

20. Borde, *Histoire de l'île de la Trinidad*, vol. 2 p. 295; AHS SG **7236** 8.7.1788.

21. TTHS **465** 12.8.1787.

22. ASHM **7006** No. 5–2–1–6 8.7.1788; AHS SG **7236** 8.7.1788.

23. Borde, *Histoire de l'île de la Trinidad*, vol. 2 p. 298.

24. AGN IERH **20** f.89–121 21.4.1782.

25. Borde, *Histoire de l'île de la Trinidad*, vol. 2 pp. 195–6.

26. Borde, *Histoire de l'île de la Trinidad*, vol. 2 p. 269.

27. AGN IERH **20** f.337 21.7.1782, 21 ff.165–6 2.10.1782; AGI CAR **9** 30.9.1784.

28. TTHS **465** 12.8.1787.

29. Joseph, *A History of Trinidad*, p. 123; Borde, *Histoire de l'île de la Trinidad*, vol. 2 pp. 195–6.

30. AGI CAR **153** 25.10.1794; Zapatero, *La guerra del Caribe*, p. 42.

31. Zapatero, *La guerra del Caribe*, p. 138; Pérez Aparicio, *Pérdida de la Isla de Trinidad*, pp. 42–7.

32. AGI CAR **9** 5.9.1787.

33. Ponte, *Bolivar y Ensayos*, p. 43.

34. AGI CAR **394** 8.4.1785, CAR **975** 28.10.1785, CAR **24** 14.11.1791. The parish of San Fernando was so-called after the newly-born Spanish prince.

35. AGI CAR **975** 28.10.1785, 20.2.1786.

36. AAC **17** 7.7.1790.

37. CO **295/2** 22.3.1802, **295/50** *ca.* 1820.

38. CO **295/56** 24.11.1783.

39. AGI CAR **443** 2.1.1778.

40. AGI CAR **394** 7.9.1784.

41. AGI SD **1032** 16.7.1793.

42. AGI CAR **975** 28.10.1785.

43. AGI CAR **443** 20.1.1778.

44. AGI CAR **153** 3.11.1794.

45. Joseph, *A History of Trinidad*, p. 166.

46. TTHS **445** 4.10.1790 *Cédula* 17.5.1789.
47. Parry, *The Spanish Seaborne Empire*, p. 326.
48. ASHM **7006** no. 5–2–1–6 8.7.1788.
49. AHNM **4819** 14.4.1796.
50. Borde, *Histoire de l'île de la Trinidad*, vol. 2 pp. 197–8
51. AGN IERH **20** f.312–5 15.7.1782.
52. AGI CAR **9** 7.1.1788.
53. CO **295/56** 27.7.1785.
54. Borde, *Histoire de l'île de la Trinidad*, vol. 2 p. 196. Papelones are blocks of raw sugar.
55. Pérez Aparicio, *Pérdida de la isla de Trinidad*, pp. 95–107.
56. CO **295/2** 18.2.1802.
57. AGI CAR **394** 7.9.1784.
58. BM ADD **36,806** f.64 1781.
59. AGI CAR **153** 3.11.1784; CO **295/2** 18.2.1802.
60. Borde, *Histoire de l'île de la Trinidad*, vol. 2 pp 273–5; Mörner, *Race Mixture*, p. 123.
61 AGI CAR **150** 3.9.1776, CAR **443** 13.4.1779.
62. Given an increase of nearly 1200 freemen including women and children and assuming that land grants were given to the heads of households, which probably consisted of an average of four to five persons, the number of grants made was probably between 250 and 300.
63. CO **295/56** 24.11.1783.
64. CO **295/41** and TDD **1816** 20.6.1816.
65. CO **295/41** and Table XV.
66. AGI CAR **152–121** 30.6.1787 Proclamation 27.7.1785.
67. CO **295/56** 27.7.1785; AGI CAR **152–121** 30.6.1787; Williams, *History of the People of Trinidad*, p. 46.
68. AHS SG **7236** 25.2.1788.
69. AGI CAR **152–86** 1.3.1787; CO **295/48** 28.10.1788.
70. AGI CAR **150–24** 22.2.1785, CAR **24** 1973/4; CO **318/71** 1824.
71. CO **295/41** 17.9.1816.
72. The distribution and size of land grants made under Spanish administration are included in Table XV. The amount of land granted from 1781– in *quarrées* was:

1781	11.0	1787	3404.9
1782	891.3	1788	5475.9
1783	1703.3	1789	5653.4
1784	785.0	1790	2486.8
1785	3519.1	1791	1767.7
1786	4159.4	1792	1552.6

1793	3654.8	1795	2749.4
1794	2355.2	1796	1175.5
		1797	1232.1

73. AGI CAR **152** 22.11.1784.
74. AGI CAR **152** 25.9.1787.
75. AGN RO **8** f.152–4 13.9.1783.
76. TTHS **605** 5.7.1784.
77. AGI CAR **24** 30.1.1786.
78. TTHS **445** 4.9.1790 *Cédula* 17.5.1789.
79. AGI CAR **23** 24.11.1791.
80. AGI CAR **152** 22.11.1784.
81. For example AGI CAR **23** 12.12.1778, 2.11.1781, 28.2.1784, 7.3.1786, 12.7.1788, CAR **533–26** 25.4.1787; AGN IERH **21** f.241–2 10.10.1782.
82. CO **295/11** 13.12.1805.
83. AGI CAR **394** 7.9.1784.
84. CO **295/37** 1815.
85. AGI CAR **443** 16.10.1778, 17.1.1780; McCallum, *Travels in Trinidad*, p. 31.
86. AGN IERH **20** f.327–335 21.7.1782.
87. McCallum, *Travels in Trinidad*, p. 31.
88. CO **295/13** 20.12.1805.
89. AGI CAR **23** 12.12.1778.
90. AGI CAR **152–30** 3.3.1785.
91. AGI CAR **24** 3.10.1784, CAR **152–30** 3.3.1785, CAR **6–24** 5.11.1787, CAR **444** 13.12.1787.
92. AGI CAR **23** 4.3.1792.
93. AGI ERH **21** f.276 26.8.1782, 20.10.1782.
94. AGI CAR **533–4–15** 22.3.1786 *Cédula* 28.7.1784.
95. AGI CAR **24** 17.11.1784.
96. AGI CAR **443** 23.12.1778.
97. AGI CAR **750** 1792.
98. AGI CAR **750** 13.5.1793, CAR **752** 1795.
99. See Table XVIII.
100. Davy, *The West Indies*, p. 320.
101. AHNM **4819** 14.4.1796.
102. AGI CAR **153** 19.7.1796.
103. AGI CAR **150** 3.9.1776.
104. AGI CAR **443** 30.10.1780.
105. AGI CAR **151** 2.1.1795.
106. AGN RO **8** f.254 10.1.1784.
107. AGI CAR **533** 3.3.1791, CAR **153** 1795. For the values of commercial and subsistence crops produced between 1786 and 1795 see Tables XVI and XVII.

108. AGI CAR **443** 16.10.1778.
109. ANHM **2845** no. 1 1777; Dauxion-Lavaysse, *A statistical, commercial and political description*, p. 338; Borde, *Histoire de l'île de la Trinidad*, vol. 2 p. 280.
110. Anon, *A gentleman of the island*, p. 62; CO **295/24** 14.2.1810; Montlezum, *Souvenirs des Antilles*, p. 279.
111. AHNM **4819** 14.4.1796, ASHM **7006** no. 5-2-1-6 8.7.1788.
112. AGI CAR **153–94** 1.6.1790; CO **295/2** 12.4.1802.
113. AGI EST **66** 25.6.1795.
114. AGI CAR **394** 4.4.1777.
115. AGI CAR **975** 28.10.1785, 16.9.1786.
116. McCallum, *Travels in Trinidad*, p. 58; Borde, *Histoire de l'île de la Trinidad*, vol. 2 p. 281.
117. TTHS **175** 20.1.1788; CO **295/2** 12.4.1802; TTHS **385** 7.6.1804; Borde, *Histoire de l'île de la Trinidad* vol. 2 p. 281.
118. As early as 1778 a resident observed that many lands had been opened up and dedicated to the cultivation of cotton AGI CAR **443** 2.1.1778.
119. AGI CAR **975** 28.10.1785, CAR **444** 18.8.1792; CO **295/2** 12.4.1802.
120. AGI CAR **24** 27.6.1787 *Cédula* 24.10.1785.
121. AGI CAR **152** 22.11.1784, CAR **153** 1789.
122. AGI CAR **153–94** 1.6.1790.
123. AGI CAR **444** 18.8.1792.
124. AGI CAR **443** 23.12.1778, CAR **975** 28.10.1785, EST **66** 25.9.1787, AHS SG **7236** 25.2.1788, AGI CAR **444** 1.5.1792.
125. AGI CAR **153–94** 1.6.1790.
126. AHNM **4819** 14.4.1796; TTHS **385** 7.6.1804.
127. AHNM **4819** 14.4.1796.
128. AGI CAR **444** 1.8.1792; Davy, *The West Indies*, p. 312.
129. Montlezum, *Souvenirs des Antilles*, p. 314; Halliday, *The West Indies*, p. 298; Davy, *The West Indies*, p. 312; Clark, *Ière*, p. 71.
130. AGI CAR **153, 444** 1792–5.
131. AGI CAR **435** 1799; Borde, *Histoire de l'île de la Trinidad*, vol. 2 pp. 278–9.
132. AGI CAR **444** 1.5.1792; AHNM **4819** 14.4.1796; TTHS **867** 30.7.1799.
133. AGI CAR **153–94** 1.6.1790.
134. Despite claims by Halliday, *The West Indies*, p. 298, Hart, *Trinidad*, p. 197, Borde, *Histoire de l'île de la Trinidad*, vol. 2 pp. 279–80, and Clark, *Ière*, p. 71 that it was introduced into Trinidad from Martinque in 1782, Cheesman maintains in *The history of the introduction of the more important West Indian staples*, p. 73 that this is unlikely since it was only established in the latter island in 1792.
135. Fraser, *History of Trinidad*, p. 149.
136. TTHS **385** 7.6.1804.

137. AHNM **4819** 14.4.1796.

138. AGI CAR **443** 23.12.1778, CAR **152** 22.11.1784, CAR **795** 28.10.1785, CAR **153–94** 1.6.1790, CAR **444** 18.8.1792, CAR **153** 15.4.1793.

139. Montlezum, *Souvenirs des Antilles*, p. 315; Dauxion Lavaysse, *A statistical, commercial and political description*, p. 338.

140. Mallet, *Descriptive account*, 1802.

141. AGI CAR **443** 23.12.1778.

142. AGI CAR **443** 23.12.1778, ASHM **7006** no. 5–2–1–6 8.7.1778, AHNM **4819** 14.4.1796, AHS SG 7236 25.2.1788.

143. AGI CAR **934** 4.4.1777, CAR **153** 14.1.1790.

144. AGN IERH **20** f.203 1782.

145. AHNM **4819** 14.4.1796; Coke, *A history of the West Indies*, p. 44.

146. AGI CAR **153** 16.6.1793.

147. Dauxion-Lavaysse, *A statistical, commercial and political description*, p. 330.

148. AGN IERH **9** f.130–8 4.10.1782; McCallum, *Travels in Trinidad*, p. 43. For exports of food crops to the mainland see Table XIX.

149. Purseglove, *Tropical Crops*, pp. 379–80.

150. CO **295/8** 27.8.1804.

151. CO **295/14** 17.4.1806.

152. TTHS **723** 24.6.1768; Purseglove, *Tropical Crops*, p. 392.

153. CO **295/14** 17.4.1806.

154. Harris, "Plants, animals and man" p. 118.

155. AGI CAR **150** 3.9.1776, 15.11.1777; AGN IERH **19** f.268–9 no date.

156. AGI CAR **443** 2.1.1778, CAR **150** 11.6.1778.

157. AGN IERH **20** f.1–45 1782, f.151 7.5.1782.

158. AGI CAR **5** 24.9.1784 *Cédula* 28.7.1784.

159. AGI CAR **24** 1786–1787.

160. AGN IERH **19** f.282 9.4.1782, **20** f.89–121 21.4.1782, AGI CAR **533–56** 23.9.1787.

161. AHNM **4819** 14.4.1796.

162. CO **295/33**, TDD **1814** no. 55 3.10.1814.

163. CO **295/6** 1802, **295/35** 1781–1797.

164. CO **295/2** 13.2.1802.

165. de Verteuil, *Trinidad*, pp. 114–5, 166–7, 421; McCallum, *Travels in Trinidad*, p. 97.

166. AGI CAR **150** 3.9.1776; AGN IERH **20** f.329 21.7.1782.

167. Halliday, *The West Indies*, p. 309.

168. AGI CAR **152–11** 28.10.1785.

169. AGI CAR **765** 1787–1790.

170. AGN IERH f.327–335 21.7.1782.

171. AGI CAR **896** 1788–1794; Pérez Aparicio, *Pérdida de la isla de Trinidad*, pp. 42–7.

172. TTHS **175** 20.1.1788, 3.8.1788.
173. AGI CAR **765** 8.3.1790, CAR **24** 14.8.1792; CO **295/1** 1.10.1805.
174. Haring, *The Spanish Empire*, pp. 339–41.
175. AGI CAR **150** 3.9.1776, CAR **24** 16.11.1776.
176. AGI CAR **152–36** 24.3.1779.
177. AGI CAR **23** 10.3.1789; Hussey, *The Caracas Company*, pp. 296–8.
178. CO **295/56** 25.11.1783.
179. AGI CAR **24** 30.1.1786.
180. AGI CAR **975** 16.9.1786.
181. TTHS **629** 3.6.1788.
182. AGI CAR **444** 13.8.1791 *Cédula* 20.4.1791.
183. AGI CAR **153** 26.4.1791.
184. TTHS **493** 1.5.1787.
185. TTHS **175** 20.1.1788.
186. TTHS **465** 12.8.1787.
187. AGI CAR **24** 30.1.1786.
188. AGI CAR **911** 19.7.1796.
189. AGI CAR **152–32** 3.3.1785, CAR **896** 1788–1794, CAR **896** 1794.
190. AGI CAR **153** 18.5.1795.
191. CO **295/2** 22.3.1802.
192. AGI CAR **533** 22.3.1786, CAR **441** 4.9.1786 *Cédula* 31.5.1786.
193. AGI CAR **23** 18.2.1784.
194. AGI CAR **152** 8.10.1784, CAR **394** 17.4.1785.
195. AGI CAR **394** 17.4.1785.
196. AGI CAR **152** 8.10.1784, 19.12.1784.
197. AGI CAR **152–87** 10.3.1787; Joseph, *A History of Trinidad*, p. 169.
198. AGI CAR **325** 29.12.1788; Acosta Saignes, *Vida de los esclavos negros*, pp. 49–50.
199. AGI CAR **152–87** 10.3.1787.
200. AGI CAR **23** 13.3.1787, CAR **533–26** 25.4.1787.
201. AGI CAR **23** 20.2.1791.
202. AGI CAR **23** 20.2.1791, 24.11.1791.
203. TTHS **637** 20.4.1790.
204. AGI CAR **543** 28.1.1777 *Cédula* 15.9.1776, CAR **443** 20.1.1778.
205. AGI CAR **153** 14.1.1790.
206. AGI IERH **21** f.15 5.8.1782.
207. AGI CAR **911** 27.12.1796.
208. AGI CAR **23** 28.2.1789.
209. AHS SG **7326** 8.7.1788.
210. AGI CAR **896** 1788–1794.
211. AGI CAR **152–76** 15.1.1787, CAR **24** 8.2.1791 *Cédula* 24.8.1790.
212. ASHM **7006** no. 5–2–1–6 24.11.1787.

213. AGI CAR **349** 13.5.1793.
214. AGI CAR **911** 26.4.1791, CAR **153** 26.10.1796.
215. AGI CAR **153** 25.7.1794.
216. AGI CAR **152** 22.11.1784.
217. AGI CAR **896** 1788–1790.
218. AGI CAR **908** 1790.
219. AGI CAR **153** 28.6.1794.
220. AGI CAR **150** 15.11.1777; Mallet, *Descriptive account,* 1802
221. AGI CAR **975** 28.10.1785.
222. AGI CAR **975** 28.10.1785.
223. AGI CAR **444** 28.10.1785; CO **295/28** 17.10.1802.
224. AGI CAR **152** 16.6.1793.
225. AGI CAR **32** 11.8.1787.
226. AGI CAR **394** 3.8.1783.
227. AGI CAR **24** 11.1.1786.
228. See Appendix 5 Coleridge, *Six months in the West Indies,* p. 78, J.E.A., *Sketches of voyages,* p. 129.
229. AGI CAR **152** 1786, CAR **24** 1793/4.
230. CO **318/71** April 1824.
231. AGI CAR **152** December 1784, CAR **24** 1790–4.
232. For changes in the indian population 1777–1797 see Table **XXI**.
233. AGI CAR **24** 8.10.1790.
234. AGN IERH **20** f. 327–335 21.7.1782.
235. AGI CAR **32** 11.8.1787.
236. AGI CAR **150** 15.11.1777, CAR **975** 28.10.1785.
237. AGI CAR **32** 1774–1784.
238. AGI CAR **260** 1777.
239. AGI CAR **32** 11.8.1787.
240. AGI CAR **24** 14.11.1791.
241. TTHS **628** 27.5.1788.
242. TTHS **175** 20.1.1788.
243. AGI CAR **394** 3.8.1783.
244. TTHS **204** July 1803.
245. AGI CAR **253** 8.12.1776.
246. AGI CAR **260** 1777.
247. AGI CAR **394** 3.8.1783.
248. AGI CAR **152–33** 22.2.1785, CAR **24** 1732–1800.
249. AGI CAR **153** 10.9.1795; TDD **3** 12.11.1818; CO **318/71** April 1824.
250. AGI CAR **260** 1777, CAR **153** 16.6.1793; CAR **24** 1793–4.
251. AGI CAR **394** 3.8.1783; TDD **3** 12.11.1819.
252. AGI CAR **394** 3.8.1783.
253. AHS SG **7326** no date.

254. AGI CAR **394** 3.8.1783.

255. AGI CAR **150** 13.6.1777, CAR **975** 8.12.1783, CAR **895** 1786.

Chapter 11, pages 227–237

1. Sahlins and Service, *Evolution and Culture*, p. 75.
2. See Terrien and Mills, "The effect of changing size", pp. 11–13 and Carneiro, "On the relationship between size", p. 239.
3. Sahlins and Service, *Evolution and Culture*, p. 54.
4. Service describes a similar situation in colonial Paraguay in "The Encomienda in Paraguay" and *Spanish–Guarani relations*.
5. Steward, "Levels of socio-cultural integration".
6. Harris, "Agricultural systems", p. 6.
7. CO **295/3** 17.12.1802.
8. CO **295/28** 17.10.1802.
9. CO **295/28** 17.10.1802.

Glossary

alcabala: sales tax
alcalde: magistrate
alcalde de barrio: justice of the peace of a ward
alcalde de hermandad: justice of the peace of a rural area
alcalde de monte: justice of the peace of a rural area
alcalde mayor: district officer with political and judicial authority
alcalde ordinario: leading magistrate of a *cabildo*
alférez: standard bearer, member of a *cabildo*
alguacil: constable, police officer
alguacil mayor: chief constable, usually attached to a *cabildo*
almojarifazgo: import and export duty
armador de corso: officer in charge of a privateering cruise
arroba: weight equivalent to about 25 lb
asesor: advisor to the governor
asiento: formal contract made by the Spanish Crown for the introduction of slaves to the New World
audiencia: high judicial court and governing body of a region; by extension the region itself

brea: pitch

caballería: unit of land measurement. According to Diffie, *Latin American Civilisation*, pp. 67–8, it measured between 500 and 1000 acres. Although the size and quality of land grants were laid down in 1513 the precise size varied with time and place
cabildo: town council
cacique: arawak term for an indian leader
capitán: indian leader
capitán poblador: in Trinidad officer in charge of the non-native indian villages with similar functions to a *corregidor*

casa de cabildo: town hall

casa de contratación: Board of Trade, which administered trading between Spain and the Empire, and was located in Seville

casa real: governor's residence

cédula: decree

chenilla: insect which devours the leaves and boll of cotton plants

ciudad: city

code noir: code for the protection of slaves formulated in the French colonies

conquistador: conqueror, conquistador

conuco: a plot of land in active cultivation in a shifting cultivation cycle

corregidor: district officer with administrative and judicial authority

corregidor de indios: Spanish official encharged with the protection of indians, and with the collection of tribute and regulation of labour under the *mita*

consejo de hacienda: council of finance, exchequer

contador: accountant and auditor in the colonial exchequer

cura: priest

cura doctrinero: priest encharged with the conversion and instruction of indians

duro: dollar

encomendera/o: recipient of an *encomienda*

encomienda: a grant of indians given to eminent colonists as a personal reward for services or merits. In return for the protection and instruction given to them by the *encomendero*, the indians were under the obligation to pay the latter tribute in the form of goods, money or labour services

escribano: notary

fanega: weight of about 110 lb. Also an area measurement; the area necessary to sow a *fanega* of grain/seed—about $6\frac{1}{2}$ acres in Trinidad

fuero: the *fuero ecclesiastico* and the *fuero militar* bestowed certain privileges on clerics and soldiers respectively, including exemption from tithe payment and trial in civil courts

grifo: offspring of a negro and an indian

hacienda: landed property or estate

labranza: small plots cultivated for long periods and generally found in the vicinity of settlements

libro beccero: book in which land grants were registered

limpieza de sangre: purity of blood or race

mano: pestle for grinding maize

mestizo: offspring of a white and an indian

metate: curved stone on which maize was ground

mita: draft labour system under which each indian villages was to make available a proportion of its male population, originally one-seventh, at a time to work for fixed wages on public works

mitayo: indian working under the *mita*

montón: mound of soil constructed to loosen the soil for the planting of tubers, to improve soil drainage, and in areas of thin soil to provide sufficient humus

moreno: brown-skinned person. Euphemistic term used in the eighteenth century to describe a person of mixed racial ancestry

mulato: offspring of a white and a negro

naboría: term used by the Spanish in Hispaniola to describe a slave possessed by an indian

pardo: dark-skinned person. Euphemistic term used in the eighteenth century to describe a negro or mulato

partido: smaller administrative unit and component of an Intendancy

patronato: patronage. The Patronato Real was the royal patronage and rights over ecclesiastical matters granted by the Pope

peninsular: a person from Spain

peonía: unit of land measurement equivalent to about 100 acres.

peso: monetary unit of variable value

principal: indian leader

procurador: solicitor

procurador general: solicitor attached to a *cabildo*

quarrée: unit of area measurement equivalent to about $3\frac{1}{3}$ acres

real: monetary unit. Eight *reales* were equivalent to one *peso*

regidor: councillor attached to a *cabildo*

republicano: the term was commonly used to denote the American birth of a Spaniard. It was used synonymously with the term *criollo* in the early colonial period but it later came to have political connotations

residencia: judicial review of an officers conduct at the end of his term of office

subdelegado: officer at the head of a *partido*

vecino: householder. When towns were founded land was distributed among the first inhabitants who became *vecinos*. The status conferred municipal rights. Not all the male inhabitants of towns were *vecinos*

visita: inspection of an area by royal officials

zambo: offspring of an indian and a negro

Bibliography

a. Primary sources

1. ARCHIVES

Archivo General de Indias, Sevilla (AGI)
  Sections:

Audiencia de Santo Domingo (SD)
Legajos: 24, 25, 26, 27B, 54, 55, 65, 71, 74, 77, 86, 166, 168, 172, 173,
  179, 180, 185, 575, 576, 581, 582, 583, 588, 590, 608, 615, 623, 627,
  632, 635, 641, 643, 645, 646, 647, 648, 649, 650, 660, 663, 666, 677,
  678, 869, 874, 881, 883, 895, 900, 1032.

Audiencia de Caracas (CAR)
Legajos: 2, 3, 5, 6, 8, 10, 20, 23, 24, 30, 32, 53, 57, 87, 150, 151, 152, 153,
  190, 198, 200, 203, 216, 253, 260, 314, 325, 349, 394, 422, 435, 443,
  444, 445, 469, 481, 533, 537, 543, 632, 733, 734, 735, 736, 737, 738,
  739, 740, 741, 744, 746, 748, 750, 752, 753, 765, 862, 878, 879, 880,
  895, 896, 908, 911, 943, 946, 947, 971, 975.

Audiencia de Santa Fé (SF)
Legajos: 13, 100, 101, 215, 216, 218, 219, 222, 227, 240, 255, 322, 423,
  498, 528, 529, 531, 540, 678.

Patronato (PAT)

Legajos:	Ramo:	No:
18	1	9
18	3	9
18	6	9
26	–	33
51	–	4

314

Contaduría (CONTAD)
Legajos: 1675, 1677, 1678

Contratación (CONT)
Legajo: 2617

Escribanía de Camara (EC)
Legajos: 701A, 705B, 712B, 715B, 1011, 1185.

Estado (EST)
Legajo: 66

Indiferente General (IG)
Legajo: 473–3

Mapas y Planos (MP)
Legajo: 185.

Archivo Histórico Nacional, Madrid (AHNM)
Legajos: 2845, 4819.

Biblioteca Nacional, Madrid (BNM)
Nos: 2,326, 3,851, 5,361, 18,178 lib. 3, 18,719[31]

Real Academia de Historia, Madrid (RAHM)

Colección Muñoz (CM)
Vos: 79 A/106, 80 A/107, 86 A/113

Museo Naval, Madrid (MNM)
Trinidad

Archivo de Servicio Histórico Militar, Madrid (ASHM)
Legajo: 7006, no.5–2–1–6

Archivo Histórico, Simancas (AHS)
Secretaría de Guerra (SG)
No: 7326

Secretaría de Estado de Inglaterra (SEI)
Nos: 6,965, 6,969

VENEZUELA

Archivo General de la Nación, Caracas (AGN)

Intendencia de Ejército y Real Hacienda (IERH)
Legajos: 9, 19, 20, 21.

Reales Ordenes (RO)
Legajo: 8.

Academia Nacional de Historia, Caracas (AHNC)
Vols: II–31, II–32.

Archivo Arquidiocesano, Caracas (AAC)
Legajo: 17.

TRINIDAD

Trinidad and Tobago Historical Society (TTHS)
Transcripts nos: 14, 22, 57, 67, 73, 81, 82, 93, 113, 121, 132, 137, 166,
    168, 169, 170, 175, 204, 281, 380, 385, 401, 421, 445, 465, 493, 552,
    602, 605, 628, 629, 637, 721, 767, 804, 867.

National Archive, Port of Spain

Trinidad Duplicate Dispatches (TDD)
Vols: 1, 2, 3.

LONDON

British Museum (BM)

Additional Manuscripts (ADD)
Vols: 36,315, 36,324, 36,806.

Public Record Office

Colonial Record Office (CO)
Vols: 28/6, 295/1, 295/2, 295/3, 295/5, 295/6, 295/8, 295/11, 295/13,
    295/24, 295/28, 295/33, 295/35, 295/37, 295/41, 295/45, 295/50,
    295/56, 295/71.

Calendar of State Papers (*America and West Indies*) (CSP (AWI))
Vols: 39, 86, 93, 97, 98, 108, 116, 117.

2. PRINTED DOCUMENTS AND CONTEMPORARY WORKS

ACOSTA, JOSÉ DE (1894). *Historia natural y moral de las Indias*. R. Anglés, Madrid.
AGUADO, PEDRO DE (1963). *Recopilación Historial de Venezuela*. Biblioteca de la
    Academia Nacional de la Historia, 2 vols, nos. 62 and 63, Caracas.
ALCEDO, ANTONIO DE (1786–9). *Diccionario geográfico-histórico de las Indias
    Occidentales ó América*. Manuel Gonzáles, Madrid.

ANDREWS, K. R., ed. (1939). English Privateering Voyages to the West Indies 1588–1595. *Hakluyt Society Series* II vol. CXI, Cambridge.

ARELLANO MORENO, Antonio (1964). *Relaciones geográficas de Venezuela*. Biblioteca de la Academia Nacional de la Historia no. 70, Caracas.

ARMELLADA, CESÁREO (1961). *Por la Venezuela indígena de ayer y hoy*. Sociedad de Ciencias Naturales la Salle, Monografías no. 5, Caracas.

BBBV (1896). *British Blue Book. Venezuela* no. 1. Documents and correspondence relating to the question of the boundary between British Guiana and Venezuela, London.

CAMPBELL, JOHN (1793). *Candid and impartial considerations on the nature of the sugar trade; the comparative importance of the British and French Islands in the West Indies*. R. Baldwin, London.

CASTELLANOS, JUAN DE (1955) *Elegías de varones ilustres*. 4 vols. Editorial A.B.C., Bogotá.

CAULÍN, ANTONIO (1966). *Historia corográfica, natural y evangélica de la Nueva Andalucía*. Biblioteca de la Academia Nacional de la Historia no. 81, Caracas.

CODIN (1864–1884). *Colección de documentos inéditos relativos al discubrimiento conquista y organización de las antiguas posesiones españoles de América y Oceania*. Madrid.

DÍAZ DE LA CALLE, JUAN (1646). *Memorial y Noticias Sacras y Reales del Imperio de las Indias Occidentales*. Madrid.

D'OLWER, L. N. (1963). *Cronistas de las culturas precolumbinas*. Fondo de cultura económica, México–Buenos Aires.

ENCISO, M. F. (1897). *Descripción de las Indias Occidentales por Martín Fernández de Enciso 1519* ed. J. T. Medina. Elzeviriana, Santiago, Chile.

ESPINOSA, VÁSQUEZ DE (1942). Compendium and description of the West Indies. *Smithsonian Miscellaneous Collection* no. 102, Washington D.C.

FERNÁNDEZ DE NAVARRETE, MARTÍN (1829). *Colección de viajes y discubrimientos* 5 vols., Madrid.

FERNÁNDEZ DE OVIEDO Y VALDÉS, GONZALO (1959). *Natural History of the West Indies*, translated and edited by S. A. Stoudemire University of North Carolina Studies in the romance languages and literatures no. 32.

HAKLUYT, RICHARD (1904). *The principal navigations voyages traffiques and discoveries of the English nation* vol. X James MacLehose and Sons, Glasgow.

HANKE, L. (1967). The New Laws 1542, in *History of Latin American Civilisation: Sources and Interpretations* vol. 1 The Colonial Experience pp. 144–149. Little, Brown and Co., Boston.

HARLOW, V. T. ed. (1925). Colonising expeditions to the West Indies and Guiana 1623–1667. *Hakluyt Society Series* II vol. LVI, London.

HARLOW, V. T. (1928). *The Discoverie of Guiana by Sir Walter Raleigh*. Argonaut Press, London.

LABAT, JEAN BAPTISTE (1742). *Nouveau voyage aux isles de l'Amerique.* 2nd ed. 8 vols. Paris.

LAET, J. DE (1640). *L'histoire de Nouveau Monde: ou description des Indes Occidentales.* Leyde.

LAS CASAS, BARTOLOMÉ DE (1951) *Historia de las Indias.* (eds A. Millares Carlo and L. Hanke) 3 vols. Fundo de cultural económica, México–Buenos Aires.

LAS CASAS, BARTOLOMÉ DE (1965). *Tratados.* 2 vols. Fundo de cultural económica, México–Buenos Aires.

LINAGE, JOSÉ DE (1944). *Norte de la Contratación de las Indias Occidentales* Publicaciones de la Comision Argentina de Fomento Interamericana, Buenos Aires.

MALLET, CAPT. F. (1802). *Descriptive account of the island of Trinidad.* W. Faden, London.

NUTTALL, Z. (1922). Royal Ordinances concerning the layout of New Towns. *Hispanic American Historical Review* vol. 5 pp. 249–254.

PELLEPRAT, PIERRE (1965). *Relato de las misiones de los Padres de la Compañía de Jésus en las Islas y en la Tierra Firme de América Meridional.* Biblioteca de la Academia Nacional de la Historia no. 77, Caracas.

POYNTZ, CAPT. JOHN (1683). *The present Prospect of the Island of Tobago.* London.

PURCHAS, SAMUEL (1906). *Hakluytus Posthumus or Purchas his Pilgrimes* vol. 16 James MacLehose and Sons, Glasgow.

RAMOS PÉREZ, DEMETRIO (1946). *El tradado de límites de 1750 y la expedición de Iturriaga al Orinoco.* Consejo Superior de Investigaciones cientificas. Instituto Juan Sebastián Elcano de Geografía. Gráficas Versal, Madrid.

RAYNAL, G. T. F. (1776). *A philosophical and political history of the settlements and trade of the Europeans in the East and West Indies.* Translated from the French by J. Justamond 2nd edition 5 vols. London.

RIONEGRO, F. DE (1918). *Relaciones de las Misiones de los P.P. Capuchinos en las antiguas provincias españolas—hoy—República de Venezuela 1650–1817.* 2 vols. Tip. "La Exposición", Sevilla.

RIONEGRO, F. DE (1929). *Misiones de los Padres Capuchinos: Documentos 1646–1817.* Hijo de Luis Martínez, Pontevedra.

SERRANO Y SANZ, MANUEL (1928). *Relaciones históricas de las misiones de padres capuchinos de Venezuela siglos XVII y XVIII.* V. Suárez, Madrid.

SIMÓN, PEDRO (1963). *Noticias Historiales de Venezuela.* Biblioteca de la Academia Nacional de la Historia 2 vols nos 66 and 67. Caracas.

SMITH, JOHN (1630). *The true travels, adventures and observations of Capt. John Smith in Europe, Asia, Africa and America from A.D. 1593 to 1629.* J.H., London.

VELASCO, JUAN LÓPEZ DE (1894). *Geografía y Descripción Universal de las Indias desde el año de 1571 al de 1574.* Boletín de la Sociedad Geográfica de Madrid. Fortanet, Madrid.

DE VERTEUIL, L. A. A. (1858). *Trinidad: its Geography, Natural Resources, Administration, Present Condition and Prospects.* Ward and Lock, London.

WARNER, G. F. ed. (1899). The voyage of Sir Robert Dudley to the West Indies 1594–5. *Hakluyt Society Series* II vol. III.

b. Secondary sources

ACOSTA SAIGNES, MIGUEL (1961). *Estudios de etnología antigua de Venezuela,* 2nd edition. Universidad Central de Venezuela Ediciones de la Biblioteca, Caracas.

ACOSTA SAIGNES, MIGUEL (1967). *Vida de los escalvos negros en Venezuela.* Hesperides, Caracas.

ALBRECHT, A. C. (1946). Indian–French relations at Natchez. *American Anthropologist* **48**, 321–384.

ALEXANDER, C. S. (1958). The geography of Margarita and adjacent islands, Venezuela. *University of California Publications in Geography* **12** (2), 85–192.

ALLEN, G. M. (1911). Mammals of the West Indies. *Bulletin of Museum of Comparative Zoology,* Harvard 54 (6), 175–263.

ALLEN, J. A. and CHAPMAN, F. M. (1893). On a collection of mammals from the Island of Trinidad, with description of new species. *Bulletin of the American Museum of Natural History* 5, 203–34.

ALLEN, J. A. and CHAPMAN, F. M. (1897). On a second collection of mammals from the Island of Trinidad with a description of new species and a note on some mammals from the Island of Dominica, W.I. *Bulletin of the American Museum of Natural History* **9**, 13–20.

ALLISON, D. A. (1962). *A report on the need for conservation and discussion of the methods to achieve it in the Northern range of Trinidad.* D.T.A. report. School of Tropical Agriculture, St. Augustine, Trinidad.

ALVARADO, LISANDRO (1945). *Datos etnográficos de Venezuela.* Biblioteca Venezolana de Cultura. Colección "Viajes y Naturaleza", Caracas.

ALVARADO, LISANDRO (1953). Glosario de voces indígenas de Venezuela. *Obras completas de Lisandro Alvarado* vol. 1 Ministerio de Educación, Caracas.

ANDERSON, EDGAR (1967). *Plants, man and life,* 2nd edition. Melrose, London.

ANGLO–AMERICAN COMMISSION (1945). *An experimental fishery survey in Trinidad, Tobago and British Guiana.* Washington.

ANON. (1807). *A gentleman of the island: A political account of the Island of Trinidad from its conquest by Sir Ralph Abercrombie in the year 1797 to the present time in a letter to His Grace the Duke of Portland.* Cadell and Co., London.

ARCILA FARÍAS, EDUARDO (1950). *Comercio entre Venezuela y México en los siglos XVI y XVII.* El Colegio de México, México.

BAILEY, L. H. (1938). *Manual of cultivated plants*. Macmillan, London.

BAIN, F. M. (1934). *The rainfall of Trinidad*. Government Printing Office, Port of Spain, Trinidad.

BDA (1919). The avocado pear. *Bulletin of the Department of Agriculture*, Trinidad **18**, 113–21.

BEALS, R. (1953). Acculturation. In *Anthropology Today* (eds A. L. Kroeber *et. al.*), pp. 621–641 Chicago, University of Chicago Press.

BEARD, J. S. (1941). Land Use Survey of Trinidad. *Caribbean Forester* **2** (4), 182–7.

BEARD, J. S. (1945). *Ecological relationships of natural grasslands in the American Tropics*. Manuscript in Forest Department, Long Circular Road, Port of Spain, Trinidad.

BEARD, J. S. (1945–6). The Mora forests of Trinidad. *Journal of Ecology* **33** (2), 173–92.

BEARD, J. S. (1946) "The natural vegatation of Trinidad. *Oxford Forestry Memoir* no. 20.

BEARD, J. S. (1953). The savanna vegetation of northern tropical South America. *Ecological monographs* **23**, 149–215.

BEARD, J. S. (1955). The classification of tropical American vegetation types. *Ecology* **36**, 89–100.

BEEBE, W. (1952). Introduction to the ecology of the Arima Valley, Trinidad, British West Indies. *Zoologica* **37**, (4), 157–83.

BOESMAN, M. (1960). The fresh water fishes of the Island of Trinidad. *Studies on the fauna of Curaçao and other Caribbean Islands* no. 48, 72–153.

BOLTON, H. E. (1917). The mission as a frontier institution in Spanish American colonies. *American Historical Review* **23**, 42–61.

DE BOOY, T. (1917). Certain archaeological investigations in Trinidad, British West Indies. *American Anthropologist* **19** (4), 471–86.

BORDE, P. G. L. (1876). *Histoire de l'île de la Trinidad sous le Gouvernement Espagnol*. vol. I 1876, vol. II 1882. Maisoneuve et Cie, Paris.

BRETON, ADELE (1921). The Aruac Indians of Venezuela. *Man* **21**, 9–12.

BRITO FIGUEROA, F. (1963). *La estructura económica de Venezuela colonial*. Instituto de Investigaciones, Facultad de Economía, Universidad Central de Venezuela, Caracas.

BROOKS, R. L. (1933). Trinidad Mora. *Forestry Department Leaflet* no. 5, Trinidad.

BROWN, H. H. (1942). The Sea Fisheries of Trinidad and Tobago. *Development and Welfare in the West Indies*. Bulletin no. 2. Advocate Printing Co., Bridgetown, Barbados.

BULLBROOK, J. A. (1927). The Aborigines of Trinidad. In *Discovery Day Celebration*, compiled by Alfred Richards pp. 66–72, Port of Spain, Trinidad.

BULLBROOK, J. A. (1940). *The Ierian Race.* Public lectures delivered under the auspices of the Historical Society of Trinidad and Tobago during the session 1938–9; Port of Spain, Trinidad.

BULLBROOK, J. A. (1940b). *Letter to W. Fred Taylor, Jamaica, B.W.I.* 6th July 1940. Manuscript in the Library, University of the West Indies, St. Augustine, Trinidad.

BULLBROOK, J. A. (1949). The aboriginal remains of Trinidad and the West Indies. *Caribbean Quarterly* **1** (2), 10–16. Port of Spain, Trinidad.

BULLBROOK, J. A. (1960). The aborigines of Trinidad. *Royal Victoria Institute Museum Occasional Papers* no. 2. Port of Spain, Trinidad.

BULLBROOK, J. A. and ROUSE, I. (1953). On the excavation of a shell mound at Palo Seco, Trinidad, British West Indies. *Yale University Publication in Anthropology* no. 50.

CALDWELL, D. K. and CALDWELL, M. C. (1964). Fishes from the collection of Southern Caribbean collected by Velero III in 1939. *Allan Hancock Expedition Report* no. 10 University of Southern California Press, Los Angeles.

CÁRDENAS, A. L. (1966). *Geografía física de Venezuela.* Ariel, Barcelona, Venezuela.

CARLOZZI, C. A. and CARLOZZI, A. A. (1968). *Conservation and Caribbean Regional Progress.* Antioch Press, Ohio.

CARMICHAEL, G. (1961). *The history of the West Indian Islands of Trinidad and Tobago 1498–1900.* Alvin Redman, London.

CARNEIRO, R. L. (1956). Slash and Burn Agriculture: a closer look at its implications for settlement patterns. In *Men and Cultures* (ed. A. F. C. Wallace). Selected Papers of the 5th Congress of Anthropological and Ethnological Sciences, pp. 229–234.

CARNEIRO, R. L. (1961). Slash-and-burn cultivation among the Kuikuru and its implications for cultural development in the Amazon Basin. In *The Evolution of Horticultural Systems in Native South America: Causes and Consequences* (ed. J. Wilbert). *Antropologica* Supplement no. 2 Caracas pp. 47–67.

CARNEIRO, R. L. (1967). On the relationship between size of population and complexity of social organisation. *Southwestern Journal of Anthropology* **23**, 234–43.

CARR, A. (1968). *The Turtle: A Natural History of Sea Turtles.* Cassell, London.

CATER, J. C. (1939). Deforestation and soil erosion in Trinidad. *Tropical Agriculture* **16** (10), 230–2.

CHAGNON, N. A. (1967). Yanomamö Social Organisation and Warfare. In *War* (eds M. Fried, M. Harris and R. Murphy), pp. 109–59. Natural History Press, New York.

CHAPMAN, F. (1894). On the birds of the island of Trinidad. *Bulletin of the American Museum of Natural History,* **6**, 1–86.

CHAUNU, P. (1959), *Seville et l'Atlantique 1504–1650*. 9 vols. S.E.V.P.E.N., Paris.

CHEESMAN, E. E. (1940). *The history of the introduction of the more important West Indian Staples*. Public lectures delivered under the auspices of the Trinidad and Tobago Historical Society 1938/9. Government Printer A. L. Rhodes, Trinidad.

CLARK, G. and HASWELL, M. (1966). *The economics of subsistence agriculture*. Macmillan, London.

CLARK, H. J. (1893). *Ïëre, the land of the humming bird, being a sketch of the island of Trinidad*. Government Printing Office, Port of Spain, Trinidad.

COKE, T. (1810). *A history of the West Indies*. 3 vols. Vol. 1 Nutall, Fisher and Dixon, Liverpool; Vols 2 & 3: London.

COLERIDGE, H. N. (1826). *Six months in the West Indies*. John Murray, London.

COLL Y TOSTE, CAYETANO (1907). *Prehistoria de Puerto Rico*. San Juan.

CONKLIN, H. C. (1957). *Hanunóo Agriculture; A report of an Integral System of Shifting Cultivation in the Philippines*. F.A.O., Rome.

CÓRDOVA, E. (1968). La encomienda y la disaparición de los indios en las Antilles Mayores. *Caribbean Studies* **8** (3), 23–49.

CÓRDOVA-BELLO, E. (1962). *Aspectos históricos de la ganadería en el Oriente Venezolano y Guyana*. Companía Shell de Venezuela. Ediciones Historia, Caracas.

CORTÉZ SEVILLA, V. (1958). Los indios caribes en el siglo XVI. *Proceedings of the 32nd Congress of Americanists* 1956, 727–31.

CRUXENT, J. M. and ROUSE, I. (1961). Arqueología cronológica de Venezuela 2 vols. *Estudios monográficos* 6. Union Panamericana, Washington D.C.

CRUXENT, J. M. and ROUSE, I. (1969). Early Man in the West Indies. *Scientific American.* **221** (5), 42–52.

DAVIS, N. D. (1896). English colonies in Trinidad. Reprint from Timehri, *Journal of the Royal Agricultural and Commercial Society*. Argosy Press, George-town, Demerara.

DAVY, J. M. D. (1854). *The West Indies, before and since slave emancipation*. W. and F. G. Cash, London.

DAUXION-LAVAYSSE, J. F. (1820). *A statistical, commercial and political description of Venezuela, Trinidad, Margarita and Tobago*. G. and W. B. Whittaker, London.

DEERR, N. (1949). *The History of Sugar*. 2 vols. Chapman and Hall, London.

DELGADO, J. (1968). El impacto cultural de España en la América indígena. In *Las raices de América* (ed. J. M. Gómez-Tabanera), 315–43. Instituto español de Antropología aplicada, Madrid.

DIFFIE, BAILEY W. (1967). *Latin-American civilisation: colonial period*, 2nd edition. Octagon Books, New York.

DOBYNS, H. F. (1966). Estimating aboriginal American population: an appraisal of techniques with a new hemispheric estimate. *Current Anthropology* **7** (4), 395–449.

DRUCKER, P. (1958). The native brotherhoods: modern intertribal organisations on the north-west coast. *Bulletin of the Bureau of American Ethnology*, no. 168 Smithsonian Institution, Washington D.C.

DUMOND, D. E. (1965). Population growth and cultural change. *Southwestern Journal of Anthropology* **21** (4), 302–24.

EDWARDS, C. R. (1965). Aboriginal watercraft on the Pacific coast of South America. *Ibero-Americana* no. 47. University of California Press, Berkeley and Los Angeles.

EGGAN, F. (1941). Some aspects of culture change in the northern Philippines *American Anthropologist* **43**, 11–18.

ELKIN, A. P. (1951). Reaction and interaction: a food gathering people and European settlement. *American Anthropologist* **53**, 164–86.

ESPINET, A. (1950). Life and Habits of the Arawak. *Trinidad Guardian* 13.8. 1950. Port of Spain, Trinidad.

FERNÁNDEZ DE NAVARRETE, MARTÍN (1937). *Viajes de los españoles por la costa de Paria*. Madrid.

FEWKES, J. W. (1914). Prehistoric objects from a shell heap at Erin Bay, Trinidad. *American Anthropologist* **16**, 200–20.

FEWKES, J. W. (1922). A prehistoric island culture area of America. *Annual Report of the Bureau of American Ethnology*, 1912–13 no. 34, 35–268. Washington.

FONAROFF, L. S. (1968). Man and Malaria in Trinidad. *Annals of the Association of American Geographers* **58**, 526–55.

FORTES, M. (1936). Culture contact as a dynamic process *Africa* **9**, 24–55.

FOSTER, G. M. (1960). Culture and Conquest: America's Spanish Heritage. *Viking Fund Publication in Anthropology* no. 27. New York.

FRASER, L. M. (1891). *History of Trinidad* 2 vols. Port of Spain, Trinidad.

FRIED, MORTON H. (1967). *The evolution of political society: an essay in political anthropology*. Random House, New York.

FRIEDERICHI, G. (1960). *Amerikanistiches Wörterbuch mit Hilfswörterbuch für den Amerikanisten* 2nd edition. Universität Hamburg.

GEERTZ, C. (1963). *Agricultural Involution: The process of ecological change in Indonesia*. University of California Press, Berkeley and Los Angeles, California.

GILMORE, R. M. (1950). Fauna and Ethnozoology of South America. *In* Handbook of South American Indians, Vol. 5 pp. 345–464. *Bulletin of the Bureau of American Ethnology*, no. 143 U.S. Government, Washington.

GOODING, E. G. B., LOVELESS, A. R. and PROCTOR, G. R. (1956). Flora of Barbados. *Ministry of Overseas Development Overseas Research Publication* no. 7 H.M.S.O., London.

GOSLINGA, C. Ch. (1971). *The Dutch in the Caribbean and on the wild coast, 1580–1680* University of Florida Press, Gainesville.

GOULD, R. C., FOWLER, D. D. and FOWLER, C. S. (1972). Diggers and Doggers: Parallel Failures in Economic Acculturation. *Southwestern Journal of Anthropology* **28** (3), 265–281.

GRISEBACH, A. H. R. (1859–1864). *Flora of the British West Indian Islands.* London.

HALLIDAY, SIR ANDREW (1837). *The West Indies: The natural and physical history of the Windward and Leeward colonies.* London.

HANKE, L. (1949). *The Spanish Struggle for justice in the conquest of America.* University of Philadelphia Press, Philadelphia.

HANKE, L. (1959). *Aristotle and the American Indian.* Hollis and Carter, London.

HARING, C. H. (1947). *The Spanish Empire in America.* Oxford University Press, New York.

HARRIS, D. R. (1965). Plants, animals and man in the outer Leeward Islands, West Indies: An Ecological Study of Antigua, Barbuda, and Anguilla. *University of California Publications in Geography* **18**.

HARRIS, D. R. (1969). Agricultural systems, ecosystems and the origins of agriculture. In *The Domestication and Exploitation of Plants and Animals.* (eds P. J. Ucko and G. W. Dimbleby), pp. 3–15. Duckworth, London.

HARRIS, D. R. (1971). The ecology of swidden cultivation in the upper Orinoco rain forest, Venezuela. *Geographical Review* **61**, 475–495.

HARRIS, D. R. (1972). Swidden systems and settlement. In *Man, Settlement and Urbanism.* (eds P. J. Ucko, R. Tringham and G. W. Dimbleby), pp. 245–262 Duckworth, London.

HART, D. (1866). *Trinidad and other West Indian islands and colonies* 2nd edition. Trinidad.

HATT, G. (1941). Had West Indian rock carvings a religious significance? *Ethnographical Studies, National museets Skrifter Ethnografisk Raekke* 1 pp. 166–202.

HEISER, C. B. (1965). Cultivated plants and cultural diffusion in Nuclear America. *American Anthropologist,* **67** (4), 930–49.

HENDRY, G. W. (1934). The source literature of early plant introduction into Spanish America. *Agricultural History* **8** (2), 64–72.

HERKLOTS, G. A. C. (1961). *The Birds of Trinidad and Tobago.* Collins, London.

HODGE, W. H. and TAYLOR, D. (1957). The ethnobotany of the Island Caribs of Dominica. *Webbia* **12**, 513–644.

HOLLIS, SIR ALFRED (1941). *A brief history of Trinidad under the Spanish Crown.* Government Printer, Trinidad.

HUNTER, M. (1934). Methods of study of culture contact *Africa* **7**, 335–350.

HUSSEY, R. P. (1934). *The Caracas Company 1728–1784: a study in the history of Spanish monopolistic trade.* Harvard University Press, Cambridge, Massachusetts.

Im Thurn, E. (1883). *Among the Indians of Guiana*. Kegan Paul, Trendh Co., London.

James, P. E. (1925). The Climate of Trinidad. *Monthly Weather Review* **42**, 71–75. U.S. Department of Commerce Weather Bureau, Washington D.C.

J.A.S.T.T. (1967). A short history of cacao and chocolate. *Journal of the Agricultural Society of Trinidad and Tobago* **76** (1), 15–17.

J.E.A. (1833). *Sketches of voyages and travels in the Western Hemisphere*. London.

Johnson, J. J. (1943). Introduction of the Horse into the Western Hemisphere. *Hispanic American Historical Review* **23**, 587–610.

Joseph, E. L. (1837). *A History of Trinidad*. Trinidad.

Joyce, T. A. (1916). *Central American and West Indian Archaeology*. Philip Lee Warner, London.

Junge, G. C. A. and Mees, G. F. (1958). The avifauna of Trinidad and Tobago. *Zoologische Verhandlingen* no. 37. Leiden.

Kendrew, W. G. (1953). *Climates of the Continents* 4th edition. Clarendon Press, Oxford.

Kenny, J. S. (1969). The amphibia of Trinidad, *Studies on the fauna of Curaçao and other Caribbean Islands* no. 108, pp. 1–78.

Kirkpatrick, F. A. (1934). *The Spanish Conquistadores*. A. and C. Black, London.

Kubler, G. (1946). The Quechua in the Colonial World. In *Handbook of South American Indians* vol. 2, pp. 487–543 *Bulletin of the Bureau of American Ethnology*, Vol. 143 U.S. Government, Washington D.C.

Kugler, H. G. (1956). Trinidad. In *Handbook of South American Geology* (ed. William F. Jenks) *The Geological Society of America Memoir* 65. New York.

La Farge, O. (1940). Maya Ethnology: The Sequence of Cultures. In *The Maya and Their Neighbours* 2nd edition. D. Appleton-Century Co., New York.

Lathrap, D. W. (1968). The "Hunting" Economies of the Tropical Forest Zone of South America: An attempt at Historical Perspective. In *Man the Hunter* (eds R. B. Lee and I. De Vore), pp. 23–29. Aldine, Chicago.

Lathrap, D. W. (1970). *The Upper Amazon*. Thames and Hudson, London.

Leeds, A. (1961). Yaruro Incipient Tropical Forest Horticulture: Possibilities and Limits. In *The Evolution of Horticultural Systems in Native South America: Causes and Consequences* (ed. J. Wilbert) *Antropologica* supplement no. 1, pp. 13–46. Caracas.

Levi-Strauss, Claude (1950). The use of wild plants in tropical South America In *Handbook of South American Indians* vol. 5, pp. 465–86 *Bulletin of the Bureau of American Ethnology* no. 143. U.S. Government, Washington D.C.

Liddle, R. A. (1928). *The geology of Venezuela and Trinidad*. McGowan, Texas.

LODARES, BALTAZAR DE (1929). *Los franciscanos capuchinos en Venezuela* 3 vols. Caracas.

LOVÉN, SVEN (1935). *Origins of the Tainan Culture, West Indies*. Elanders Bokfryckeri Aktiebolag, Göteborg.

LOWE, R. H. (1962). The fishes of the British Guiana Continental Shelf, Atlantic coast of South America, with notes on their natural history. *Journal of the Linnaean Society of London (Zoology)* **44** (301), 661–700.

LYNCH, J. (1958). *Spanish Colonial Administration 1782–1810: the Intendant System in the Viceroyalty of the Río de la Plata*. University of London Historical Studies, no. 5. Athlone Press, London.

McALISTER, L. N. (1963). Social structure and social change in New Spain. *Hispanic American Historical Review* **43**, 349–70.

McARDLE, REV. (1936–7). *The Dominicans in the West Indies*. Public lectures delivered under the auspices of the Trinidad and Tobago Historical Society, Port of Spain.

McCALLUM, PIERRE F. (1805). *Travels in Trinidad during the months February, March and April 1803*. Liverpool.

McKUSICK, M. B. (1960). Aboriginal canoes in the West Indies. *Yale University Publications in Anthropology* no. 63.

MAIR, L. (1935). The village census in the study of culture contact *Africa* **8**, 20–33.

MARSHALL, R. C. (1934). The physiography and vegetation of Trinidad and Tobago. *Oxford Forestry Memoir* no. 17.

MASON, P. (1970). *Patterns of Dominance*. Oxford University Press, London.

MEGGERS, B. J. (1954). Environmental limitation on the development culture. *American Anthropoligist* **56**, 801–24.

MÉNDEZ-AROCHA, A. (1963). *La Pesca de Margarita*. Estación de Investigaciones Marinas de Margarita. Fundación la Salle de Ciencias Naturales, Caracas.

MERCADAL, J. G. (1959). *Lo que España llevó a América*. Series "Ser y Tiempo" no. 14 Taurus ediciones S.A., Madrid.

MERRILL, E. D. (1954). The Botany of Cook's Voyage. *Chronica Botanica* vol. 14, pp. 161–384.

MERRILL, G. C. (1958). The historical record of man as an ecological dominant in the Lesser Antilles. *Canadian Geographer* **11**, 17–22.

MIKESELL, M. W. (1967). Geographic perspectives in Anthropology. *Annals of the Association of American Geographers* **57**, 617–634.

MILLETTE, J. C. (1970). *The Genesis of Crown Colony Government: Trinidad, 1783–1810*. Moko Enterprises, Trinidad.

MIRANDA, J. (1962). Importanicia de los cambios experimentados por los pueblos indígenas desde la conquista in *Akten des 34 Internationalen Amerikanisten-kongresses*, Wien, pp. 147–152.

MONTLEZUM, BARON DE (1818). *Souvenirs des Antilles*. Chez Gide fils, Paris.

MORALES PADRON, F. (1957). Descubrimiento y papel de Trinidad en la penetración continental. *Anuario de Estudios Americanos* **14**, 93–159.

MORALES PADRON, F. (1960). Trinidad en el siglo XVII. *Anuario de Estudios Americanos* **17**, 133–180.

MORISON, S. E. (1942). *Christopher Columbus, Admiral of the Ocean Sea*. Oxford University Press, London.

MÖRNER, M. (1961). Teoría y práctica de la segregación racial en la América colonial española. *Boletín de la Academia Nacional de la Historia, Caracas*, **44**, 278–285.

MÖRNER, M. (1967). *Race Mixture in the History of Latin America*. Little and Brown, Boston.

MÖRNER, M. (1970). *La corona española y los foraneos en los pueblos de indios*. Instituto de Estudios Ibero-Americanos, Estocolmo. Serie A Mongrafías no. 1 Almqvist and Wiksell, Stockholm.

MOSK, S. A. (1938). Spanish pearl fishing operations on the pearl coast in the 16th century. *Hispanic American Historical Review* **18** (3), 392–400.

MURPHY, R. F. and STEWARD, J. H. (1956). Tappers and Trappers: Parallel process in acculturation. *Economic Development and Cultural Change* **4**, 335–55.

NAIPAUL, V. S. (1969). *The Loss of El Dorado: A history*. Andre Deutsch, London.

NAVARRO, J. G. (1955). *Los franciscanos de la conquista y colonisación de América*. Ediciones Cultura Hispanica, Madrid.

NEWCOMB, W. W. (1960). Towards an understanding of war. In *Essays in the Science of Culture in honor of Leslie A. White* (ed. G. E. Dole), pp. 317–36. Thomas Y. Crowell, New York.

NOEL, J. A. (1967). *Spanish Colonial Administration and the socio-economic foundation of Trinidad 1777–1797*. Ph.D. Thesis, University of Cambridge.

NOEL, J. A. (1972). *Trinidad, Provincia de Venezuela*. Biblioteca de la Academia Nacional de la Historia no. 109, Caracas.

NYE, P. H. and GREENLAND, D. J. (1960). The soil under shifting cultivation. *Commonwealth Bureau of Soils, Technical Communication* no. 51.

OJER, P. (1966). *La formación del Oriente Venezolano* vol. 1 *Creación de las Gobernaciones*. Biblioteca de Estudios Universitarios no. 6. Universidad Católica "Andres Bello" Facultad de Humanidades y Educación Instituto de Investigaciones históricas, Caracas.

OLSEN, F. (1973). On the trail of the Arawaks, *Proceedings of the 4th International Congress for the study of pre-Columbian cultures of the Lesser Antilles*, St. Lucia, pp. 181–191.

PARRA PÉREZ, C. (1964). *El regimen español en Venezuela* 2nd edition. Ediciones cultura hispanica, Madrid.

PARRY, J. H. (1955). Plantation and Provision Ground: An historical sketch of the introduction of food crops into Jamaica. *Revista de Historia de América* **39**, 1–20.

PARRY, J. H. (1966). *The Spanish Seaborne Empire.* Hutchinson, London.

PARSONS, J. J. (1962). *The Green Turtle and Man.* Gainesville, Florida.

PATIÑO, V. M. (1963). *Plantas cultivadas y animales domesticos en América equinoccial* 2 vols. Imprenta departmental, Cali, Colombia.

PÉREZ APARICIO, J. (1966). *Pérdida de la isla de Trinidad.* Escuela de Estudios Hispano-Americanos. Colección Anuario no. 165. Sevilla.

PICHARDO MOYA, F. (1956). *Los aborigenes de las Antillas.* Fondo de Cultura Económica, México—Buenos Aires.

PONTE, A. F. (1919). *Bolivar y Ensayos.* Cosmos, Caracas.

POPENOE, H. (1964). The pre-industrial cultivator in the tropics. *International Union for the Conservation of Nature and Natural Resources. Proceedings and Papers of the 9th Technical Meeting: The ecology of man in the tropical environment,* pp. 66–73.

PRESTOE, H. (1870). *Catalogue of plants in the Royal Botanical Gardens.* Trinidad.

PUENTE Y OLEA, MANUEL DE (1900). *Los trabajos geográficos de la Casa de Contratación.* Escuela tipográfica y librería Salesianas, Sevilla.

PURSEGLOVE, J. W. (1965). The spread of tropical crops. In *The genetics of Colonising Species* (eds H. G. Baker and G. L. Stebbins), pp. 375–86. Academic Press, New York.

PURSEGLOVE, J. W. (1968). *Tropical Crops: Dicotyledons* 2 vols. Longmans, London.

RAMDIAL, B. S. (1964). *Shifting Cultivation and its Effects on Soil.* Master of Forestry Thesis, Yale University.

RENVOIZE, B. S. (1970). *Manioc (Manihot esculenta Crantz) and its Role in the Amerindian Agriculture of Tropical America.* M.Phil. Thesis, University of London.

RICHARDS, P. W. (1952). *The Tropical Rain Forest, an Ecological Study.* Cambridge University Press.

ROBERTSON, J. A. (1927). Some notes on the transfer by Spain of plants and animals to its colonies overseas. *James Sprunt Historical Studies.* **19**, (2), 7–21.

ROGERS, DAVID J. (1965). Some Botanical and Ethnological considerations of *Manihot esculenta. Economic Botany* **19**, 367–77.

ROTH, W. E. (1915). An inquiry into the animism and folklore of the Guiana indians. In *Annual Report of the Bureau of American Ethnology,* 1908–9, no. 30, pp. 103–386.

ROUMAIN, J. (1942). Contribution a l'étude de l'ethnobotanique précolombienne des Grandes Antilles. *Bulletin du Bureau d'Etnologie de la Republique d'Haiti* no. 1.

ROUSE, I. (1947). Pre-history of Trinidad in relation to adjacent areas. *Man* **47** (103), 93–98.

ROUSE, I. (1948). The West Indies. In *Handbook of South American Indians* vol. 4, pp. 49–565. *Bulletin of the Bureau of American Ethnology*, 143. U.S. Government, Washington D.C.

ROUSE, I. (1951). Pre-historic Caribbean culture contact as seen from Venezuela. *Transactions of the New York Academy of Sciences* **13** (82).

ROUSE, I. (1956). Settlement Patterns in the Caribbean Area. In Prehistoric Settlement Patterns in the New World. *Viking Fund Publication in Anthropology* no. 23, pp. 165–72.

ROUSE, I. (1956). Settlement Patterns in the Caribbean Area. In Prehistoric. *Publications in Anthropology* no. 61.

ROUSE, I. (1963). Final Technical Report. NSF-G24049: Dating of Caribbean Cultures. July 31st 1963. Mimeo.

ROUSE, I. (1964a). Prehistory of the West Indies. *Science* **144** (3618), 499–513.

ROUSE, I. (1964b). The Caribbean Area. In *Prehistoric Man in the New World* (eds J. D. Jennings and E. Norbeck), pp. 389–417. University of Chicago Press, Chicago.

ROUSE, I. (1969). Radio-carbon dates from Trinidad. November 26th 1969. Mimeo.

ROUSE, I. and CRUXENT, J. M. (1963). *Venezuelan Archaeology*. Yale University Press, New Haven and London.

ROWE, J. H. Inca culture at the time of the Spanish conquest. In Handbook of South American Indians vol. 2 pp. 183–329. *Bulletin of the Bureau of American Ethnology*, no. 143. U.S. Government: Washington D.C.

SAHLINS, M. D. (1962). *Moala: cultures and nature on a Fijian island.* University of Michigan Press, Ann Arbor.

SAHLINS, M. D. and SERVICE, E. R. (1960). *Evolution and Culture.* University of Michigan Press, Ann Arbor.

SANDERS, W. T. and PRICE, B. J. (1968). *Mesoamerica: The evolution of a civilisation.* Random House, New York.

SANOJA, M. and VARGAS, I. (1968–9). Orinoco Project. 1st General Report. Universidad Central de Venezuela, Caracas. Mimeo.

SAUER, C. O. (1950). Cultivated Plants of South and Central America. In *Handbook of South American Indians* vol. 5, pp. 487–543. *Bulletin of the Bureau of American Ethnology*, 143. U.S. Government, Washington D.C.

SAUER, C. O. (1963). *Land and Life.* University of California Press, Berkeley and Los Angeles.

SAUER, C. O. (1966). *The Early Spanish Main.* University of California Press, Berkeley and Los Angeles.

DE SCHLIPPE, PIERRE (1956). *Shifting cultivation in Africa: the Zande system of agriculture.* Routledge and Paul, London.

SERVICE, E. R. (1951). The Encomienda in Paraguay. *Hispanic American Historical Review* **31**, 230–52.

SERVICE, E. R. (1954). *Spanish–Guarani relations in Early Colonial Paraguay*. University of Michigan Press, Ann Arbor.

SERVICE, E. R. (1962). *Primitive Social Organisation: An Evolutionary Perspective*. Random House, New York.

SERVICE, E. R. (1968). The prime-mover of cultural evolution. *Southwestern Journal of Anthropology* **24**, 396–407.

SHIELS, W. E. (1961). *King and Church, the rise and fall of the Patronato Real*. Loyola University Press, Chicago.

SIMPSON, L. B. (1952). *The Encomienda in New Spain: the beginning of Spanish Mexico*. University of California Press, Berkeley and Los Angeles.

SLUITER, E. (1948). Dutch–Spanish rivalry in the Caribbean Area 1594–1609. *Hispanic American Historical Review* **28** (2), 165–96.

SMITH, R. C. (1955). Colonial towns of Spanish and Portuguese America. *Journal of the Society of Architectural Historians* **14**, 3–12.

SOCIAL SCIENCE RESEARCH COUNCIL (1954). Acculturation: An Exploratory Formulation. *American Anthropologist* **56**, 973–1000.

SPENCER, J. E. (1966). Shifting Cultivation in Southeastern Asia. *University of California Publications in Geography* **19**.

SPICER, E. H. (1962). *Cycles of Conquest: The impact of Spain, Mexico and the United States on the indians of the South West* 1533–1960. University of Arizona Press, Tucson.

STEWARD, J. H. (1949). South American cultures: An interpretative summary. In *Handbook of South American Indians* vol. 6, pp. 669–772. *Bulletin of the Bureau of American Ethnology*, no. 143 U.S. Government, Washington D.C.

STEWARD, J. H. (1951). Levels of Sociocultural Integration: An Operational Concept. *Southwestern Journal of Anthropology* **7**, 374–90.

STEWARD, J. H. (1955). *Theory of culture change: the methodology of multilinear evolution*. University of Illinois Press, Urbana.

STEWARD, J. H. (1968). Causal factors and processes in the evolution of pre-farming societies. In *Man the Hunter* (eds R. B. Lee and I. De Vore), pp. 321–34. Aldine, Chicago.

STURTEVANT, W. C. (1961). Taino Agriculture. In *The Evolution of Horticultural systems in Native South America: Causes and Consequences* (ed. J. Wilbert). *Antropologica* supplement 3, pp. 69–82. Caracas.

STURTEVANT, W. C. (1969). The ethnography of some West Indian starches. In *The Domestication and Exploitation of Plants and Animals* (eds P. J. Ucko and G. W. Dimbleby), pp. 177–99. Duckworth, London.

SUÁREZ, M. M. (1968). *Los Warao: Indígenas del Delta del Orinoco*. Departmento de Antropología, Instituto Venezolano de Investigaciones Científicas, Caracas.

SUTER, H. H. (1960). *The general and economic geology of Trinidad, British West Indies* 2nd edition. Colonial Office, Colonial Geological Surveys, London.

TAYLOR, D. and ROUSE, I. (1955). Linguistic and Archaeological Time Depth in the West Indies. *Internationational Journal of American Linguistics* **21**, 105–15.

TERRIEN, F. W. and MILLS, D. L. (1955). The effect of changing size upon the internal structure of organisations. *American Sociological Review* **20**, 11–13.

THOMPSON, R. W. (1959). Pre-British place-names in Trinidad. *De West-Indische Gids* **XXXIX**, pp. 138–65. Martinus Nijhoff, The Hague.

TUDELA, JOSÉ (1954). *El llegado de España a América* 2 vols. Ediciones Pegaso, Madrid.

TWIST, T. F. (1953). Weather of the eastern Caribbean. *Weather* **8**, 303–4.

VAYDA, A. P. (1961). Expansion and warfare amongst swidden agriculturalists. *American Anthropologist* **63**, 336–58.

VESEY-FITZGERALD, D. (1936). Trinidad Mammals. *Tropical Agriculture* **13**, (6), 161–5.

WALL, G. P. and SAWKINS, J. G. (1860). *Report on the Geology of Trinidad or part one of the West Indian Survey 1860.* Geological Survey, London.

WATSON, J. B. (1952). Cayuá culture change. *American Anthropological Memoir* no. 73.

WATTERS, M. (1933). *A history of the Church in Venezuela* 1810–1930. University of North Carolina Press, Chapel Hill.

WATTS, D. (1966). Man's Influence on the Vegetation of Barbados 1627 to 1800. *University of Hull Occasional Papers in Geography* no. 4.

WHITE, L. A. (1959). *The Evolution of Culture.* McGraw Hill, New York, Toronto, London.

WILLIAMS, ERIC (1962). *History of the People of Trinidad and Tobago.* P.N.M. Publishing Co., Port of Spain, Trinidad.

WILLIAMS, R. O. and CHEESMAN, E. E. (1938) (onwards) *The Flora of Trinidad and Tobago* (unfinished). Department of Agriculture, Port of Spain, Trinidad.

WILLIAMS, R. O. and WILLIAMS, R. O. (1951) *The Useful and Ornamental Plants in Trinidad and Tobago* 4th edition. Guardian Commercial Printery, Port of Spain, Trinidad.

WING, E. (1962). *Succession of Mammalian Faunas on Trinidad, West Indies.* Ph.D. Thesis, University of Florida.

WING, E. (1967). Aboriginal fishing in the Windward Islands. *Proceedings of the 2nd International Congress for the Study of pre-Columbian Cultures in the Lesser Antilles* pp. 103–15. Barbados Museum and Historical Society, Barbados.

ZAPATERO, J. M. (1965). *La guerra del Caribe en el siglo XVIII.* Instituto de cultura puertorriqueña, San Juan, Puerto Rico.

ZERRIES, O. (1968). Primitive South America and the West Indies. In *Pre-Columbian American Religions* (eds W. Krickeberg, H. Trimborn, W. Muller and O. Zerries), pp. 230–316. Weidenfeld and Nicholson, London.

Archaeological collections

Yale University, New Haven, U.S.A.

1. John Goggin's collection, mainly from the middens at St. Joseph, Mayo and Bontour, in the Department of Anthropology.
2. Personal collection of Prof. I. Rouse from various middens throughout the island.

Florida State Museum, University of Florida, Gainesville, Florida, U.S.A.

Personal collection of Dr. Bullen.

National Museum, Port of Spain, Trinidad

Great variety of artefacts from all parts of the island.

British Museum

Collections from middens at Point Fortin, Morne Diablo, Tarouba, Palo Seco.

Index